S0-BRT-596

Multicultural Education
Fourteenth Edition

EDITOR

Fred Schultz
University of Akron (Retired)

Fred Schultz, former professor of education at the University of Akron, attended Indiana University to earn a B.S. in social education in 1962, an M.S. in the history and philosophy of education in 1966, and a Ph.D. in the history and philosophy of education and American studies in 1969. His B.A. in Spanish was conferred by the University of Akron in May 1985. He is actively involved in researching the development and history of American education with a primary focus on the history of ideas and social philosophy of education. He also likes to study languages.

SCHOOL OF EDUCATION
CURRICULUM LABORATORY
UM-DEARBORN

Boston   Burr Ridge, IL   Dubuque, IA   New York   San Francisco   St. Louis
Bangkok   Bogotá   Caracas   Kuala Lumpur   Lisbon   London   Madrid   Mexico City
Milan   Montreal   New Delhi   Santiago   Seoul   Singapore   Sydney   Taipei   Toronto

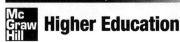
Higher Education

ANNUAL EDITIONS: MULTICULTURAL EDUCATION, FOURTEENTH EDITION

Published by McGraw-Hill, a business unit of The McGraw-Hill Companies, Inc., 1221 Avenue of the Americas, New York, NY 10020.
Copyright © 2008 by The McGraw-Hill Companies, Inc. All rights reserved. Previous edition(s) 1994–2007. No part of this publication may be reproduced or distributed in any form or by any means, or stored in a database or retrieval system, without the prior written consent of The McGraw-Hill Companies, Inc., including, but not limited to, in any network or other electronic storage or transmission, or broadcast for distance learning.

Some ancillaries, including electronic and print components, may not be available to customers outside the United States.

Annual Editions® is a registered trademark of the McGraw-Hill Companies, Inc.
Annual Editions is published by the **Contemporary Learning Series** group within the McGraw-Hill Higher Education division.

This book is printed on recycled, acid-free paper containing 10% postconsumer waste.

1 2 3 4 5 6 7 8 9 0 QPD/QPD 0 9 8

ISBN 978–0–07–339747–4
MHID 0–07–339747–4
ISSN 1092–924X

Managing Editor: *Larry Loeppke*
Production Manager: *Beth Kundert*
Developmental Editor: *Dave Welsh*
Editorial Assistant: *Nancy Meissner*
Production Service Assistant: *Rita Hingtgen*
Permissions Coordinator: *Shirley Lanners*
Senior Marketing Manager: *Julie Keck*
Marketing Communications Specialist: *Mary Klein*
Marketing Coordinator: *Alice Link*
Project Manager: *Jean Smith*
Design Specialist: *Tara McDermott*
Senior Administrative Assistant: *DeAnna Dausener*
Senior Operations Manager: *Pat Koch Krieger*
Cover Graphics: *Maggie Lytle*

Compositor: Laserwords Private Limited
Cover Image: Comstock/PictureQuest and Thinkstock Images/JupiterImages

Library in Congress Cataloging-in-Publication Data
Main entry under title: Annual Editions: Multicultural Education. 2008/2009.
   1. Multicultural Education—Periodicals. I. Schultz, Fred, *comp.* II. Title: Multicultural Education.
658′.05

www.mhhe.com

Editors/Advisory Board

Members of the Advisory Board are instrumental in the final selection of articles for each edition of ANNUAL EDITIONS. Their review of articles for content, level, currentness, and appropriateness provides critical direction to the editor and staff. We think that you will find their careful consideration well reflected in this volume.

Preface

In publishing ANNUAL EDITIONS we recognize the enormous role played by the magazines, newspapers, and journals of the public press in providing current, first-rate educational information in a broad spectrum of interest areas. Many of these articles are appropriate for students, researchers, and professionals seeking accurate, current material to help bridge the gap between principles and theories and the real world. These articles, however, become more useful for study when those of lasting value are carefully collected, organized, indexed, and reproduced in a low-cost format, which provides easy and permanent access when the material is needed. That is the role played by ANNUAL EDITIONS.

In this fourteenth edition of *Annual Editions: Multicultural Education,* we confront many, if not most, of the same issues that confronted us at the beginning of this decade. Multicultural Education, a multi-disciplinary area of study, is continuing its efforts to be an integrated part of school, college, and university studies. The effort to achieve transformative influence in the content and direction of schooling will continue. All voices are welcome as we address the need to prepare young persons for an increasingly diverse national social structure. How to help young people as well as adults face this need effectively is still a primary question before us.

The concept of multicultural education evolved and took shape in the United States out of the social travail that wrenched the nation in the late 1960s, and has continued through the decades to the present. The linkages between diverse and coexisting ethnic, racial, and socioeconomic heritages have been explored. There has been enthusiastic support for the idea of a volume in this Annual Editions series exclusively devoted to multicultural education. Having been teaching and studying multicultural education for 33 years, it is a pleasure to serve as editor of *Annual Editions: Multicultural Education.*

The critical literature on gender, race, and culture in educational studies increases our knowledge base regarding the multicultural mosaic that so richly adorns North American cultures. When the first courses in multicultural education were developed in the 1960s, the United States was in the midst of urban and other social crises, and there were no textbooks available. Educators who taught in this area had to draw heavily from academic literatures in anthropology, sociology, social psychology, social history, sociolinguistics, and psychiatry. Today, there are textbooks available in the area, but there is also a need for a regularly, annually published volume that offers samples from the recent journal literature in which the knowledge bases for multicultural education are developed. This volume is intended to address that need.

The National Council for the Accreditation of Teacher Education (NCATE) in the United States has in place national standards requiring that accredited teacher education programs offer course content in multicultural education. A global conception of the subject is usually recommended, in which prospective teachers are encouraged to develop empathetic cultural sensitivity to the demographic changes and cultural diversity that continues to develop in the public schools as a result of dramatic demographic shifts in the population.

In this volume we first explore the social contexts for the development of multicultural education. Its role in teacher education is then briefly defined in the essays in Unit 2. In Unit 3 the nature of multicultural education as an academic discipline is discussed, and several issues related to this topic are explored. The readings in Unit 4 look at multicultural education from the perspective of people in the process of developing their own unique personal identities, in the context of their interactions with their own as well as others' cultural heritages and personal life experiences. The readings in Unit 5 focus on curriculum and instruction in multicultural perspective. Unit 6 addresses special topics relevant to development of multicultural insight, and the essays in Unit 7 explore alternative visions for multicultural education and the need for a critically conscious quest for emancipatory educational futures for all people of all cultural heritages.

Once again we are including important *Internet References* sites that can be used to further explore article topics. These sites are cross-referenced by number in the topic guide.

This year I would like to acknowledge the very helpful contributions of the advisory board members. Their assistance in finding useful sources is appreciated. I would also like to acknowledge Dr. Stephen H. Aby, research librarian at the University of Akron, whose assistance is greatly valued.

This volume will be useful in courses in multicultural education at the undergraduate and graduate levels. It will add considerable substance to the sociocultural foundations of education, educational policy studies and leadership, as well as to coursework in other areas of preservice and inservice teacher education programs. We hope you enjoy this volume, and we would like you to help us improve future editions. Please complete and return the form at the back of the book. We look forward to hearing from you.

Fred Schultz

Fred Schultz
Editor

Contents

UNIT 1
The Social Contexts of Multicultural Education

The concepts in bold italics are developed in the article. For further expansion, please refer to the Topic Guide.

UNIT 2
Teacher Education in Multicultural Perspective

The concepts in bold italics are developed in the article. For further expansion, please refer to the Topic Guide.

UNIT 3
Multicultural Education as an Academic Discipline

UNIT 4
Identity and Personal Development: A Multicultural Focus

The concepts in bold italics are developed in the article. For further expansion, please refer to the Topic Guide.

UNIT 5
Curriculum and Instruction in Multicultural Perspective

The concepts in bold italics are developed in the article. For further expansion, please refer to the Topic Guide.

UNIT 6
Special Topics in Multicultural Education

The concepts in bold italics are developed in the article. For further expansion, please refer to the Topic Guide.

UNIT 7
For Vision and Voice: A Call to Conscience

The concepts in bold italics are developed in the article. For further expansion, please refer to the Topic Guide.

The concepts in bold italics are developed in the article. For further expansion, please refer to the Topic Guide.

Topic Guide

This topic guide suggests how the selections in this book relate to the subjects covered in your course. You may want to use the topics listed on these pages to search the Web more easily.

On the following pages a number of Web sites have been gathered specifically for this book. They are arranged to reflect the units of this *Annual Edition*. You can link to these sites by going to the student online support site at *http://www.mhcls.com/online/*.

ALL THE ARTICLES THAT RELATE TO EACH TOPIC ARE LISTED BELOW THE BOLD-FACED TERM.

Adolescence
7. The Biology of Risk Taking
15. Beyond Promise: Autobiography and Multicultural Education
26. Assessing English Language Learners' Content Knowledge in Middle School Classrooms
28. Family and Consumer Sciences Delivers Middle School Multicultural Education

African American History
19. Making Connections with the Past
37. Researching Historical Black Colleges

Asian American Teachers
12. Asian American Teachers

Autobiography and schooling
15. Beyond Promise: Autobiography and Multicultural Education
25. Rewriting "Goldilocks" in the Urban, Multicultural Elementary School

Black colleges
37. Researching Historical Black Colleges

Canadian schools
8. Dare to Be Different
20. Affirming Identity in Multilingual Classrooms

Critical theoretical perspective
6. Hitting the Ground Running
13. The Human Right to Education
17. Whose World Is This
36. Toward a Pedagogy of Transformative Teacher Education

Cross-cultural communication
14. Knowing, Valuing, and Shaping One's Culture

Culturally responsive teaching
34. Why Are "Bad Boys" Always Black
35. The Culturally Responsive Teacher

Cultural diversity
1. Five Trends for Schools
9. The Cultural Plunge
10. Ain't Nothin' Like the Real Thing
11. Collaborative Recruitment of Diverse Teachers for the Long Haul—TEAMS
16. Expanding Appreciation for "Others" Among European-American Pre-Teacher
20. Affirming Identity in Multilingual Classrooms
23. As Diversity Grows, So Must We
25. Rewriting "Goldilocks" in the Urban, Multicultural Elementary School
29. Public Education in Philadelphia
31. Standards-Based Planning and Teaching in a Multicultural Classroom

Cultural issues
1. Five Trends for Schools
2. In Urban America, Many Students Fail to Finish High School
3. In Rural America, Few People Harvest 4-Year Degrees
4. Colorblind to the Reality of Race in America
10. Ain't Nothin' Like the Real Thing
11. Collaborative Recruitment of Diverse Teachers for the Long Haul—TEAMS
14. Knowing, Valuing, and Shaping One's Culture
16. Expanding Appreciation for "Others" Among European-American Pre-Teacher

Cultural politics of education
15. Beyond Promise: Autobiography and Multicultural Education
16. Expanding Appreciation for "Others" Among European-American Pre-Teacher
18. A Developing Identity
36. Toward a Pedagogy of Transformative Teacher Education

Cultural values
1. Five Trends for Schools
2. In Urban America, Many Students Fail to Finish High School
3. In Rural America, Few People Harvest 4-Year Degrees
14. Knowing, Valuing, and Shaping One's Culture
15. Beyond Promise: Autobiography and Multicultural Education
16. Expanding Appreciation for "Others" Among European-American Pre-Teacher
21. Myths and Stereotypes about Native Americans
23. As Diversity Grows, So Must We

Curriculum and instruction
23. As Diversity Grows, So Must We
24. Arts in the Classroom
25. Rewriting "Goldilocks" in the Urban, Multicultural Elementary School
26. Assessing English Language Learners' Content Knowledge in Middle School Classrooms
27. Promoting School Achievement among American Indian Students throughout the School Years
28. Family and Consumer Sciences Delivers Middle School Multicultural Education
30. Assessing English-Language Learners in Mainstream Classrooms
31. Standards-Based Planning and Teaching in a Multicultural Classroom
34. Why Are "Bad Boys" Always Black

De Facto Segregation
14. Knowing, Valuing, and Shaping One's Culture

Demographic change
1. Five Trends for Schools
9. The Cultural Plunge
23. As Diversity Grows, So Must We

Internet References

The following Internet sites have been carefully researched and selected to support the articles found in this reader. The easiest way to access these selected sites is to go to our student online support site at *http://www.mhcls.com/online/*.

AE: Multicultural Education 14/E

The following sites were available at the time of publication. Visit our Web site—we update our student online support site regularly to reflect any changes.

General Sources

Administration for Children and Families
http://www.acf.dhhs.gov

This site provides information on federally funded programs that promote the economic and social well-being of families, children, and communities.

Children's Defense Fund (CDF)
http://www.childrensdefense.org

At this site of the CDF, an organization that seeks to ensure that every child is treated fairly, there are reports and resources regarding current issues facing today's youth, along with national statistics on various subjects.

Educational Resources Information Center
http://www.eric.ed.gov

This invaluable site provides links to all ERIC sites: clearinghouses, support components, and publishers of ERIC materials. You can search the ERIC database, find out what is new, and ask questions about ERIC.

Education Week on the Web
http://www.edweek.org

At this *Education Week* home page, you will be able to open archives, read special reports, keep up on current events, look at job opportunities, and access a variety of articles of relevance in multicultural education.

Global SchoolNet Foundation
http://www.gsn.org

Access this site for multicultural education information. The site includes news for teachers, students, and parents, as well as chat rooms, links to educational resources, programs, and contests and competitions.

National Education Association
http://www.nea.org

Something about virtually every education-related topic can be accessed at or through this site of the 2.3-million-strong National Education Association.

National MultiCultural Institute (NMCI)
http://www.nmci.org

NMCI is one of the major organizations in the field of diversity training. At this Web site, NMCI offers conference data, resource materials, diversity training and consulting service information, and links to other related sites.

Phi Delta Kappa
http://www.pdkintl.org/home.shtml

This important organization publishes articles about all facets of education. By clicking on the links at this site, for example, you can check out the journal's online archive.

UNIT 1: The Social Contexts of Multicultural Education

American Psychological Association
http://www.apa.org/topics/homepage.html

By exploring the APA's "Resources for the Public," you will be able to find links to an abundance of articles and other resources that are useful in understanding the factors that are involved in the development of prejudice.

Association for Moral Education
http://www.amenetwork.org/

AME is dedicated to fostering communication, cooperation, training, curriculum development, and research that links moral theory with educational practices. From here it is possible to connect to several sites on ethics, character building, and moral development.

Center for Innovation in Education
http://www.center.edu

This is the home page of the Center for Innovation in Education, self-described as a "not-for-profit, non-partisan research organization" focusing on K–12 education reform strategies. Click on its links for information and varying perspectives on numerous reform initiatives.

International Project: Multicultural Pavilion
http://curry.edschool.virginia.edu/curry/centers/multicultural/papers.html

Here is a forum for sharing stories and resources and for learning from the stories and resources of others, in the form of articles on the Internet that cover many of the racial, gender, and multicultural issues that arise in the field of multicultural education.

National Black Child Development Institute
http://www.nbcdi.org

Resources for improving the quality of life for African American children through public education programs are provided at this site.

UNIT 2: Teacher Education in Multicultural Perspectives

Awesome Library for Teachers
http://www.awesomelibrary.org/teacher.html

Open this page for links and access to teacher information on many topics of concern to multicultural educators.

Education World
http://www.education-world.com

Education World provides a database of literally thousands of sites that can be searched by grade level, plus education news, lesson plans, and professional-development resources.

Teacher Talk Forum
http://education.indiana.edu/cas/tt/tthmpg.html

Visit this site for access to a variety of articles discussing life in the classroom. Clicking on the various links will lead you to electronic lesson plans covering a variety of topic areas from Indiana University's Center for Adolescent Studies.

UNIT 3: Multicultural Education as an Academic Discipline

Goals 2000: A Progress Report
http://www.ed.gov/pubs/goals/progrpt/index.html

Open this site to survey a progress report by the U.S. Department of Education on the Goals 2000 reform initiative. It provides a sense of the goals that educators are reaching for as they look toward the future.

Teachers Helping Teachers
http://www.pacificnet.net/~mandel/

This site provides basic teaching tips, new teaching methodology ideas, and forums for teachers to share their experiences. Download software and participate in chat sessions. It features educational resources on the Web, with new ones added each week.

UNIT 4: Identity and Personal Development: A Multicultural Focus

Ethics Updates/Lawrence Hinman
http://ethics.acusd.edu

This site provides both simple concept definition and complex analysis of ethics, original treatises, and sophisticated search engine capability. Subject matter covers the gamut, from ethical theory to applied ethical venues. There are many opportunities for user input.

Kathy Schrock's Guide for Educators
http://school.discovery.com/schrockguide/

This classified list of Web sites is useful for enhancing curriculum and professional growth of teachers.

Let 100 Flowers Bloom/Kristen Nicholson-Nelson
http://teacher.scholastic.com/professional/assessment/100flowers.htm

Open this page for Kristen Nicholson-Nelson's discussion of ways in which teachers can help to develop children's multiple intelligences. She provides a useful bibliography and resources.

The National Academy for Child Development
http://www.nacd.org

This international organization is dedicated to helping children and adults reach their full potential. This page presents links to various programs, research, and resources.

UNIT 5: Curriculum and Instruction in a Multicultural Perspective

American Indian Science and Engineering Society
http://www.aises.org

This is the AISES "Multicultural Educational Reform Programs" site. It provides a framework for learning about science, mathematics, and technology by which minority students and their teachers can make meaningful cultural connections to teaching and learning. It also provides Web links.

Child Welfare League of America
http://www.cwla.org

The CWLA is the United States' oldest and largest organization devoted entirely to the well-being of vulnerable children and their families. This site provides links to information about issues related to the process of becoming multicultural.

STANDARDS: An International Journal of Multicultural Studies
http://www.colorado.edu/journals/standards/

This fascinating site provides access to a seemingly infinite number of international archives.

UNIT 6: Special Topics in Multicultural Education

American Scientist
http://www.amsci.org/amsci/amsci.html

Investigate this site to access a variety of articles and to explore issues and concepts related to race and gender.

American Studies Web
http://lumen.georgetown.edu/projects/asw/

This site provides links to a wealth of resources on the Internet related to American studies, from gender studies to race and ethnicity. It is of great help when doing research in demography and population studies.

CYFERNet: National Network for Family Resiliency Program & Directory
http://www.agnr.umd.edu/nnfr/home.html

This page will lead you to a number of resource areas of interest for learning about resiliency: General Family Resiliency, Violence Prevention, and Resiliency Topics for Young Children are a few.

National Institute on the Education of At-Risk Students
http://www.ed.gov/offices/OERI/At-Risk/

The At-Risk Institute supports research and development activities designed to improve the education of students at risk of educational failure due to limited English proficiency, race, geographic location, or economic disadvantage.

U.S. Department of Education
http://www.ed.gov/pubs/TeachersGuide/

Explore this government site for examination of institutional aspects of multicultural education. National goals, projects, grants, and other educational programs are listed here as well as many links to teacher services and resources.

UNIT 7: For Vision and Voice: A Call to Conscience

Classroom Connect
http://www.classroom.net

This is a major Web site for K–12 teachers and education students, with links to schools, teachers, and resources online. It includes discussion of the use of technology in the classroom.

www.mhcls.com/online/

EdWeb/Andy Carvin
http://edwebproject.org

The purpose of EdWeb is to explore educational reform and information technology. Access educational resources world-wide, learn about trends in education policy, and examine success stories of computers in the classroom.

Online Internet Institute
http://www.oii.org

A collaborative project among Internet-using educators, proponents of systemic reform, content-area experts, and teachers who desire professional growth, this site provides help for integrating the Web with individual teaching styles.

We highly recommend that you review our Web site for expanded information and our other product lines. We are continually updating and adding links to our Web site in order to offer you the most usable and useful information that will support and expand the value of your Annual Editions. You can reach us at: *http://www.mhcls.com/annualeditions/.*

UNIT 1

The Social Contexts of Multicultural Education

Unit Selections

Key Points to Consider

- Should the federal government institute a national standard of accountability for public schooling?

- What facets of the history of the human struggle for civil rights should be taught to students?

- Should affirmative action be discontinued? Why or why not?

- Why has there been a recent increased level of racial segregation in the United States? What does this mean for public education?

- What impact do changing racial configurations in population have on education?

Student Web Site
www.mhcls.com/online

Internet References
Further information regarding these Web sites may be found in this book's preface or online.

American Psychological Association
   http://www.apa.org/topics/homepage.html
Association for Moral Education
   http://www.amenetwork.org/
Center for Innovation in Education
   http://www.center.edu
International Project: Multicultural Pavilion
   http://curry.edschool.virginia.edu/curry/centers/multicultural/papers.html
National Black Child Development Institute
   http://www.nbcdi.org

The social contexts of multicultural populations are so complex and interrelated (usually but not always) that they are very difficult to describe adequately. Nonetheless, this is the situation in many urban areas of the United States and some rural areas of the nation. The same may be said for Canada, and there are some other nations that share this experience. Culture is the most powerful social influence on human life. As we become more culturally diverse as societies, we experience unique social phenomena that can affect how we define ourselves as national social orders.

Multicultural national communities face special challenges in daily life. Such societies also have unique opportunities to develop truly great culturally pluralistic national civilizations in which the aesthetic, artistic, literary, and moral standards of each cultural group can contribute to the creation of new standards. Groups can learn from one another, they can benefit from their respective strengths and achievements, and they can help one another to transcend problems and injustices of the past. We ought, therefore, to see the multicultural national fabric that is our social reality as a circumstance of promise, hope, and pride.

In examining the social context of multicultural education, we need to help teachers and education students to sense the promise and the great social opportunity that our multicultural society presents. We have the task of empowering students with a constructive sense of social consciousness and a will to transcend the social barriers to safety, success, and personal happiness that confront, in one form or another, almost one-third of them. It is essential that we invest in all the children and young adults of multicultural nations, in order that great social promise and hope may be brought to future fulfillment.

We can ask ourselves certain very important questions as we work with children and young adults in our schools. Are they safe? Are they hungry? Are they afraid? Are they angry? Do they have a sense of angst; are they filled with self-doubt and uncertainty as to their prospects in life? For far too many children and adolescents from all socioeconomic groups, social classes, and cultural groups the answers to these questions are "yes." Far greater numbers of children from low-income minority cultural groups answer "yes" to at least some of these questions than do children from higher socioeconomic families.

Having done this, educators and civic leaders should consider a few questions. What are the purposes of schooling? Are schools limited to their acknowledged mission of intellectual development? Or, are schools also capable of advancing, as did classical Greek and Roman educators, education in honor, character, courage, resourcefulness, civic responsibility, and social service? This latter concept of the mission of schooling is still the brightest hope for the full achievement of our great promise as a multicultural society in an interdependent world community of nations.

What are the obstacles to achieving this end? Each child must be able to advance intellectually in school as far as may be possible. We need to help children develop a sense of honor, self-respect,

The McGraw-Hill Companies, Inc./Jean Smith, photographer

and pride in their own cultural heritage, which will lead them in their adult years to want to serve, help, and heal the suffering of others. We need intellectually curious and competent graduates who are knowledgeable about their own ethnic heritages and committed to social justice for all persons, in their own nation as well as in the community of nations.

The problems we face in achieving such an intellectual and social end are significant. Developing multicultural curriculum materials for schools and integrating them into the course content and activities can help to sensitize all students to the inherent worth of all persons. All youth deserve the opportunity to learn about their own cultural heritages.

North American nations have qualitative issues to face in the area of intercultural relations. Our problems differ because of very different national experiences and very different school systems. Around the world other nations have to wrestle with providing adequate opportunity for minority populations while maintaining high intellectual standards. The articles in this unit attempt to discuss all of these concerns, and they attempt to address the thoughtful concerns of those who have studied the rhetoric of debate over multiculturalism in school curricula.

There have been dramatic demographic changes in the characteristics of the world's population and in the interdependence of the world's nations in a global economy. We must reconsider how we develop human talent in our schools, for young people are the ones who will be the most basic resource in the future. Some unit essays give important background on the history of the civil rights movement in the United States as well as on the origins of many racial and cultural stereotypes that have inhibited the efforts of educators to help young people become more accepting of cultural diversity.

The unit essays are relevant to courses in cultural foundations of education, educational policy studies, multicultural education, social studies education, and curriculum theory and construction.

Five Trends for Schools

Schools in the United States grapple with change as demographics alter the education landscape.

Shelley Lapkoff and Rose Maria Li

On October 17, 2006, the U.S. population officially reached 300 million, double the nation's population in 1950. The United States houses less than 5 percent of the world's population, but it is the third most populous country in the world, after China (1.3 billion) and India (1.1 billion). The United States is expected to be the only developed country on the top-10 list of most populous countries by 2050 (U.S. Census Bureau, 2002a), at which point its population is expected to exceed 420 million.[1]

In addition to the rapid growth of the U.S. population, there have been dramatic changes in the population's composition in the last 50 years: Americans are growing older, more educated, and more diverse. These trends have implications for school districts in terms of enrollment levels, student characteristics, and the resources available for education. Five demographic trends in the United States are influencing school districts around the country.

Trend 1:
The Enrollment Roller Coaster

As many long-time school administrators know firsthand, enrollment fluctuations can seem like a roller-coaster ride. U.S. enrollments increased throughout the 1950s and 1960s, peaked in 1970, and fell from the early 1970s through the mid-1980s. This caused many districts to close schools and reduce their teaching staffs. But then enrollment increases accelerated in the late 1980s and grew for the next decade, causing school districts to open new schools, reopen old ones, or otherwise cope with overcrowding.

By the late 1990s, elementary enrollments had leveled off (U.S. Census Bureau, 2007). Today, many districts are experiencing the results of the low birthrate of a decade ago. Most of the children born in 1997—a year that saw the fewest U.S. births in recent years—are now in 4th grade. In many districts, this will be the smallest cohort of students. A recent upward trend in U.S. births may reverse the elementary enrollment decline in a few years.

Meanwhile, many districts are experiencing a high school "bubble" as cohorts born around 1990 reach the high school grades. But high school enrollments will head downward during the next decade and then level off or inch up again, following the elementary trends.

U.S. birth patterns always have some effect on the nation's school districts, but local conditions can sometimes overpower the national trend. Despite national increases in the number of children of high school age, enrollments did not increase in some urban areas. For example, in Oakland, California, the expected high school bubble never materialized because large numbers of families moved out of the area after the dot-com bust. And California's Palo Alto Unified School District is experiencing higher—not lower—elementary enrollments due in part to the attractions of Stanford University and some of the state's highest test-scoring public schools. Moreover, the district has seen an increase in immigrant Asian and Indian households, many of which have larger families than U.S.-born households.

Enrollment declines are often painful for districts, especially when the decline warrants school closures. In general, urban areas have been hardest hit, as families leave the cities and birthrates fall. Even if school buildings remain open, declining enrollments usually mean reduced funding for schools, which can result in teacher losses and program reductions.

Trend 2:
Immigration and Diversity

Fertility and mortality rates are relatively low in the United States. When a nation reaches these low levels, which is the case in most developed countries, its population grows slowly and may even decline. At this point, immigration plays a crucial role in population growth.

In 2002, net migration to the United States (the difference between the numbers entering and leaving) was over one million, more than three times higher than the next highest-receiving countries: Afghanistan (300,000), which saw many refugees returning in 2002; Canada (190,000); Germany (180,000); Russia (140,000); United Kingdom (130,000); Italy (120,000); and Singapore (120,000; U.S. Census Bureau, 2002b).

The 1965 amendments to the U.S. Immigration and Nationality Act created a major shift in both the number of arrivals to the United States and their countries of origin, fueling increases in the numbers of entrants from Latin America and Asia. Moreover, once these populations arrive, family reunification laws make it likely that more people from these countries will follow.

A diverse U.S. population will engender fresh perspectives.

In 1970, more than 60 percent of the nation's 9.6 million foreign-born people originated in Europe, 19 percent in Latin America, 9 percent in Asia, and 10 percent in other areas. By 2000, only 15 percent of the 28.4 million foreign-born population came from Europe. More than half originated in Latin America—with Mexico accounting for more than half of this group—and more than one-quarter came from Asia (primarily from China, the Philippines, India, Vietnam, and Korea; U.S. Census Bureau, 2002a).

Immigrants continue to be attracted to a handful of states—California, New York, Florida, Texas, New Jersey, and Illinois—and half of the nation's foreign-born population resided in five metropolitan areas in 2000—Los Angeles, New York, San Francisco, Miami, and Chicago (U.S. Census Bureau, 2002a). However, since 2000, the long-standing concentration of Hispanics and Asians in port-of-entry metropolitan areas has been eroding as these two groups disperse inland toward more suburban metropolitan areas (Frey, 2006) and new immigrant hot spots, such as North Carolina, Georgia, and Nevada (Martin & Midgley, 2006).

The advantages and challenges of an ethnically diverse population are being felt throughout the United States. A diverse U.S. population may engender an entrepreneurial spirit and fresh perspectives conducive to new discoveries and approaches. At the same time, the recent influx of Hispanics and Asians to the United States has resulted in greater demands for social and education services, including English as a second language (ESL) instruction. The 2000 Census reported 380 categories of single languages or language families other than English spoken at home. Spanish is the most common, with more than 28 million speakers among the U.S. population 5 years and older, followed by Chinese (2 million); French (1.6 million); German (1.4 million); and Tagalog (1.2 million; Shin & Bruno, 2003).

In 2004, 9.9 million school-age children (ages 5–17) spoke a language other than English at home, representing 19 percent of all children in this age-group, a 9 percent increase from 3.7 million in 1979 (U.S. Department of Education, 2006). More than 67 percent of Hispanic children and almost 63 percent of Asian/Pacific Islander children spoke a language other than English at home, compared with only about 5 percent of their white and black counterparts. Of the children who spoke a language other than English at home in 2004, a disproportionate share were U.S.-born or naturalized U.S. citizens (81 percent); poor or near-poor (57 percent); and living in the West (40 percent) and South (29 percent) of the United States. About 2.8 million, or 28 percent of children who spoke a language other than English at home, reportedly spoke English less than "very well."

Virtually all children and grandchildren of immigrants accept the necessity of learning English (Alba, Logan, Lutz, & Stults, 2002). On the other hand, children in immigrant families are well positioned to become proficient bilingual speakers, for which there is a growing need in an increasingly multilingual world. From one-quarter to more than one-half of children in immigrant families speak English well and, at the same time, speak a language other than English at home (Hernandez & Denton, 2005). In 2000, 92 percent of the U.S. population ages 5 and older had no difficulty speaking English (Shin & Bruno, 2003).

An often-overlooked characteristic of migration is that immigrant populations generally assimilate rapidly. Research has shown that second- and third-generation children assimilate on several economic and social measures, such as learning English at young ages, closing the college attendance gap with native-born whites, and achieving more than 50 percent home ownership in middle age.

In terms of residential segregation, generational status also makes a difference. Although immigrants tend to cluster in neighborhoods, second-generation Hispanic adults are about half as clustered as their parents, whereas many Asian groups are even more integrated into the general population. This suggests that ethnicity has less of an effect on indicators of economic and social well-being than does generation, age of arrival, or country of birth (Myers, 2007). Also, the continual flow of new immigrants might mask the fact that Hispanics and Asians are assimilating. Some third-and-greater-generation Hispanics may not even identify themselves as Hispanics, further complicating efforts to measure assimilation.

Trend 3:
The Varied Home Front

Three family characteristics in the United States materially influence a child's situation: the presence of married parents in the household, poverty, and secure parental employment. Children who live with two married parents generally have access to better economic and social resources and experience more favorable health and education outcomes (Carlson, 2006; Fields & Smith, 1998). Today, more than two-thirds of children ages 0–1.7 live in households with two married parents. The percentage has been stable since the mid-1990s but with striking and persistent differences by race and ethnicity (Federal Interagency Forum on Child and Family Statistics, 2006). In 2005, 76 percent of white-alone, non-Hispanic children lived with two married parents, compared with 35 percent of black-alone children and 65 percent of Hispanic children (who may be of any race).[2] For at least the past decade, children with one or more foreign-born parents were more likely to live in two-parent households (81 percent in 2005) than native-born children (68 percent in 2005; Federal Interagency Forum on Child and Family Statistics, 2006).

Children in married-couple families are much less likely to live in poverty than children living with only one parent. In 2004, 9 percent of children in married-couple families lived below the poverty threshold, compared with 42 percent of children in single-mother families (Federal Interagency Forum on Child and Family Statistics, 2006). Nationally, 17 percent of children under age 18 lived in families with incomes below the poverty threshold.

The proportion living below poverty generally has declined for all household types nationally since the 1990s. This is good news because economic deprivation is associated with a variety of poor outcomes for children at all stages of development, from low birth weight to problems with cognitive development, school achievement, and emotional well-being (Duncan Brooks-Gunn, 1997).

The period between 1980 and 2004 saw a steady increase in the percentage of children who lived with at least one parent who worked full-time year-round (Federal Interagency Forum on Child and Family Statistics, 2006). Of children living in families with two parents, the percentage with both parents working full-time year-round increased from 17 percent in 1980 to 33 percent in 2000. Since 2000, however, the percentage has slightly dropped.

An increase in parental employment may be a mixed blessing. When both parents work full-time, the family has greater economic resources, and parents may share child-care responsibilities. However, the family's schedule may be more stressful, and parents may be less nurturing, less emotionally available, and less likely to set limits for their children (Schor, 1995).

To improve student performance, schools may need to look increasingly beyond the academic curriculum and offer support to children of working parents outside of normal school hours. This might take the form of after-school enrichment opportunities, organized athletic activities, or meaningful volunteer or community-service projects. Support would also include high-quality child care before and after school, particularly for elementary school students.

Trend 4:
An Aging Population

The baby-boom generation will soon reach retirement age. The 55- to 64-year-old population group is projected to be the fastest-growing segment of the U.S. adult population during the next decade. By 2030, the over-65 population will most likely be twice as large as its 2000 counterpart, growing to 71.5 million, or nearly 20 percent of the total U.S. population.

Americans are living longer than ever before. A baby born in 2004 can expect to live almost 78 years, up from 71 years in 1970 (National Center for Health Statistics, 2006). Despite such impressive gains in survival, racial/ethnic and gender

disparities persist, although they have narrowed. By far, the largest variation in death rates is by education attainment: In 2002, the age-adjusted death rate for people with fewer than 12 years of schooling was four times higher than that for people ages 25–64 with at least 13 years of schooling (National Center for Health Statistics, 2005).

Each succeeding cohort of older individuals has higher education attainment. Today, 19 percent of people age 65 and over have a college education, compared with only 5 percent of that age-group in 1965. And the trend continues: When the baby-boom generation retires, more than 30 percent will have been college educated (Federal Interagency Forum on Child and Family Statistics, 2006). Higher levels of education are usually associated with higher incomes, higher standards of living, above-average health, and longer life expectancy.

The soon-to-retire baby boomers offer great opportunities for schools.

The aging of the population necessarily offers challenges for schools. First, districts may lose a large proportion of their most-experienced teachers and administrators during the next two decades. In anticipation of potential labor shortages in K–12 districts, various colleges and some states are developing new programs to encourage second careers in teaching (Poster, 2003). For example, Virginia's community colleges are providing a statewide "career switcher" initiative. Second, an aging population could diminish school funding for education because older and childless voters are generally less supportive of public school funding than are voters with school-age children (Poterba, 1998). In California, most districts exempt seniors from special local parcel or bond taxes. In close elections, this helps ameliorate the potentially negative senior vote on school funding initiatives. Districts in other states with significant proportions of older residents may want to consider adopting similar approaches to protect school budgets.

But the soon-to-retire baby boomers also offer great opportunities for schools. Well-educated, committed, and healthy, many could serve as volunteers in local communities or embark on second careers as teachers and school administrators. Retiree volunteers could help boost a declining education workforce (see The Longevity Dividend). The flexibility of part-time work and creative job situations may appeal to prospective teachers in this age-group.

Trend 5:
Obesity

Despite the generally positive circumstances of older Americans, unaddressed health issues foreshadow potential problems. Between 1999 and 2002, almost two-thirds of adults (ages 20–74) were considered overweight; almost one-third were considered obese; (National Center for Health Statistics, 2005).[3]

Schools should place greater emphasis on health, nutrition, and physical activity during the elementary school years.

This problem begins in childhood for many people. According to data from the 1999–2002 National Health and Nutrition Examination Surveys, which collect data from physical examinations throughout the United States, nearly 16 percent of children were considered obese (National Center for Health Statistics, 2005). The historical trend is troublesome; only 4 percent of children were considered obese in the early 1970s. The high percentage of Americans who are physically inactive raises significant concerns because overweight and obesity are risk factors for many chronic diseases and disabilities, including heart disease, hypertension, diabetes, some types of cancers, and back pain. To counter these trends and help establish health-promoting habits early in life, schools should consider placing greater emphasis on health programs, nutrition, and physical activity during the elementary school years.

The Two Ends of the Spectrum

Compared with 20 years ago, the average child entering school today is less likely to live in a family with two married parents but is more likely to have a living grandparent, reside in a non-poor family with secure parental employment, encounter classmates of other races and ethnicities who speak a language other than English at home, and become obese. At the other end of the age spectrum, older adults in the United States are, on average, more educated and can expect to live longer and be healthier than previous generations. As involved community members, older adults can serve as intergenerational role models. They can also help schools face the challenges of the 21st century by sharing their skills and experiences and contributing to improving school and after-school learning environments in their neighborhoods.

Notes

1. In contrast, the population in more than half of the world's developed countries is expected to decline over the next 50 years. By 2050, Germany's current population of 82 million and Japan's current population of 127 million are expected to fall below 74 million and 100 million, respectively (U.S. Census Bureau, 2006).

2. The "white-alone" and "black-alone" categories refer to those who indicate only one racial category.

3. For adults, obese is defined as a body mass index greater than or equal to 30; overweight (including obese) is a body mass index greater than or equal to 25.

The Longevity Dividend

With the growth of an elderly population destined to live longer and healthier, it makes sense to harness the experience and social capital of older adults—not just for the benefit of future generations but also for their own good health. One key to successful psychological aging is "generativity," the opportunity to leave the world better for future generations through productive, meaningful engagement (Fried et al., 2004). Generative roles not only give meaning and purpose but also provide social engagement, which has been shown to maintain cognition, decrease disability, and delay mortality. Findings also indicate that loneliness has implications for health (Cacioppo et al., 2002).

The challenge for our aging society is to provide opportunities for the elderly to engage in meaningful roles after retirement. Experience Corps (www.experiencecorps.org) does just that (see "The Value of Experience" Educational Leadership, March 2005). Launched in 1995, the program seeks to

- Channel the talent and energy of growing numbers of older adults into public and community service.
- Provide significant benefits for the older people who participate.
- Achieve real outcomes in the community.

Now active in 19 U.S. cities, the program enlists volunteers ages 55 years and older to serve in public elementary schools (grades K–3).

Volunteers ideally commit to at least 15 hours each week for a full school year and are paid a monthly stipend to cover expenses. Experience Corps projects place a critical mass of tutors and mentors at each school so that the presence of the older adults influences the climate of the entire school. Volunteers are involved in academic support (literacy, math, and computer support; working in school libraries); behavioral support (conflict resolution, positive attention); school attendance, parental outreach, and public health (asthma club).

Initial results suggest that high-intensity volunteerism can lead to improvements in the level of physical activity among previously physically inactive volunteers. The program also can lead to meaningful improvements in student reading scores and to a reduction in student behavior problems. Moreover, as Experience Corps members engage with students and teachers and take on key leadership roles, they create healthier and more positive perceptions about aging in the schools and communities in which they work.

References

Cacioppo, J. T., Hawkley, L. C., Crawford, L. E., Ernst, J. M., Burleson, M. H., Kowalewski, R. B., et al. (2002). Loneliness and health: Potential mechanisms. *Psychosomatic Medicine, 64,* 407–417.

Fried, L. P., Carlson, M. C., Freedman, M., Frick, K. D., Glass, T. A., Hill, J., et al. (2004). A social model for health promotion for an aging population: Initial evidence on the Experience Corps. *Journal of Urban Health, 81,* 64–78.

References

Alba, R., Logan, J., Lutz, A., & Stults, B. (2002). Only English by the third generation? Mother-tongue loss and preservation among the grandchildren of contemporary immigrants. *Demography, 39,* 467–484.

Carlson, M. J. (2006). Family structure, father involvement, and adolescent behavioral outcomes. *Journal of Marriage and Family, 68*(1), 137–154.

Duncan, G. J., & Brooks-Gunn, J. (Eds.). (1997). *Consequences of growing up poor.* New York: Russell Sage Foundation.

Federal Interagency Forum on Child and Family Statistics. (2006). *America's children in brief. Key national indicators of well-being, 2006.* Available: http://childstats.gov/americaschildren

Fields, J. M., & Smith, K. E. (1998). *Poverty, family structure, and child well-being: Indicators from the SIPP* (Population Division Working Paper No. 23). Washington, DC: U.S. Bureau of the Census. Available: www.census.gov/population/www/documentation/twps0023.html

Frey, W. H. (2006). *Diversity spreads out: Metropolitan shifts in Hispanic, Asian, and black populations since 2000.* Washington, DC: Brookings Institution. Available: www.frey-demographer.org/reports/Brook06.pdf

Hernandez, D., & Denton, N. (2005). *Geography and resources for children in immigrant families.* Presentation at the National Institute of Child Health and Human Development.

Martin, P., & Midgley, E. (2006). Immigration: Shaping and reshaping America (2nd ed.). *Population Bulletin, 61*(4).

Myers, D. (2007). *Immigrants and boomers: Forging a new social contract for the future of America.* New York: Russell Sage Foundation.

National Center for Health Statistics. (2005). *Health, United States, 2005.* Washington, DC: Author. Available: www.cdc.gov/nchs/data/hus/hus05.pdf

National Center for Health Statistics. (2006). Deaths: Preliminary data for 2004. *National Vital Statistics Reports, 54*(19). Available: www.cdc.gov/nchs/data/nvsr/nvsr54/nvsr54%5f19.pdf

Poster, J. (2003, January). *Teacher supply and demand: How do career-changers preparation programs really work?* Paper presented at the Hawaii International Conference on Education, Honolulu, HI. Available: www.hiceducation.org/Edu%5fProceedings/John%20B.%20Poster.pdf

Poterba, J. (1998). Demographic change, intergenerational linkages, and public education. *American Economic Review, 88,* 315–320.

Schor, E. (1995). *Caring for your school-age child, ages 5 to 12.* Elk Grove, IL: American Academy of Pediatrics. Available: www.aap.org/pubed/zzzusdqqbac.htm

Shin, H. B., & Bruno, R. (2003). *Language use and English-speaking ability: 2000* (Census 2000 Brief C2KBR-29). Washington, DC: U.S. Census Bureau.

U.S. Census Bureau. (2002a). *Global Population Profile: 2002.* Washington, DC: Author. Available: www.census.gov/ipc/prod/wp02/wp-02003.pdf

U.S. Census Bureau. (2002b). *Coming to America: A profile of the nation's foreign born (2000 Update)* (Census Brief: Current Population Survey, CENBR/01-1) Washington, DC: Author.

U.S. Census Bureau. (2006). International Data Base. Available: www.census.gov/ipc/www/idbnew.html

U.S. Census Bureau. (2007). *Table A-1. School enrollment of the population 3 years old and over, by level and control of school, race, and Hispanic origin: October 1955 to 2005.* Washington, DC: Author. Available: www.census.gov/population/www/socdemo/school.html

U.S. Department of Education, National Center for Education Statistics. (2006). *The condition of education 2006* (NCES 2006-071). Available: http://nces.ed.gov/programs/coe/2006/pdf/07%5f2006.pdf

SHELLEY LAPKOFF is President and Principal of Lapkoff & Gobalet Demographic Research Inc., Berkeley, California; lapkoff@aol.com. **ROSE MARIA LI** is a demographer and President of Rose Li and Associates Inc.; rose@roseliassociates.com.

In Urban America, Many Students Fail to Finish High School

Faced with a deteriorating pipeline of students, colleges in cities like Compton, Calif., struggle to serve their local neighborhoods

KARIN FISCHER

E dith J. Negrete's big dreams defy her modest means. In those dreams, Ms. Negrete is an anesthesiologist, earning a comfortable salary that pays for a fancy car and a nice home for her 8-year-old son, Joshua.

Her reality is more complicated. Ms. Negrete, who dropped out of high school at age 15 to get married, recently lost her job as a clerk at a moving company here and has moved in with her father to make ends meet. Now 27, she is raising Joshua on her own and getting a divorce from her husband, who is in prison.

But Ms. Negrete says she has hope for the future, in the form of the local community college, El Camino College Compton Center. Inspired by a former co-worker, who studied for a psychology degree during lunch breaks, Ms. Negrete enrolled at the college three years ago. Eventually, she wants to transfer to the University of California at Los Angeles.

"As you get older, you really know what you want," says Ms. Negrete, who is the first in her family to attend college. "Once you have an education, have a paper in your hand, then a lot of doors open."

The situation Ms. Negrete faced mirrors what is happening in low-income urban centers across America. Hindered by poor-performing public schools, many residents drop out before earning a high-school diploma, and with it, the all-important ticket to the bevy of higher-education institutions often located in and around urban areas.

In this Southern California city, part of an arc of low-income neighborhoods on Los Angeles' southern tier, only one-third of residents 25 years or older are high-school graduates; fewer than seven in 100 have a bachelor's degree. Nationwide, 84 percent of Americans hold a high-school diploma, and 27 percent are four-year-college graduates.

Faced with that deteriorating pipeline, urban colleges, both two-year and four-year, have struggled to serve large swaths of their local neighborhoods. Just 382 Compton students attend the nearest California State University campus, at Dominguez Hills, making up about 4 percent of the undergraduate popula-tion there, while 134 go to the campus in Long Beach, accounting for less than 1 percent of its student body. As for UCLA, Ms. Negrete's top choice, just seven of the university's nearly 25,000 undergraduates are from Compton.

Even as a college degree becomes an ever more indispensable vehicle out of poverty, the share of English-language learners, members of racial and ethnic minorities, and other groups historically underrepresented in higher education is growing in inner-city schools. The small number of students who enroll in college often struggle to succeed, battling poor preparation and juggling work and family responsibilities. And factors outside the classroom can also depress scholastic achievement. This fall alone, Compton's public-school district was notified of 460 new foster-care placements among its students.

"Increasingly, there is a gulf between the haves and the have-nots," says Houston D. Davis, project director for the national Educational Needs Index, which paints a county-by-county portrait based on educational, economic, and population data. "In cities . . . there are pockets, there are populations, that have very real needs, and those needs are getting greater."

Changing Expectations

The Compton Unified School District's slogan is "excellence in progress," and, by many measures, the city schools have far to go. The district's graduation rate lags behind the statewide average. Twenty-five percent of students drop out before graduation day. Fewer than a quarter of high-school seniors complete requirements for admission to either of California's two public-university systems, and just 27 percent of students who graduated last spring went on to a four-year college.

Despite those daunting numbers, Jesse L. Gonzales, the district's superintendent, says he wants to send the message that a college degree can open doors beyond Compton, where the unemployment rate is 11 percent, well above the national average. Partnerships have been established with local colleges, and liaisons have been appointed at each of the district's three high schools to help parents, most of whom never attended college, understand the college application process. When Mr. Gonzales visits Compton elementary schools, he says, his question to students is, "Where are you going to college?"

"It is better to set standards too high and miss them," he says, "than to set them too low and hit them."

On the face of it, Compton graduates have a multitude of postsecondary options—after all, Los Angeles County is home to more than 50 two- and four-year colleges.

But the factors holding inner-city students back can be both practical and parochial. Many Compton students are illegal residents and are not eligible for state or federal financial aid. For others, earning an immediate paycheck is more important than an eventual degree, while some struggle to balance work schedules, child care, and a three-bus commute.

For first-generation students, the "nuts and bolts" of applying for college admission and financial aid can also be a deterrent, says Robert L. Caret, president of the Coalition of Urban and Metropolitan Universities, a group of colleges that are located in, and primarily draw from, metropolitan areas.

"No one in their family or their peer group has done it, and they don't know how to begin," says Mr. Caret, who is president of Towson University, near Baltimore.

Beating the Odds

At Compton High School, every morning before classes begin, the principal, Jesse Jones, stands outside its gates, greeting each student with a booming "Good morning." He says he never misses a day.

"Many of these kids have no stability in their lives," says Mr. Jones, who came out of retirement three years ago to run the school. "It's about the image you are sending. They have to start believing in you."

The students streaming onto the campus look very much like the population of Compton as a whole. Nearly 69 percent are Hispanic, and 29 percent are black. One-third speak English as a second language.

Originally a predominantly white, middle-class community, which counts the former president George H.W. Bush among its past residents, the complexion of the area has changed significantly in recent decades. By the 1970s, the city's population was largely African-American. Today an influx of immigrants, mainly from Mexico, and the migration of Latino families from elsewhere in the Los Angeles metropolitan region have led to rapid growth of the Hispanic population, especially among school-age children.

Compton's changing demographics have brought special challenges. Although the student body is now predominantly Latino, much of the district's staff is black. In some cases, that has meant retraining teachers to adjust to students' new learning styles.

Under the now five-year watch of Mr. Gonzales, the superintendent, more Advanced Placement and college-preparatory classes have been added to the curricula of the high schools, while the most academically at-risk ninth-grade students have been singled out for extra instruction in reading and mathemat-ics. Students in kindergarten through the third grade have two hours of "protected" reading time each day.

There is some evidence that Mr. Gonzales's efforts are working: Since 2002, Compton students have shown improvement on California's two statewide accountability assessments.

Second Chances

Ms. Negrete says she didn't get that kind of encouragement when she went to public school here. Now she is trying to give her son the kind of support she never received. Joshua, she says proudly, is at the top of his class and wants to be an archaeologist. Occasionally, when her aunt cannot watch him, Joshua comes with her to classes at El Camino College Compton Center.

"Sometimes he complains," she says, "but I tell him that if you want to succeed, you have to have a degree."

With busy schedules and sometimes unreliable child care, Ms. Negrete is not alone in bringing a child with her to classes on the campus. On a recent sunny day, students' children darted across the college's sunny courtyard as a live band played a rollicking beat. The occasion was Fiesta Latina, part study break, part celebration of the college's continued existence after its predecessor, Compton Community College, lost its accreditation last July. Faculty and staff members joined the queue for homemade tostadas and pupusas, gathering in small clusters to scoop the food off paper plates.

"It would have been a disaster if the college had closed," says Hilda Gaytan, president of the student government, which sponsored the event. Ms. Gaytan, 50 and a Mexican immigrant, came to Compton Community College after she lost her job in the garment industry three years ago. "We all came here for a second chance."

The community college has been providing second chances to students in Compton and the surrounding towns for nearly 80 years. The community's pride in the college is palpable. Everyone, it seems, knows a young person who appeared destined to go down the wrong path but was turned around by Compton Community College professors. At night, residents stroll the parklike campus, a safety zone in a city that last year ranked as one of the nation's deadliest, with 72 murders for 97,833 residents.

In 2002, voters in Compton, where the per capita income is just $12,617, voted overwhelmingly for a $100-million bond, essentially taxing themselves for the next two decades to pay for new classroom buildings and a tutoring facility on the campus. But the amount of revenue from all sources that Compton is able to spend is about 10 percent below that of other California community colleges.

A Community's College

Community colleges in urban areas often face a struggle to make ends meet, says Alicia C. Dowd, an assistant professor of education at the University of Southern California. Ms. Dowd has found that community colleges in large cities have per-student revenues 13 percent to 18 percent lower than two-year colleges elsewhere.

Part of the reason for that, she says, is that urban colleges often lack the political clout to fight for larger state appropriations. They also might not have skilled administrators who can compete for grants from private foundations or federal and state governments.

Federal student-aid policy can also work against some types of urban postsecondary institutions, says John B. Lee, an education consultant. He notes that for-profit colleges have been pulling out of central cities since a change in financial-aid rules in the 1990s made serving at-risk students with high student-loan default rates too costly. The percentage of full-time students enrolled in proprietary schools in cities declined by 11 percent between 1996 and 2000. Meanwhile, enrollments at for-profit institutions in suburban areas increased 18 percent during the same period.

Mr. Lee says he is concerned that the loss of these institutions, which frequently offered training programs that lasted just a few months, leaves inner-city students with fewer educational options. "I worry these students are being abandoned," he says.

In Compton, an agreement to combine Compton Community College with El Camino College ensured a continued local higher-education presence in the city. The accreditation fight ended in July when Compton officials decided to drop their appeal of the decision a year earlier by the Western Association of Schools and Colleges' Accrediting Commission for Community and Junior Colleges. But that battle the subsequent merger have left a bitter taste with some city residents. They question whether El Camino, with its largely middle-class, transfer-oriented student body, can be sensitive to the needs and to the challenges of the Compton community, where students are far more likely to be pursuing a vocational degree or certification.

Because only courses approved for El Camino can be offered at the Compton center, this fall's session began without a number of basic-skills and English-language courses or its popular licensed vocational nurse-training program. (The center has since entered into an agreement with another area college, Los Angeles Trade-Technical College, to offer the practical-nursing program, and El Camino is fast-tracking approval of about 20 courses before the next semester.)

"This is our community's college," says Bruce A. Boyden, a graduate of the college and a member of the Committee to Save the Compton Community College District, a group that pushed for the college to remain independent. "Compton took disenfranchised young people and empowered them to become employable in the community in which they live. At El Camino, they are preparing doctors, lawyers, and Indian chiefs."

A Basic-Skills Gantlet

But if Compton is the community's college, it is also a reflection of the community's struggles.

One out of every five courses taken at the college is a basic-skills course. In all of California, by contrast, remedial math and writing courses account for only about 7 percent of community-college enrollment. What's more, many students appear to become mired in these remedial courses without ever making it to for-credit course work. Only about one-quarter of Compton College students who took a basic-skills class in their first year took and passed a college-level course in the same subject area within three years.

The last three years for Ms. Negrete, for instance, have largely been catching up. She is also pursuing her general-equivalency diploma and estimates it will take her another two years before she has earned the credits to transfer to a four-year college.

Becoming bogged down in remedial courses can discourage students from earning a community-college degree or going on to a four-year university, says Estela Mara Bensimon, director of the Center for Urban Education at the University of Southern California.

"The biggest barrier to success for black and Latino community-college students is basic skills," says Ms. Bensimon. "Basic skills is a gantlet."

At Compton Community College, that problem was exacerbated because writing was not integrated throughout the curriculum, says Toni Wasserberger, a professor of English at the college. Instead, many faculty members would rely on other measures of assessment, such as multiple-choice exams or short-answer responses.

As a solution, college officials decided to pair a number of courses in the English department, including some at the basic-skills level, with some in other disciplines, including history, psychology, and even math. Students take the paired courses, which have complementary syllabi and writing assignments that reinforce each other, during the same semester. The two professors leading each course review students' papers and general progress together.

With the upheaval at the college over the last two years, it is difficult to accurately measure the success of the linked courses, says Ms. Wasserberger, a tiny woman with hip eyeglasses and energy to spare. Some students, she notes, had to drop out of the linked program because of the difficulty of taking two classes while working full time.

Still, for Ms. Wasserberger, who has been at the college since 1970, helping at-risk community-college students succeed seems to be as much of an art as a science.

A student wanders into the English department's outer office, interrupting Ms. Wasserberger midthought. "Just a minute," she says, "I've got to go give this student a hug."

The student, a slender woman who appears to be in her late 20s, is equally effusive. "You're my mentor," she says, before seeking some advice on English course offerings. After she leaves, Ms. Wasserberger returns to her seat.

"She was in my class," Ms. Wasserberger says of the student. "She literally could not write a sentence."

"You don't make up for what they didn't have," she says. "You make progress."

In Rural America, Few People Harvest 4-Year Degrees

Big Bend Community College tries to improve college enrollment and fight poverty as its area's minority population grows

SARA HEBEL

This wide, arid expanse of central Washington State is filled with rolling rows of alfalfa, potatoes, and other crops, irrigated by the Columbia River and its tributaries. Most of the fields have been harvested now but, in the orchards, apples are ripe for the picking.

The region's close ties to the land and to the seasonal cycles of agriculture have long shaped its economy, which, in turn, has defined its educational landscape. As in many rural parts of the country, that picture is often bleak. Compared with the nation as a whole, few jobs here require bachelor's degrees, and few residents have earned them. Poverty rates are high. For many residents, the prospect of attending college seems remote.

In Mattawa, a town of about 3,300 people tucked amid orchards, vineyards, and fields at the southwestern edge of Grant County, the school district's classrooms are swelling this fall as migrant families fill the town for the apple harvest.

School administrators are trying to help their students with reading, vocabulary, and other basic academic skills, despite a language barrier. For more than half of the students here, Spanish is their first language. More than four-fifths qualify for federal free or reduced-price lunch programs, and the students are often expected to contribute to their families' incomes. Many of their parents never graduated from high school, much less attended college, and the students are unfamiliar with the application process for admissions or financial aid. Many are reluctant to travel far from home; the nearest public colleges—Big Bend Community College, Yakima Valley Community College, and Columbia Basin College, and Central Washington University—are all about an hour's drive away.

Across Grant County, only about one in eight adults hold bachelor's degrees. Residents' average annual per-capita income is close to $17,700, about 34 percent below the statewide average.

Administrators at Big Bend Community College—which includes Mattawa in its service area—are trying to reach beyond the nearly 2,700 students enrolled there, to attract both traditional-age students and adults by persuading them of the economic benefits of a college education. But many residents must struggle to carve out the time and money needed for a degree, or for work-force-training programs, as they juggle jobs and raising children.

Across the nation, rural populations as a whole have consistently lagged behind the rest of the country in the proportion of adults holding bachelor's degrees. The gap has widened slightly in the past decade, according to the U.S Department of Agriculture. In 2000, 15.5 percent of adults living outside of metropolitan areas held bachelor's degrees, compared with 26.6 percent of adults in metropolitan areas.

Robert M. Gibbs, a regional economist in the Agriculture Department, says many rural economies are beginning to slowly broaden beyond their historic roots in occupations like farming and mining. But those areas, from Appalachia and the Deep South to the Great Plains and Southwest, still do not tend to offer the social or physical amenities needed to support rapid growth in the number of knowledge-based jobs.

Compared with the rest of the nation, Mr. Gibbs says, "they're not really catching up."

Most rural populations have few colleges nearby, leaving residents without the broad array of academic programs available to residents of more densely populated urban and suburban areas.

The city of Seattle alone contains three public community colleges, the University of Washington, and 10 private institutions. Students there can take programs in subjects as varied as boat making, hotel-restaurant management, and culinary arts, says José A. Esparza, coordinator of student recruitment and outreach at Big Bend. His two-year college, whose service area covers 4,600 square miles, offers 20 associate-degree programs and 13 certificate programs. But it does not provide offerings in some fields that students often request, like dental hygiene, forensics, and interior design.

"Sometimes students will have to change what they want to do to fit with what we have," he says.

Barriers to Preparation

In rural Washington, one of the challenges in improving the college-going rate materializes at public elementary and secondary schools. Over the past 15 years, Mattawa, for example, has seen rapid growth in its Hispanic population. At the town's Wahluke High School, the racial composition of the student body has gone from about 80 percent white to 20 percent Hispanic in the early 1990s to the reverse proportion now.

Gary Greene, superintendent of the Wahluke School District, is focused on raising his students' reading skills and college ambitions at an early age. Every morning three second-graders show up at his

Educational Disparities Among Counties

Here is how some of the nation's urban and rural counties compare with each other, and lag behind the nation as a whole, in their populations' highest levels of educational attainment:

	National average	Urban sample average	Rural sample average
■ Proportion of 18- to 24-year-olds with at least a high-school diploma	82.5%	75.0%	74.0%
■ Proportion of 25- to 64-year-olds with an associate degree	7.2	6.0	6.1
□ Proportion of 25- to 64-year-olds with a bachelor's degree or higher	26.5	22.0	13.2

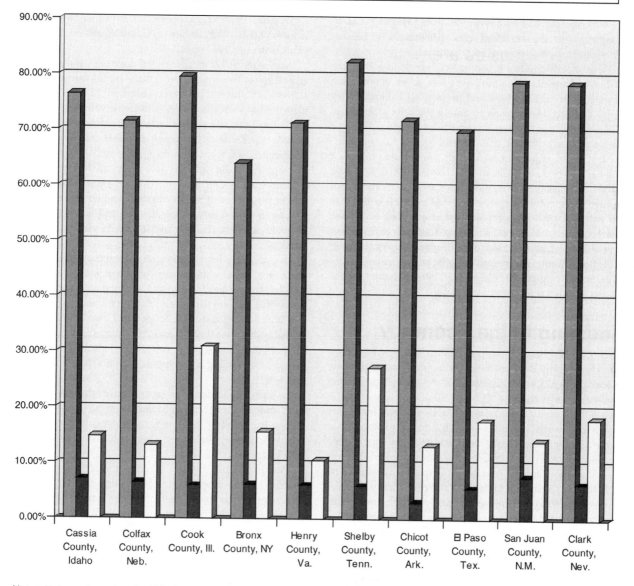

Notes: Data are based on the U.S. Census.
Bachelor's-degree-attainment rates for urban counties tend to be higher than those for rural counties, in part because higher-education participation often varies widely across metropolitan neighborhoods.

Source: Educational Needs Index.

office to read him their favorite books. He makes sure that reading is taught for 90 minutes per day from kindergarten through the eighth grade. By the 10th grade, he notes, the district's students have begun to show marked improvements in their standardized-test scores in reading.

But progress is slow. Mr. Greene struggles to compete with more densely populated communities for good teachers who can speak Spanish. And gaps in attendance among the district's migrant children, who make up more than one-third of the students, lead them to lose much of what they learn. Mr. Greene himself jumped in and out of schools as a youth, as part of a migrant family that followed fruit and other crop harvests around the state.

The migrant life can also limit the college dreams of students. Esteban Cabrera, an intervention specialist at Wahluke High School who grew up as a migrant worker, says those students who are not legal residents especially believe they do not have much of an educational future. What's more, they may not have top grades—in part because of their inconsistent attendance—and they are ineligible for federal and state financial aid for college.

"Some students are really bummed out about that and ask, What's the use of me graduating?" he says.

Mr. Cabrera understands some of this struggle. When he was young, every fall his work in the harvest would lead him to arrive at school a month late, and each spring he would rise at 1 A.M. to help cut asparagus so he could attend school. He was always behind, always tired, and his grade-point average suffered.

Even so, he was determined to pursue a college degree. But, like many of his students now, "I wasn't sure how to go about doing that," he recalls. Eventually he found his way to Yakima Valley Community College. He went on to earn a bachelor's degree at Central Washington and a master's degree in education at Heritage University, a private institution near Yakima.

Now Mr. Cabrera wants to convince his students that there is a path to higher education for them, too. He points students to private scholarships and makes sure they consider short-term vocational programs and community colleges, which tend to be less costly than four-year colleges. Only 28 percent of the senior class in 2004–5 (the most recent figure available) went on to four-year colleges, but 44 percent of the graduates planned to enroll at community colleges.

Dale Hedman, Wahluke's principal, says he tries to make the economic significance of going to college clear: "We're trying to say to them, This is your ticket away from the orchard."

Connecting to the Economy

The ability of higher education to open doors to better-paying jobs is also central to what Big Bend counselors and administrators promote as they seek to recruit greater numbers of the region's adults and traditional-age college students.

Patrick Kelly, a senior associate at the National Center for Higher Education Management Systems, says such a message is crucial for institutions in rural communities to communicate if they hope to draw more students and better serve their regions. One of the main barriers to college attainment in rural populations is that many adults who earn a GED never go beyond that high-school-equivalency degree.

Before being able to take college courses for credit, those adults often need to pay for at least a year of remedial study, he says. "That just starts to add up," he says, "and is perceived as being too long of a road to finish."

He cites one program offered at Big Bend, and elsewhere in Washington, as having promise for both attracting and retaining more residents who have not traditionally pursued higher education. It seeks to help the state's immigrant populations by allowing them to learn English as well as a trade, like welding or commercial driving, simultaneously. The skills are taught in the same classrooms during an intensive, 10- or 11-week program.

"We are seeing a population that otherwise would not walk through our doors," says Sandy Cheek, Big Bend's director of basic skills. The integrated programs are drawing many male Hispanic adults, who have been underrepresented at the college, she says. More than one in five students at the college are Hispanic, compared with almost 37 percent of the population of the counties that Big Bend serves.

Josë Cortes says the opportunity to learn English and gain a commercial driver's license was appealing because it held out the hope of a better life for him, his wife, and their three children.

"I wanted to take a better job, and I was tired of working in the orchards," says Mr. Cortes, 38, an immigrant from Mexico, where he had gained a sixth-grade-level education. After completing the program, he landed a job driving trucks and operating other equipment for a construction company.

He earns about $2,300 per month, more than twice what he made in the orchards. "We can buy toys, clothes, and everything," he says. "This is the life that I seek."

Across the state, the integrated program's students have earned an average of five times more college credits than English-language learners in traditional programs. They were 15 times as likely to complete their work-force training and earn certificates.

At Big Bend, 93 percent of the 29 students enrolled in the integrated commercial-driving program in 2004–5 completed it and gained certification, while none of the English-language learners in the traditional programs did so. Thirty-four percent of the integrated program's students made both reading and listening gains in their English skills, almost twice as many as those in more-traditional programs.

The shortened time frame and practical nature of the integrated program, says Ms. Cheek, make it "a really viable next step for them to take."

In deciding what vocations to offer through the integrated program, Big Bend administrators say they wanted to train residents in jobs that are available in the area and in occupations in which residents could envision themselves. Even though the region could use more nursing assistants, for example, many Hispanic male adults probably don't see themselves in that role as easily as they might see themselves driving a truck, college officials say. So the college first focused on building up programs in fields like commercial driving and welding.

In terms of academic programs, rather than tailor them to prepare students for specific jobs that might be locally available in the future, Big Bend officials hope that increasing the general level of education among the region's population will itself be a draw for new businesses.

Another factor driving the college's decisions about program offerings is the need to find instructors to staff them. Like the administrators at the Wahluke School District, Big Bend officials say they struggle to attract aspiring faculty members. For those who are single, there isn't much of a dating scene, and many of the area's social activities are family-oriented. For couples, the problem is finding employment for their spouses.

This fall the college advertised for over a month for an instructor in the integrated commercial-driving program and for one in the integrated-welding program. But less than two weeks before those programs were set to begin, no likely candidates had yet applied—"goose eggs," says Kara Garrett, dean of education, health, and language skills.

At the last minute, she says, a qualified candidate for the commercial-driving position "walked in off the street." To give him

Rural and Urban Communities Often Fall Behind in Education

Densely populated urban centers and sparsely populated rural regions face similar demographic situations and educational challenges, which often lead those communities to lag behind the rest of the nation in college preparation and participation. Here is how two communities, one urban and one rural, compare with the nation as a whole. Data are from 2005 unless otherwise noted.

	RURAL Grant County, Wash.	**NATIONAL**	**URBAN** Compton, Calif.
Highest level of educational attainment among adults 25 or older			
High-school diploma	28.1%	29.6%	33.4%
Some college, no degree	21.6%	20.1%	13.6%
Associate degree	10.1%	7.4%	9.8%
Bachelor's degree or higher	12.5%	27.2%	6.9%
Economic profile			
Proportion of people living in poverty	16.4%	13.3%	21.9%
Proportion of children under 18 living in poverty	23.4%	18.5%	29.7%
Per capita personal income	$17,667	$25,035	$12,617
Unemployment rate	11.6%	6.9%	11.1%
Student profile	**Wahluke School District**		**Compton Unified School District**
Proportion of students eligible for federal free- or reduced-price-meal programs	84.0%	40.0%	93.0%
Proportion of students who speak English as a second language	57.7% (2006)	18.8% (2004)	54.0% (2006)
High-school-graduation rate	69.0%	73.9% (2003)	65.1%
Proportion of graduates going to a four-year college	28.0%	44.2%	26.9%

Teacher profile

The Wahluke School District struggles to attract experienced teachers, especially Spanish-speaking ones, and to keep them, says Gary Greene, the superintendent. More than half of the district's teachers have fewer than three years of experience, and their tenure in the district averages between two and three years, Mr. Greene says.

The Compton Unified School District has tried to increase its proportion of teachers fully certified by the State of California, says the superintendent, Jesse L. Gonzales. Still, in the 2004–5 academic year, just half of the district's core academic courses were taught by teachers with full state certification and demonstrated knowledge of the subject areas, as is required by the federal No Child Left Behind law. Over all, 74.6 percent of Compton teachers are fully certified.

Population, by race

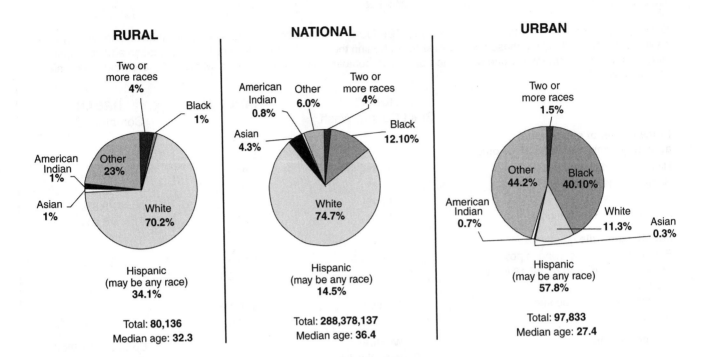

RURAL

Two or more races 4%

Black 1%

American Indian 1%

Asian 1%

Other 23%

White 70.2%

Hispanic (may be any race) 34.1%

Total: 80,136
Median age: 32.3

NATIONAL

American Indian 0.8%

Other 6.0%

Two or more races 4%

Asian 4.3%

Black 12.10%

White 74.7%

Hispanic (may be any race) 14.5%

Total: 288,378,137
Median age: 36.4

URBAN

Two or more races 1.5%

Other 44.2%

Black 40.10%

American Indian 0.7%

White 11.3%

Asian 0.3%

Hispanic (may be any race) 57.8%

Total: 97,833
Median age: 27.4

time for orientation, the college delayed the program's start date by a week. The position for the welding course still has not been filled on a permanent basis. The college was able to start that program on time by finding a part-time instructor to fill in for the fall quarter.

Patchwork of Programs

The college is accustomed to finding ways to plug gaps, whether in terms of staff or of financial resources. This year the dean of arts and sciences, Rachel Anderson, found out that a technical assistant who was helping out in an evening program has a master's degree in marine biology. She hired him to be a part-time mathematics instructor.

Administrators say they are almost constantly applying for federal, state, and private grants and contracts, which make up about half of Big Bend's budget, to patch together community services and aid programs. College administrators just got word, for instance, that they will receive four years of support from a federal education program to help migrant workers. And a new state Opportunity Grant Program will allow the college to help low-income students pay for such services as child care, allowing them to attend class.

Big Bend, like other colleges in rural areas around the country, also offers programs to help students deal with distance. Students in some far-flung communities can avoid drives to Big Bend of as much as two hours each way by taking classes in an interactive, tele-vised setting, with their local classrooms linked by fiber-optic line to instruction at Big Bend.

The enrollment in those interactive classes and online courses has grown to some 1,700 in 2005–06.

Still, distance education does not bridge all gaps. Many courses, from welding to laboratory sciences, require hands-on training with

an instructor. And students who need extra help in any course often find it easier to get assistance in person. Sometimes the region's residents find that they just have to commit to a long drive if they are going to be able to reach their educational and economic goals.

'Lots of Obstacles'

For the past year, Rosa Fabian has been driving her Oldsmobile 40 minutes each way to a job-skills center in Moses Lake, where Big Bend is located, to take information-technology classes that the college offers there.

She says she has wanted to further her education since 1989, when she came to the United States from El Salvador, where she had finished a high-school education. "I always loved to better myself, and it's always been my wish to," she says. "But I found lots of obstacles."

Ms. Fabian, 45, is a single mother of two and, until a year ago, had not gained legal status as a U.S. resident. She arrived in the United States not knowing much English or how to drive.

She also didn't know how to go about enrolling in a college or vocational-training program, until a friend told her about Big Bend's information-technology offering. Now she expects to complete the program in March, earning a certificate. She hopes to land a job in an office, perhaps doing clerical work.

But for Ms. Fabian, as for so many other low-income residents here, the path to a better education is still not easy. Her car died in October. She replaced it with a used Chevrolet, with worn tires, man-aging to pay for it with her income as a part-time cook's assistant.

The journey to her information-technology certificate may seem even longer for Ms. Fabian once the freezing rains of a Washington winter begin to fall. But she is determined to keep going, to finish her education, bad tires or not.

Colorblind to the Reality of Race in America

IAN F. HANEY LÓPEZ

How will race as a social practice evolve in the United States over the next few decades? The American public, and indeed many scholars, increasingly believe that the country is leaving race and racism behind. Some credit Brown v. Board of Education, the revered 1954 U.S. Supreme Court decision pronouncing segregated schools unequal, and the broad civil-rights movement of which the decision was a part, with turning the nation away from segregation and toward equality. Others point to changing demographics, emphasizing the rising number of mixed-race marriages and the increasing Asian and Hispanic populations that are blurring the historic black-white divide.

My sense of our racial future differs. Not only do I fear that race will continue to fundamentally skew American society over the coming decades, but I worry that the belief in the diminished salience of race makes that more likely rather than less. I suspect that the laws supposedly protecting against racial discrimination are partly to blame, for they no longer contribute to racial justice but instead legitimate continued inequality. We find ourselves now in the midst of a racial era marked by what I term "colorblind white dominance," in which a public consensus committed to formal antiracism deters effective remediation of racial inequality, protecting the racial status quo while insulating new forms of racism and xenophobia.

The Jefferson County school district, in Kentucky, covers Louisville and surrounding suburbs. A target of decades of litigation to eradicate Jim Crow school segregation and its vestiges, the district has since 2001 voluntarily pursued efforts to maintain what is now one of the most integrated school systems in the country. But not everyone supports those efforts, especially when they involve taking race into consideration in pupil assignments. In 2004 a white lawyer named Teddy B. Gordon ran for a seat on the Jefferson County School Board, promising to end endeavors to maintain integrated schools. He finished dead last, behind three other candidates. Indifferent to public repudiation, he is back—this time in the courtroom. Gordon's argument is seductively simple: Brown forbids all governmental uses of race, even if designed to achieve or maintain an integrated society.

He has already lost at the trial level and before an appellate court, as have two other sets of plaintiffs challenging similar integration-preserving efforts by school districts in Seattle and in Lynn, Mass. But Gordon and the conservative think tanks and advocacy groups that back him, including the self-styled Center for Equal Opportunity, are not without hope. To begin with, over the past three decades the courts have come ever closer to fully embracing a colorblind Constitution—colorblind in the sense of disfavoring all uses of race, irrespective of whether they are intended to perpetuate or ameliorate racial oppression. More immediately, last June the Supreme Court voted to review the Louisville and Seattle cases—Meredith v. Jefferson County Board of Education and Parents Involved in Community Schools v. Seattle School District.

Roger Clegg, president and general counsel of the Center for Equal Opportunity, is thrilled. As he gleefully noted in The National Review, there's an old saw that the court does not hear cases it plans to affirm. The Bush administration, too, supports Gordon and his efforts. The U.S. solicitor general recently submitted a friend-of-the-court brief urging the justices to prevent school districts across the country from paying attention to race.

At issue is a legally backed ideology of colorblindness that could have implications beyond schools—for higher education and the wider society. Yes, in a narrowly tailored decision three years ago, the Supreme Court allowed the University of Michigan to consider race as one factor in law-school admissions. But since then, conservative advocacy groups have used the threat of lawsuits to intimidate many institutions into halting race-based college financial-aid and orientation programs, as well as graduate stipends and fellowships, and those groups are now taking aim at faculty hiring procedures. This month Michigan voters will decide whether to amend the state constitution to ban racial and gender preferences wherever practiced. And looming on the horizon are renewed efforts to enact legislation forbidding the federal and state governments from collecting statistics that track racial disparities, efforts that are themselves part of a broader campaign to expunge race from the national vocabulary.

Gordon predicts that if he prevails, Louisville schools will rapidly resegregate. He is sanguine about the prospect. "We're a diverse society, a multiethnic society, a colorblind society," he told The New York Times. "Race is history."

But the past is never really past, especially not when one talks about race and the law in the United States. We remain a racially stratified country, though for some that constitutes an argument for rather than against colorblindness. Given the long and sorry history of racial subordination, there is tremendous rhetorical appeal to Justice John Marshall Harlan's famous dissent in Plessy v. Ferguson, the 1896 case upholding segregated railway cars: "Our Constitution is color-blind, and neither knows nor tolerates classes among citizens."

Contemporary proponents of colorblindness almost invariably draw a straight line from that dissent to their own impassioned advocacy for being blind to race today. But in doing so, partisans excise Harlan's acknowledgment of white superiority in the very paragraph in which he extolled colorblindness: "The white race deems itself to be the dominant race in this country. And so it is, in prestige, in achievements, in education, in wealth and in power. So, I doubt not, it will continue to be for all time." That omission obscures a more significant elision: Harlan objected not to all governmental uses of race, but to those he thought would unduly oppress black people.

As viewed by Harlan and the court, the central question was where to place limits on government support for the separation of racial groups that were understood to be unequal by nature (hence Harlan's comfortable endorsement of white superiority). He and the majority agreed that the state could enforce racial separation in the "social" but not in the "civil" arenas; they differed on the contours of the spheres. Harlan believed that segregated train cars limited the capacity of black people to participate as full citizens in civic life, while the majority saw such segregation only as a regulation of social relations sanctioned by custom. The scope of the civil arena mattered so greatly precisely because state exclusions from public life threatened to once again reduce the recently emancipated to an inferior caste defined by law.

For the first half of the 20th century, colorblindness represented the radical and wholly unrealized aspiration of dismantling de jure racial subordination. Thus Thurgood Marshall, as counsel to the National Association for the Advancement of Colored People in the late 1940s and early 1950s, cited Harlan's celebration of colorblindness to argue that racial distinctions are "contrary to our Constitution and laws." But neither society nor the courts embraced colorblindness when doing so might have sped the demise of white supremacy. Even during the civil-rights era, colorblindness as a strategy for racial emancipation did not take hold. Congress and the courts dismantled Jim Crow segregation and proscribed egregious forms of private discrimination in a piecemeal manner, banning only the most noxious misuses of race, not any reference to race whatsoever.

In the wake of the civil-rights movement's limited but significant triumphs, the relationship between colorblindness and racial reform changed markedly. The greatest potency of colorblindness came to lie in preserving, rather than challenging, the racial status quo. When the end of explicit race-based subordination did not eradicate stubborn racial inequalities, progressives increasingly recognized the need for state and private actors to intervene along racial lines. Rather than call for colorblindness, they began to insist on the need for affirmative race-conscious remedies. In that new context, colorblindness appealed to those opposing racial integration. Enshrouded with the moral raiment of the civil-rights movement, colorblindness provided cover for opposition to racial reform.

Within a year of Brown, Southern school districts and courts had recognized that they could forestall integration by insisting that the Constitution allowed them to use only "race neutral" means to end segregation—school-choice plans that predictably produced virtually no integration whatsoever. In 1965 a federal court in South Carolina put it squarely: "The Constitution is color-blind; it should no more be violated to attempt integration than to preserve segregation."

Wielding the ideal of colorblindness as a sword, in the past three decades racial conservatives on the Supreme Court have increasingly refought the battles lost during the civil-rights era, cutting back on protections against racial discrimination as well as severely limiting race-conscious remedies. In several cases in the 1970s—including North Carolina State Board of Education v. Swann, upholding school-assignment plans, and Regents of the University of California v. Bakke—the court ruled that the need to redress the legacy of segregation made strict colorblindness impossible. But as the 1980s went on, in other cases—McCleskey v. Kemp, which upheld Georgia's death penalty despite uncontroverted statistical evidence that African-Americans convicted of murder were 22 times as likely to be sentenced to death if their victims were white rather than black, and City of Richmond v. Croson, which rejected a city affirmative-action program steering some construction dollars to minority-owned companies despite the fact that otherwise only two-thirds of 1 percent of city contracts went to minority companies in a city 50 percent African-American—the court presented race as a phenomenon called into existence just when someone employed a racial term. Discrimination existed only but every time someone used racial language. Thus the court found no harm in Georgia's penal system, because no evidence surfaced of a specific bad actor muttering racial epithets, while it espied racism in Richmond's affirmative-action program because it set aside contracts for "minorities."

That approach ignores the continuing power of race as a society-altering category. The civil-rights movement changed the racial zeitgeist of the nation by rendering illegitimate all explicit invocations of white supremacy, a shift that surely marked an important step toward a more egalitarian society. But it did not bring into actual existence that ideal, as white people remain dominant across virtually every social, political, and economic domain. In 2003 the poverty rate was 24 percent among African-Americans, 23 percent among Latinos, and 8 percent among white people. That same year, an estimated 20 percent of African-Americans and 33 percent of Latinos had no health insurance, while 11 percent of white people were uninsured. Discrepancies in incarceration rates are particularly staggering, with African-American men vastly more likely to spend time in prison than white men are.

Or forget the numbers and recall for a moment the graphic parade of images from Hurricane Katrina. Or consider access to country clubs and gated communities, in-group preferences for jobs and housing, the moral certainty shared by many white folks regarding their civic belonging and fundamental goodness. Or, to tie back to Louisville, reflect on what you already know about the vast, racially correlated disparities in resources available to public (and still more to private) schools across the country. Racial dominance by white people continues as a central element of our society.

What may be changing, however, is how membership in the white group is defined. The term "white" has a far more complicated—and fluid—history in the United States than people commonly recognize. For most of our history, whiteness stood in contrast to the nonwhite identities imposed upon Africans, American Indians, Mexican peoples of the Southwest, and Asian immigrants, marking one pole in the racial hierarchy. Simultaneously, however, putative "racial" divisions separated Europeans, so that in the United States presumptions of gross racial inferiority were removed from Germans only in the 1840s through 1860s, the Irish in the 1850s through 1880s, and Eastern and Southern Europeans in the 1900s to 1920s. The melding of various European groups into the monolithic, undifferentiated "white" category we recognize today is a recent innovation, only fully consolidated in the mid-20th century. Now white identity may be expanding to include persons and groups with ancestors far beyond Europe.

Perhaps we should distinguish here among three sorts of white identity. Consider first persons who are "fully white," in the sense that, with all of the racially relevant facts about them widely known, they would generally be considered white by the community at large. (Obviously, racial identity is a matter not of biology but of social understandings, although those may give great weight to purportedly salient differences in morphology and ancestry.) In contrast to that group, there have long been those "passing as white"—people whose physical appearance allowed them to claim a white identity when social custom would have assigned them to a nonwhite group had their ancestry been widely known. Of people of Irish and Jewish descent in the United States, for example, one might say that while initially some were able to pass as white, now all are fully white.

Today a new group is emerging, perhaps best described as "honorary whites." Apartheid South Africa first formally crafted this identity: Seeking to engage in trade and commerce with nations cast as inferior by apartheid logic, particularly Japan, South Africa extended to individuals from such countries the status of honorary white people, allowing them to travel, reside, relax, and conduct business in South African venues that were otherwise strictly "whites only." Persons who pass as white hide racially relevant parts of their identity; honorary whites are extended the status of whiteness despite the public recognition that, from a bioracial perspective, they are not fully white.

In the United States, honorary-white status seems increasingly to exist for certain people and groups. The quintessential example is certain Asian-Americans, particularly East Asians.

Although Asians have long been racialized as nonwhite as a matter of law and social practice, the model-minority myth and professional success have combined to free some Asian-Americans from the most pernicious negative beliefs regarding their racial character. In part this trend represents a shift toward a socially based, as opposed to biologically based, definition of race. Individuals and communities with the highest levels of acculturation, achievement, and wealth increasingly find themselves functioning as white, at least as measured by professional integration, residential patterns, and intermarriage rates.

Latinos also have access to honorary-white identity, although their situation differs from that of Asian-Americans. Unlike the latter, and also unlike African-Americans, Latinos in the United States have long been on the cusp between white and nonwhite. Despite pervasive and often violent racial prejudice against Mexicans in the Southwest and Puerto Ricans and other Hispanic groups elsewhere, the most elite Latin Americans in the United States have historically been accepted as fully white. With no clear identity under the continental theory of race (which at its most basic identifies blacks as from Africa, whites from Europe, reds from the Americas, and yellows from Asia), and with a tremendous range of somatic features marking this heterogeneous population, there has long been relatively more room for the use of social rather than strictly biological factors in the imputation of race to particular Hispanic individuals and groups.

It seems likely that an increasing number of Latinos—those who have fair features, material wealth, and high social status, aided also by Anglo surnames—will both claim and be accorded a position in U.S. society as fully white. Simultaneously, many more—similarly situated in terms of material and status position, but perhaps with slightly darker features or a surname or accent suggesting Latin-American origins—will become honorary whites. Meanwhile, the majority of Latinos will continue to be relegated to nonwhite categories.

The continuing evolution in who counts as white is neither particularly startling nor especially felicitous. Not only have racial categories and ideologies always mutated, but race has long turned on questions of wealth, professional attainment, and social position. A developing scholarship now impressively demonstrates that even during and immediately after slavery, at a time when racial identity in the United States was presumably most rigidly fixed in terms of biological difference and descent, and even in the hyperformal legal setting of the courtroom, determinations of racial identity often took place on the basis of social indicia like the nature of one's employment or one's choice of sexual partners.

Nor will categories like black, brown, white, yellow, and red soon disappear. Buttressed by the continued belief in continental racial divisions, physical features those divisions supposedly connote will remain foundational to racial classification. The stain of African ancestry—so central to the elaboration of race in the United States—ensures a persistent special stigma for black people. Honorary-white status will be available only to the most exceptional—and the most light-skinned—African-Americans, and on terms far more restrictive than those on which whiteness will be extended to many Latinos and Asian-Americans.

Those many in our society who are darker, poorer, more identifiably foreign will continue to suffer the poverty, marginalization, immiseration, incarceration, and exclusion historically accorded to those whose skin and other features socially mark them as nonwhite. Even under a redefined white category, racial hierarchy will continue as the links are strengthened between nonwhite identity and social disadvantage on the one hand, and whiteness and privilege on the other. Under antebellum racial logic, those black people with the fairest features were sometimes described as "light, bright, and damn near white." If today we switch out "damn near" for "honorary" and fold in a few other minorities, how much has really changed?

In the face of continued racial hierarchy, it is crucial that we understand the colorblind ideology at issue in the school cases before the Supreme Court. "In the eyes of government, we are just one race here," Justice Antonin Scalia intoned in 1995. "It is American." That sentiment is stirring as an aspiration, but disheartening as a description of reality, and even more so as a prescription for racial policies. All persons of good will aspire to a society free from racial hierarchy. We should embrace colorblindness—in the sense of holding it up as an ideal. But however far the civil-rights struggle has moved us, we remain far from a racially egalitarian utopia.

In this context, the value of repudiating all governmental uses of race must depend on a demonstrated ability to remedy racial hierarchy. Colorblindness as a policy prescription merits neither fealty nor moral stature by virtue of the attractiveness of colorblindness as an ideal. In the hands of a Thurgood Marshall, who sought to end Jim Crow segregation and to foster an integrated society, colorblindness was a transformative, progressive practice. But when Teddy Gordon, Roger Clegg, the Bush administration, and the conservative justices on the Supreme Court call for banning governmental uses of race, they aim to end the efforts of local majorities to respond constructively to racial inequality. In so doing, they are making their version of colorblindness a reactionary doctrine.

Contemporary colorblindness is a set of understandings—buttressed by law and the courts, and reinforcing racial patterns of white dominance—that define how people comprehend, rationalize, and act on race. As applied, however much some people genuinely believe that the best way to get beyond racism is to get beyond race, colorblindness continues to retard racial progress. It does so for a simple reason: It focuses on the surface, on the bare fact of racial classification, rather than looking down into the nature of social practices. It gets racism and racial remediation exactly backward, and insulates new forms of race baiting.

White dominance continues with few open appeals to race. Consider the harms wrought by segregated schools today. Schools in predominantly white suburbs are far more likely to have adequate buildings, teachers, and books, while the schools serving mainly minority children are more commonly underfinanced, unsafe, and in a state of disrepair. Such harms acccumulate, encouraging white flight to avoid the expected deterioration in schools and the violence that is supposedly second nature to "them," only to precipitate the collapse in the tax base that in fact ensures a decline not only in schools but also in a range of social services. Such material differences in turn buttress seemingly common-sense ideas about disparate groups, so that we tend to see pristine schools and suburbs as a testament to white accomplishment and values. When violence does erupt, it is laid at the feet of alienated and troubled teenagers, not a dysfunctional culture. Yet we see the metal detectors guarding entrances to minority schoolhouses (harbingers of the prison bars to come) as evidence not of the social dynamics of exclusion and privilege, but of innate pathologies. No one need talk about the dynamics of privilege and exclusion. No one need cite white-supremacist arguments nor openly refer to race—race exists in the concrete of our gated communities and barrios, in government policies and programs, in cultural norms and beliefs, and in the way Americans lead their lives.

Colorblindness badly errs when it excuses racially correlated inequality in our society as unproblematic so long as no one uses a racial epithet. It also egregiously fails when it tars every explicit reference to race. To break the interlocking patterns of racial hierarchy, there is no other way but to focus on, talk about, and put into effect constructive policies explicitly engaged with race. To be sure, inequality in wealth is a major and increasing challenge for our society, but class is not a substitute for a racial analysis—though, likewise, racial oppression cannot be lessened without sustained attention to poverty. It's no accident that the poorest schools in the country warehouse minorities, while the richest serve whites; the national education crisis reflects deeply intertwined racial and class politics. One does not deny the imbrication of race and class by insisting on the importance of race-conscious remedies: The best strategies for social repair will give explicit attention to race as well as to other sources of inequality, and to their complex interrelationship.

The claim that race and racism exist only when specifically mentioned allows colorblindness to protect a new racial politics from criticism. The mobilization of public fears along racial lines has continued over the past several decades under the guise of interlinked panics about criminals, welfare cheats, terrorists, and—most immediately in this political season—illegal immigrants. Attacks ostensibly targeting "culture" or "behavior" rather than "race" now define the diatribes of today's racial reactionaries. Samuel P. Huntington's jeremiad against Latino immigration in his book Who Are We?: The Challenges to America's National Identity rejects older forms of white supremacy, but it promotes the idea of a superior Anglo-Protestant culture. Patrick J. Buchanan defends his latest screed attacking "illegal immigrants," State of Emergency: The Third World Invasion and Conquest of America, against the charge of racism by insisting that he's indifferent to race but outraged by those with different cultures who violate our laws. My point is not simply that culture and behavior provide coded language for old prejudices, but that colorblindness excuses and insulates this recrudescence of xenophobia by insisting that only the explicit use of racial nomenclature counts as racism.

Contemporary colorblindness loudly proclaims its antiracist pretensions. To actually move toward a racially egalitarian society, however, requires that we forthrightly respond to racial inequality today. The alternative is the continuation of colorblind white dominance. As Justice Harry Blackmun enjoined in defending affirmative action in Bakke: "In order to get beyond racism, we must first take account of race. There is no other way."

Ian F. Haney López is a professor at the Boalt Hall School of Law at the University of California at Berkeley. New York University Press has just issued a 10th-anniversary edition of his White by Law: The Legal Construction of Race, with a new chapter on colorblind white dominance.

To actually move toward a racially egalitarian society requires that we forthrightly respond to racial inequality today. The alternative is the continuation of colorblind white dominance.

As seen in the *Chronicle of Higher Education,* November 3, 2006, pp. B6–B9. Excerpted from *White By Law,* 10th Anniversary edition (New York University Press, 2006) Copyright © 2006 by Ian F. Haney López. Reproduced with permission of the author.

Metaphors of Hope

Refusing to be disheartened by all the negative press surrounding education today, Ms. Chenfeld travels the country and encounters one inspiring educator after another. She tells four of their stories here.

MIMI BRODSKY CHENFELD

On the Big Island of Hawaii, there's a forest of lava-crusted hills and bare corpses of trees called Devastation Trail. Old volcanic eruptions burnt the Ohia trees and left this once-lush terrain barren and ashen.

Walking on the wooden paths through the devastation, one could easily miss the tiny flowers remarkably pushing through the charred earth. The markers that identify these flowers read: Thimbleberry, Swordfern, Creeping Dayflower, and Nutgrass. While others aimed their cameras at the stark, mysterious lava hills, I focused on the flowers. In the midst of such a desolate scene, these perky "signs of life" seemed to be symbols of courage and persistence.

Reading daily the bleak headlines and articles that stress the stress by focusing on bullying, violence, gangs and cliques, and numerous random acts of unkindness and hostility in our seemingly devastated educational landscape, one could easily sink into despair. However, as a stubborn optimist, I always search for markers of thimbleberry, swordfern, creeping dayflower, and nutgrass—metaphors of hope!

When Mr. T (also known as Tom Tenerovich) was moved upstairs after years of teaching kindergarten classes, he observed that second-graders were more vocal, more argumentative, more opinionated! A voracious reader of books about education, he was familiar with many theories and programs. *But reading about ideas is different from doing.*

One idea that intrigued Mr. T was that of Town Meeting. He and his students discussed building a structure that would enable all voices to be heard, problems to be solved, and good listening habits to be formed.[1]

The class added mayor and assistant mayor to the list of jobs on their classroom helpers board. During the year, every student would be assigned to these jobs for a one-week term of office.

The Town Meeting works this way: each week, the mayor and assistant mayor, along with Tom, write an agenda for two, 30- to 40-minute Town Meetings. Any student can submit a proposal for discussion, but it has to be written and include name, date, and the issue to be discussed. Some of the issues concerning the students have included changing seats, playground rules,

classmates being hurtful, picking team members, and activities for "Fun Fridays."

At the Town Meeting, the class discusses the topic and votes to resolve the issue. "Even if they disagree, it's so sweet to hear how they disagree," Tom reports. "They're really beginning to listen to each other." He continues,

> It's amazing the way it works out. None of the kids are bossy when they become mayor. Even our most timid children became good mayors. Believe it or not, one of my most high-maintenance tough kids was the best mayor! He took charge in a fair way—he knew what to do—he behaved appropriately.
>
> Even I became an agenda issue! One of the kids reminded me that I hadn't done something I promised. That was important to the children, and I had to remedy it.

Committees formed from discussions: academic committees, playground committees (to see that no students were left out of games or weren't chosen for teams), and classroom improvement committees. Tom was thrilled to see how the twice-weekly Town Meetings honoring the feelings and agendas of the students carried over into the everyday life of the group. "This really is democracy in action! Points of view are freely expressed. All opinions are valued and respected. You can see and feel the increase of courtesy and kindness."

The school mascot is a bobcat. Tom and his second-graders added the idea of Bobcat Purrs to their Town Meeting. Like "warm fuzzies," pats on the back, recognition of positive acts, observations of improvements, Bobcat Purrs were "built into our meetings," Tom explains, "and became part of our culture. Children wrote up a 'purr,' decorated it, and handed it to the mayor, who read it and presented it. No one was ever left out. We promised *not* to just recognize our best friends. Children looked for what their classmates were doing well. They were very specific."

One student, who had experienced alienation, low self-image, and loneliness in earlier years and whose posture defined his feelings, received a Bobcat Purr during a Town Meeting that stated how proudly he was standing. He was standing up straight! The boy beamed!

Another student who had difficulty finishing her work received a Bobcat Purr from a classmate honoring her for finishing *all* of her work. Everyone rejoiced.

When children live in a climate that accentuates the positive, their eagle eyes catch the flickering light of flames that are almost burnt out.

The picture I want to snap for my Album of Hope is of a proud second-grader standing up straight with the mayor, assistant mayor, his teacher, and all of his classmates honoring him with a Bobcat Purr during the Town Meeting.[2]

Swordfern: Cathy

Cathy Arment and her first-graders are not involved in the building of structures like Town Meetings. With their teacher, this group of students from diverse cultures, races, and religions works hard and plays hard together. Cathy described a memorable scene in a telephone message: "I was reading the children Jonathan London's *Froggy's First Kiss*—you know, for Valentine week. Mim, I looked up from the story to see the children sitting in clusters, their arms around each other, their eyes wide as I turned the pages, so totally involved. I almost began to weep at the sight of their beauty."

Here we have students with Ethiopian, Mexican, Appalachian, Southeast Asian, and African American backgrounds. How did such a diverse group of children learn to love one another?

Here we have students with Ethiopian, Mexican, Appalachian, Southeast Asian, and African American backgrounds—children who are newcomers, some from dysfunctional homes, some from foster homes, some with hardship home lives, some at risk. How did such a diverse group of children learn to love one another?

Cathy and I talked at length. With all the realities of alienation, anxiety, insecurity, and mean-spiritedness that these students face, *how is such a warm and loving environment created?* What is the strategy? What are the techniques? Cathy thought long and hard about these questions. She realized that she did not have a preconceived plan for helping her students build positive classroom relationships. She hadn't adopted a program specifically aimed at such outcomes. Nowhere in her plan book were consciously chosen activities based on proven behavior management theories. *She just did what she did because of who she was and what she believed.* Reviewing her ideas, she said:

All I can think of is that from day one, we are together. We verbalize feelings—good and bad. We're not afraid to share. From our first moment together, we talked about respecting everyone. Some of my children have heavy accents. They are "different." Many of them have been

made fun of. We talk about how hurtful it is to be teased, to put people down and to be put down. We begin to listen to each other. To care about each other. *My children never, ever tease!* And—I'm a human being, too—I share with them. They'll ask me, "Teacher, what did YOU read? What did YOU do over the weekend? Did YOU have a fun holiday?" When a child has a low day, we all try to cheer that child. Sometimes I have a gray day. The kids will go out of their way to brighten me. They know we stick together, that I care for them very deeply. They know that we are all safe in our room.

When the children wrote and illustrated their "I Have A Dream" papers inspired by Dr. Martin Luther King, Jr.'s famous speech, many of them expressed the warm feelings they experienced in the classroom and wrote dreams like these: "I have a dream to be with my family and to give love to everybody and to care about everybody" (Abigail). "I have a dream that people would be nice to other people and, if people are hurt, other people could help them just like other people help me" (Carissa).

The Israeli-Yemenite dancer Margolith Ovid once said, "The greatest technique in the universe is the technique in the human heart."

The picture I would snap for my Album of Hope is of Cathy's kids, arms around each other, sitting in clusters, listening to Froggy's First Kiss.[3]

Creeping Dayflower: Ms. Gibson

Before the new school year even begins, Dee Gibson sends warm *Welcome to the Family* cards to her future students! These fortunate first-graders know—from everything said and done, from words and actions, activities and discussions, planning and projects—that their class is a second family in which each and every family member is important and connected to everyone else. This is not a theme or a curriculum item or a subject area—*it's the way it is* in Ms. Gibson's class. Because she is passionate, articulate, and committed to creating, with her children and families, a safe, encouraging, caring community that really is a second family (and for some children over the years, a first family!), the experiences of her students are very special. They help one another. They cooperate. They plan and talk together. They are totally involved in the life they share together in this home away from home.

We can't take the environment for granted. We are the architects of the culture of the school, of the program.

When the children were asked such questions as "What is it like being in this kind of class family? What do you do? How do you feel?" the responses were honest and forthcoming:

We're all together. We get in pods. We work together. If two kids are having an argument, the whole class stops till we work it out. We really feel like everyone cares about each other.—*Jay*

***

We're like teamwork. We help each other with work and to pick up. Everyone here sticks together —*Lauri*

***

All the kids are friends. Arguing doesn't really happen much—everyone cooperates.—*Ryan*

***

Our teacher treats people fair. The other kids act very kind together. She teaches us how to work together.—*Barrett*

***

We don't really get in fights!—*Nikki*

***

Everybody is nice to each other, and they act like a family. Ms. Gibson is like one of the family.—*Danielle*

The language in this class is the language of respect, acceptance, courtesy, responsibility, and cooperation. It's not limited to a week's celebration of a theme! It's the vocabulary of a close-knit family. That's an everyday reality.

The picture I want to take for my Album of Hope is of the children holding up their summer "Welcome to the Family" cards. A sequel to that picture is of children discovering that the welcome cards were not a gimmick! They were the real thing.[4]

Nutgrass: Anne and Claudette

Partners in Educating All Children Equally (PEACE), Anne Price and Claudette Cole travel to schools, programs, and conferences, spreading very simple messages—especially to administrators who too often don't attend workshops that are aimed directly at the heart. Anne and Claudette remind those directors, managers, principals, and superintendents that their influence in the creation of positive, life-affirming school climates is immeasurable. They *really can* make the difference between the life and death of an entire program or school.

Claudette and Anne discuss ways of helping teachers to develop positive relationships with their students and to motivate the students to develop caring and respectful relationships with one another. What are some suggestions for doing so? Usually, without hesitation, most of the administrators offer such actions as recognizing students, paying attention to them, appreciating their talents and efforts, encouraging them to cooperate with and be considerate of one another, and inviting students to share ideas and input so that they are directly involved in the success of the school.

Claudette and Anne gently turn these ideas around, directing them to the administrators. "Just as we advocate developmentally appropriate practices for teaching children, so we have to apply those ideas to our staff." Anne explains their simple, direct approach: "It's our responsibility to pay attention to the needs of staff so they can meet the children's needs."

What are some of the greatest trouble spots in the dynamics of any school or program? Absenteeism, turnover, bullying, discipline problems, low morale, lack of trust, miscommunication—to name just a few. It's so obvious to Anne and Claudette that these problems, often reflecting a disconnected and resentful staff, carry over to the students and poison the atmosphere. (Think lava!)

Think of ways to inspire and create a healthy workplace for all who spend time there. Claudette asks, "Does the staff feel appreciated? Respected? Do they feel they have ownership of and an investment in the success of the program? Are their efforts and contributions valued? Do we keep all avenues of communication open? Do we trust enough to be honest with each other without fear of reprisal?"

Anne reminds participants in her workshops that we can't take the environment for granted. *We are the architects of the culture of the school, of the program.* "You'll see the difference in an environment where children, staff, families, and communities are nurtured and respected. Ideas flow freely, teamwork flourishes, staff feels open and trusting with each other and with the administration—now, will the turnover be as great? The absenteeism? The low morale?" She challenges her groups to talk honestly about these vital components that make for a healthy, positive school culture.

"And," she warns, "you can't give it if it's not in you to give. That's why we constantly have to think about our commitments, beliefs, and goals. How we feel about those deeper questions will generate our behavior."

Claudette and Anne inspire those who lead to look deeply into their own hearts and souls and honestly find whether their beliefs, actions, and words are in harmony. Their decisions will shape the culture of their schools, affecting children, staff, families, and neighbors.

The image for my Album of Hope is a group of administrators exchanging ideas and experiences, sharing feelings, and being energized by the process and promise of making a real difference in the lives of those they guide.[5]

These are just four examples of courageous, confident, hopeful educators who, like our four brave little flowers, insist on growing through hardened and lava-crusted times! I must tell you, I have gathered hundreds and hundreds of examples of educators throughout the land who inspire and nurture caring, compassionate communities of learners.

All of them give themselves wholly to this "holy" process. Their words aren't slogans. Their promises are not bulletin-board displays or mottos. Their commitments are demonstrated every day by how they meet and greet, listen and talk, share and care in their numerous interactions with children and adults.

They know that nothing is to be taken for granted. Tom's Town Meeting is not guaranteed to succeed. A teacher who does not teach in the "key of life," who doesn't listen to or respect the students, who is rigid and devoid of joy and humor, can follow the recipe for a Town Meeting to the last syllable, but it will yield nothing that will teach the children, *through doing,* the art of building positive classroom relationships.

I have gathered hundreds and hundreds of examples of educators throughout the land who inspire and nurture caring, compassionate communities of learners.

Cathy didn't adopt a specific program. She and her children *are* the program, and their mutuality, kindness, and concern for one another are expressed in everything they do. There is no place for bullying in the safe place of Cathy's classroom. She teaches by heart!

Unless one believes it deeply and demonstrates that belief in everything he or she does (from the smallest acts to the largest), even a stellar concept like *family* will be another act of betrayal. Dee Gibson truly believes in establishing a second family with her children. This is not a once-a-month, set-aside time slot; it's the air they breathe and everything they do. Children are acutely alert to hypocrisy. They know when their teachers speak empty words. Lip service is disservice! They learn those lessons well.

Anne and Claudette, in their workshops, invite administrators to examine their own beliefs, motivations, and actions. Joanne Rooney, in her excellent article "Principals Who Care: A Personal Reflection," wrote:

> Good principals model care. Their words and behavior explicitly show that caring is not optional. Nothing can substitute for this leadership. Phoniness doesn't cut it. No principal can ask any teacher, student, or parent to travel down the uncertain path of caring if the principal will not lead the way.[6]

The way through these often grim times is through dedication and commitment, courage, persistence and fierce optimism. Just as Swordfern, Nutgrass, Creeping Dayflower, and Thimbleberry push their bright colors through seemingly solid lava, countless teachers and administrators shine their lights—brightening the sacred spaces they influence, dotting the charred landscape with blossoms of hope.

Notes

1. Tom was inspired by A. S. Neill, *Summerhill School* (New York: St. Martin's Griffin, 1992).

2. Tom Tenerovich and his second-graders enjoyed their Town Meetings at the Royal Palm Beach Elementary School, Royal Palm Beach, Fla. Tom currently teaches second grade at Equestrian Trails Elementary school in Wellington, Fla.

3. Cathy Arment and her loving first-graders listened to *Froggy's First Kiss* at the Etna Road School, Whitehall-Yearling Public Schools, Whitehall, Ohio, where she was voted Teacher of the Year 2004.

4. Dee Gibson and her family of first-graders thrive in the Walden School, Deerfield Public Schools, Deerfield, Ill. Dee was featured in my guest editorial, "Welcome to the Family," *Early Childhood Education Journal,* Summer 2003, pp. 201–2.

5. Anne Price and Claudette Cole are PEACEmakers in Cleveland, Ohio. You can contact Anne and Claudette at www.peaceeducation.com.

6. Joanne Rooney, "Principals Who Care: A Personal Reflection," *Educational Leadership,* March 2003, p. 77.

Mimi Brodsky Chenfeld began teaching in 1956. She works and plays with people of all ages and grade levels throughout the country. Among her books are *Teaching in the Key of Life* (National Association for the Education of Young Children, 1993), *Teaching by Heart* (Redleaf Press, 2001), and *Creative Experiences for Young Children,* 3rd ed. (Heinemann, 2002). She lives in Columbus, Ohio. She dedicates this article to the memory of Pauline Gough, whose life's work, brightening the way for educators and children, is a stellar example of metaphors of hope.

Hitting The Ground Running

Why Introductory Teacher Education Courses Should Deal With Multiculturalism

MARTA I. CRUZ-JANZEN AND MARILYN TAYLOR

The Problem

I know I still have a lot to learn but I have a foundation. I know that I don't know a lot and need to learn more. I have to accept that I have biases, I cannot feel guilty because that is what I was taught growing up. But I know that I have to examine myself. Like you always said, "critical introspection and critical reflection." I remember when I didn't know what that was. All teachers must do this. It must start inside with you, then out with the students. Whenever I am writing a lesson plan or getting materials for my class I remember the forms of bias and ask who is being left out here. I ask if I was in any way biased. This course prepared me for that and I am glad it was the very first course I took. I know teachers in schools today that still don't know this. Don't even have a clue the damage they do to kids. I try to tell them but they think they know it all and some think I want to be smarter than them. A friend just graduated from [another institution], never took a single course in multicultural education. I see it in her classroom and the things she does. She always wonders where I learned all these things. How can anyone become a teacher and not learn these things? It should be required! (Spring 2000).

These are the comments of a teacher candidate who completed the introduction to education course at the institution where this study was conducted. This candidate's comments suggest intentional reflection, awareness of personal biases, and purposeful curriculum monitoring to ensure inclusiveness. This candidate is aware that not all teachers examine bias as he/she does, and that not all programs prepare teachers for this task. Like this candidate, others with a foundation in multicultural education agree that we have a problem.

Teachers are not being adequately prepared, before or after entering the profession, to work effectively with the increasingly diverse student population they encounter in public P/K–12th schools. Experienced administrators and teachers consistently express a need for teachers who are better prepared to work with a "diverse student mix" in urban settings (Truog, 1998). The current study was conducted to assess and strengthen one program's approach to multicultural education to meet this need.

Many multiculturalists point out that White/Caucasian, monolingual, middle class teachers' life experiences differ markedly from most of their students (Banks, 1991; Derman-Sparks & Phillips, 1997; Howard, 1999; Lawrence, 1997; Ooka Pang, 2001). Most acknowledge the importance of teachers stepping outside of their own cultural framework, knowing about, and respecting the diverse cultures, races, languages their students represent.

But Lipman (1993) suggests that teachers can be very resistant to change; their ideologies and convictions about children of color and their intellectual potential tend to remain unchanged in spite of information to the contrary. Zofko Lattragna (1998) found that White/Caucasian college students, particularly males, are most resistant to multicultural education. This is alarming because most students in higher education across the nation, including those pursuing the teaching profession, are White/Caucasian.

Preparation in multicultural education can occur before or after entering the profession. Still, once candidates become teachers, effective multicultural education can be hard to come by. Unless teachers enroll in continuing and/or post baccalaureate courses, they are often exposed to new information only through short, mandated in-services/workshops that take place after a long workday. Workshops tend to be superficial; termed "dog and pony shows" that do not provide the quality time needed to fully explore and understand issues of multiculturalism and are unlikely to bring about key and enduring personal changes.

To the contrary, they can serve to further trivialize the issues, focus on single fixes, and add to the confusion, frustration, distrust, and alienation already felt (Cruz-Janzen, 2000). It is agreed, that resolution of inequities in classrooms and school reform must go beyond the staff development that entertains, avoids making anyone uncomfortable, and adds a few strategies to "teachers' bag of tricks."

Thus, it becomes all the more imperative that preservice teacher candidates experience appropriate, sustained multicultural education. When they prepare, candidates have more time and course requirements to reflect. Faculty have time to develop and adjust topics adequately and in response to their class's feedback.

In the urban teacher preparation program where this study took place, faculty concurred that candidates would benefit most by beginning their study of multiculturalism before setting foot in the classroom. That way, their practicum [field experience and/or student teaching] in an actual P/K–12 classroom would be accompanied by thoughtful reflection on how teachers can best teach diverse students. Without this foundation, candidates sometimes completed methods courses without knowledge of why or how to address the unique needs of diverse learners.

This state college produced the largest number of new teachers in the state. Known as an urban "institution of access" and characterized by a diverse student body, it was recognized for its stated commitment to diversity. In an effort to prepare candidates to "hit the ground running," the program infused multiculturalism throughout the initial foundations in education course required at the very start of the teacher education sequence.

The course worked steadily to develop candidates' sociocultural understanding, essential as a basis for lifelong growth in competence as multicultural educators. Equity and multiculturalism were taught throughout the entire semester. Faculty facilitated candidates' reflection on these topics and comparisons to their own development.

Activities were designed to enhance candidates' abilities to design and implement responsive instructional practices suitable for diverse students. It allowed them to critically examine classrooms in urban multicultural schools through their connected field experience and, concurrently, reflect with peers and professors on the implications of these conditions for effective teaching and learning. In this way, the course provided initial understandings upon which candidates' further learning could be built.

Faculty teaching this course considered it essential to nurture and monitor candidates' openness to new perspectives. Thus, faculty examined the impact of their teaching and made adjustments to minimize resistance. Candidates looked at the implications of their own socialization for their role as teachers. Faculty guided candidates in the examination of their own history of family immigration and integration into mainstream U.S.A. society.

Candidates examined their own—often-unexplored—socialization into their gender, race, ethnicity, socioeconomic class, physical appearance, abilities and disabilities, and other forms of diversity. They looked at how this shaped the way they perceived others unlike them. They reflected on their own experiences in the school system and how their own diversity and that of their teachers, in turn, shaped those. They took a close look at the role of schools not only in enculturating but deculturating groups from non-Anglo Saxon Protestant European backgrounds. They studied the long—and continuing—historical battle of various groups, including women and persons of color, for educational equality and became cognizant of the effects that bias in curricular materials and programs have on students, particularly females and students of color (Sadker & Sadker, 2003).

In their field experience, candidates had the opportunity to examine race, gender, and class in a diverse urban school and community through the sociocultural lenses learned in their campus-based course.

The Study

This study examined 214 written pre- and 180 post-course surveys in which candidates described their preparation in the introductory multicultural-designated course. Candidates were either seeking bachelor's degrees concurrent with teaching licensure, or were post-baccalaureate seeking "licensure only."

The study assessed their ways of understanding and valuing multiculturalism before and after the course. Since White/Caucasian, monolingual, middle class teachers continue to constitute the majority of the teaching force, a particular interest was to examine White/Caucasian candidates' before and after responses. The study also looked at responses among candidates of color and between males and females.

The six semester credit hour course block was offered in 5–6 sections by different instructors each semester and included 60 hours of field experience in a diverse urban middle or high school. Three of the six instructors were persons of color: African American, Latino/a, and Native American.

Candidates in several course sections completed anonymous surveys during the first and last week each semester starting in fall 1997 through spring 2000. Two demographic identifiers were race/ethnicity and gender. One race category titled "Other" enabled candidates to select Interracial/Interethnic with lines provided for the possible combinations. The survey questions were as follows:

The Survey Questions:

1. What do you hope to acquire/learn from this course? (pre-survey)
   What do you feel you acquired/learned from this course? (post-survey)
2. Multicultural education means:
3. Multicultural education IS/IS NOT needed because:
4. Multicultural education DOES/DOES NOT benefit "minority" students because:
5. Multicultural education DOES/DOES NOT benefit European American [White/Caucasian] students because:
6. Multicultural education DOES/DOES NOT benefit female students because:
7. Multicultural education DOES/DOES NOT benefit male students because:
8. Multicultural education DOES/DOES NOT benefit me because:
9. Multicultural education DOES/DOES NOT benefit society because:
10. Other Comments:

Narrative responses per candidate per survey question were categorized as positive or negative. Positive comments conveyed openness to multiculturalism and indicated, in the post-course survey, that candidates experienced learning that enabled them to see the *benefits* of multicultural education to their careers and/or personal lives. Negative comments expressed aversion, lack of interest, and/or resistance to the topic.

Findings

The findings are summarized in representative narrative responses and reported in tables. Disaggregated annual data is reported in the Appendices to this paper. The first column presents ratios. For example, a ratio of 21:57 indicates 27 of the 57 participants wrote positive comments. It does not mean the remaining 36 wrote negative ones; perhaps they didn't write any at all. The next column—"% Total"—translates this ratio to the percent of positive comments from the total participants. Horizontally, the tables are divided into pre- and post-survey. Horizontally across, responses are further disaggregated by gender. Moving down the columns, responses are disaggregated by race/ethnicity.

Table 1 shows the number of respondents, their race/ethnicity, and gender across the six semesters.

It is important to note that across all semesters several candidates changed racial/ethnic identity and those self-identifying as "Other" increased. This finding is further discussed in the conclusions.

Pre- and Post-Course Survey

A limitation of the study is the small number of participants. Therefore, the focus was on qualitative analysis of actual comments to support course and program improvement and identify areas for further study.

Table 2 indicates the ratio of positive comments to the first question. It shows that, across the six semesters, 65 of 144 White/Caucasian candidates responded positively in the pre-course survey. Most of these comments indicated lack of awareness with a strong desire to learn. Candidates were, overall, far more positive across all semesters in both the pre- and post-course survey.

Some of the pre-course comments include:

White/Caucasian:

"I want to learn how to be comfortable teaching and learning in such an environment."

"Everything. . . . I have never studied multicultural and don't even know what it is."

"To better assess the needs and wants of multicultural students and parents to help their educational progress. Basic techniques of teaching in a diverse school. The do's and don'ts."

Latino/Hispanic:

"Receive an experience working with secondary students that come from diverse backgrounds."

"The differences in cultures and traditions and how important it is as a teacher to be fair in presenting information to students in your class."

African American:

"This class should be given to all Americans so we can understand the whole world communities. Others need to understand what other groups have experience so they have a better understanding of how hard it is to be of color in this world."

Native American Indian:

"Because our society is racist. This racism is eating away at any unity. This country could have. Without addressing this issue we will kill each other in a race war."

Other:

"How do you teach multiculturalism in a predominantly White school? Or predominantly Black? Or male? My personal experience was immersion, quite literally, and the availability of having students give personal accounts."

In answer to post-survey question #3, most candidates responded positively showing increased awareness and learning. Most White/Caucasian candidates wrote that the course helped them realize that they, too, are multicultural and living in a multicultural world. Post-survey comments indicate that most candidates, of all backgrounds, found the course personally and professionally beneficial, like this respondent:

"That my education of cultural diversity will never end. It's a life long process."

White/Caucasian candidates and candidates of color responded in various ways in the post-survey:

White/Caucasian:

"Multicultural is far more important than many realize. We all live in a multicultural world! Even I am diverse!"

"Much about cultures and about the way that they interact. Better understanding on the effects of education. It opened my eyes and figure out ways to teach to many different kinds of people and to be sure that I don't forget or offend anyone."

"Get rid of the Old Boys' network." "Avoiding forms of bias, which leads to more sensitive and responsible behavior. I continue to learn to respect others' beliefs even if I disagree."

Table 1   Composite Survey Participants Race/Ethnicity and Gender

	PRE-COURSE			POST-COURSE		
	Total	**Male**	**Female**	**Total**	**Male**	**Female**
EA	144	51	93	116	39	77
AꜰA	12	5	7	6	3	3
L/H	31	9	22	24	7	17
NA	4	0	4	5	2	3
AsA	1	0	1	0	0	0
Other	22	10	12	29	15	14
	214			180		

EA = European American [White/Caucasian]; AꜰA = African American;
L/H = Latino/Hispanic; NA = Alaskan Native/Native American Indian; AsA = Asian
American; Other.

Table 2 Cumulative Positive Responses to Question # 1

	PRE	POST
EA	65:144	82:116
AғA	5:12	6:6
L/H	17:31	19:24
NA	2:4	3:5
AsA	0:1	0:0
Other	10:22	16:29
	99:214	126:180

EA = European American [White/Caucasian]; AғA = African American; L/H=Latino/Hispanic; NA = Alaskan Native / Native American Indian; AsA = Asian American; Other.

"I am aware of biases that occur that I was blind to before. I have become aware of my own prejudices and make a conscious effort to omit them."

"That I have stereotypes and that I have the capacity to hinder the education of my students by doing so. I was taught to be aware of my own stereotypical assumptions and other things so that I can learn to teach individual kids."

"Very deep. I learned a great deal. Issues minorities are facing, ideas on how to approach these issues."

Latino/Hispanic:

"Multicultural education is fun, interactive, and exciting. It really is the only way to educate in today's changing society."

"Multicultural education is a **must** for everyone. We as teachers owe it to our children to teach them about themselves and about others. The process to better our world starts with our children. If things don't change, we are sure to destroy one another. We need to teach love for all, not hate!"

"Hopefully by presenting multicultural education we will be more sensitive to other genders and races and value them as they value themselves."

African American:

"The makeup of our society is constantly incorporating new immigrants, which allows for their stories & history to be told by themselves instead of someone who did not take the time to correctly learn their history."

Native American Indian:

"The more we know about those who are different from us, the more likely we will be able to understand their perspective."

"The oppression felt by others is not understood and at least multicultural education provides some understanding. This

country does not change and I personally feel sorry for Whites."

"To be sensitive to other cultures. To understand why Whites act the way they do. Education is based on economics and not on the true value of education. Education is not a right, or treated as a right, because all children in the U.S. do not benefit from it."

Other:

"This class is helpful to all groups. Equipping future teachers with ways to deal with their own biases, with curriculum bias, with societal influence—are all beneficial for **any** teacher of any gender, race, ethnicity."

Over the six semesters, negative remarks emerged after the course from 10 of the 180 respondents (5%). While limited, these were examined carefully each year (see Table 3).

Emergent Themes

Multiple responses reflected three themes:

1. The first was a pattern of narratives, like the following, showing that candidates encountered difficult challenges within themselves and/or their families and friends as their awareness of diversity and societal injustices increased.

"It was an extremely thought-provoking class. My husband and I got in an argument **every time** I came home from it because my perspective changed enough to make him uncomfortable."

"My boyfriend and I got into some pretty bad arguments. He didn't want to accept that I am multiracial. He says I am White, just White. We finally broke up. I don't think he was ready for that. It would have been a problem later on."

"My mother is always making racist comments. I used to pretend not to hear her. Now it really bothers me."

"I am married to a really bigoted guy. How can I help him see what I have learned this semester without losing my marriage? I feel like he has to know and learn too."

2. The second pattern conveyed candidates' concerns that unless multicultural education courses are taught "the way [it] should be," greater problems may be created.

"I feel like multicultural education is beneficial but it is going to be a long time before it's presented in a way it should be. People need to get past the hate and ignorance before they can learn these things and before they can teach these things effectively."

"Multicultural education is a very sensitive area and if taught & presented correctly could be beneficial to all. If not, I believe, it could cause deep barriers between many."

3. The third pattern indicated that candidates considered having instructors of color a definite advantage.

"This was my best I favorite class of the semester. I appreciated the forum format that existed each day. The teacher's insights were great. Her perspectives and philosophy were challenging and beneficial to me."

"First-hand knowledge is always helpful. I love to hear [the professor's] stories and experiences about multicultural education."

"Thank you from the bottom of my heart for touching my soul. You are a teacher of power, wisdom, and all around beauty. I admire your strength and your spirit that has already moved mountains. Thank you."

Post-Survey Follow Up

As candidates moved through the remainder of the teacher preparation program, they were surveyed informally during advising. Many commented that the introductory multicultural course should be required of all prospective teachers, no matter what college or university. Course completers wrote, anonymously, about how the introductory multicultural course continued to impact their subsequent teacher preparation program:

"I was able to write lesson plans and take learning styles and other diversities into consideration. I was always asking whom am I leaving out? I want to help all students. But we learned in your class that we may omit someone because we are socialized to do it without being aware. I am now aware and stop to ask myself."

"Sometimes, if the instructor forgets, we (the students) remind them, hey what about the students of color, what about learning disabled, non-English speakers."

"In one class the students had to tell the professor that he was prejudiced. He was using all these Stereotypic materials, doing and saying all these things. He was teaching us everything we knew not to do. It was pretty sad. We told him to take your course."

Survey Year 1: 1997–1998

In academic year 1997–1998, only 25 of 82 (30.4%) candidates initially indicated a specific interest in learning about multiculturalism while 39 of 66 (59.1%) expressed growth at the end of the course. Composite results are reported in Tables A.1 through A.3 of the Appendix. There were no negative comments in the pre-course and only three post-course.

"How frustrating, annoying, and angry the amount of diversity that was dealt with made me." White/Caucasian female (aged 18–22 years).

"I resent always having to talk about race. If only they worked as hard as other people that also came here with nothing. We don't owe them anything and I resent all the talk about special treatments for them." White/Caucasian male (aged 23–27).

Looking only at responses to "Other comments," only 16 of 82 (19.5%) candidates responded positively in the pre-course survey. This increased to 22 of 66 (33.3%). The only negative post-course comment follows:

"I really got upset and frustrated with the amount of diversity. Is it really necessary to constantly pick everyone out and set them in a group? It is a good idea to learn more about different cultures but if we are a melting pot, please let us melt and not separate so like oil and water, never being able to mix." White/Caucasian female (23–27 age group).

In this year White/Caucasian candidates responding positively increased from 36.8% (21:57) to 60.0% (27:45). Positive comments from White/Caucasian females increased from 46.9% (15:32) to 74% (20:27). Positive comments from White/ Caucasian males were fewer before the course and showed a smaller increase from 24% (6:25) to 38.9% (7:18).

Survey Year 2: 1998–1999

Composite results for 1998–1999 are reported in Tables B.1 through B.3 of the Appendix. This year, 61 of 99 (61.6%) candidates responded positively in the pre-course survey. This number grew to 76 of 87 (87.3%). White/Caucasian candidates showed a gain from 55.9% (38:68) to 82.5% (47:57). White/Caucasian males' increased from 52.4% (11:21) to 88.2% (15:17). White/Caucasian females' increased from 59.6% (28:47) to 80.0% (32:40).

In year two, 43 of 99 (43.4%) participants made positive comments to item # 10. This ratio increased to 73 of 87 (83.9%). Of 76 total comments, only three were negative:

"Multicultural education is very valuable, however, I do not feel that an entire class should be devoted to this area. It

Table 3 Negative Comments Regarding Value of Multicultural Education

1997–98		1998–99		1999–00	
PRE	POST	PRE	POST	PRE	POST
N = 0/82	N = 3/66	N = 0/99	N = 3/87	N = 0/33	N = 4/27
	White/Caucasian Female (2)				White/Caucasian Female (1)
	White/Caucasian Male (1)		White/Caucasian Male (2)		White/Caucasian Male (2)
			African American Female (1)		
					Latino/Hispanic Male (1)

could easily be incorporated into a section of an education class and the importance would not be lost." White Caucasian male (43–47 age group).

"I wasn't raised that way. I was raised in a Christian home. I am educated. It doesn't happen to me." African American female (18–22 age group).

"We need to say things they were they were. If Whites came here and did what they did, we have to admit that they were pretty brave and hard working. And we have to admit that everyone was doing the same to everyone else. The Africans were enslaving other Africans and selling them too. The Indians here also had slaves. That's just the way it was. I don't have to be made feel ashamed of my White ancestors. I wasn't there, I didn't do anything wrong and I can't change any of that now. So get off it!" White/Caucasian male (33–37 age group).

Survey Year 3: 1999–2000

In 1999–2000, the final year of the study, 13 of 33 (39.4%) candidates initially indicated a specific interest in learning about multiculturalism, and 21 of 27 (77.8%) responded positively in this area at the end. Overall, White/Caucasian candidates increased from 6:19 (31.5%) to 8:14 (57.1%). White/Caucasian males increased from 40.0% (2:5) to 75.0% (3:4). White/Caucasian females increased from 28.6% (4:14) to 50.0% (5:10). Disaggregated results are reported in Tables C.1 through C.3 of the Appendix. Three negative comments were made to, "What do you feel you acquired/learned from this course:"

"I don't ever want to have to take another multicultural course." White/Caucasian male (23–27 age group).

"Affirmative Action is going the wrong way. Why do they need special rights?" White/Caucasian male (33–37 age group).

"I am tired of having to deal with this over and over. By emphasizing all of this and the differences, we are maintaining the separations. Why can't we all just get along and see people for the content of their character rather than their skin color?" Latino/Hispanic male (23–27 age group).

In response to "Other Comments," while only 11 of 33 (33.3%) candidates indicated a specific interest in learning about issues of multiculturalism before the course, 15 of 27 (55.6%) reported positively afterwards. Of twenty-seven comments, only two were negative:

"I think you are pretty bias[ed] yourself. Where do you get your information? I hope I never have to sit through another one of your classes again. I was angry all the time" White/Caucasian female (23–27 age group).

"I can now see why people don't want to take these courses. We are constantly being told what we did wrong, what our ancestors did. I personally think they did a pretty darned good job. We are the most advanced country in the world. Other countries would like to have what we do. Why is Africa the poorest country in the world? Why are people starving in India? I feel very proud of my ancestry and what White people have done. Wherever they went it's a prosperous nation. You have to be pretty darned good to be able to do that." White/Caucasian male (23–27 age group).

Conclusions

Results indicated that the vast majority of teacher candidates, in all three years, were more positive about the importance of multicultural education at the end of the course than at the start. Only five percent made negative comments after the course. The findings support the notion that, with few exceptions, teacher candidates were favorably impacted by these courses, both professionally and personally.

Comments describe a generally favorable impact on White/ Caucasian males and females, as well as other racial/ethnic groups. As instructors had planned, candidates' comments suggest they emerged with enhanced sociocultural understanding, clearer sense of self-identity, openness to new perspectives, and awareness of the implications of multicultural education on their work as teachers. Comments further suggest candidate growth in awareness of what it takes to help all students.

Candidates' growing sociocultural awareness, apparent in post-course comments, may have accounted for the increased number of respondents who, at the end of the course, affirmed their interracial and/or interethnic heritage. A number of candidates, who at the beginning classified themselves as "White" or as members of only one racial or ethnic group, began to affirm multiple heritages by the end of the course.

During the timeframe of this study, instructors developed their ability to support a variety of candidates facing difficult challenges within themselves or their families and adjusted the course in response to candidate needs. Still, there were some exceptions—candidates who were negative at the close of the course, a finding in keeping with Lipman (1993) and Zofko Lattragna (1998).

While resistant candidates were limited, a concern is that they did move on to student teach and take teaching positions in diverse schools and classrooms. Further research is needed to explore the impact of emerging teachers' negative attitudes toward multicultural education on the students they later teach.

While this study documents their resistance, the causes are less clear. Resistance may have been caused by an interfering worldview that became intensified by the course experience. Comments showed that White/Caucasian candidates who resisted perceived that the course was designed to make them feel guilty for being White. They reacted against instructors whom they perceived as preaching at them, judging them, or giving them false information. Comments suggested resentment of a perceived 'overemphasis' on multiculturalism and study of topics perceived as not concerning them. They felt anger, fatigue, resentment, and frustration. They held a more negative view of difference, considering it divisive and harmful. With these negative comments as guides, course faculty considered whether further adjustments in the courses could lessen resistance, or whether other solutions exist.

Each year's results demonstrated similar patterns—mostly positive. Year One (1997–1998) supports the appropriateness of providing multicultural education to White/Caucasian preservice teacher candidates. The year's discrepancy in female and male responses suggested the need for course adjustments, and for further comparative research to examine differences in male and female candidates' needs at the start of courses and their learning at the end.

Faculty first arrived at the understanding of the need to apply known theories of gender and racial socialization and enculturation in the design of multicultural courses and field experiences. Faculty saw the need to better match learning and teaching styles to assure that courses nurture both male and female candidates' openness.

Year Two results confirmed general patterns from year one and reflected the effectiveness of changes implemented in response to year one data. It signified a small victory for faculty teaching the course. When they used the results from year one—showing a smaller gain for men than women in responsiveness to multicultural education—to change the course, their courses appeared to have a more positive impact on male candidates.

In revisions to the course in year two, faculty integrated more male issues. Candidates explored gender socialization as well as the impact of the media on both men and women in U.S.A. society. They viewed videos dealing with the increase of male—especially boys'—violence in our society and schools. Further, they examined media portrayal of minority ethnic groups, stereotypes that impact human aspirations, and ways the media affect life and learning from an early age. In turn, they learned how gender socialization and teacher expectation and interactions impact educational achievement and career options.

To facilitate exploration of topics and maximize candidates' engagement, faculty implemented several discussion structures, including dyads between two candidates, small groups of 5–7 candidates, whole class, and individual written reflections. Additionally, small support groups created safe environments for candidates to get to know each other and feel more comfortable reflecting on the various topics. Candidates used timers and had equal time to speak without interruption. No one could speak more than once until everyone in the group had spoken. Candidates could not react and/or respond to each other's comments. Discussions could not be taken out of the classroom and if they were, the individual person(s) originating the topic had to agree. Written reflections were shared anonymously.

The overarching goal was to release silenced voices: inner and each other's. These structures and ground rules paved the way for candidates to speak their minds freely, without fear of criticism, and empowered many to disclose personal experiences. Male candidates voiced frustration with "male bashing" and affirmative action. Females discussed persistent sexism in society. Stories by candidates of color were often poignant "eye-openers" for everyone, particularly White/Caucasians who often expressed lack of awareness.

Year Three results replicate the general pattern of Year Two, showing gains for both White/Caucasian men and women in their positive response to multicultural education.

The follow up comments from course completers suggested the required introductory course that infused multiculturalism was effective at the start of the teacher education sequence by opening their eyes and minds to multiple perspectives valuable for their growth and in preparing them for critical reflection and analysis through all subsequent courses.

Closing Remarks

The study was conducted to assess and improve an introductory multicultural-designated course in an urban teacher preparation program. The course aimed to promote candidates' positive response to multiculturalism, especially White/Caucasian candidates. Results suggest that this approach effectively laid the foundation for almost all candidates' further growth as multicultural educators. The study suggested that an introductory course combined with field experience and focused on critical issues and self-identity development established an effective basis for career-long learning in multicultural education.

Clearly, with increased concerns about student achievement and school effectiveness, particularly cultural and language minorities and low socioeconomic students in urban schools, more research needs to be conducted to ascertain how to best prepare prospective and current teachers to work effectively with students from different backgrounds than their own.

References

Banks, J. A. (1991). Multicultural education: It's effects on students' racial and gender attitudes. *Handbook on research on social studies teaching and learning.* New York: Macmillan, pp. 459–569.

Cruz-Janzen, M. I. (2000). Preparing preservice teacher candidates for leadership in equity. *Equity & Excellence, 33* (1), 94–101.

Derman-Sparks, L. & Phillips, C. B. (1997). *Teaching/learning anti-racism: A developmental approach.* New York: Teachers College Press.

Howard, G. R. (1999). *We can't teach what we don't know: White teachers, multicultural schools.* New York: Teachers College Press.

Lawrence, S. M. (1997). Beyond race awareness: White racial identity and multicultural teaching. *Journal of Teacher Education, 48*(2) 108–115.

Lipman, P. (1993). *The influence of restructuring teachers' beliefs about and practices with African American students.* Dissertation. University of Wisconsin, Madison.

Ooka Pang, V. (2001). *Multicultural education: A caring-centered, reflective approach.* Boston: McGraw-Hill.

Sadker D. M. & Sadker, M. P. (2003). *Teachers, schools, and society.* Needham Heights, MA: Allyn & Bacon.

Truog, A. (1998). Principals' perspectives on new teachers' competencies: A need for curricular reform. *Teacher Educators, 34* (1), 54–69.

Zofko Lattragna, P. (1998). The impact of gender and race on student perceptions of classroom interactions, instruction, and curriculum: A multicultural perspective. Research study at Rutgers University, Camden Campus. Presented at the National Conference on Race & Ethnicity in American Higher Education. May 30, 1998. Denver, CO.

MARTA I. CRUZ-JANZEN is an associate professor of multicultural education with the College of Education at Florida Atlantic University, Boca Roton, Florida. **MARILYN TAYLOR** is dean of the College of Education Center for Teacher Education at the University of Alaska Southeast, Juneau, Alaska.

Appendix A

Table A.1 Survey Participants, Fall 1997 & Spring 1998

	PRE			POST		
	Total	Male	Female	Total	Male	Female
EA	57	25	32	45	18	27
AFA	4	2	2	1	1	0
L/H	10	4	6	7	2	5
NA	2	0	2	3	2	1
AsA	1	0	1	0	0	0
Other	8	2	6	10	5	5
	82			66		

Ea = European American [White/Caucasian]; AFA = African American; L/H = Hispanic/Latino; NA = Alaskan Native / Native American Indian; AsA = Asian American; Other.

Table A.2 Fall 1997 & Spring 1998

A. What do you hope to acquire/learn from this course?
B. What do you feel you acquired/learned from this course?

	A. PRE				B. POST			
	Total	% Total	Male	Female	Total	% Total	Male	Female
EA	21:57	36.8	6:25	15:32	27:45	60.0	7:18	20:27
AFA	0:4	00.0	0:2	0:2	1:1	100	1:1	0:0
L/H	2:10	20.0	1:4	1:6	3:7	42.9	0:2	3:5
NA	0:2	00.0	0:0	0:2	1:3	33.3	0:2	1:1
AsA	0:1	00.0	0:0	0:1	0:0	N/A	0:0	0:0
Other	2:8	25.0	0:2	2:6	7:10	70.0	2:5	5:5
	25:82	30.4			39:66	59.1		

Ratio = # Positive comments dealing with diversity & multiculturalism : group size (N)

Table A.3 Fall 1997 & Spring 1998, General Comments By Participants (Question #10 in Survey)

	PRE				POST			
	Total	% Total	Male	Female	Total	% Total	Male	Female
EA	9:57	15.79	4:25	5:32	16:45	35.56	8:18	8:27
AFA	1:4	25.0	1:2	0:2	1:1	100	1:1	0:0
L/H	1:10	10.0	1:4	0:6	0:7	00.0	0:2	0:5
NA	1:2	50.0	0:0	1:2	2:3	66.6	1:2	1:1
AsA	0:1	00.0	0:0	0:1	0:0	N/A	0:0	0:0
Other	4:8	50.0	1:2	3:6	3:10	30.0	0:5	3:5
	16:82	19.5			22:66	33.3		

Ratio = # Positive comments dealing with diversity & multiculturalism : group size (N)

APPENDIX B

Table B.1 Survey Participants Fall 1998 & Spring 1999

	PRE			POST		
	Total	Male	Female	Total	Male	Female
EA	68	21	47	57	17	40
AғA	6	2	4	4	2	2
L/H	13	2	11	11	2	9
NA	1	0	1	1	0	1
AsA	0	0	0	0	0	0
Other	11	7	4	14	8	6
	99			87		

Table B.2 Fall 1998 & Spring 1999

A. What do you hope to acquire/learn from this course?

B. What do you feel you acquired/learned from this course?

	A. PRE				B. POST			
	Total	% Total	Male	Female	Total	% Total	Male	Female
EA	38:68	55.9	11:21	28:47	47:57	82.5	15:17	32:40
AғA	5:6	83.3	2:2	3:4	4:4	100	2:2	2:2
L/H	10:13	76.9	1:2	9:11	10:11	90.9	1:2	9:9
NA	1:1	100	0	1:1	1:1	100	9	1:1
AsA	0	0	0	0	0	0	0	0
Other	7:11	63.6	4:7	3:4	14:14	100	8:8	6:6
	61:99	61.1			76:87	87.3		

Ratio = # Positive comments dealing with diversity & multiculturalism : group size (N)

Table B.3 Fall 1998 & Spring 1999, General Comments by Participants (Item #10 in the Survey)

	PRE				POST			
	Total	% Total	Male	Female	Total	% Total	Male	Female
EA	30:68	44.1	10:21	20:47	48:57	84.2	15:17	33:40
AғA	4:6	66.6	1:2	3:4	4:4	100	1:2	3:2
L/H	5:13	38.5	1:2	4:11	9:11	81.8	2:2	7:9
NA	1:1	100	0:0	1:1	1:1	100	0:0	1:1
AsA	0	0	0	0	0	0	0	0
Other	3:11	27.3	1:7	2:4	11:14	78.6	3:8	8:6
	43:99	43.4			73:87	83.9		

Ratio = # Positive comments dealing with diversity & multiculturalism : group size (N)

APPENDIX C

Table C.1 Survey Participants Fall 1999 & 2000

	PRE			POST		
	Total	**Male**	**Female**	**Total**	**Male**	**Female**
EA	19	5	14	14	4	10
AFA	2	1	1	1	0	1
L/H	8	3	5	6	3	3
NA	1	0	1	1	0	1
AsA	0	0	0	0	0	0
Other	3	1	2	5	2	3
	33			27		

Table C.2   Fall 1999 & Spring 2000

A. What do you hope to acquire/learn from this course?
B. What do you feel you acquired/learned from this course?

	A. PRE				**B. POST**			
	Total	**% Total**	**Male**	**Female**	**Total**	**% Total**	**Male**	**Female**
EA	6:19		2:5	4:14	8:14		3:4	5:10
AFA	0:2		0:1	0:1	1:1		0:0	1:1
L/H	5:8		1:3	4:5	6:6		3:3	3:3
NA	1:1		0	1:1	1:1		0:0	1:1
AsA	0		0	0	0		0	0
Other	1:3		1:1	2:2	5:5		2:2	3:3
	13:33	39.4			21:27	77.8		

Ratio = # Positive comments dealing with diversity & multiculturalism : group size (N)

Table C.3   Fall 1999 & Spring 2000, General Comments by Participants (Item #10 in Survey)

	PRE				POST			
	Total	**% Total**	**Male**	**Female**	**Total**	**% Total**	**Male**	**Female**
EA	8:9	42.1	2:5	6:14	8:14	57.1	2:4	6:10
AFA	0:2	0	0:1	0:1	1:1	100	0:0	1:0
L/H	2:8	25.5	1:3	1:5	3:6	50.0	1:3	2:3
NA	1:1	100	0:0	1:1	1:1	100	0:0	1:1
AsA	0	0	0	0	0	0	0	0
Other	0:3	0.0	0:1	0:2	2:5	40.0	0:2	2:3
	11:33	33.3			15:27	55.6		

Ratio = # Positive comments dealing with diversity & multiculturalism : group size (N)

The Biology of Risk Taking

For help in guiding adolescents into healthy adulthood, educators can look to new findings in the fields of neuroscience and developmental psychology.

LISA F. PRICE

I celebrate myself,
And what I assume you shall assume,
For every atom belonging to me as good belongs
to you.

—Walt Whitman, *Leaves of Grass*

Adolescence is a time of excitement, growth, and change. Whitman's words capture the enthusiasm and passion with which teenagers approach the world. Sometimes adolescents direct this passion toward a positive goal, such as a creative essay, an art project, after-school sports, or a healthy romance. At other times, they divert their passions to problematic activities, such as drug experimentation, reckless driving, shoplifting, fights, or school truancy.

Why do adolescents take risks? Why are teens so passionate? Are adolescents just young adults, or are they fundamentally different? Advances in developmental psychology and neuroscience have provided us with some answers. We now understand that adolescent turmoil, which we used to view as an expression of raging hormones, is actually the result of a complex interplay of body chemistry, brain development, and cognitive growth (Buchanan, Eccles, & Becker, 1992). Moreover, the changes that teenagers experience occur in the context of multiple systems—such as individual relationships, family, school, and community—that support and influence change.

Educators are in a pivotal position to promote healthy adolescent growth. Understanding the biological changes that adolescents undergo and the behaviors that result can provide the foundation for realistic expectations and effective interventions.

The Impact of Puberty

The hormonal changes of adolescence are often considered synonymous with puberty. The word *puberty* comes from the Latin term *pubertas,* meaning "age of maturity." As implied by the word's etymology, the changes of puberty have long been understood to usher in adulthood; in many cultures, puberty and the capacity to conceive continue to mark entry into adulthood. In contrast, puberty in modern Western culture has become a multistep entry process into a much longer period of adolescence (King, 2002).

Hormonal changes of adolescence include adrenarche, gonadarche, and menarche (Dahl, 2004; King, 2002). Adrenarche refers to the increased production of adrenal hormones and occurs as early as age 6–8. These hormones influence skeletal growth, hair production, and skin changes. Gonadarche refers to the pulsatile production of a cascade of hormones and contributes to driving the growth spurt and genital, breast, and pubic hair development. Menarche refers to the beginning of girls' menses, which generally occurs late in girls' pubertal development.

The Stages and Ages of Puberty

The clinician J. M. Tanner developed a system for classifying male and female pubertal growth into five stages (Tanner I–V). In the 1960s, he identified a trend of progressively earlier age at menarche across cultures (1968). Since then, investigators have identified similar trends of earlier arrival of other markers of puberty, such as breast and pubic hair development (Herman-Giddens et al., 1997). These trends have diverged across race in the United States, with proportionately more African American girls experiencing earlier-onset puberty than white girls. The implications of these trends have ranged from debates over the threshold for premature puberty to investigations into factors that contribute to earlier-onset puberty (Kaplowitz & Oberfield, 1999).

Boys who enter puberty at an earlier age experience certain advantages, including higher self-esteem, greater popularity, and some advances in cognitive capabilities (King, 2002). These same boys may also be more likely to engage in risk-taking behavior, possibly because they often socialize with older boys (Steinberg & Morris, 2001). Girls, on the other hand, often have more problems associated with earlier entry into puberty, including lower self-esteem and elevated risk for anxiety, depression, and eating disorders. These girls are also more likely to engage in risk-taking behaviors, including earlier sexual intercourse.

Don't Blame It on Hormones

In the past, hormones were believed to be in a state of great flux, which presumably caused adolescents to be dramatic, erratic, intense, and risk-prone. Evidence suggests, however, that only minimal association exists between adolescent hormone levels and emotional/behavioral problems (Buchanan et al., 1992; King, 2002). Youth with higher levels of hormones do not appear to be at higher risk for emotional or behavioral problems (Dahl, 2004).

Adolescence is a time of excitement, growth, and change.

Today, adolescent specialists view emotional intensity and sensation-seeking as normative behaviors of adolescence that are more broadly linked to pubertal maturation than to hormone levels. Pubertal stage rather than chronological age is linked to romantic and sexual pursuits, increased appetite, changes in sleep patterns, and risk for emotional disorders in girls. One group of investigators studying teen smoking and substance use found that increased age had no correlation with increased sensation-seeking or risky behavior (Martin et al., 2002). Instead, they determined that pubertal maturation was correlated with sensation-seeking in boys and girls, which, in turn, led to a greater likelihood of cigarette smoking and substance use.

Pubertal stage was clearly linked to difficulties that Derek began experiencing in school. He had been a solid student in 6th grade who scored in the average range and generally turned his homework in on time. He socialized with a group of same-age friends and was teased occasionally because he was skinnier and shorter than his peers. By 7th grade, however, he had begun his growth spurt. He was now a few inches taller and had developed facial hair. Although he appeared more confident, he also seemed more aggressive and was involved in several fights at school. He began to spend part of his time with a few 8th grade boys who were suspected of writing graffiti on a school wall.

A teacher who had a good relationship with Derek took him aside and spoke with him about the change in his behavior from 6th to 7th grade. Derek was able to talk about his own surprise at the changes, his wish for more respect, and his ambivalence about entering high school—he was worried about what teachers would expect of him. Derek and the teacher agreed to talk periodically, and the teacher arranged for Derek to meet with the school counselor.

The Adolescent Brain

Neuroscientists used to believe that by the time they reached puberty, youth had undergone the crucial transformations in brain development and circuitry. Data obtained through available technology supported this view, identifying similar brain structures in children and adults. The adolescent brain seemed entirely comparable to the adult brain.

This view of adolescent brain development has undergone a radical shift during the last decade, with the identification of ongoing brain changes throughout adolescence, such as synaptic pruning and myelination. People have the mature capacity to consistently control behavior in both low-stress and high-stress environments only after these neurobiological developments are complete. This maturation does not take place until the early 20s.

Synaptic pruning refers to the elimination of connections between neurons in the brain's cortex, or gray matter. In the 1990s, researchers determined that during adolescence, up to 30,000 synapses are eliminated each second (Bourgeois & Rakic, 1993; Rakic, Bourgeois, & Goldman-Rakic, 1994). The removal of these redundant synaptic links increases the computational ability of brain circuits, which, in turn, enhances a function intricately connected to risk taking: the capacity to regulate and rapidly stop activity. Myelination, which refers to the wrapping of glial cell membranes around the axon of neurons, results in increased speed of signal transmission along the axon (Luna & Sweeney, 2004). This facilitates more rapid and integrated communication among diverse brain regions.

Synaptic pruning and myelination, along with other neurobiological changes, facilitate enhanced cognitive capacity as well as behavioral control, also known as *executive function*. Executive function is the ability to interact in a self-directed, appropriate, organized, and purposeful manner. The prefrontal cortex plays a vital role in guiding executive function, which is also influenced by such areas of the brain as the hippocampus (which coordinates memory), the amygdala (which coordinates emotional processing), and the ventral striatum (which coordinates reward-processing). The prefrontal cortex is less mature, however, in young adolescents than in adults.

Given these three factors—an inability to completely regulate and refrain from certain activities, an absence of fully integrated communication among the various regions of the brain, and a less developed prefrontal cortex—it is not surprising that adolescents biologically do not have the same capacities as adults to inhibit their impulses in a timely manner.

Biology and Thrill-Seeking

By their mid-teens, adolescents appear to have achieved many decision-making abilities seen in adults (Steinberg & Cauffman, 1996). In fact, studies have found that teens can identify the same degree of danger in risky activities that adults can—driving while intoxicated, for example (Cauffman, Steinberg, & Woolard, 2002). However, certain methodological flaws in studies of adolescents may have prevented investigators from accurately assessing adolescent risk taking (Steinberg, 2004). These flaws include evaluating teens individually rather than in the context of a group, within which most risk-taking behavior occurs; asking teens to evaluate theoretical situations, which may not sufficiently represent the challenges of actual situations; and evaluating teens in settings that reduce the influence of emotion or induce anxiety rather than generate the exhilaration associated with risk taking.

One result of these flaws may be that measures of adolescents' cognitive abilities—particularly their evaluation of risk—do not adequately reflect their actual cognitive and emotional processes in real time. Consequently, teens *appear* to have the cognitive capacities of adults yet continue to engage in more risky behaviors.

The emotional lives of adolescents also appear to shift during these years. Adolescents seek more intense emotional experiences than children and adults do. They appear to need higher degrees of stimulation to obtain the same experience of pleasure (Steinberg, 2004). Developments in an area of the brain called the limbic system may explain this shift in pursuit and experience of pleasure (Spear, 2000).

Teenagers generally thrive in reasonable, supportive environments that have a predictable, enforced structure.

Ongoing cognitive development and emotional shifts result in a biologically based drive for thrill-seeking, which may account for adolescents' continued risk taking despite knowledge of the accompanying hazards. Some interventions attempt to reduce the potential for risky behavior through external means—laws and rules, for example—rather than placing sole emphasis on the practice of educating teens in risk assessment (Steinberg, 2004). Others have considered teens' ability to reason well in "cool" circumstances but their failure to do so when in "hot" situations that arouse the emotions. Providing adolescents with sufficient scaffolding, or a good balance of support and autonomy, may be particularly important (Dahl, 2004).

This kind of scaffolding would be especially effective with a student like Shauna. Shauna raised the concerns of school faculty soon after she started 9th grade. Her attendance, class participation, and assignment completion were erratic. She had also run away from home during the summer and received a warning for shoplifting. The school counselor learned that Shauna's parents had separated over the summer and that her mother was struggling to set limits in the absence of Shauna's father. The school counselor, several teachers, and the vice principal decided to meet with both of Shauna's parents.

Although tension between the parents was evident, both parents agreed that Shauna should come home immediately after school instead of going to the mall, which she had recently started to do. Both parents also felt strongly that she needed to regularly attend school and complete assignments. The parents arranged to meet with Shauna together to discuss their shared expectations for her. The parents and teachers agreed to stay in contact with one another regarding Shauna's attendance and homework. The group also decided that a home-based reward system might encourage Shauna's success at school. The reward system would involve outings to the mall and to friends' homes, with incrementally less adult supervision and more autonomy as she continued to succeed.

The Role of Educators

These new findings suggest some beneficial approaches that educators might follow to guide adolescents into healthy adulthood.

- *Ensure that schools provide adolescents with vital support.* School bonding provides a protective influence for youth. The mentorship of a teacher can make the difference in a teen's course.
- *Keep a long view.* Researchers have found that the benefits of successful interventions may disappear for a few years in adolescence to reappear in later adolescence (Masten, 2004). Other teens are late bloomers whose troubled earlier years are followed by success.
- *Prioritize your concern.* The junior who has never been a problem and gets into trouble once is at a different level of risk than the 7th grader who has a long history of worrisome behaviors, such as fights, school truancy, mental illness, exposure to trauma, loss of important adult figures, or absence of stable supports. Act early for adolescents with long histories of risk taking.
- *Remember that puberty is not the same for all teens.* Some adolescents enter puberty earlier than others, giving them a perceived social advantage as well as possible disadvantages. There may be a biological drive to risk taking in teens, which is expressed by individual teens at different ages.
- *Remember that teens are not adults.* Having the scientific evidence to support the view that teens are not adults can be helpful to educators working with families, adolescents, or other professionals who may have unrealistic expectations for adolescents.
- *Take advantage of adolescent passion.* Direct adolescents' enthusiasm toward productive ends. A teen's passion can become a bridge to learning about such topics as music theory, history, politics, race relations, or marketing.
- *Reduce risk with firm structure.* Although teenagers dislike rules, they generally thrive in reasonable, supportive environments that have a predictable, enforced structure. For example, an authoritative stance in parenting—which reflects firmness coupled with caring—has repeatedly been found to be the most effective parenting strategy. Continue to maintain school rules and expectations, even when an adolescent continues to break the rules.
- *Collaborate to solve problems.* Working with risk-taking adolescents can be demanding, taxing, and worrisome. Talk regularly with colleagues for support. Contact appropriate consultants when your concern grows. Teens who see teachers collaborate with other adults benefit from these healthy models of problem solving.

It's important for educators to keep in mind that up to 80 percent of adolescents have few or no major problems during this period (Dahl, 2004). Remembering that most adolescents do well can encourage the positive outlook that educators need to effectively work with youth during this exciting and challenging time in their lives.

References

Bourgeois, J-P., & Rakic, P. (1993). Changes of synaptic density in the primary visual cortex of the macaque monkey from fetal to adult stage. *Journal of Neuroscience, 13,* 2801–2820.

Buchanan, C. M., Eccles, J. S., & Becker, J. B. (1992). Are adolescents the victims of raging hormones? *Psychological Bulletin, 111,* 62–107.

Cauffman, E., Steinberg, L., & Woolard, J. (2002, April 13). *Age differences in capacities underlying competence to stand trial.* Presentation at the Biennial Meeting of the Society for Research for Adolescence, New Orleans, Louisiana.

Dahl, R. E. (2004). Adolescent brain development: A period of vulnerabilities and opportunities. *Annals of the New York Academy of Science, 1021,* 1–22.

Herman-Giddens, M. E., Slora, E. J., Wasserman, R. C., Bourdony, C.J., Bhapkar, M. V., Koch, G. G., et al. (1997). Secondary sexual characteristics and menses in young girls seen in office practice. *Pediatrics, 99,* 505–512.

Kaplowitz, P. B., & Oberfield, S. E. (1999). Reexamination of the age limit for defining when puberty is precocious in girls in the United States. *Pediatrics, 104,* 936–941.

King, R. A. (2002). Adolescence. In M. Lewis (Ed.), *Child and adolescent psychiatry* (pp. 332–342). Philadelphia: Lippincott Williams & Wilkins.

Luna, B., & Sweeney, J. A. (2004). The emergence of collaborative brain function: fMRI studies of the development of response inhibition. *Annals of the New York Academy of Science, 1021,* 296–309.

Martin, C. A., Kelly, T. H., Rayens, M. K., Brogli, B. R., Brenzel, A., Smith, W. J., et al. (2002). Sensation seeking, puberty, and nicotine, alcohol, and marijuana use in adolescence. *Journal of the American Academy of Child and Adolescent Psychiatry, 41,* 1495–1502.

Masten, A. S. (2004). Regulatory processes, risk, and resilience in adolescent development. *Annals of the New York Academy of Science, 1021,* 310–319.

Rakic, P., Bourgeois, J-P., & Goldman- Rakic, P. S. (1994). Synaptic development of the cerebral cortex. *Progress in Brain Research, 102,* 227–243.

Spear, P. (2000). The adolescent brain and age-related behavioral manifestations. *Neuroscience and Biobehavioral Reviews, 24,* 417–463.

Steinberg, L. (2004). Risk taking in adolescence: What changes, and why? *Annals of the New York Academy of Science, 1021,* 51–58.

Steinberg, L., & Cauffman, E. (1996). Maturity of judgment in adolescence. *Law and Human Behavior, 20,* 249–272.

Steinberg, L., & Morris, A. S. (2001). Adolescent development. *Annual Review of Psychology, 52,* 83–110.

Tanner, J. M. (1968). Early maturation in man. *Scientific American, 218,* 21–27.

LISA F. PRICE, MD, is the Assistant Director of the School Psychiatry Program in the Department of Psychiatry at Massachusetts General Hospital, 55 Fruit St., YAW 6900, Boston, MA 02114. She is also an Instructor in Psychiatry at Harvard Medical School.

UNIT 2

Teacher Education in Multicultural Perspective

Unit Selections

Key Points to Consider

- Why is multicultural education so frequently seen as an isolated and segregated part of teacher education programs?
- What are the reasons for so much resistance to coursework in the area of multicultural education in teacher education programs?
- What can we learn about teaching styles and methods from case studies of teachers from cultures other than our own?
- Is the concept of social justice a topic suitable for a multicultural classroom? Explain.
- What seem to be the major points of disagreement about the role of multicultural education in teacher education programs?
- What attitudes need to change regarding multicultural education? Explain.

Student Web Site

www.mhcls.com/online

Internet References

Further information regarding these Web sites may be found in this book's preface or online.

Awesome Library for Teachers
http://www.awesomelibrary.org/teacher.html

Education World
http://www.education-world.com

Teacher Talk Forum
http://education.indiana.edu/cas/tt/tthmpg.html

At a time when the minority student body at the elementary and secondary school levels is beginning to approach a majority of the school population, fewer students from cultural minorities are choosing teaching as a career. This social reality within teacher education programs in the United States only underscores the need for multicultural education, as well as for coursework in specific cultural studies areas in the education of American teachers.

Multicultural educational programming of some sort is now an established part of teacher education programs, but debate continues as to how it can be integrated effectively into these programs. The National Council for the Accreditation of Teacher Education (NCATE) has established a multicultural standard for the accreditation of programs for teacher education in the United States. Many educators involved in teaching courses in multicultural education have wondered why such coursework is so often a segregated area of teacher education curricula. And many who are involved in multicultural teacher education believe that all teacher educators should become knowledgeable in this area. Teaching preservice teachers to respect cultural diversity can enhance their ability to respect individual students' diversity in learning styles and beliefs. Prospective teachers need to be sensitized to the reality of cultural diversity and to the need to learn about the values and beliefs of their students.

There is still much misunderstanding within the teacher education establishment as to what multicultural education is. This will continue as long as many of its opponents consider it a political rather than an intellectual or educational concept. If all children and young adults are to receive their educational experiences in schools that nourish and respect their respective heritages as people, all teachers must learn those intellectual and affective skills that can empower them to study and to learn about diverse cultures throughout their careers. Multicultural education course content in teacher education programs is about both cultural diversity and individual students from differing cultural heritages.

Teachers will have to consider how each student's development is shaped by the powerful force of those values prevailing in his or her home and neighborhood. In a civilization rapidly becoming more culturally pluralistic, resistance to overwhelmingly Eurocentric domination of social studies and language arts curricula in the schools will continue. About 5 billion of the projected 6 billion people on Earth are people with a non-Eurocentric conception of the world. Scholars in the social sciences, humanities, and teacher education in North America, who study minority-majority relations in the schools, now realize that the very terms "minority" and "majority" are changing when we speak of the demographic realities of the cultural configurations existent in most major urban and suburban educational systems. This is also true when we consider minority-majority relations in vast isolated rural or wilderness areas where those of western or northern European descent can be found to be "minorities" in the midst of concentrations of indigenous peoples. Many teachers will teach students whose values and views of the world are very different from their own, hence the relevance of teachers learning how to learn about human cultures and belief systems in order that they can study the lives and heritages of their students in the schools.

Many teachers of European ethnic heritage are having difficulty understanding the importance of the fact that North American society

Anderson Ross/Getty Images

is becoming more culturally pluralistic. From a multicultural perspective, one of the many things course content seeks to achieve is to help all prospective teachers realize the importance of becoming lifelong learners. The knowledge base of multicultural education is further informed by the history of the struggle for civil rights in North American societies. Multicultural educational programming in teacher education programs seeks to alter how prospective teachers perceive society as a whole, not just its current minority members. We must take a broad view of multicultural education. Culturally pluralistic themes need to be apparent throughout teacher education programs and integrated into the knowledge bases of teacher education. Broadly conceived, multicultural education seeks to help members of all ethnic, cultural backgrounds to appreciate one another's shared human concerns and interrelationships; it should not be conceived as simply the study of minority cultural groups. Teachers need to be prepared in such a manner that they learn genuine respect for cultural as well as personal diversity.

Teachers should be prepared to take a global perspective of the world and to think critically about the issues confronting them, their students, and society as a whole (seen as part of an interdependent community of nations). Multicultural education should not be politicized. It should be a way of seeing the world as enriched by cultural and personal diversity. Preservice teachers should learn from case studies that exemplify and report on the differing cultural traditions in child rearing, entry into adulthood (rites of passage), and varying cultural styles of child-adult interaction in school settings.

The essays in this unit explore why it is important not to see multicultural education as just a political concept, but rather as an area of critical inquiry from which we can all learn alternative diverse styles of teaching appropriate to the learning styles and cultural backgrounds of students. The articles stress the importance of teachers being able to learn differing ways, share in social interaction in classroom settings, and to see the impact of race, gender, and social class on their ideas about themselves as teachers, how they perceive other teachers, and how they perceive their students.

This unit's articles are relevant to courses that focus on introduction to the cultural foundations of education, educational policy studies, history and philosophy of education, and curriculum theory and construction, as well as methods courses in all areas of teacher education programs.

Dare to Be Different

Can a school choose its own path despite the pressures of accountability? In the end, Ms. Wassermann says, it is possible to act on our beliefs within the constraints that bind us.

Selma Wassermann

Charles Dickens Elementary School, with its scarlet brick exterior, is a hundred-year-old relic from a time when schools were built as no-nonsense fortresses to contain and socialize a swelling immigrant population. In spite of its down-at-the-heels condition, it manages to retain its grandeur, wearing its red coat as a banner of bravado: Dare to Be Different. For Charles Dickens Elementary is as distinct in its ethos as in its appearance from most other public schools in the city of Vancouver—and perhaps throughout the entire province of British Columbia.

The Vietnamese pho shops and other low-rent cafés that hawk sushi, samosas, pizza, and dim sum on the Kingsway, just up the block, manifest the diversity of the area and signal the ethnic mix of the children in the school. Many of them are new Canadians; some speak English as yet haltingly; others, not quite yet. In Annie O'Donaghue's class of third- through fifth-graders, a children-drawn world map on the bulletin board shows the students' countries of origin: El Salvador, Honduras, India, Canada, Portugal, China, Vietnam, Philippines, Ireland. Many of the children who are identified as coming from Canada are of First Nations heritage.

Dickens is not the school one would have picked as most likely to defy every new curriculum du jour handed down by school boards and ministries of education over the last 30 years. It is certainly not the school one would have picked to remain true to its child-centered roots, facing off against such educational tsunamis as the back-to-basics movement, Madeline Hunter's direct instruction, and now the high-stakes testing madness that is passing for educational quality. And this is certainly not the school, given the challenges of the student population, that one would have picked to demonstrate such high performance levels, showing us once again what many educators know: that given the "right stuff"—the right teachers, the right administration, the right conditions—all children can be successful learners.

I came to visit Charles Dickens and left humbled at what I saw, for surely this is the kind of school and the quality of education that we all say we want for our children. I wanted to know what made it "work" and how, in the past 20 years, it has held onto its autonomy and endured as a beacon of what a school can and should be.

Scenes from the School

I walk up the steep stone steps and enter a large hallway, looking for the general office. The floor is patterned linoleum worn by the footsteps of hundreds and thousands of winter boots, but the visitor's eye is immediately drawn to the colors—children's art on every wall, including large-scale murals painted directly on the hallway lockers. Even the tops of the lockers are used to display children's dioramas. The colorful exhibits speak of the value put on children's creative work, and it is obvious that the students themselves, not the teachers, have put this art on display. In the rear area of the hallway, under the staircase, an old couch, some easy chairs, and a small bookcase containing paperback books and magazines make an informal reading corner. No one is on guard here; all the doors are unlocked, and the school can be entered from any side. There is a sense of "non-orderliness" here—not sloppy or unclean, but put together by children. The informality of it all is striking, and it is immediately clear that children own this environment and that order and control are not key issues in this school.

John Perpich, principal of Charles Dickens Elementary School for the last six years, escorts me upstairs to Annie O'Donaghue's classroom. Like every other class in the school, this is a multi-age grouping: grades 3, 4, and 5 combined. The rationale for multi-age grouping, Perpich says, is that the numbers of same-age children in the school population of 455. children do not allow for even distribution into grade-level classes. He smiles when he says this, suggesting a hidden agenda, which he immediately reveals. This school believes in multi-age grouping. It is a mainstay of the program. Insofar as logistics permit, teachers work with the same group of children over a three-year period, getting to know them well enough to understand individual learning needs and provide appropriate instruction that addresses those needs. Perpich says that in single-year transitions, it often takes teachers about six weeks to "learn" the learning styles of each new student. In the multi-age arrangement, teachers and students simply pick up in September where they left off in June—a seamless continuum rather than a brand-new experience. It is the kind of organization that allows for and facilitates continuous student learning.

Another advantage of multi-age grouping is that it implants in students the notion that their classroom is a family, in which the older children look out for the younger ones, caring for them, helping them out socially and educationally, and taking responsibility for being the "older brothers and sisters." This outlook filters down through the ages, so that when the "littles" move up the chronological ladder and become the "olders," they too take on the mantle of helpers and caretakers. It becomes natural for children to work with those of their own age, with some who are younger, and with some who are older. Age demarcations that contribute to unhealthy social attitudes simply do not exist here.

My eyes scan the classroom. Bulletin boards "owned" by the children display poems, stories, artwork, and newspaper clippings with headlines such as "Don Baker, 41, Pleads Guilty to Raping Prostitutes, Sex with Kids," and "Huge Crowds Throng St. Peter's Square," and "Canada's Leading Architect Arthur Erikson Puts His Touch on New Tower." I am immediately reminded of Sylvia Ashton-Warner's advice to teachers: "Let life come in the door."[1] If these are the headlines that children see on newsstands and on the kitchen tables in their homes, why should they not be put under thoughtful scrutiny in the classroom?

After each reading, the children offer feedback, and I hear critiques that go to the heart of what makes a poem good—descriptor words, imagery, cadence, the ability to evoke pictures in the mind.

The informality I observed in the corridor carries over into the classroom. Annie sits on a low chair, and the children gather around her. They are having "writer's workshop," in which they share their poetry with one another and solicit informed feedback. Their poems reflect a previous lesson on alliteration and imagery, and it appears that even children new to English can use language in spectacular and powerful ways. After each reading, the children call on their classmates who raise their hands to offer feedback, and I

hear critiques that go to the heart of what makes a poem good—descriptor words, imagery, cadence, the ability to evoke pictures in the mind. These poems are first drafts, and the children, after reading and feedback, will have an opportunity to redraft until the poems reach their final, polished stage. In this group of 24 mixed-age children, there is no sign of restlessness or inattention. In fact, there is a calmness here and an interest in the work that is palpable. Critical feedback is focused on what's good and what might be added to strengthen the poem. It is always respectful, a learned skill, and a key aspect of "writer's workshop." After the readings, the children leave the whole group to work individually to redraft their poems. When Annie has to leave the room, the children seem unaware that she has gone; they simply continue with their work, interacting with one another, talking quietly, and some coming over to visit with me, swarming like butterflies.

"So how old are you, anyway?" Rahul asks, looking me over as if I were last week's hamburger.

"Hmm," I look him in the eye. "What would you think?"

The children appraise me and I wonder if I haven't given them license to stretch the truth.

"I think you're 49," Christina says in all seriousness.

"Forty-nine!" I gasp, astonished at this gift.

"But don't worry," she quickly replies. "You only look 45."

They are as close to Ashton-Warner's "natural child" as I have seen in many, many school visits.[2]

Back at the office, Perpich hands me the recent evaluations of students' progress in "meeting writing goals." The table for spring 2005 presents data on writing development in grades 5, 6, and 7. At the grade-7 level, a total of four children have been recorded as "not meeting expectations." Seventeen children are "minimally meeting expectations." Fifty-three children are "meeting expectations." And 26 children are "exceeding expectations," making a total of 96% of seventh-graders who are "meeting or exceeding the standards for that grade level." Perpich says that "we are still working on the total of 36% from combined grades 5, 6, and 7 who are not yet, or minimally, meeting expectations, which is largely due to the numbers of ESL children in that group." In the last year, there was a 40% increase in the number of children meeting or exceeding expectations in literacy, and the expectation is that the coming year will show similar if not better results.

Keys to the School Operation

When parents enroll their children at Charles Dickens, they are handed a brochure with the mission statement of the school, developed by the previous principal, Corine Clark, her staff, and a group of parents. On the front of the brochure, a photo of the school caps the statement: "Together we bring alive our commitment to develop each child's potential in all domains through a long-established philosophy built on mutual respect, continuous learning, and opportunities for leadership within a child-centered, multi-aged framework." This statement is expanded in the list of beliefs that underlie the operating practices of me school:

- Learning requires the active participation of the learner.
- People learn in different ways and at different rates.
- Learning is built on individual and social processes.
- The learner is the focus of education, not the curriculum.
- The integration of subjects is necessary.
- Curiosity, creativity, and cooperation should be nurtured.
- Creative and critical problem-solving skills should be taught.
- Play is a condition of learning.
- Questions should be valued.
- A sense of responsibility in decision making should be fostered.
- A sense of self as an individual and as part of the group is important.

The brochure introduces parents to the specific features of the school that are based on these beliefs: an orientation toward continuous progress; appropriate evaluation of progress; schoolwide team-teaching; anecdotal reporting to parents, instead of letter grades; a collegial and collaborative working relationship between teachers and administrators, with consensus decision making in staff meetings; mentoring for student teachers who come from me two major universities' teacher training programs; advocacy teams to recommend school policy directions and school improvement plans; an active student council; and a parent involvement advocacy team and parent advisory council. Reading the brochure, I am reminded of the quote "What a wise and good parent will desire for his own child, a nation must desire for all children"[3] and think sadly how far so many schools have strayed from that standard.

While any child from the school catchment area may attend Charles Dickens Elementary School, out-of-district parents who are interested in having their children attend Dickens can apply for admission. There is currently a waiting list of applicants; many parents willingly drive their children across the city to attend the school.

A Little History

John Wormsbecker, former assistant superintendent of schools in Vancouver, talked to me about early days, when "open education" was being looked to as an antidote to the "crisis in the classroom" arising from too much emphasis on silence, obedience, and workbook and textbook exercises that numbed the mind and depleted the soul.[4] In the early Seventies, groups of educators from North America under-

took educational pilgrimages to the U.K. to see firsthand the child-centered programs that were part of the British Primary School movement. (After more than 20 successful years of operation, open education in Great Britain was swept away by the broom of the "iron lady," Prime Minister Margaret Thatcher, who gleefully presided over its demise. This was not a matter of what was good for children; it was purely a matter of economics and budget cutting.)

During the 1970s, Wormsbecker and others from the Vancouver District Office went to England to see for themselves what the British primary classroom looked like and had to offer teachers and students in Vancouver. When they returned, they brought over specialists to give workshops and provide support to teachers and schools in Vancouver that tilted in favor of more child-centered programs. The child-centered philosophy then spread throughout British Columbia (as it did in places in the U.S.), and more child-centered programs appeared in provincial public school classrooms. While many Vancouver schools were initially involved, the programs began to falter during the reactive "back-to-basics" thrust of the 1980s. Although one can still find classrooms throughout the province where teachers remain wedded to their child-centered practices, it is rare today to find an entire school that is wholly consistent in its dedication to such principles.

When the honeymoon with open education was over, Dickens found itself, like other schools, with a few teachers outside the mainstream whose practice was guided by their open education philosophy. The arrival in 1988 of George Rooney, the new principal, changed all of that. Rooney, credited with the resurrection of open education at Charles Dickens, stood by his child-centered beliefs and, slowly but surely, took the steps that would ensure that Dickens became a lighthouse school for child-centered education. Rooney, who retired in 1995, was succeeded by Tom Robb and then Corine Clark, both of whom committed themselves to carrying on the child-centered programs. When John Perpich took over the administrative reins, he willingly accepted the responsibility of keeping it all alive.

What Makes Dickens Run?

Dickens has officially been granted "alternative school" status by the ministry of education and the Vancouver school board. This designation gives them more degrees of freedom and allows them to depart, in giant steps, from mainstream practices seen throughout the district. For example, standardized tests, such as the CAT (Canadian Achievement Tests), the CTSB (Canadian Tests of Basic Skills), and the Stanford Achievement Test, used in Vancouver and other provincial schools as means of assessing performance, are rejected in favor of the professional judgments of teams of teachers, based on their day-to-day observations and evaluations of students' work. (The Foundation Skills Assessments [FSA], a provincewide test, is mandated for all schools, and Dickens is not exempt from this requirement.) When I asked about how this approach was possible in such a climate of high-stakes testing, Perpich told me, "Of course, we are required to document a student's levels of achievement. And as long as I can document the children's progress and successful performance, 'downtown' is happy. Of course, there are many ways to do this." I was astonished to learn that each school in the district has many options with respect to providing high-quality education for all students and evaluating student performance. Perpich and his staff have chosen "continuous progress." Other schools have chosen differently. I wonder what it takes to dare to march to the drummer of one's educational beliefs.

Because there is no "grade-level curriculum," each child's learning needs are met along a continuum of progress.

Most of the school's 30 teachers teach in teams of two and sometimes three. Team-teaching creates opportunities for teachers to examine and discuss instructional strategies, the assessment of learning needs, appropriate interventions, teacher/student interactions, and "whether the plans are working." Every classroom is a learning laboratory, every teacher a professional.

As noted earlier, teachers remain with the same group of children for three years. Thus they get to know the students better and to become familiar with their individual learning needs and styles. Because there is no "grade-level curriculum," each child's learning needs are met along a continuum of progress. The teachers use a "theme" approach to curriculum, so that each child may work at his or her own level. In the continuous progress system, no child is a failure who would be subject to the ridicule of his or her classmates. Perpich says, "Our school does not use a 'deficit' model; here, we emphasize efficacy and success."

Perpich tells the story of "Mike," a boy who transferred from another school. Mike had been branded as a "five-er"— that is, a child with letter grades of "E" based on gradewide tests given three times a year, which he consistently failed. After transferring to Dickens, where the pressure to achieve on standardized tests was removed, Mike began to succeed. This is not miraculous or anomalous but is simply an example of learning that builds on success rather than failure.

As explained in the parents' brochure, there are no grades given at Dickens Elementary School. Parents receive anecdotal reports written by the teachers. Attached to these reports are the students' self-evaluations of their performance. Both the principal and the teachers have observed that in such a climate of openness and respect, children evaluate themselves with great honesty and perception—and are often less generous in their assessments than are their teachers.

And the parents' response to narrative reporting? Parents claim that the narratives tell them much more than letter grades about how and what their children are learning. Some parents still ask for letter grades, and the school does provide them if requested. However, such requests are rare.

There are observable effects on children's behavior in this school. I'm told, "There's no attitude problem here; what's more, as the kids go on into secondary school, there's no attitude problem there, either." Perpich tells me that, as principal in his previous school, he would return from lunch to face a long line of children waiting outside his office to be "disciplined" for biting, kicking, punching, hair pulling, and on and on. At Dickens, there is no line of children, and his disciplinary work is virtually nonexistent.

The Teachers Hold the Keys

It is not difficult to see that the critical force in initiating and maintaining a child-centered philosophy in a school is the teaching staff. Without like-minded teachers who perform at the highest levels and are respected as professionals, no educational program, let alone a child-centered one, can endure. Teachers must see the school as a place where all children can satisfy their curiosity, develop their abilities and talents, pursue their interests, and, through their interactions with their teachers and the older children around them, get a glimpse of the great variety and richness of life.[5]

When Rooney stepped in as principal of Dickens Elementary, he actively searched for and recruited teachers with such a perspective. Rather than rely on résumés and interviews, he actually visited classrooms and watched teachers in action. Based on his observations, he hired his initial Dickens staff. Teachers who "came with the school" and did not share the child-centered philosophy were invited to transfer to other, more congenial schools in Vancouver, and 11 teachers left when Rooney established the operating principles for the school.

Rooney was able to gather a critical mass of teachers who could be counted on to be strong advocates of open education and whose classroom practices matched those principles. Once those teachers were in place, the school began to attract attention for its students' academic success, its high regard in the parent community, and its status in the academy, with both universities in the area vying for student teacher placements. Dickens eventually became a magnet for other like-minded teachers, and recruitment and sustainability were no longer problems.

The staff at Dickens is exceptional in many ways. Teachers share decision making with respect to policy and practice in the school, and their professional autonomy is unquestioned. They function on an extremely high level in virtually every area of teacher expertise. In deciding class makeup for the next school year, for example, teachers are more than willing to accept their share of the "more difficult" children. Children who present the greatest challenges are not "dumped" on teachers who are new to the school; decisions about placement are based on which teacher is best qualified to meet a particular child's needs.

Perpich tells me that in the staff room, when teachers talk about students, they never complain or make negative comments. These teachers, Perpich says, love what they do, and it shows. When there is an opening for a new teacher, several members of the staff join the principal in the interview process. This practice goes to the edge of the envelope of what the union allows, but Perpich is willing to take the risk to get the teachers he wants. The school's job postings these days are worded in a way that will very nearly ensure that only those teachers sharing a like-minded philosophy will even apply.

It Takes Two to Tango

If the staff holds the keys to the successes of Charles Dickens, it is the principal who supports, encourages, facilitates, and explicitly appreciates what the teachers do. The teachers could not function at such a high level without strong administrative support, and Rooney, Robb, Clark, and Perpich have all been exemplary in providing it.

A successful alternative school requires an educational leader who is willing to take a stand on what he or she believes and stay the course. As Joanna McClelland Glass writes in her brilliant play, *Trying,* "You just lace up your skates and hit the ice."[6] Of course, the principal must be clear about his or her beliefs and be able and willing to act on them. As noted earlier, Dickens had to obtain special permission from the school board for some of its practices, such as anecdotal reporting instead of letter grades, and this was granted. Much of what is done at Dickens, however, is done without special permission. "We are quiet about it; my strategy is to do it first and then beg forgiveness after," Perpich tells me. The school is left largely to its own devices because of two essential conditions: there is no flak from parents or kids because they are well satisfied, and the kids are clearly cared about and performing at high levels of achievement.

Perpich is in his last year as principal before he retires, but he already has plans in the works for recruiting and hiring the principal who will replace him. He and his staff will decide on who will next carry the ball to keep the spirit and practice of Charles Dickens Elementary School alive and well.

But What Happens in Secondary School?

Because Charles Dickens has been in operation for nearly 20 years, there is now a history of reports about students who graduate from grade 7 and go on to junior and senior secondary schools in the district. In June 2004, for example, more than 50% of those who graduated from Dickens and applied to the secondary "mini schools" (schools-within-schools that offer special programs and enroll a small cadre of talented and high-functioning students) were accepted. The feedback from teachers at the mini schools and other high schools accepting Dickens students is that these young people are well-rounded, can carry on good discussions focused on the "big ideas," are good leaders, are good team players, are autonomous, are flexible and make good adjustments to high school, and are personally responsible. These reports remind me of the descriptions of the high school graduates from the Eight-Year Study program, which emphasized a richer and learner-centered curriculum and a healthy respect for student autonomy.[7]

Good News and Bad News

My observations at Dickens and interviews with the principal, teachers, and former district officials have provided a richly textured view of how a school with a highly challenging student population has not only survived but flourished. In the face of the prevailing educational ethos, which celebrates the trivial and downplays much of what we know is right and good for kids, Dickens has maintained its dedication to a child-centered program that actively reveres children and treats them with the respect that they deserve while ensuring that each one learns to his or her greatest ability. It's not a big mystery. All that is needed is the will, the instructional talent, the treatment of teachers as the high-functioning professionals they are, the administrative leadership, and the expertise to pull it all together to make it work. But none of this is news; this is what we, as educators, have known all along—from the early days of the Eight-Year Study to studies of the open classroom in the 1970s to more recent studies of single schools' alternative programs.[8]

So what is the bad news? From the safe haven of my office and desk, where I can look out at the cruise ships making their way up the inland waterway to Alaska, I feel sadness in recognizing that there is no magic formula that others can use to replicate what happens in this school. Dickens exists because a group of educators made tough decisions about what they thought was right and good for children. They stood by their decisions and played clean (and a little dirty) to get what they wanted. They never backed down.

In the end, it all conies down to choices—and educators have more choices than they might realize. It's one thing to knuckle under and accept what we hate and put that into practice, knowing all the while that we don't believe in it and wish it would go away. It's another thing to find out what options we do have and see how best we can maneuver to maintain and act on our beliefs within the constraints that bind us.

What can we do? And how far can we go? It may be possible to go much farther than we at first thought, if we can stand up and say, "This is what we believe. This is what's right." Having the toughness to do that is perhaps easy for me to advocate but hard in the field. For what it takes is "stand-up" leadership from principals, who must buffer the school from district and provincial demands. It takes school boards and provincial and state authorities who aren't afraid to give the professionals in the field the autonomy to follow a different pathway in meeting rigorous standards. Without such mettle, we will continue to bend and sway with the winds of change, and children will be the losers.

Notes

1. Sylvia Ashton-Warner, *Teacher* (New York: Simon & Schuster, 1962).

2. Sylvia Ashton-Warner, *Spearpoint: Teacher in America* (New York: Knopf, 1972).

3. Mary Brown and Norman Precious, *The Integrated Day in the Primary School* (London: Ward Lock, 1970), p. 36.

4. Charles Silberman, *Crisis in the Classroom* (New York: Random House, 1970).

5. Brown and Precious, p. 42.

6. Joanna McClelland Glass, *Trying* (Toronto: Playwrights Canada Press, 2005).

7. Wilford M. Aiken, *The Story of the Eight-Year Study* (New York Harper & Brothers, 1948).

8. See, among others, Deborah Meier, *The Power of Their Ideas: Lessons for America from a Small School in Harlem* (Boston: Beacon Press, 2003); Mary Ann Raywid, "Central Park East Secondary School: The Anatomy of Success," *Journal of Education for Students Placed at Risk,* vol. 4, 1999, pp. 131–51; and Charles Silberman, *The Open Classroom Reader* (New York: Random House, 1970).

SELMA WASSERMANN is a professor emerita, Simon Fraser University, Vancouver, B.C. She wishes to thank Larry Cuban, John Persich, Linda McLean, and Anne Luckhart for their feedback on earlier drafts of this article.

The Cultural Plunge

Cultural Immersion as a Means of Promoting Self-Awareness and Cultural Sensitivity among Student Teachers

Jesús Nieto

Introduction

"The depth of this class to me has been the cultural plunges. I learned so much in those plunges that no other course at (this university) could even remotely compete with. What I learned in the plunges about myself and accepting others is something that I will carry through life ... after I forget the statistics and psychological tests in my other classes."

The number of K–12 students from culturally and linguistically diverse backgrounds continues to increase exponentially (Major & Brock, 2003). Much attention has been focused on the ever-increasing disparity between the diverse student population and the predominantly white teaching force (Steeley, 2003). Most students entering the field of teaching continue to be white, monolingual, middle-class women (Glazier, 2003). Female European-American teachers will thus continue to comprise the great majority of educators for some time to come, but will be teaching students increasingly different from themselves in terms of ethnicity and social class. Latinos are the fastest growing segment of the nation's population, but just over 10% have a college education, compared to over 25% for all Americans (Brown, Santiago, & Lopez, 2003). It has been noted that students from the lower end of the socioeconomic spectrum face the greatest educational challenges (Prince, 2002), have much less access to quality education (Lin, 2001), and perform more poorly in school (Davis, 1989; Ornstein & Levine, 1989).

Linguistic diversity is receiving an increasing amount of attention from educators, and it has been noted that students who speak a language other than English and have limited proficiency in English are the fastest-growing population in U.S. public schools. From 1991 to 1999, the number of language-minority schoolaged children in the U.S. increased from 8 million to 15 million and the number of K–12 students who are classified as being limited-English-proficient (LEP) rose from 5.3 million to 10 million students (Smith-Davis, 2004).

Disability continues to be equated with inferiority and to lead to exclusion (Fitch, 2002). Disability issues are becoming increasingly important to "regular" teachers, as children with disabilities are being increasingly mainstreamed. According to a recent report from the U.S. Department of Education, more than 95% of students with disabilities are now served in regular schools, with 52% spending most of the school day in general education classrooms (Klotz, 2004).

Although many have voiced concern about the need for teacher education to sensitize future teachers to cultural and social concerns, few have offered concrete strategies for doing so. There has been a lack of effective teacher preparation for working with diverse, high-need students (Shinew & Sodorff, 2003); and although most teacher education programs report that they have thoroughly incorporated multicultural content and perspectives in their curriculum, this is not borne out by external examinations (Cochran-Smith, 2003).

Experiential Learning in Teacher Education

Several authors have urged the utilization of experiential learning in teacher education, often as a means of increasing cultural sensitivity. Baker (1989) believes that experiential learning is beneficial because students learn best when thinking, feeling and doing are all combined. Bergen (1989) has stated that no student teacher should be considered fully qualified for teaching until she or he has spent the equivalent of one semester involved in a "foreign" culture, and posits that Americans are very ethnocentric and thus in great need of becoming more culturally aware. Wilson (1982) believes that "Cross-cultural experiential learning should be a component of every teacher education program" (p. 184), and she outlines cultural immersion activities which are used to train members of the Peace Corps and other organizations.

Mio (1989) describes a program at a Southern California university where graduate students were matched with immigrant and refugee students in a cultural exchange. Socializing on campus, exploring ethnic restaurants in the area together, and visiting one another's homes were among the program's activities, after which participants wrote a paper about their experience. Such approaches are congruent with calls to reach unmotivated students by using educational strategies which are interesting, meaningful and at a level of difficulty that is challenging but attainable and which elicit expression of students' opinions, experiences and feelings (Berlin, 2004). These innovations in teacher training are made all the more important because many teachers have had little if any contact with students from different racial or cultural backgrounds (Milner, 2003).

The Cultural Plunge

For some years several professors at San Diego State University have been using a cultural immersion activity called a *cultural plunge*. They have used this activity in a sociology program (Gillette, 1990), in counselor education (Cook, 1990; Malcolm, 1990) and most recently, as described here, in teacher education. The author has been using the cultural plunge in teacher education since 1989, at which time he incorporated it in classes in that department, and several other teacher education faculty now use it as well. While faculty who utilize the cultural plunge tend to do so in a similar manner, there are some differences among the approaches. This article describes the way in which he approaches this activity.

Simply put, a cultural plunge is individual exposure to persons or groups markedly different in culture (ethnicity, language, socioeconomic status, sexual orientation, and/or physical exceptionality) from that of the "plunger." Most plunges last about one hour and there are a total of four required in my course. Important criteria for cultural plunges as described in my course syllabus are: (1) the majority of people there are from the focal group; (2) you are on the turf of the focal group (not in a school or restaurant); (3) this must be a type of experience you've never done before; (4) the plunge takes place after this course begins (credit cannot be given for past experiences); (5) you do not take notes; and (6) the plunge lasts at least one hour.

While the number and type of plunges I require have varied over the years, the most recently required are: (1) Attend a service at the largest African American church in the city; (2) Attend a religious ceremony in a language which you do not understand (Spanish and Vietnamese are recommended, as they constitute the two most widely spoken languages among English Learners); (3) Interact with homeless people; and (4) Interact with people with disabilities.

Cultural plunges have four major objectives which are stated in the course syllabus: (a) to have direct contact with people who are culturally different from oneself in a real-life setting which represents the target group's "turf"; (b) to gain insights into circumstances and characteristics of the focal community; (c) to experience what it is to be very different from most of the people one is around, and (d) to gain insight into one's values, biases, and affective responses.

Cultural Plunge Papers

Because people who engage in cultural immersion activities heighten their learning when they reflect upon their experience (Barrett, 1993), students write a 3-page reaction paper for each plunge. On page one, students list 10 popular stereotypes about the focal group and indicate what prior contact they've had with it. On page two, students describe their emotional response to the experience and any insights on why they reacted emotionally the way they did. Page three begins with discussion of whether the plunge experience reinforced or challenged the popular stereotypes of the focal group. The cultural plunge paper is concluded with exploration of "implications for my career." This last section is particularly significant because students often overlook the implications of the plunge experience for the classroom or other career setting. Upon further reflection, they often realize such things as the importance of greeting students warmly, learning to speak a few words of diverse languages as a sign of respect and interest in various cultures, and, most importantly, the crucial nature of not prejudging others.

Students' Reactions to the Cultural Plunge

Students' reactions to the plunges are described in detail in their cultural plunge reaction papers and tend to follow a progression of fear, excitement, and finally, appreciation. While most participants are generally afraid initially to go on cultural plunges, they almost invariably are glad they did after completion of the assignment, and tend to rate them as among the most important learning experiences they have ever had. The author surveyed 93 students enrolled in his spring and summer 2004 multicultural education classes. They were asked a variety of questions about their reaction to the course, including items about cultural plunges. They were asked to rate specific types of cultural plunges as well as the cultural plunge in general. Table 1 reports results from those surveys.

As all ratings reported on Table 1 range from 4.2 to 4.9, it is evident that cultural plunges had a "great" or "very great" impact on most respondents. These findings are similar to those of prior surveys done by the author with hundreds of students from 1989 to 1993, wherein cultural plunges received ratings ranging from 4.5 to 4.9 on a 5-point scale. In addition, cultural plunge papers have also been rated highly (4.2 to 4.5) in numerous surveys over the years.

Excerpts from Student Reaction Papers

Going beyond quantitative data, perhaps the following excerpts from students' plunge papers can best illustrate the impact that

Table 1 Impact of Cultural Plunges on Students

	Mean*	N
African American cultural plunge	4.4	93
Other Language cultural plunge	4.5	93
Homeless plunge	4.5	93
Disabled plunge	4.5	93
Gay/lesbian plunge	4.4	93
Cultural Plunge overall	4.6	93

*Ratings Code 1 = None 2 = Some 3 = Moderate 4 = Great 5 = Very Great

such experiences have on participants. The excerpts are organized around stated plunge objectives:

To Learn about the Target Community

[Farrakhan discussed] . . . some of the 'lies' that the whites use to keep African Americans down, and aren't they clever at making the blame all fall upon these people. The media portrays mainly blacks as gang members and drug dealers and this perpetuates the 'lie' and grinds away at all African Americans' sense of respect and self-esteem.

Many of my friends view Hispanics as lazy people. Nothing could be further from the truth. I saw many people, men and women, young and old, working their hearts out. Their community . . . was . . . a place of pride. As for family, when Pam told us about his family, I could see the pride and respect in his eyes.

Students are often quite surprised, even shocked, to learn that communities they visit are very different than what they had anticipated. They become intensely aware of how little they know about people unlike themselves, and often feel very ashamed about their ignorance. They often report a new desire to learn more about different cultural groups. Given the fact that gay students are among the most vulnerable students in middle school and high school (Weller, 2004), experiences which help future teachers to develop an awareness about the gay community are of particular significance.

To Experience Being an Outsider

Arriving at the church, . . . I immediately felt out of place and almost apologetic for being there. It was a strange feeling to he the minority in the group, something I have never experienced before to such a degree.

I realize much clearer now how it really must feel to be a minority. I've just taken my color for granted. It's not something I have to deal with everyday.

I can now understand more thoroughly what it is like to be in the minority, rather than the majority. The sense of isolation and loneliness is horrible, and it makes me sick to think some people live with that feeling everyday.

The underlying theme in these quotes is clearly fear. Most students who embark on cultural plunges are very anxious and occasionally even express concern for their lives. When I telephoned a student who dropped my summer, 1993 class after the first day, she told me that a big reason was because she was afraid to do the required plunge in an African American community, and both she and her husband were afraid that she might be physically harmed. Another student verbally expressed similar fears on the first day of that same class, but she decided to stay in the class and in fact had a great time on that plunge, as do almost all students.

The sad fact is that many European American students in my classes have usually managed to avoid ever going into a setting where the predominant ethnicity is different from their own, and many students of color have socialized primarily with members of their own ethnic group. Due to the influence of parents, peers, and mass media images, many White students have a profound fear of people of color and particularly of African-Americans, as these quotes reflect. Students of color are not exempt from such fears either, and they often are very anxious about visiting a community of a different ethnic group. The reality is that we all learn the same lies, and students tend to have the same biases about people different from themselves.

As these quotes indicate, cultural plunges are often the first experiences that many European American students have had of not being in the majority. Intense discomfort and a desire to leave immediately are common responses. The value of this particular lesson is profound. Students often write in their plunge reaction papers that they are now keenly aware of the importance of reaching out to their students who are ethnic outsiders. This realization is usually deepened when someone from the community reaches out to them on their plunges, which is usually the case. They thus learn firsthand what a positive impact a friendly gesture can make to a student who is culturally different from most others in a new setting, and they determine to be especially welcoming to ethnically diverse children in their future classes.

To Become More Aware of One's Values and Biases

I sat quietly in my chair listening to the conversation of the [African American] ladies around me. I really don't know what I was expecting, but these women did the same things in their lives that I did and they talked about the same things I do. It's amazing how because someone else may look different than you do you think that they act differently, too.

Throughout the (funeral) service, I was angry because I didn't see anyone cry, not even relatives. Then I learned that Buddhists believe in reincarnation; their spirit comes back to life in a form of human or animal, depending on your karma. Well, this helped me understand. I had already judged them, thinking they were morbid and insensitive people. This is where the danger lies; one starts to judge and stereotype out of ignorance or lack of understanding, which in turn, can lead to prejudice.

It caused me to reexamine how I interact with people of different cultures and how I unconsciously favor or respond better to those that relate better to my values. I also realize that while I try not to be "colonial" in mentality, I do want to be acknowledged and appreciated. Since visiting the conference and discovering this about myself, I have tried harder in communicating and listening and I have found I get far less defensive, I work far better with non-middle class students, I no longer expect acknowledgement, and I am far happier in my relations across cultural lines.

Students have many different types of insights about their values and biases as a result of cultural plunges. Whether discovering basic differences in world view, custom, or belief, or becoming more aware of similarities that exist across ethnic lines, students learn firsthand that their ideas about others are very often erroneous. They are able to discover some of their own fundamental assumptions, and are often very surprised that they were so unaware of their own values and biases.

Further Impact of Cultural Plunges: Effects on Motivation and Behavior

While the foregoing quotes from student cultural plunge reaction papers speak to three of the objectives of the plunge activity, there is another type of quote which warrants inclusion. This kind of quote speaks to the effects of cultural plunges on students' motivation and on their future behavior with people different from themselves:

That Saturday evening will stay with me for a long time. Both in my mind and in my heart. It's so easy to be oblivious and unaffected, when we don't think about things that don't concern ourselves. The thing is . . . that they do concern us, and I don't think I can forget that, or better yet, I don't want to forget!

I don't think I will ever be able to not think about what I saw on this day. No, as a matter of fact, I believe I will think about it often and I'm glad, because that means I will have to do something about it to be able to live with the images.

This cultural plunge really made me experience how the so called "minority" groups feel in our society. And hopefully this experience will stay with me forever so that I'm more sensitive when I'm teaching my students about the many different cultures in our society who all have an equal place here.

In all, I thought this experience was definitely worth it. I felt what it was like to be in the "minority." If this is what people of different races feel like when they are in the presence of a majority of whites, then something ought to be done to change attitudes. If this is a realistic goal, I don't know. All I know is what I have in my hands to control and I am definitely going to try.

These reactions indicate the lasting impression which cultural plunges leave on many students, and the degree of resolve which students feel to act on their newfound sensitivity. Unforgettable images, exposure to previously unknown crucial issues, and the experience of having been an outsider for the first time provide intense motivation to behave in new ways. The most commonly expressed new goals are to reach out to all students, attempt to promote increased communication and understanding between different ethnic groups, and become involved in social change efforts. All of these behaviors can significantly improve teachers' effectiveness with culturally diverse students and those students' communities.

Discussion

Cultural plunges engender a level of learning that is not possible with standard teaching methods such as lecture, texts, or discussion. Although plunge papers varied in terms of student reactions and emotional intensity, the overwhelming majority reported positive learning resulted from the experiences. This was true for students of varying ethnicity, color, gender, sexual orientation, socioeconomic status, physical attributes, religion and political views. Student enthusiasm for cultural plunges was very high, and a number of students recommended that more cultural plunges be required in the author's classes. One student stated in a reaction paper that "cultural plunges . . . should be a requirement for all future teachers," and this sentiment was quite widespread.

Perhaps the most compelling validation of cultural plunges comes from the words of students themselves. The author's students write a course reaction paper in lieu of a final examination in which they have total freedom to state their reactions to any aspects of the class which they care to comment upon. They are encouraged to be as frank as possible and to offer criticism and suggestions for improvement. Almost all students write about their cultural plunges and what they got out of them. The following excerpts are taken from course reaction papers:

> The cultural plunges are the best type of homework that one can do in order to truly learn about other cultures, customs and creeds. The benefit one obtains after such an experience is very great; more than if one had simply read an article or a book. All these plunges create that direct highway to the human heart.

> The plunges that we were sent on helped me face my fears, biases, and most of all the truth. It is amazing what first hand experience can do to a person . . . The plunges that I experienced have changed the way I think and look at things forever.

> The plunges give you that crucial first-hand experience that reading a textbook will never give you. I began to think about what kind of implications these plunges have for my career, and I became excited about how I would address these issues in my own classroom.

The learning which takes place from cultural plunges can be greatly enhanced via lectures, texts and videos. The author uses a number of powerful videos which address homelessness, discrimination against African Americans, violence against women, war, CIA experiments with drugs and diseases on Americans (including soldiers) without their knowledge or consent, and conditions in Third World sweatshops. These shocking depictions of the realities of diverse populations help to open minds and hearts and to create more empathy and compassion in future teachers. Many students have stated that the combination of lecture, video and cultural plunge has had a profound effect of their views towards homeless people and other populations.

Limitations

In the face of these results it is important to remember that there are limits to any teaching method, and the cultural plunge is no exception. One ought not overgeneralize from what one experiences on a single outing in any community, and cultural plunges certainly do not make cultural experts of anyone. Some students do not get as much out of these experiences as others, and are not very impressed with them. A few students view their plunges as negative experiences which they wish they had not been through. They might not have felt welcome, might disagree with a sermon in a church service or might strongly dislike church services in general. Such reactions are quite infrequent, however, and limited to a very small number of students (probably less than 5%). I make every effort to accommodate student concerns and requests for alternative plunges. For example, some students who are atheists have attended African America cultural events rather than go to the Baptist church service. In these types of situations, I brainstorm with the students for options which will be meaningful as well as acceptable, and leave the final decision in the hands of the student.

Conclusion

Plunges represent a type of education that is experiential, meaningful, interesting, challenging, confidence-building, growth-inducing and rewarding for most students. They represent a significant means towards students' greater understanding and acceptance of others, as well as of enhancing self-awareness; they thus have great potential as a viable educational approach in a full range of academic, business and government training programs. The fact that most plunges are one or two hours long makes their use very practical, and numerous students have said that they have gotten more out of plunges than out of service work requiring much more of a time commitment. Given the myriad challenges that confront teacher education in terms of preparing future teachers for the increasingly diverse students they will serve, the cultural plunge provides one means of helping to sensitize student teachers to social and cultural realities, to their own values and biases, and to the students of today's and tomorrow's classrooms.

References

Baker, F. (1989). How can you have experiential learning without experiential teaching? *Teacher Education Quarterly, 16*(3), 35–43.

Barrett, M. (1993). Preparation for cultural diversity: Experiential strategies for educators. *Equity & Excellence, 26*(1), 19–26.

Bergen, Jr., T. J. (1989). Needed: A radical design for teacher education. *Teacher Education Quarterly, 16*(1), 73–79.

Berlin, B. A. (2004). Reaching unmotivated students. *The Education Digest, 69*(5), 46–47.

Brown, S., Santiago, D., & Lopez, E. (2003). Latinos in higher education. *Change, 35*(2), 40–46.

Cochran-Smith, M. (2003). The multiple meanings of multicultural teacher education: A conceptual framework. *Teacher Education Quarterly, 30*(2), 7–26.

Cook, V. (1990). Personal interview. San Diego, June.

Davis, A. (1989). Teaching the disenfranchised child: The limitations of positivist research on instruction. *Teacher Education Quarterly, 16*(1), 5–14.

Fitch, E. F. (2002). Disability and inclusion: From labeling deviance to social valuing. *Educational Theory, 52*(4), 463–477.

Gillette, T. (1990). Telephone Interview. San Diego, May.

Glazier, J. (2003). Moving closer to speaking the unspeakable: White teachers talking about race. *Teacher Education Quarterly, 30*(1), 73–93.

Klotz, M. B. (2004). Help kids welcome disabled students. *The Education Digest, 69*(6), 41–42.

Lin, Q. (2001). Towards a caring-centered multicultural education within the social justice context. *Education, 122*(1), 107–114.

Major, E. & Brock, C. (2003). Fostering positive dispositions toward diversity: Dialogical explorations of a moral dilemma. *Teacher Education Quarterly, 30*(4), 7–27.

Malcolm, D. (1990). Personal interview. San Diego, April.

Milner, R. (2003). This issue. *Theory into Practice, 42*(3), 170–172.

Mio, J. S. (1989). Experiential involvement as an adjunct to teaching cultural sensitivity. *Journal of Multicultural Counseling and Development, 17*(1), 39–45.

Ornstein, A. C. & Levine, D. U. (1989). Social class, race, and school achievement: Problems and prospects. *Journal of Teacher Education, 40*(5), 17–23.

Prince, C. (2002). Attracting well-qualified teachers to struggling schools. *American Educator, 25*(4), 16–21.

Shinew, D. & Sodorff, C. (2003). Partnerships at a distance: Redesigning a teacher education program to prepare educators for diverse, high-need classrooms. *Action in Teacher Education, 25*(3), 24–29.

Smith-Davis, J. (2004). The new immigrant students need more than ESL. *The Education Digest, 69*(8), 21–26.

Steeley, S. (2003). Language minority teacher preparation: A review of alternative programs. *Action in Teacher Education, 25*(3), 59–68.

Weller, E. M. (2004). Legally and morally, what our gay students must be given. *The Education Digest, 69*(5), 38–43.

Wilson, A. (1982). Cross-cultural experiential learning for teachers. *Theory Into Practice, 21*(3), 184–192.

Jesús Nieto is an associate professor in the School of Teacher Education at San Diego State University, San Diego, California.

From *Teacher Education Quarterly,* Winter 2006, pp. 75–84. Copyright © 2006 by Caddo Gap Press. Reprinted by permission.

Ain't Nothin' Like the Real Thing
Preparing Teachers in an Urban Environment

Nancy Armstrong Melser

In her first journal reflection, Stephanie, a preservice teacher, described her initial impression of the urban school in which she was working. She wrote, "To be totally honest, my first impression was that I have never seen so many black people in my entire life!" While this comment may be surprising and jarring, Stephanie was being upfront about what many of my students were feeling in their first days of the Urban Semester Program at Ball State University.

According to the National Center for Education Statistics (2000), almost 40 percent of the total U.S. public school population is made up of students of color; in many metropolitan school districts, that number exceeds 80 percent. However, as the demographics of schools in the United States are changing, the population of preservice teachers remains much the same. As Roman (1999b) states:

> The student body in the United States is becoming more diverse than ever, while the teaching population is becoming less so. Teachers of European American background have had very little experience with bicultural students, and they may in fact harbor negative or stereotypical ideas about them. Further, many teacher education programs have a poor record of educating teachers for diversity. (p. 97)

With a growing number of African American students as well as those from other cultures, who will teach the children in large urban schools? Most likely, it will be young, white, females who are fresh out of college, with little experience and with little knowledge about those children's cultures.

The student body in the United States is becoming more diverse than ever, while the teaching population is becoming less so.

Colleges and universities are presented with the problem of preparing teachers for diverse classrooms on a daily basis. As educators, we realize the importance of teaching preservice teachers about diversity. We offer courses in multicultural training, we teach about black history, and we even teach students about using appropriate classroom materials that are not biased or prejudiced. However, the majority of this education is offered in small parts and isolated courses. According to Abdal-Haqq (1998):

> Isolated courses in multicultural education are unlikely to equip teachers for such work [work with diverse populations]. Many such courses appear to take the "music appreciation" approach to diversity. They promote acceptance, tolerance, and even respect for diversity, but they do not necessarily affirm it. (p. 68)

The lack of preparation for teaching in urban settings is one problem. In addition, research indicates that many new teachers in urban schools will leave within their first years of teaching. Since "as many as 50% of beginning teachers [are] leaving urban schools within the first five years" (Allen, 2003, p. vii), colleges and universities must prepare preservice teachers to work with students of various races and cultures. Teaching future educators to survive in a variety of settings is a key factor in their success or failure as urban educators. According to Watzke (2003):

> "Survival" has been characterized by many researchers as an initial stage in teacher development, marked by stress and issues of classroom management, an obstacle that must be overcome in order to advance in teaching practice. Veenman (1984) described this stage as one of reality shock-new teachers must adapt to the realities of classroom teaching from which they have been sheltered through traditional teacher education programs. (p. 223)

At Ball State University, we wanted to make this "reality shock" less severe for our preservice teachers, and better prepare them for the children they would someday teach. We knew that something had to be done to place preservice teachers in an alternate environment where diversity training occurred on a daily basis. Thus, the Urban Semester Program at Ball State University began.

The Urban Semester Program

The Urban Semester Program is an immersion program for junior level students. In this immersion experience, participants take a semester of classes while spending all day, five days a week, working in one of two elementary schools in the Indianapolis

Public Schools System. The populations of the two elementary schools are largely poor (96 percent and 94 percent free and reduced meal eligibility) and largely African American (89 percent and 88 percent), in sharp contrast to the university population of preservice teachers, who are mostly European American (95 percent). The Indianapolis school system was chosen for this collaborative project because it represented a true urban setting, had a diverse population of students, and was located only an hour from the Ball State campus. The goals of this partnership were to debunk the myths about teaching in an urban location while also promoting positive attitudes about teaching in such a setting. The ultimate goal was to recruit students for job openings in the urban environment by preparing them through field placements in diverse surroundings.

The student teachers learn about children in urban settings and how to become more empowered in reaching and teaching them on a daily basis.

By working side by side with experienced urban teachers, the college students learn about real-life issues teachers face while completing methods classes. The students are able to apply what they have learned with the children in the classrooms while obtaining immediate feedback about their lesson plans. The classes the preservice teachers complete in the Urban Semester include Math Methods, Science Methods, Social Studies Methods, Introduction to Special Education, and Classroom Management. College students attend all of these classes in their elementary buildings, and the professors travel from campus to teach and supervise field experiences. When they are not in college classes, the students participate in every aspect of teaching while assigned to one elementary classroom. They teach lessons, create teaching materials, attend teacher inservice sessions, and learn to manage the classroom on their own. Most important, they learn about children in urban settings and how to become more empowered in reaching and teaching them on a daily basis. Opportunities to develop relationships with families are another focus of the semester. Preservice teachers participate in parent-teacher conferences and extracurricular and community events where, for the first time, they have the opportunity to dialogue with children's families and members of the urban community.

The students in this program tell us that they learn more in a semester of urban experience than they do from years of on-campus classes. The following pages describe lessons they have learned.

Attitude Is Everything

As in the journal entry previously mentioned, many of the preservice teachers come to this program with existing stereotypes and preconceived notions. One of the best ways to change these ideas is to immerse the students into every

aspect of the school and community through such practices as Back to School Night and parent-teacher conferences. All Urban Semester students participate in these events and in the discussions that are held afterwards. The day after parent-teacher conferences, for example, several students reported that few parents had attended, therefore concluding that the parents "just didn't care!" Many preservice educators hold such beliefs, according to Ann Scott (1999). In her essay titled "Reaction to Ethnic Notions," she states:

Because of their cultural uniformity, and unless there are conscious strategies to the contrary, pre-service programs often serve as a mechanism for reproducing negative and racist attitudes and beliefs that later get translated into teaching approaches that continue to create unequitable education, (p. 31)

Scott goes on to state that "the general assumption among preservice teachers was that the parents did not really care about their children or their children's education" (p. 31). To debunk this notion, we held a brainstorming session in the Urban Semester Program about *why* the parents did not attend, and the students eventually realized that the parents may have been working at a second or third job, may not have been able to secure transportation to the school, or may not have had child care for their children at home. Over time, the preservice teachers understood that the urban parents, in most cases, were truly doing the best they could to provide for their children, even though they did not attend all school events.

Materials Do Matter

Another area that is strongly addressed in the Urban Semester Program is that of using culturally responsive materials in lessons and bulletin boards. Since the majority of the preservice teachers in this program are white, a major focus of our classes is to expose them to multicultural literature, diverse learners, and the contributions of all people, regardless of color, gender, or race. In the elementary education course, for example, students create a multicultural literature pack, which must include a book that appropriately represents a culture other than their own. In class, we discuss examining materials for bias and stereotypes and making appropriate curriculum decisions for the learners in their classrooms. In science class, the students create lessons about famous inventors who are not the stereotypical "dead white males" whom they often learn about in school. The students draw on material about people from other cultures, in the process learning a great deal about other cultures so they can transfer this information to the children they teach. By participating in the Urban Semester, the preservice teachers learn about developmentally and culturally appropriate teaching in ways that are not possible on campus.

Kids Are Key

The immersion in the urban setting also shows the preservice teachers that it is hard to teach students with whom you have not yet connected. According to Delpit (1995), culturally diverse students find themselves at a disadvantage for many reasons, including the fact that:

> Nowhere do we foster inquiry into who our students really are or encourage teachers to develop links to the often rich home lives of our students; yet teachers cannot hope to begin to understand who sits before them unless they can connect with families and communities from which their students come. (p. 179)

By getting to know the communities in which the children live, taking part in home visits, and initiating family events, our preservice teachers are learning about the students they teach and making connections to the lives of the children in their classrooms.

One event, called Family Fun Night, was created by the students in our program to bring parents, families, and community members into the schools to participate in hands-on science activities that can be easily duplicated at home. This event allows preservice teachers to interact with families and learn more about the children they are teaching, and it provides a rewarding teaching experience. This event also provides an opportunity for rich professional growth in the area of community building among our students, and creates parent and family involvement experiences that are often lacking in traditional college courses.

Management Is Major

A fourth lesson learned by participants in the Urban Semester Program is that of managing a classroom of diverse learners. At the beginning of the semester, many of the students in this program are unsure of their discipline approaches, are shy about correcting students, and are hesitant to reprimand children for misbehavior because they do not want the students to dislike them. While this attitude is typical among all beginning teachers, the students in the Urban Semester Program soon learn to put aside their fears.

During their placements, the preservice teachers learned that their disciplinary methods were often different than those of the teachers in their classrooms. For example, the preservice teachers often worry about "being mean" when telling a student to do something, while the veteran urban teachers are more direct in their approaches and don't worry about winning popularity contests with their students. Also, the preservice teachers are often quiet and timid when correcting students, while the practicing teachers use a firmer and often louder voice. Finally, the veteran teachers are often more culturally responsive to the children and know more about the discipline techniques that work with children in an urban environment.

According to Lisa Delpit, the author of *Other People's Children: Cultural Conflict in the Classroom* (1995), this is indeed a normal reaction of teachers who are placed in a different culture than their own (p. 121). However, by learning about the discipline strategies that are used in urban settings, the preservice teachers soon learned that the behaviors of children are often reflective of their culture and are best dealt with directly. This approach also validates the research of Weinstein, Tomlinson-Clarke, and Curran (2004), who state that:

> A lack of multicultural competence can exacerbate the difficulties that novice (and even more experienced teachers) have with classroom management. Definitions and expectations of appropriate behavior are culturally influenced, and conflicts are likely to occur when teachers and students come from different cultural backgrounds. (p. 26)

The authors also point out that very little is written in management texts about how to deal with cultural diversity and cultural conflict in classrooms. Our Urban Semester students learn about what works with a variety of children, and can practice these techniques on a daily basis. The professors also learn to teach more current methodology and processes that are culturally appropriate to the learners in this environment. By working daily with students and teachers of diverse backgrounds and cultures, our students learn a great deal about management that will assist them in their future teaching careers.

Conclusion

Overall, the immersion of preservice teachers into an urban setting has many benefits. The most important one, however, is learning the culture and pedagogy of the students whom one teaches. By working hand in hand with urban students, the preservice teachers learn lessons that cannot be taught in a book, and cannot be learned in a lecture hall. As Roman (1999a) states:

> To have knowledge of another culture does not mean to be able to repeat one or two words in a student's language, nor is it to celebrate an activity or sing a song related to their culture. To acknowledge and respect is to be able to understand and apply this knowledge to everyday classroom activities. It is to be able to make changes in one's curriculum or pedagogy when the needs of the students have not been served. It is to be patient, tolerant, curious, creative, eager to learn, and most important, non-authoritarian with students. In order for a teacher to promote excellence in education, there has to be a real and honest connection between the needs of cultural values of teachers and students. (p. 144)

In brief, the Urban Semester Program helps preservice teachers make these connections to students, staff, and self. We know it is working when several students each year take jobs in urban settings and when the final journal entries appear different than the first. In Stephanie's case, the unease reflected in her initial journal entry changed to the following sentiment:

> Now I know why I took these classes. Sure, I still see colors and differences, but now I know to celebrate them and assist the children in learning to the best of my abilities. I *know* that an urban school is where I belong and I am sure that I can make a difference!

References

Abdal-Haqq, I. (1998). *Professional development schools: Weighing the evidence.* Thousand Oaks, CA: Corwin Press.

Allen, E. (2003). *Surviving and thriving in the beginning years as an urban educator.* Bloomington, IN: 1st Books Library Publishers.

Delpit, L. (1995). *Other people's children: Cultural conflict in the classroom.* New York: The New Press.

National Center for Education Statistics. (2000). *Fast facts* (available at www.nces.ed.gov). Washington, DC: U.S. Department of Education.

Roman, L. (1999a). Cultural knowledge and culturally responsive pedagogy. In S. Nieto (Ed.), *The light in their eyes: Creating multicultural learning communities* (pp. 144–146). New York: Teachers College Press.

Roman, L. (1999b). Social class, language, and learning. In S. Nieto (Ed.), *The light in their eyes: Creating multicultural learning communities* (pp. 90–97). New York: Teachers College Press.

Scott, A. (1999). Reaction to ethnic notions. In S. Nieto (Ed.), *The light in their eyes: Creating multicultural learning communities* (pp. 22–32). New York: Teachers College Press.

Watzke, J. L. (2003). Longitudinal study of stages of beginning teacher development in a field-based teacher education program. *The Teacher Educator, 38*(3), 223–229.

Weinstein, C. S., Tomlinson-Clarke, S., & Curran, M. (2004). Toward a conception of culturally responsive classroom management. *Journal of Teacher Education, 55*(1), 25–38.

NANCY ARMSTRONG MELSER is Assistant Professor of Elementary Education, Ball State University, Muncie, Indiana.

Collaborative Recruitment of Diverse Teachers for the Long Haul—TEAMS

Teacher Education for the Advancement of a Multicultural Society

Marci Nuñez and Mary Rose Fernandez

The recruitment of qualified teachers is an immense and demanding job, particularly for high-poverty urban schools. Urban schools often turn to the common practice of recruiting teachers who are underqualified, most of them with no teaching experience and limited training. Because of their lack of preparation, coupled with the difficult working conditions they face and the inadequate support within their schools, these beginning teachers are likely to leave the profession soon after they enter. The attrition data is challenging: 33% of beginning teachers leave within the first three years of teaching, and almost 50% leave within five years. This attrition in turn produces yet more recruitment, again of a new group of under-prepared teachers, creating a "revolving door" phenomenon that has come to characterize the teaching profession. Thus, students in high-poverty schools often see new, under-prepared teachers year after year, despite the fact that these very students are in most need of quality, experienced teachers. These students are denied the opportunity to learn from well-prepared, committed teachers who are in the profession for the long haul.

The TEAMS (Teacher Education for the Advancement of a Multicultural Society) Teaching Fellowship Program is a collaborative model of positive recruitment that prepares diverse teachers, paraprofessionals, and counselors for service in urban, public school with the goal of increasing the academic success of all students. The TEAMS Program has evolved a unique model that provides a winning situation for all who are involved by using creative partnering to recruit, prepare, and support a confident, critical, and diverse teaching force prepared to tackle the challenges of inner-city teaching for the long haul.

Background

TEAMS has provided a network of teachers, like-minded educators, and resources for a diverse group of professionals who are attempting to create change in today's school system. TEAMS not only provides critical financial support for honorable work going on in the classroom, but helps teachers reach out to each other to receive the learning that they need to become better equipped to serve their students. Without the commitment of programs such as TEAMS, educators such as me would not be able to network and develop as effectively as leaders of social change and diversity.

—Angela Devencenzi

For over eight years, TEAMS has implemented a model of teacher development that attempts to defy these disheartening recruitment and attrition rates by annually enrolling more than 400 teachers along the West Coast in the program. The program model rests on the assumption that by providing financial support to acquire a teaching credential, focusing training activities on diversity, multiculturalism, and effective teaching strategies for urban schools, developing a network of like-minded educators, and intentionally targeting communities of color for recruitment, a diverse group of capable teachers committed to a career in public school teaching will emerge.

Our unique collaboration of higher education institutions, K–12 public school districts, and community-based organizations is led by the University of San Francisco (USF). We seek to develop a highly qualified teaching force that is reflective of the racial and ethnic diversity of students in urban K–12 schools up and down the West Coast, with a particular focus in the San Francisco Bay Area, Los Angeles, San Diego, and Seattle-Tacoma metropolitan areas.

Established in 1998 by the USF School of Education, the Multicultural Alliance, and several K–12 schools, TEAMS was created to address the critical shortage of teachers of color in San Francisco Bay Area urban schools. After the closure of the Multicultural Alliance in 2000, USF assumed a leadership role in TEAMS by becoming its fiscal agent and host institution. Creatively leveraging the resources that each of our partners brings to the collaborative, the program has been able to provide this unique combination of financial, educational, career, and professional development support to over 3000 aspiring and new teachers during its existence.

We are primarily funded by AmeriCorps, a program of the Corporation for National and Community Service. This AmeriCorps funding is the most significant way we are able to provide financial support for new teachers. Each year we receive an operating grant along with 400 AmeriCorps Education Award slots for Fellows. Fellows earn an education award of $4,725 each year for two years to use towards their teacher education by serving in an urban public school as a teacher of record, paraprofessional educator, or counselor.

Seeking Diversity in Teacher Recruitment

It is apparent that the increasingly diverse student population in urban public schools requires not only teachers who are credentialed, but also those who reflect the racial and ethnic diversity. Currently, students of color make up one third of our nation's schools while people of color comprise only 13% of the teaching force. In urban schools, students of color make up 75% of the student body while people of color represent only 36% of the teaching force. Furthermore, the increase in students of color is expected to continue at a significant rate. Nationally, predictions put the numbers of students of color at half of the student population by 2020[1] while the percentage of teachers of color is not expected to increase.[2]

We in TEAMS have always believed and insisted that any discussion on teacher quality must necessarily include a focus on teacher diversity if the racial achievement gap and growing student diversity is to be addressed in a meaningful way. In the "Assessment of Diversity in America's Teaching Force: A Call to Action," the National Collaborative on Diversity in the Teaching Force points out that "although teacher quality has been accepted and internalized as a mantra for school reform, the imperative for diversity is often marginalized rather than accepted as central to the quality equation in teaching." One of the key findings of the study is that "students of color tend to have higher academic, personal, and social performance when taught by teachers from their own ethnic groups" Furthermore, the study found that the academic achievement of students of color increased significantly when taught by teachers using culturally responsive strategies.

Breaking Down Financial Barriers

TEAMS was developed to intentionally and systematically address diversity in its recruitment process by targeting communities of color and reducing the financial and access barriers that commonly face candidates of color. The AmeriCorps Education Award provides an incentive for each stakeholder in the recruitment process. For potential teachers, it provides financial support for the educational costs of pursuing and attaining their teaching credentials as well as an incentive to work in urban schools and serve the community.

TEAMS Partners in Education—both teacher education programs and urban school districts—also have an incentive to recruit members to the program, thereby providing the individual advisement and referrals needed to attract TEAMS applicants. The Education Award provides teacher education programs with the means to offer an alternative source of financial aid to prospective candidates, which helps recruitment efforts, particularly among people of color. For urban school districts, which are already employing non-credentialed teachers to meet their immediate needs, both the program components and its education award are a means to improve the quality and preparation of their non-credentialed teachers and to support career-ladder programs for paraprofessional educators.

We have also been fortunate in using the Education Awards as leverage to get some of our higher education partners to provide matching funds in the form of scholarships to Fellows enrolled in their teacher education programs. Other forms of financial support we have been able to provide for Fellows include a housing subsidy, funded by the Teachers' Housing Cooperative of San Francisco, and in past years, mini-grants for service-learning projects. In a recent survey of Fellows completing the program, a majority (63%) responded that the financial support offered by the Program was the top reason why they joined and over 70% pointed to it as a very important factor in their development as a teacher. As voiced by one participant, TEAMS "was the only way for me to pay for my continuing educational goals."

Outreach and Credentialing

Outreach is critical to recruit the diverse population we support, including those who might not necessarily see themselves reflected in the teaching profession or might not think they have the means to do it. Many of the candidates we recruit are people of color, first generation college students, people from lower socio-economic backgrounds, and/or people moving into teaching from other careers (including para-educators who seek to advance their career). We rely heavily on personal connections and relationships for this recruitment. It is surprising how successful Fellows are in recruiting other teachers by simply sharing with them their experience in TEAMS. Other recruitment methods include referrals from partner institutions, holding of informational sessions, and participation in career and graduate school fairs.

For candidates who have considered teaching as a profession, but have not pursued it because of a lack of understanding about the process or lack of financial capacity to afford teacher credentialing, our recruitment information focuses more on the different teacher education institutions that TEAMS partners with, thereby offering a variety of locations for potential Fellows to pursue their credential, the financial incentives available, and information on the steps to become licensed.

Each year, about 70% of the Fellows who participate are people of color. One higher education partner not only tripled the diversity in its program, but also doubled its teacher education enrollment in the first year of partnership with TEAMS. It is important to note that we do not see recruitment and development efforts as separate from one another. Candidates must be enrolled in one of our partner credential programs and must be placed in an urban public school before being officially accepted into the program. Thus, academic coursework, practical experience, and the additional training and support are what we offer to prepare teachers for a long-term career in the teaching field.

Teacher Preparation and Culturally Responsive Pedagogy

Our primary pedagogy encourages Fellows to be educational leaders by helping them to understand the impact that teachers have in the classroom, in the school, and in the community. Also, by understanding the impact of policies and other external factors on the ability of teachers to be effective, Fellows are motivated to act as change agents in educational reform. Overall, the purpose is not just to develop the teacher, but also to help the teacher become more effective in developing diverse students in urban schools.

Methodology: Providing the Missing Link

TEAMS utilizes four specific methods to prepare teachers: (1) Enrollment in a credential program; (2) Service as a teacher or school counselor; (3) Attendance at pedagogical seminars; and (4) Completion of a service-learning project. We recognize that teaching service provides important practical training for new teachers, particularly when that service occurs while teachers are also gaining academic preparation. Thus, Fellows receive both the preparation offered by the teacher education program and the experience of working in an urban public school.

Below, we describe the professional development training opportunities provided by TEAMS, in particular, the pedagogical seminars, the family network, the service-learning projects, and the Cesar Chavez Service and Leadership Initiative. Through pedagogical seminars and service-learning projects, key components are offered that are often "missing links" for new teachers in urban schools.

Pedagogical Seminars

The TEAMS pedagogical seminars are designed to help Fellows build teaching skills, address critical issues in urban education, and network with peers and experts in the field. Topics addressed in the pedagogical seminars vary from year to year, but always retain a focus on multiculturalism, social justice, and youth empowerment while exploring teaching strategies that have been effective in diverse, urban classrooms.

Examples of previous seminar themes include: "Critical Curriculum Planning," "Moral Commitment and Ethical Action in the Classroom," "Building Diversity in Public Education," "Teachers as Visionaries and Change Agents," "Culturally Responsive Pedagogy," and "Transforming Hearts, Minds, and Society in a Standards-Based, High Stakes Climate," among others. At each seminar, a practitioner, researcher/scholar, teaching veteran, or educational leader is invited to address the group and the theme.

Each seminar incorporates an aspect of four areas: network, theory, practice, and motivation. The seminars provide opportunities for Fellows to interact with other new teachers and with experienced teachers. Presentations, discussions, and small group work provide opportunities to exchange ideas and develop relationships.

Service-Learning

The TEAMS program in a large sense kept me in the teaching profession. The service-learning project has enabled me to work with students in a building a community. It has been essential in keeping me more focused on real teaching. It has enhanced my teaching of Pre-Algebra and Science because I can link it to the community.

—Dante Ruiz

In addition to attending the seminars, each Fellow is required to complete at least one service-learning project per year with his or her students. Through the pedagogical seminars, Fellows learn about the *Youth Empowerment Model* of service-learning. Examples of actual projects implemented by Fellows in the past are presented so Fellows can see how the project impacted the classroom, school, community, and student learning. Service learning projects help Fellows develop practical skills in building community in the classroom, collaboration with other community members, and creative approaches to curriculum development.

The service-learning projects often become the highlight of the Fellows' experience, many of them receiving local and even national recognition. It is not surprising that a majority of Fellows have reported that the service-learning training they received and the project they undertook were a positive transformative process for them as teachers and also for their students. As echoed by one Fellow,

TEAMS gave me real world experience with service-learning projects that I otherwise would not have had. Me and another Fellow took the students out of the classroom and into their community to try and teach them about community responsibility and pride. I believe that this out-of-class curriculum was more beneficial than anything that could have been accomplished with a book in a classroom.

The following are two examples of community action projects that took place in the San Francisco Bay Area:

A Public Health Campaign: Wendy Ginsburg, a Fellow from 2004–2006, worked with her students to educate families in the Mission District of San Francisco about the dangers of a popular candy that contained lead. This candy was widely sold in stores around the neighborhood. Wendy decided to do her service-learning project in her 5th grade math class, where she wanted students to be able to compare, analyze, and interpret different data sets (math standard 1.0). The students did candy consumption surveys, tallied the data, created charts, and formulated conclusions based on their data. In addition, Wendy arranged a partnership with the local Department of Public

Health (DPH) to help students learn more about the effects of lead, and also to gain access to educational materials that the DPH had on the topic.

Armed with their new knowledge, the students decided to do an educational campaign, which included presentations to the school, talking to merchants in the neighborhood to urge them to stop selling the lead-tainted candy, and making fliers and posters warning about the dangers of the candy. Wendy was able to get through her academic content by this very creative process, one that engaged the students in a "real-world" situation and in service to others. Their project gained them a spot on the local news and in the newspaper.

A Youth-Friendly Resource Guide: Another Fellow described how her service-learning project in publishing a youth-friendly resource guide to San Francisco enabled her students to impact their community through research, reflection and creative expression:

> Impact High students were engaged in a community building research project that brought them together as a group of teenagers in the juvenile justice system to look at the issues that contributed to their contact with the system. My students came to the conclusion in their research that one of the main issues that drives students into the system is a lack of resources. Out of this came the idea to create a youth-friendly resource guide for San Francisco youth.
>
> In this way students were able to strengthen their own sense of community, develop their resourcefulness while researching what services exist for youth in San Francisco, publish their writing as a way to get their voices and perspectives that have been historically marginalized heard, and learn about what it takes to publish a magazine. The service activity was based in writing and research so it furthered my curricular goals for my writing workshop class. Writing for an authentic audience and knowing that their writing would be published pushed otherwise unmotivated students to draft and be thoughtful about their poetry and prose.
>
> The students completed the magazine, which was a compilation of student poetry and other writing and a guide to resources and services available to youth in the San Francisco area ranging from employment to health. A community publishing event was held where students provided a poetry performance and food to the community as a way to distribute their resource guide. The magazine was impressive and the students came away with a great sense of accomplishment knowing that their work truly made a significant impact on their peers and community.

Both of these projects illustrate the youth empowerment approach (YEA) to service-learning that we adopted and implemented which evolved from a partnership with REAL (Revitalizing Education and Learning), a community-based organization involved in youth development. The YEA model involves students in a problem posing, creative planning, action, reflection cycle that encourages intelligent engagement with social problems and mirrors Paulo Freire's concept of praxis. Through service-learning projects, students are engaged in their own learning process while contributing to their schools, the families their schools serve, and the broader community beyond their schools. Fellows are encouraged and provided with resources to work with other Fellows, other teachers in their schools, parents, and community agencies to plan and implement the service projects.

The Cesar Chavez Leadership and Service Initiative

The Cesar Chavez Leadership and Service Initiative is an optional program for TEAMS Fellows in California to implement a project specific to the United Farm Workers labor leader Cesar Chavez, in addition to or to meet their service-learning requirement. Fellows receive resources and training that highlights his life and work. It is another example of the youth empowerment model of service-learning.

Service-learning projects based on this initiative begin with a study on the life and work of Chavez, the social struggles he was engaged in, and a consideration of how those struggles manifest in the communities students live in today. TEAMS Fellows and curriculum consultants share lesson plans on Chavez that meet content standards for various grade levels.

The process engages students by having them identify community needs and how they will address problems through their service. It works to build community in the classroom as students dialogue, brainstorm, and work as a team to reach consensus. Fellows utilize interdisciplinary approaches to experiential learning, such as social studies and history for the Chavez lesson, math and science for students to study the chosen problem and assess results, and writing for the after-service reflection.

In years past, the initiative culminated in the Cesar Chavez Conference on Service and Leadership for middle and high school students in the San Francisco Bay Area who have been involved in service learning. Held at USF, 100 middle and high school students participated in an all-day conference of workshops and mural-making that depicted the ten values of Cesar Chavez. The murals that were created went beyond our expectations. The students not only conceptualized the content and design, they also created the actual murals, which turned out to be stunning pieces of art. The murals were mobile, designed to travel to different schools to raise awareness about Chavez, the impact of the labor movement he led, and to serve as an example of student work.

There were other significant outcomes from the Conference, most notably, the high school students, many of whom had not been to a college campus before, had their interest piqued because of their experience with their college student hosts that day, and asked numerous questions about how to get in to college (USF specifically, but also college in general). Of equal significance, the USF college students (students of color from a multicultural on-campus group called FACES) who had volunteered as hosts to the high school students reported that the experience inspired them to work with young people in the future.

Teacher Support

Teachers need programs like this to continue motivating themselves while receiving financial support. So many things prevent people from entering and staying in the education field, I feel TEAMS bridges this gap and gives so many people the opportunity to become and stay an educator.

—Renata Elmore

Support for teacher development is tied to recruitment, preparation and development, and long-term retention. Newly hired, inexperienced teachers who do not receive induction and mentoring are more than twice as likely to leave their position after the first year, and a higher percentage leave the teaching field entirely as opposed to moving to another position. Among the key reasons teachers leave the profession, lack of support and a poor working environment are factors that are often cited.

Not surprisingly, the support that we generate through seminars and a support network are important factors in TEAMS Fellows' decisions to stay in teaching:

This program was a tremendously helpful teacher education and teacher support program. I had the support of the TEAMS staff, fellow teachers, and all the leaders and presenters. This program helps teachers who teach in urban schools. We felt respected and we all realized that we were all struggling with the same things. The program helps us learn how to be more effective with our schools, students, and families. My teaching has been greatly affected and I am a better teacher for it.

Families

Fellows are grouped into "families" that meet consistently throughout the program year. Families are organized by grade level, subject area, or teaching specialty (Special Education, Bilingual Education). Within families, Fellows develop deeper relationships with a smaller group of teachers who share a similar teaching context. A family leader who is a veteran teacher, current practitioner, and/or teacher educator facilitates each family group. The program has engaged TEAMS alumni in the role of family leader as well.

Within their families, Fellows build community, discuss issues brought up in the seminars, share best practices and resources, and troubleshoot problems. Families are encouraged to communicate with and support each other outside of the seminars. Some families use their network to visit each other's classroom, exchange lesson plans and teaching strategies, or meet socially for support outside of the seminars.

The theoretical aspect introduces new knowledge and intellectual engagement, while practice helps Fellows to build skills in applying that knowledge. Presenters share best practices on effective teaching strategies and facilitate hands-on approaches to content development. Lastly, it is an important way for Fellows to have the opportunity to reflect upon their learning, be inspired and challenged, and strengthen their commitment to the field of teaching.

Developing Professionals

Furthermore, we strive to emphasize professionalism among our Fellows and encourage them to continue their development through research and collaborative projects. For example, through a grant acquired by the program, a group of Fellows, alumni and TEAMS Staff co-presented a service-learning workshop at the National Service Learning Conference in 2004, focusing on the outcomes of their Cesar Chavez-focused service-learning projects.

Alumni are also encouraged to stay connected to the program, to share their expertise, and mentor new Fellows. They are regularly invited to present workshops to current Fellows at pedagogical seminars, thus keeping them active participants in TEAMS and vital resources of support for Fellows as our network grows.

Teacher Network

We consistently work to foster and strengthen connections among Fellows in their cohort community that extend into the TEAMS network to include past Fellows, mentor teachers, other teachers at schools where Fellows are placed, and other educators, administrators, politicians, parents, and community members who support TEAMS. We nurture this network through public forums, social events, invitations to participate in Fellows' service-learning projects, an online community (including an area for sharing of curriculum and lesson plans, a job board, and chat room), and leadership development for network members by sharing their expertise at seminars.

Kate Shoemaker, an alumnus of the program, described the importance of the this network in this way:

TEAMS provided me with professional support during my first two years of teaching. I was overwhelmed when I entered my own classroom. Knowing I had TEAMS seminars to look forward to and compatriots with whom to consult made the tough times manageable. Now, I have a fantastic life-long network of professional resources.

Hanging in for the Long Haul

Through innovative collaboration, an intentional focus on diversity and culturally responsive pedagogy, and a training design focused on providing teachers with the tools to be successful in urban public schools, we have created in TEAMS an innovative model of teacher development and a strong network of dedicated teachers. However, the work does not stop there. We receive many more requests for support from Fellows than we have the capacity to provide. Many Fellows want the opportunity to observe other's classrooms, be mentored by a master teacher, and be able to see examples of great teaching in a high-stakes, highly scripted curriculum. Furthermore, as testing continues to be a focus of teacher credentialing, we will need to provide opportunities for our Fellows to be well prepared to pass those tests, as well as be able to afford them, while helping them not lose sight of the reason why they are in the profession: their students.

Everyone interested in the future of public schools must pay equal attention to the problems of teacher recruitment and retention. Vigorous efforts on teacher recruitment and development must continue if we are to produce enough qualified teachers to meet current and future needs. At the same time, teacher retention must also be addressed if the "revolving door" of recruitment and attrition is to be stopped and well-prepared, critically-minded, and professionally-supported teachers will hang in for the long haul.

Notes

1. Borman, G. D., Stringfield, S., & Rachuba, L. (2000). *Advancing minority high achievement: National trends and promising practices.* New York: College Board.

2. National Collaborative on Diversity in the Teaching Force. (2004). *Assessment of Diversity in America's Teaching Force: A Call to Action.* Washington, DC: Author.

MARCI NUÑEZ is assistant director of student activities and **MARY ROSE FERNANDEZ** is director of the TEAMS Program, both at the University of San Francisco, San Francisco, California.

Asian American Teachers

Do they impact the curriculum? Are there support systems for them?

Hema Ramanathan

Introduction

The significance and importance of global education and a culturally relevant curriculum have been thrown into relief by the events of Sept. 11, 2001, emphasizing the urgency to understand and be accepting of diverse cultures. This has a strong bearing on the "enculturation" role of schools, as agents of cultural reproduction.

The traditional curriculum transmits Euro-American norms that are seen as the primary American culture. The possible positive effects of a culturally responsive and diverse curriculum (CDC) have been detailed, including affirming the value of cooperation, helping students and teachers build an identity by comparing what they have learned in the classroom with their own experiences, and the importance of a caring community (Gay, 2000; Ladson-Billings, 1992b; Sleeter & Grant, 1991; Zimpher & Ashburn, 1984).

There is little doubt that schools should be more inclusive and that school-based personnel should appreciate and affirm what minority teachers bring to facilitate the development of a culturally relevant curriculum that is academically rigorous (Quiocho & Rios, 2000) but there is no systemic effort to genuinely shift from a Western perspective to include other perspectives and materials (Foster, 1994, cited in Quiocho & Rios, 2000; Gay, 2000).

However, adopting CDC or culturally congruent approaches to teaching has its own pitfalls. They can render teachers suspect by the broader school community since such approaches do not conform to the mainstream (Conner, 2002; Foster, 1994; Lipka, 1994, cited in Quiocho & Rios, 2000). Further, race and race-related pedagogy are not considered appropriate topics for discussion among faculty members, and issues regarding them are not raised in faculty forums (Foster, 1994, cited in Quiocho & Rios, 2000).

Where there is no self-examination, there is unlikely to be an expectation of overt support. The result is that the voices of minority teachers have been silenced and many of them do not have a role as decision-makers beyond the everyday decisions that teachers make in the classroom (Goodwin, Genishi, Asher, & Woo, 1997; Irvine, 2002; Quiocho & Rios, 2000).

These issues as they relate to Asian Americans have other features that complicate the matter. The term "Asian American,"

classed as one group for purposes of census and political policy, embraces sub-groups that differ widely in matters of language, religion, and cultural practices and beliefs. This multicultural, multi-ethnic, multi-literate profile engenders a lack of coherent cultural identity so that only a narrow slice is represented in the broad spectrum of the curriculum (Gay, 2000).

In the past three decades, the Asian-American population has been overlooked in terms of the demographic profile in spite of a dramatic increase of about 63%. Of Asian Americans, nearly a fourth is under 17 and of school-going age, accounting for about 3% of the total K–12 student population (Smith, Rogers, Alsalam, Perie, Mahoney, & Martin, 1994) while accounting for only 1.2% of the nation's teaching force (Snyder & Hoffman, 1994). Their low visibility is compounded by the fact that they are not evenly represented across the country in all regions; clustered along the East and West coasts, they are largely "missing in action" in the Midwest and South (U.S. Census Bureau, 2000).

Unlike other minority communities, there is no scarcity of qualified persons in this community in which 37% aged 25 or older is college educated. Yet, specifically among Asian-American women who hold degrees, only 1% goes into teaching, a profession still dominated by women. Many of the rest opt for jobs in technical and scientific fields which are higher-paying and where discrimination is perceived to be less of a barrier to advancement (Rong & Preissle, 1997; Su, Goldstein, Suzuki & Kim, 1997).

Emerging literature on Asian Americans shows that perceptions about the community are often at odds with reality. Asian Americans desire to be 'normal,' to fit in (Gordon, 2000). Whether it is to be accepted as "honorary Whites" so as not to remain "forever foreigners," or to get by in a racist society by staying quiet and behaving so that nobody would bother them (Tuan, 1998), Asian Americans indicate a desire to assimilate and to nullify their Asian roots. Their integration seems to depend on how mainstream they are, which argues for assimilation not accommodation.

Viewed as a "model minority," self-esteem issues that are cited in support of African-American and Hispanic profiles in the curriculum may not appear to be applicable to Asian-American students. While it is true that Asian-American students by and large are academic achievers and the Asian-American community appears to be successful economically, second- and third-generation Asian-American students in schools have to contend with cultural, social, and emotional issues like any other minority group (Siu, 1996).

Among all ethnic groups, the extremely limited research that is available on Asian-American teachers is a matter of deep concern (Quiocho & Rios, 2000). The available data focus on issues of motivation, explaining why Asian Americans are drawn to teaching and what may keep them in the profession (Goodwin, Genishi, Asher, & Woo, 1997; Gordon, 2000; Rong & Preissle, 1997; Su, Goldstein, Suzuki, & Kim, 1997). There are few studies that address the effect Asian-American teachers could have on the curriculum or the issues they may have to deal with in their work environment (Gay, 2000; Goodwin, Genishi, Asher, & Woo, 1997; Quiocho & Rios, 2000).

The purpose of this descriptive study was: (1) to understand problems Asian Americans may face as minority teachers; (2) to examine any impact they may have on curricula and academic experiences at the building level; and (3) to identify support systems available to them to implement desired changes.

Methodology

A survey of 23 items based on the research questions was designed. Of the 15 of these items that dealt with issues of identity of the Asian-American teachers and other professionals in the building, five explored the respondents' perceptions of the effect of their ethnicity on the curriculum and related activities in school. Seven items focused on how peers, administrators, students, and their parents related to issues of acceptance of their identity, and support that was or could be offered. Three items questioned the respondents about their awareness of and membership in professional ethnic support groups. Since the sampling frame of Asian-American teachers available was small, the survey was piloted with African-American teachers to test for a minority perspective.

The Midwestern state chosen for study mirrored the changing national demographics with regard to the Asian-American population (U.S. Bureau of Census, 1997). A list of all Asian-American teachers, obtained from the state Department of Education, provided an initial sampling frame of 106. Deletion of those no longer teaching and additions of names suggested by respondents defined a final sample of 96.

The final survey, with a cover letter and a stamped envelope for returning the completed survey, was mailed to all participants. Reminders over a period of two months included postcards, phone calls, and duplicate surveys. Forty participants responded to the survey for a return rate of 41.7%. Four of them declined to participate; they felt their ethnic identity as Asian Americans was not relevant to their identity as teachers. Another respondent stated that since he was mistaken for a Caucasian, his responses were not relevant. A sixth respondent chose not to complete the survey since the questions dealt with "delicate issues." Eventually 34 surveys were deemed useable. The data were coded and categorized by the researcher using open coding techniques (Strauss & Corbin, 1990).

Findings and Discussion
Curricular Issues

The presence of Asian-American teachers appears to have little effect on the curriculum or the academic experiences of students, and core content courses are not affected by the presence of Asian-American teachers in schools. Given that five of the respondents stated that they did not see themselves as Asian American, it is likely that their curriculum is not affected by ethnic perspectives.

Of the 34 usable responses, only three related their ethnicity to the content formally. Two taught Japanese and Chinese languages in their schools, supporting Ladson-Billings' (1992a) statement that there is a distinct ethnic-specific cultural preference for language that teachers bring into the classroom. The Japanese language teacher was also in charge of an after-school Japanese club. A music teacher incorporated a few Japanese songs into the repertoire.

Three other respondents brought their experience and knowledge of "otherness" into the curriculum informally, reflecting the findings of Goodwin, Genishi, Asher, and Woo (1997). They referred to world literature and global issues while discussing their content; this was not a requirement of the curriculum but was made possible by their wide experience. For example, a teacher from India compared Third World conditions to the U.S. to illustrate differences in life styles and to inculcate sensitivity to environmental issues.

Any other references to the ethnicity of the Asian-American teachers were sporadic and "add-ons." Four respondents said they incorporated activities related to their culture in their classroom but were not specific about the purpose or the learning expected from the students. Eight of the 34 responded that they had been used as resource persons by other teachers in the building.

In a scenario that is easily recognized, they were invited to talk to other classes about their culture, ethnicity, and country of origin or affiliation. The topics most often included the "visible" features of culture such as food, festivals, customs, and rituals, especially of marriage. On a more personal and serious note, a Japanese American was invited to talk about the experiences of Japanese Americans interned in concentration camps in the U.S. during World War II.

Decision-Making

Asian-American teachers are curriculum deliverers (Twisleton, 2004), not involved in defining the curriculum and with no opportunity to influence either the structures or the people in their working environment.

The Japanese language teacher stated that he wished that he were included in decisions regarding establishing or abolishing a foreign language department or offering Japanese but seemed to have no belief that his wish would be granted. A second respondent was both skeptical and cautious about her presence on any decision-making body. She believed that there was a danger of "being tokenized or less than appreciated because the teachers may have little understanding of non-mainstream experiences."

With the exception of one school building which had three Asian-American teachers, all the other respondents were the only Asian Americans in their schools. This lack of critical numbers may preclude their having an impact on decision-making at the building level.

The teachers were cautious about establishing an alternative culturally-responsive pedagogy and curriculum, unlike those studied by Su (1997). Except for two respondents, none of the others expressed a desire to be involved in re-designing the curriculum with a view to incorporating Asian-American elements. Rather than see schools as sites for diversity, anti-racism, social justice, and transformation (Feuerverger, 1997; Foster, 1994; Klassen & Carr, 1997, cited in Quiocho & Rios, 2000), most of these Asian-American teachers appear to want to maintain the status quo.

Issues of Support
Administrators and Peers

Asian-American teachers appreciated the support they receive from both administrators and their peers and detailed generic teacher needs in the areas of teaching, curriculum, and discipline.

Of the 34 usable responses to this set of questions, 15 respondents stated that they were supported by their peers in two areas—professional and personal—while 12 felt that they were not. Like all teachers, they looked to the administration for help with planning and implementing their teaching responsibilities and with student discipline.

Peripheral experiences of sharing information related to their ethnicity were seen as acknowledgement by peers and administrators of their uniqueness. Thus, most of the support they asked for was not curricular re-alignment, representation in the curriculum, or cultural mores of expectation and behavior that might distinguish them from their 'mainstream' peers.

Students

Asian Americans are proud of their ethnicity and yet wish to blend in with the dominant group (Gordon, 2000b). This dichotomy of appearance and perception was clearly noticeable in their interpretation of student appreciation. Asian-American teachers were pleased both when students noticed their ethnicity and when they did not. They welcomed being treated like all other teachers regardless of their ethnicity. On the other hand, they enjoyed the attention students paid to their different cultural background.

Fully a third of the respondents indicated that their ethnic identity did not impinge itself on the students. They believed that they were successful teachers because they were like any other teachers and exhibited the same characteristics of concern and caring. As one respondent colorfully phrased it, "I could be purple and still (the students) would enjoy my class, hopefully because I teach with caring and love." Another respondent commented,

> More than 80% of my students and parents like and appreciate the things I'm doing to help my students learn. I use my lunch hour to help the slow students. I always find time to help my students.

Yet students were not entirely blind to their teachers' differences. Their curiosity was piqued by their teachers' ethnicity and the respondents saw this as an indication of a positive attitude. Students questioned their teachers about their personal background and culture. The respondents felt that sometimes students "look(ed) to me as a source of information about Asia." Students are also curious about the country of origin of the Asian-American teachers. "They love to see some real samples from China/Taiwan and hear about the Chinese zodiac."

Some respondents were also subliminally conscious that students' perceptions of race and ability are influenced by the teacher's ethnicity. Beyond seeing the teachers as sources of trivia, two clear statements made by the respondents point to their belief that minority students are conscious and appreciative of the teachers modeling a minority status. They "appreciate the fact that (the teacher) can connect with them in different ways . . . can talk about skin color and speaking languages other than English with a certain depth of understanding."

As another respondent said, "My students realize that teachers don't just come in Black and White background. Anyone with the right qualifications (education) can become a teacher."

Professional Support Groups

Eighteen of the respondents indicated that they would join a group that addressed Asian-American issues related to teaching and teachers while nine did not wish to be part of any group. There are two professional organizations already in existence that are based on Asian-American ethnicity: the Chinese Language Teachers Association and an organization for music teachers founded by one of the respondents.

Yet, except for two respondents who each identified one organization, the others were unaware of the existence of these organizations. However, respondents felt the need for such support systems that would help them in their professional life, which are not available to them at present.

Role as Interlocutors

Falling outside the "color lines" of traditional racial discourse provides Asian-American teachers a role not obviously available to African-American or European-American teachers in a school building: interlocutors in a racially-charged incident. Being neither Black nor White, they are seen either as neutral, "colorless," or as either color, as may suit the students. "I can be seen as White by White students and as Black by Black students," a participant stated.

At the very least, Asian-American teachers see themselves as a "bridge between worlds and between people." This seems to be a great advantage with parents who are not hostile or wary of their 'allegiance.' As one respondent said,

> I'm in a high-minority population school and being non-White is an advantage with African Americans, Hispanic, and Asian parents. I don't sense the immediate mistrust that I see directed towards White educators. I've been asked to sit in on conferences where the educators were all White and the parents were non-White, for that very reason.

Their strength is derived from their being perceived as impartial. As mediators, they have been able to explain grading issues to minority students, defusing potential problems. Since they do not "belong" to the "other side," their words have veracity and carry weight with all stakeholders in a school building. As two respondents said,

> (Being an Asian American helps) with my students simply because it aids me in discussing fairness of rules, policies, treatment of minorities, or any related issues from a minority perspective.

> Some of my African-American students have accused other White teachers of giving out low grades to Black students because they are prejudiced. Since I'm not White, I was able to play neutral ground and explain to them how mistaken the students were, since grades are *earned* and not *given* by the teachers.

Non-Responses

Four respondents declined to participate; they felt that their ethnic identity as Asian Americans was not relevant to their identity as teachers. Another respondent stated that since he was often mistaken for a Caucasian, his responses would not be relevant. A significant third of them are either not conscious of their ethnicity or choose not to bring them into play. Their claim to be Caucasian or mainstream distinguishes them from those who would like to see their ethnicity as a strength and would like to have active support from their peers to explore it.

A sixth respondent chose not to complete the survey though she was repeatedly assured that her anonymity and that of the school would be maintained. As she explained in a telephone conversation, the questions dealt with "delicate issues" that she did not want to talk about.

Discussion

Asian-American teachers in this study appear to be well-integrated into the school system with regard to a teacher's life, role, and responsibilities, unlike the teachers in Goodwin, Genishi, Asher, and Woo (1997). They feel accepted and supported by peers and students and believe that their concerns are heard. Their problems relating to issues of curriculum, student discipline, and professional support are no different from other teachers in U.S. schools in most respects. Thus, the Asian part of their identity does not seem to count with them at all or to be an issue, and they do not seem to be overly concerned about being underrepresented in their schools or in the curriculum.

For change to be effected a critical mass has to be achieved. The desire on the part of Asian-American teachers to maintain the status quo may be prompted by a lack on numbers in their school buildings. In most cases, as the sole representative of their community, the desire to make a change in the curriculum may not seem feasible to them and therefore may not be entertained.

Calls for a wider, more multicultural curricula have not gone unheard. It is clear that students of today will need to know more about Asia than was required of the previous generation.

The economic growth of India and China make it apparent that in the future students will have to be more familiar with the present histories and cultures of such countries.

With this in mind, schools should be more deliberate about diversifying the curriculum. It should be apparent that teaching Asia in two weeks in a high school Social Studies class will not meet these needs, and that a more equitable distribution of time, addressing various cultures, is necessary (Conner, 2002).

Content teachers should become more knowledgeable about Asian cultures and a growing body of Asian literature in English. It seems natural that Asian-American teachers would be more intentionally involved in such curricular decisions about internationalizing the curriculum and making it more globally focused.

Recent world events have shown the need for foreign language expertise in this country and that promoting a functionally monolingual education is totally inadequate. Schools could offer an Asian language as part of its curriculum. Apart from the need for students to become well-rounded adults with knowledge of the world, the growth of India and China as global economic forces make it important for them to learn about Asia. It then would seem to follow that Asian-American teachers would be a rich resource.

With minority teachers a rarity in the teaching force and growing scarcer, attracting Asian Americans into the teaching profession will require that certain features such as salaries be amended (Su, 1997). Perhaps they could be offered inducements and bonuses and differentiated contracts as is offered to math and science teachers in some school districts. Calls for increasing teacher pay have come from a wide spectrum of society (Blair, 2001; Bond, 2001; Johnson, 2000). Whether this will come to pass is a question but until the monetary benefits are appreciably increased, Asian Americans are unlikely to enter the teaching profession in any substantial numbers.

The variety of roles that teachers play in a school in providing support for each other could be limited if they are not aware of their own strengths. The ability to offer differing viewpoints and perspectives on issues so that they can act as interlocutors in race-related matters could be significant to the well-being and growth of school and society. For example, Asian-American teachers could mediate in racially-charged situations where trust is challenged and communication lines are broken. They could explicate to minority students the nuanced perspectives of the educational system and, on appropriate occasions, advocate for the perceptions of beleaguered minority students.

The larger question is about teacher professional identity in which ethnicity is assimilated or absorbed. The most common way minority groups address conflicts in identity is either by adopting the dominant mode of identification and ignoring or relegating to the background their own ethnic features.

Ethnic organizations may exist in part because of the desire of the community to maintain its identity (Barth, 1969; Gordon, 1964). The case in point of a teacher being unwilling to respond to an anonymous survey is deeply disturbing and is a telling comment on the insecurity that some Asian-American teachers deal with in their work environment. The reluctance to address what is probably an unpleasant situation may indicate a peer group or administration that could be deliberately vindictive at being portrayed in unflattering terms.

Professional support groups could help Asian-American teachers identify and retain their cultural and ethnic features without jeopardizing their career or professional persona. Exploring and affirming their identity, and in turn finding ways of understanding and valuing it, will mitigate the marginalization of Asian-American teachers. However, the practically nonexistent research on the formation of an ethnic professional identity precludes a detailed discussion in an empirical study.

Conclusion

It is increasingly apparent that the conversations about race in the U.S. cannot continue to be a Black-White issue but must include Asian Americans and Hispanic Americans. The violence inflicted on Asian Americans in the aftermath of Sept. 11 was only one in a long line of attacks on them. The incidents by the "dot-busters" in Jersey City dating from the 1980s to the ransacking of Korean shops in 1992 were unfortunately not isolated occurrences (Zia, 2000).

Asian-American teachers appear to be an untapped resource; they should recognize that they are a "salient marker" (Tuan, 1998) to their students and other stakeholders, making it essential for them not to make their ethnic identity a private affair.

The U.S. perceives itself as a unique multiracial and multiethnic society. Schools claim to help their students value and celebrate diversity. Raising the profile of the largely invisible Asian-American teachers in schools is a viable starting point in achieving these objectives. It remains to be seen what the map of a school would look like if Asian-American teachers were to emphasize their ethnicity and not conform to the generic role that a teacher is expected to play in a school.

References

American Association of Colleges of Teacher Education. (1994). *Teacher education pipeline III: Schools, Colleges and Departments of Education enrollments by race, ethnicity, and gender.* Washington, DC: Author.

Banks, J. A. (1994), Transforming the mainstream curriculum. *Educational Leadership, 51*(8), 4–8.

Banks, J. A. (Ed.) (1996). *Multicultural education, transformative knowledge, and action: Historical and contemporary perspectives.* New York: Teachers College Press.

Barth, F. (1969). *Ethnic groups and boundaries: The social organization of cultural differences.* London, UK: Allen & Unwin.

Blair, J., (2001, February 21), Lawmakers plunge into teacher pay. *Education Week.* Retrieved September 2005, from http://www.edweek.org

Bond, C. K. (2001). Do teacher salaries matter? Unpublished doctoral dissertation, Teachers College, Columbia University, New York.

Gay, G. (2000). *Culturally responsive teaching: Theory, research and practice.* New York: Teachers College Press.

Goodwin, A. L., Genishi, C., Asher, N., & Woo, K. A. (1997). Voices from the margins: Asian American teachers' experiences in the profession. In D. M. Byrd & D. J. McIntyre (Eds.) *Research on the education of our nation's teachers. Teacher education Yearbook V.* Thousand Oaks, CA: Corwin Press.

Gordon, J. (2000a). Asian-American resistance to selecting teaching as a career: The power of community and tradition. *Teachers College Record, 102*(1), 173–96.

Gordon, J. (2000b). *The color of teaching.* New York: Routledge Falmer

Gordon, M. (1964). *Assimilation in American life.* New York: Oxford University Press.

Irvine, J. J. (Ed.) *In search of wholeness: African-American teachers and their culturally specific classroom practices.* New York: New York University, Institute for Education and Social Policy.

Johnson, S. M. (2000, June 7). Teaching's next generation. *Education Week.* Retrieved September 2005, from http://www.edweek.org

Kincheloe, J. L & Steinberg, S. R. (1997). *Changing multiculturalism.* Philadelphia: Open University Press.

Ladson-Billings, G. (1992a). Culturally relevant teaching: The key to making multicultural education work. In C. Grant (Ed.), *Research and multicultural education.* London, UK: Falmer Press.

Ladson-Billings, G. (1992b). Reading between the lines and beyond the pages: A culturally relevant approach to literacy teaching. *Theory into Practice, 31,* 312–320.

Ladson-Billings, G. (1994). *The dreamkeepers: Successful teachers of African American children.* San Francisco: Jossey-Bass.

Morishima, J. K., & Mizokawa, D. T. (1980). *Education for, by, and of Asian/Pacific Americans, II.* ERIC Documents. ED199356.

Phinney, J. (2000). Ethnic identity. In A. Kazdin (Ed.), *Encyclopedia of psychology. 3.* Washington, DC: American Psychological Association.

Quiocho, A., & Rios, F. (2000). The power of their presence: Minority group teachers and schooling. *Review of Educational Research, 70*(4), 485–528.

Rong, X. L., & Priessle, J. (1997). The continuing decline in Asian-American teachers. *American Educational Research Journal, 34*(2), 267–93.

Shain F. (2003). *The schooling and identity of Asian girls.* Sterling, VA: Trentham Books.

Siu, S-F. (1996). *Asian-American students at risk: A literature review. Report No. 8.* ERIC Reproduction Services ED404406.

Sleeter, C. E., & Grant, C.A. (1991). Mapping terrains of power: Student cultural knowledge versus classroom knowledge. In C. E. Sleeter (Ed.), *Empowerment through multicultural education.* Albany, NY: State University of New York Press.

Smith, T. M., Rogers, G. T., Alsalam, N., Perie, M., Mahoney, R. P., & Martin, V. (1994). *The Condition of education, 1994.* Washington, DC National Center for Education Statistics, Department of Education. ED371491.

Snyder, T. D., & Hoffman, C. M. (1994). *Digest of education statistics, 1994.* Washington, DC National Center for Education Statistics, Department of Education. ED377253.

Strauss, A. L., & Corbin, J. M. (1998). *Basics of qualitative research: Techniques and procedures for developing grounded theory.* Thousand Oaks, CA: Sage.

Su, Z. (1997). Teaching as a profession and as a career: Minority candidates' perspectives. *Teaching and Teacher Education, 13*(3), 325–40.

Su, Z., Goldstein, S., Suzuki, G., & Kim, J. (1997). Socialization of Asian Americans in human services professional schools: A comparative study *Urban Education, 32*(3), 279–303.

Tuan, M. (1998). *Forever foreigners or honorary whites: The Asian American experience today.* New Brunswick, NJ: Rutgers University Press.

Twisleton, S. (2004). The role of teacher identities in learning to teach primary literacy. *Educational Review, 56*(2), 157–164.

U.S. Census Bureau. (2000). *Statistical abstract of the United States: 2000* (120th Edition). Washington DC: United States Department of Commerce.

Ware, F. (2002) Black teachers' perceptions of their roles and practices. In J. J. Irvine (Ed)., *In search of wholeness: African-American teachers and their culturally specific classroom practices.* New York: New York University, Institute for Education and Social Policy.

Waters, M. C. (1990). *Ethnic options: Choosing ethnic identities in America.* Berkeley, CA: University of California Press.

Yon, D. (1996). Identity and differences in the Canadian diaspora: Case study from Metropolitan Toronto. In A. Ruprecht & C. Tiana (Eds.), *The re-ordering of cultures: Caribbean, Latin America, and Canada in the hood.* Ottawa, ON: Carleton Press.

Zia, H. (2000). *Asian American dream: The emergence of an American people.* New York: Farrar, Strauss & Giroux.

Hema Ramanathan is an associate professor in the Department of Curriculum and Instruction of the College of Education at the University of West Georgia, Carrollton, Georgia.

From *Multicultural Education,* Fall 2006, pp. 31–35. Copyright © 2006 by Caddo Gap Press. Reprinted by permission.

UNIT 3

Multicultural Education as an Academic Discipline

Unit Selections

Key Points to Consider

- What should be some minimal standards of practice in the field of multicultural education?

- What should be the qualifications for persons who wish to become specialists in multicultural education?

- It has been argued that all American students should learn the multicultural reality of our nation. Why is this true? How can it be accomplished?

- Is a "melting pot" approach to multicultural education outdated? How can multicultural education be applied to the classroom?

- What issues are raised by total infusion models of multicultural education in teacher education programs?

- What should all American students know about racism and prejudice by the time they graduate from high school?

- How do we help people learn to accept cultural diversity? What can teachers do to foster acceptance of cultural differences?

Student Web Site

www.mhcls.com/online

Internet References

Further information regarding these Web sites may be found in this book's preface or online.

Goals 2000: A Progress Report
   http://www.ed.gov/pubs/goals/progrpt/index.html
Teachers Helping Teachers
   http://www.pacificnet.net/~mandel/

"Multicultural education" emerged as an area of scholarship out of the social upheavals of the 1960s and the concern of many in the scholarly community that there was a critical need for research-based knowledge of the cultural contexts of education. Much of our early knowledge base came from critically important research in anthropology and sociology (as well as psychiatric studies of the impact of prejudice and victimization on targeted racial and cultural minorities), from the 1920s to our present time. These studies examined intercultural relations in all sorts of urban, suburban, small town, and rural settings in the United States. They used ethnographic field inquiry methods developed by anthropologists and later used by some sociologists and educators. The earliest of these studies, from the 1920s through the 1950s, focused on such concerns as child-rearing practices, rites of passage into adulthood, perceptions of other cultural groups, and the social stratification systems of communities and neighborhoods. Studies of how victimized and involuntarily segregated racial and cultural groups responded to being "targeted" for discriminatory treatment documented the intercultural state of affairs in American society in the 1930s and 1940s.

As the civil rights movement of the 1950s in the United States continued to grow in momentum throughout the 1960s, continued anthropological and sociological inquiry about the education of minority cultural youth continued to develop. Out of the urban and other social crises of the 1960s emerged a belief among those educators concerned about questions of racial and cultural justice that there was a serious need for an area of educational studies, which would specifically focus on the study of intercultural relations in the schools from a "multi-" cultural perspective. It would challenge the by-then-traditional Eurocentric melting pot visions of how one became "American." The problem with the Eurocentric "melting pot" was that it was a very exclusionary pot; not everyone was welcome to jump into it. The philosophy of a culturally pluralist democracy in which all cultural heritages would be treasured and none rejected became attractive to those who witnessed the arbitrary and cruel effects of racial and cultural prejudice in schools, as well as in other areas of life in "mainstream" society.

The belief that all teachers should respect the cultural heritages of their students and that all students have the right to know their cultural heritages and to develop pride in them began to spread among socially concerned educators. The studies that had been conducted on intercultural relations among teachers and students by the early 1970s clearly demonstrated the need for an academic discipline that would focus on building knowledge bases about our multicultural social reality as well as on how to teach about other cultural heritages and to improve the quality of instruction in multicultural school settings. Many of us realize today that all young Americans need to know about the American experience from a multicultural perspective that rejects and transcends the old Anglo- and Eurocentric presuppositions of melting pot theories of assimilation into American social life.

As part of the movement for civil rights, persons from non-English-speaking backgrounds also sought to guarantee that their children would be given the opportunity to grow up both bilingual and bicultural. By the time the U.S. Supreme Court handed down its decision in *Lau v. Nichols* in 1974, there were dozens of cases in the federal court

CORBIS/Royalty-Free

system concerning the causes of bilingual education and English as a second language.

The academic leadership of the nation's cultural minorities and many other concerned scholars has forged a competent community dedicated to the task of setting standards of practice for multicultural education as an academic discipline. There is spirited dialogue going on in the field as to what these standards of practice should be as well as about what academic qualifications people ought to have to conduct multicultural education. James Banks, professor of multicultural education at the University of Washington, and others are concerned about the future survival and development of multicultural education as an academic discipline that must also maintain its focus on classroom practice as well as on defensible theoretical constructs.

Multicultural education must develop an ongoing cadre of competent scholarly leaders to direct the further development of the field as well as to ensure that attempts to merely infuse multicultural content into existing teacher education course content does not dilute the academic quality of multicultural education or the standards of practice in the field. Multicultural education is an interdiscipline that draws its knowledge base from anthropology, sociology, social history, and even psychiatry. Schools need focused and adequately prepared specialists in this new interdiscipline on their faculties in order to maintain thier academic integrity.

The essays in this unit reflect concerns regarding academic standards and goals for multicultural education, as the field continues to develop and to enter a new period in its history. The authors of these essays raise important qualitative issues that must be addressed as the time approaches when a majority of Americans will be from "minority" cultural heritages and when traditional conceptions of minority and majority relations in the United States will have little meaning.

This unit's essays are relevant to courses in curriculum theory and construction, educational policy studies, history and philosophy of education, cultural foundations of education, and multicultural education.

The Human Right to Education
Freedom and Empowerment

CAETANO PIMENTEL

Introduction

Education is widely understood as the gradual process of acquiring knowledge or the process of training through which one teaches or learns specific skills; furthermore, it can be understood as disciplining the character. It is undoubtedly the spread of knowledge and information but, more than this, the imparting of experience, knowledge, and wisdom. One of the fundamental goals of education is the transmission of culture between generations.

In a broader sense, education begins with life itself[1] and goes beyond formal or informal schooling, encompassing the struggles and triumphs of daily life. It is essential both for children and adults—in the case of the latter, to replace or prolong initial education in schools, colleges, and universities as well as in apprenticeship.[2]

Religious values, political needs, and the system of production have always determined the standards of education. Indeed, education has always been subordinated to the expectations concerning the roles individuals would perform in their social group.

But the importance of education has been acknowledged in a much broader sense:

Dakar Framework for Action:

6. (. . .)[Education] is the key to sustainable development and peace and stability within and among countries, and thus an indispensable means for effective participation in the societies and economies of the twenty-first century, which are affected by rapid globalization.(. . .)

Indeed, as a human right, education is the acknowledgement of the individual's rights rather than his or her role in the capitalist goals of the economic growth; the human right to education is the way through which one can conquer freedom and become a genuine individuated[3] being, self-aware and yet deeply and truly connected to others.

The Brazilian educator Paulo Freire formulated ideas concerning literacy (and the learning process as a whole) which became influential internationally. According to Freire, the process of learning necessarily goes along with the learner's ever-increasing awareness of his/her existential condition and of the possibility of acting independently to change it—with individuals reflecting on their values, their concern for a more equitable society, and their willingness to support others in the community. Learning process is what Freire called 'conscientization,' an empowerment of the individual.

Freire expanded education's technical-pedagogic dimension to a political one, which demands a major shift of the education paradigm into 'praxis': reflection plus action, which highlights the importance of learners becoming active subjects in the learning process, taking a position of agents.

Education throughout History[4]

Education has taken as many forms as cultural, political, and religious values have been created by human kind. In Egypt and Mesopotamia (3000 B.C.), the first formal group education appeared as Scribal schools. In primitive societies of hunters and gatherers, learning process was based on watching and imitating. Jewish religious education was a way to glorify G*d. In Greece, a man-centered approach to education was available to a privileged male few, both at home and in State schools—but, still, the whole purpose of education was to subordinate the individual to the needs of the State.

Medieval education was an evolution of Catholic catechetical schools of the second century—Monasteries were both for those preparing for a monastic vocation (oblati) and those whose aims were secular (extend); the later Middle Ages witnessed the rise of the great cathedral schools followed by the ascendancy of the universities and the complexities of scholasticism.

During the Renaissance, there was a turn back to humanistic cultural values of Classical Greece and Rome. Based mainly on parish church provisions and also found in some monasteries and palaces, primary schools were mostly limited to elites. Changes in economical relations arising at the time led to the education of some new skills, such as computation and bookkeeping.

In the following centuries, complex changes on economic, political, technological, religious, scientific, and aesthetic levels demanded a substantial increase in provisions for schooling and the access to schools. The fullest expression of the need to broaden formal educational opportunity came in calls for universal schooling. Convictions and trends moved in the direction of enlarged access despite the persistence of some conservative medieval opposition. These convictions and trends meant increasing the number of schools and putting them near potential student populations in towns and villages-and a big challenge was to find a sufficient number of competent schoolmasters.

The 18th century gave way to the emergence of the idea that schools should be instruments of social reform (Samuel Hartlib, John Dury, John Comenius), and access to them should be increased. Social and religious reforms, nationalism, commerce and industry, colonization, and scientific methods of inquiry and technological innovations were responsible for the development of a number of theories concerning education and school access, amongst them the ideas of secular universal elementary schooling and the development of critical rational thinking.

The North American colonies along the Atlantic coast (17th–18th centuries) transplanted the ideas of Renaissance (South), Reformation (North), and Enlightenment (Franklin and Jefferson), whereas earlier settlements established by Spain and France maintained a parish organization of schools. Private schools (Franklin), free public school for all (Jefferson), language teaching, and the diffusion of knowledge were some of the trends concerning education for white boys and girls.

In Brazil, Asia, and Africa, Jesuit Priests were in charge of the catechisation of natives and the children of the first colonisers. Particularly in Brazil, their mission was to teach them to read, perform labor, and organize themselves in order to protect the land occupied, which led the native culture to be nearly extinguished. The Jesuits remained in Brazil until 1759, when they were sent away from the country by Marques de Pombal, whose goals were to create an administrative elite and increase the production of raw materials and commodities (e.g., sugar) to be traded by Portugal.

Major social, political, cultural, and economical changes arose after the French and American revolutions, when four major trends to modern western democracies were established: the rise of nation states, urbanization and industrialization, secularization, and popular participation.

Nation states, with their enormous power to gather and focus both human and material resources, have come to interfere increasingly in the definition of educational policy and schooling. Industrialization and urbanization resulted in a concentration of human populations more and more diverse. secularization has meant an augmenting emphasis on rational/empirical modes of explanation. Popular participation refers to an enlarging access to involvement in the governance of public life.

These trends have not and do not come about in a linear way, nor are they alike everywhere, both in timing or scope. Changes are still operating in many western and eastern countries today, and as a result we can find four major issues that modern states are yet to sort out: social stratification and class interests, religion and ideology, race and ethnicity, and geography (i.e., localism, regionalism).

The Right to Education—A Historical Background

Educational process implies a number of actors: those who receive education, those who provide education, and those who are responsible for the ones who receive education.[5] The first legislation on educational issues were an attempt to balance the complex relations between these actors. The social, cultural, political, and economical changes brought about in the modern age by the emancipation of the individual have had a great impact on the relationship between the individual and the state. The recognition of rights of individuals and duties of state are both a reflection and a consequence of these changes.

Although we may find today the right to education enshrined in many provisions of human rights law, none of the classical civil instruments such as the British Bill of Rights of 1689, the Virginia Declaration of Rights of 1776, the American Declaration of Independence of 1776, and the French Declaration of Rights of Man contained any language specifically related to the right to education, although some recognised the freedom of teaching from state interference. Indeed,

> Public education was perceived as a means to realising the egalitarian ideals upon which these revolutions were based (. . .).[6]

Child labor in England had been subject to legal regulation since the first Factory Act in 1802 (Health and Morals of Apprentices Act), but it was not until the Factory Act of 1833 that legal provisions imposed restrictions on child labor and created the obligation of school attendance-first in textile establishments, and then the Mines Act came later in 1842.

The Constitution of the State of Indiana (1816), in its article IX, recognized the importance of education to the preservation of free government (sect. 1) and also stated goals to provide for a general system of education, free and equally open to all (sect. 2).[7]

The socialist ideas of a paternal state, drafted by Marx and Engels, and the liberal anti-clerical concepts of freedom (of science, research and teaching, among others) also influenced the definition of the educational rights by means of compulsory school attendance and similar measures. In the latter half of the 19th century the Constitution of the German Empire contained a section entitled "Basic Rights of German People," and the German Weimar Constitution of 1919 included a section on "Education and Schooling."[8]

The first provision on the human right to education with a corresponding duty of the state to provide education was in Stalin's Soviet Constitution of 1936. As a matter of fact, the right to education has been a major fundamental right in all constitutions of socialist states.[9]

As a major interest of the state and society, education turned out to be a right of the individual, rather than solely a duty of state or parents. And in the 20th century, many international and regional instruments and a number of national constitutions have recognized the right to education, which thus has become a fundamental human right.

At the international level, peaceful resolution of conflicts has always been a major concern: the International Peace Conference (The Hague, 1899), the League of Nations (Versailles, 1919), and the Declaration by United Nations (1942) to support the fight against the Axis Powers were the expression of nations' concern about peace and security.

When the Second World War was over, representatives of 50 countries met in San Francisco, in 1945, to draft the United Nations Charter. The purpose of the United Nations, set forth by the charter, comprehends not only peace and security goals, but a broader scope of actions and international cooperation efforts concerning economic, social, cultural, and humanitarian problems and, above all,

> to reaffirm faith in fundamental human rights, in the dignity and worth of the human person, in the equal rights of men and women end of nations large and small (. . .).[10]

UNESCO, the United Nations Educational, Scientific, and Cultural Organization, was born in the same year. Peace and security, justice, the rule of law and the human rights, and fundamental freedoms are clearly expressed in its declaration of purpose.

The United Nations' Universal Declaration of Human Rights (UDHR) (1948) enshrines, in its Article 26, the right of everyone to free and compulsory education and recognizes the role of education in the development of the human personality and the respect for human rights and fundamental freedoms.

The process of positivization of the rights contained in the UDHR at the international level started with the two covenants adopted in 1966. Concerning education, the International Covenant on Economic, Social, and Cultural Rights spells out in more detail the right to education, in its articles 13 and 14, including the right to free compulsory primary education, adult education, freedom to choose education, and recognition of the role of education in enabling all persons to participate effectively in a free society.

Education as a Human Right

Emphasising education as a basic human right shifts the focus from simply concentrating on the contribution that education can make to economic development. The focus on education as a fundamental human right is that the internationally agreed Human Right treaties form a common platform for enshrining equal rights to education for all citizens. In this perspective the individual in society is viewed as a stakeholder with rights and not an object of charity or investment.[11]

The international community has embraced education as a basic human right, as major international and regional instruments disclose a number of important State obligations.

The right to education is recognized as the one which empowers individuals to cope with basic needs, such as health and dignity, and which enables the full and free development of his or her personality. Also, education is required for the implementation of the collective right to development—which means that any society depends on the education of its members to enjoy satisfactory conditions of life and fully achieve its goals, to assure that they will be able to fulfil personal needs such as housing, health, and food.

Education is now recognized as the pathway to freedom, and free democratic society depends on its members' abilities to freely choose, think, and express themselves, and to actively contribute to the political and social processes in pursuit of their interests.

Education is assigned to the "second generation" of human rights, those related to equality. The nature of second generation rights is fundamentally social, economic, and cultural. In social terms, they ensure different members of the community equal conditions and treatment, securing the ability of the individual to lead a self-directed life and to pursue the development of his or her personality.[12]

Second generation Human Rights are mostly positive rights, "rights (or guarantees) to," as opposed to negative rights which are "rights from," usually freedom from abuse or oppression by others. Hence, education must be provided by a series of positive actions by others: school systems, teachers, and materials must be actively provided in order for such a right to be fulfilled, representing things that the State is required to provide to the people under its jurisdiction.

But the Right to Education can also be linked to first generation (freedom) rights, for it entitles individuals to a certain degree of liberty and autonomy before states and their institutions (the right to choose education), and to third generation (solidarity) rights: the right to self-determination, to economic and social development, and to participate in the common heritage of mankind,[13] aspiring ultimately to the full respect for and protection of all human rights. The article 8(1) of the Declaration on the Right to Development reads as follows:

> States should undertake, at the national level, all necessary measures for the realization of the right to development and shall ensure, *inter alia*, equality of opportunity for all in their access to basic resources, education, health services, food, housing, employment and the fair distribution of income. Effective measures should be undertaken to ensure that women have an active role in the development process. Appropriate economic and social reforms should be carried out with a view to eradicating all social injustices.[14] (emphasis added)

The right to education is complex and demands strong commitments at many levels to be implemented. As a result, many different aspects of the right to education have been emphasized by the international community since the Universal Declaration of Human Rights, perhaps due to a lack of full commitment to the principles related to this multifaceted right.[15]

In the subjective dimension of the right to education, we can take the definition given by Canotilho[16] to social rights:

> Social rights are subjective rights inherent to the portion of space where the citizen lives, independently of immediate justitiability or exequibility. (. . .) Neither the state nor third parties can damage re-entrant juridical positions in the ambit of protection of these rights.

In the objective dimension, the right to education, as any other social right, according to Canotilho, can be put into practice through lawmaking processes, in order to create material and institutional conditions for these rights to be granted to individuals. In addition, it must be provided as a materialization of the subjective dimension of these rights and a duty of the state to comply with its institutional obligations. These obligations range from minimum guarantees inspired by neoliberal principles to the full wide-ranging welfare model adopted by social-democracies in northern Europe, for instance.

Education Today

Albeit the repeated affirmation and recognition of education as a human right, one hundred and thirteen million children around the world are not enrolled in school and many more than that drop out before being able to read or do simple mathematics. These figures will add to the ranks of 880 million illiterate adults in the world[17] and to escalating unemployment, poverty, and income disparities. A lot has changed since the rise of nation-states, but educational policies are still ruled by economical and political interests.

Since 1950, the estimated illiteracy rates have significantly declined,[18] but as a complex right which consists of quantitative and qualitative aspects, these numbers fall short on describing how well all the purposes comprised by the Article 26 of the Universal Declaration have been fulfilled. On this matter, Joel Samoff has stated:

> The most important measures of success of an education programme are the learning that has taken place and the attitudes and values that have been developed. There is little point in reducing the cost of 'delivering education services' without attention to whether or not learning is taking place. Assessing learning and socialization is both complex and difficult. That it is difficult makes it all the more important that it be addressed systematically and critically.[19]

Although in most countries primary education is compulsory by law, it is rarely enforced. From the Proclamation of Teheran, in 1968, to the World Declaration on Education for All adopted by the World Conference on Education for All in Jomtien, Thailand in 1990, and the Dakar Framework for Action of 2000, many changes took place, specially with regard to the focus of education.[20]

Basic principles, such as "free education" and "primary education," have been distorted to exempt governments from the duty of implementing education as set by international and national law. In contrast, statements concerning the international community's agreement on the education's purpose have been considerably broadened:

> Taking into account all of the above, the vision of education's aims and purposes that has emerged over the past several decades is essentially focused on two inter-related themes. The first, which can be broadly labelled as 'Education for peace, human rights and democracy', is directly linked to—indeed, has largely been inspired by—the aims and purposes proclaimed in Article 26 of the Universal Declaration. The second, which can be broadly labelled as 'Education for development,' is linked to Article 26 in a more complex way.[21]

Right to Education v. Access to Education

According to the Annual Report 2004 by the UN Special Rapporteur on the Right to Education, Professor Katarina Tomasevski, there are many obstacles to the full realization of the right to education: the commercial approach to education (rather than a human-right approach), gender discrimination, and school drop-out are the ones which deserve special attention.

The liberalization of education, under the World Trade Organization GATS (General Agreement on Trade in Services), is within the concept of free market and competitiveness, raising a conflict between trade law and human rights law.[22] Deregulation, privatization, and reduction of public spending leads to the elimination of public funding or subsidy to public services—and that includes education. The underlying philosophy of this process leads to a change of perception from public and community good to individualism and individual responsibility.[23]

In this context, education is not regarded as a right which must be made freely available, accessible, acceptable, and adaptable. It is reflected in an altered vocabulary, as pointed out by Prof. Tomasevski, in which "access" to education does not grant free education funded by the government.[24] Education is no longer provided by the entitlement to rights; it is determined by purchasing power and the rules of self-regulation of the market, as a part of a creeping privatization of education that causes the transference of education costs to poor families. An astonishing array of education charges, from direct school fees to indirect costs for books, pencils, uniforms, and transportation, are supposed to be afforded by family units worldwide.[25]

We must take into account that the expansion of private education is creating a two-tiered system that creates inequities rooted in social class, caste, and gender-where public education, in very poor condition due to lack of resources, is only used by those who cannot afford to pay for better quality schooling provided by private institutions. This dual education system creates and perpetuates a divided society, and this division goes beyond purchasing power, for this inequality also reflects discrimination on the basis of religion, language, race, and gender.

Moreover, not every family can afford having one or more of their children going to school instead of helping the family earn more income. Very often, costs are cited by parents as the major factor in deciding to keep children out of school.[26]

Education is the way to break out of the poverty cycle: through education children, particularly girls, can ultimately help increase the family income, and stay healthier. Education is definitely the foundation for equitable human and economic development.

In developing countries, the education crisis is also a crisis of education quality. Those children who do attend school in the world's poor countries face enormous obstacles to their learning. A chronic teacher shortage most of the time results in large-sized classes, multi-graded or divided by shifts. Another problem is the inadequate supply of basic materials, such as books, desks, and benches, not to mention the lack of transportation for students and the too-often empty stomach.

Gender Inequalities

Gender issues concerning education are also a major concern,[27] for very large gender inequalities still exist in the majority of developing countries. Education not only provides basic knowledge and skills to improve health and income, but it empowers women to take their rightful place in society and the development process. It gives them status and confidence to influence household decisions—women who have been to school tend to marry later and have smaller families. Their children are better nourished and are far more likely to do well at school. Educated women can overcome cultural and social factors, such as lack of family planning and the spread of disease, which contribute to the cycle of poverty.[28]

But girls are needed at home and they contribute largely to the family income: they look after siblings, nurse sick relatives (e.g., in the context of HIV/AIDS in Africa), and do domestic tasks. Besides that, the low number of government schools and the limited public transport make distance a barrier for both boys and girls, but for reasons of safety and security, most parents are reluctant to let their daughters walk long distances to school. In some African countries, sexual abuse of girl pupils—at school and on the way to school—is one of the main reasons parents withdraw their daughters from school.[29]

Girls and women have been victimized by economic factors not only in the realm of education, as it has been pointed out by Prof. Tomasevski.[30] A major shift on many other factors is equally necessary to ensure employment and political representation opportunities—but equal access to education is a significant start to achieve gender equality.[31]

Inclusive Education

Another step in universal education goals is inclusive education: a strategy contributing towards the ultimate goal of promoting an inclusive society, one which enables all children/adults, whatever their gender, age, ability, ethnicity, refugee status, impairment or HIV status, to participate in and contribute to that society. Difference is respected and valued. Discrimination and prejudice must be actively combated in policies, institutions and behavior.[32]

Within schools inclusive education is an approach which aims to develop a child-focus by acknowledging that all children/adults are individuals with different learning needs and speeds. It leads people to learn about themselves and understand their strengths and limitations, which makes them better able to recognize and understand not only individual health and physical conditions, but also the political, economic, and social conditions that surround them. One must view oneself positively in order to move from passive to active participation.

School Drop-Out

Providing schools is only part of the problem—a huge one for sure, but still only a part of it; the drop-out phenomenon poses another challenge to schools, families, and governments, as well as to the quality of education provided in many countries.[33]

According to Paulo Freire,[34] society itself prevents students from having access to and remaining at school; indeed, dropout is nothing but "school push-out," i.e., children/adults are expelled from school for a number of social, economic, and cultural factors.

The causes that give rise to the dropout/push-out of students are many, such as to help their families, course failure, pregnancy, lack of interest, addiction to drug/alcohol, financial reasons, gender and ethnic discrimination, not getting along with teachers and/or other students, or criminality. School drop-out/push-out is an issue which concerns both developed and underdeveloped countries—and it does not refer only to minority groups such as immigrants and indigenous populations.

Effective and relevant education is important to combat school dropout/push-out. It helps the promotion of the personal development of the individual, ensuring that educational content, method, and scheduling are appropriate to the different needs and circumstances of each person—as in the case of rural areas, where harvest season can make children and adults prioritize work rather than school,[35] or school-dropout caused by the student's mere lack of interest.

Indeed, concerning this problem in China and Colombia, Prof. Tomasevski stated in her Annual Report 2004:

> (. . .) an important reason for children's dropping out of school was their dislike of the education provided them. That many children, when asked whether they liked school—rarely as this happens—answered in the negative is a sobering lesson for education authorities.

From sub-Saharan Africa to Canada, from rich to poor, from eastern to western culture countries, the world cannot refrain from dealing with education issues—such as exclusion and poor quality education—raised by many cultural, religious, ethnic, social, or economic factors, and their impact on the educational process.

The Dakar Framework for Action affirms:

> 43. Evidence over the past decade has shown that efforts to expand enrollment must be accompanied by attempts to enhance educational quality if children are to be attracted to school, stay there, and achieve meaningful learning outcomes.

To address these problems, it is necessary to promote a shift in the education paradigm. Students are not supposed to be coadjuvants to education process and schools should not be an instrument of dominant economic and political purposes.

All students in school is inclusive education in the broadest sense-regardless of their strengths or weaknesses in any area, they become part of the school community. They are included in the feeling of belonging among other students, teachers, and support staff.[36]

A New Approach to Education

The strategic objectives of UNESCO's Medium-Term Strategy for 2002–2007 provide a new vision and a new profile for education, as follows:

- Promoting education as a fundamental right in accordance with the Universal Declaration of Human Rights;
- Improving the quality of education through the diversification of contents and methods and the promotion of universally shared values;
- Promoting experimentation, innovation and the diffusion and sharing of information and best practices as well as policy dialogue in education.

It is important to highlight the concern towards the methods and contents of education, an important issue which has been raised in recent years in order to achieve the higher purpose of education, that is to say, the learner's achievement and development.

In addition, there must be developed a deeper understanding of literacy, a core educational issue, which is widely seen as essential for enabling a person to function fully in his/her society and is often reduced to the ability to read and write in the official language.

This narrow understanding of literacy, developed in the last two centuries with the formation of the nation state, industrialization, and mass schooling, does not recognize the role it plays as a key to developing a critical mind—which does not rely merely on the development of such skills, but on the liberation and full development of the individual.

Human Rights Education

Human rights education has been proclaimed in various global and regional legal instruments, such as The Charter of the United Nations, which reads:

> To achieve international co-operation in solving international problems of an economic, social, cultural, or humanitarian character, and in *promoting and encouraging respect for human rights and for fundamental freedoms* for all without distinction as to race, sex, language, or religion; (. . .)[37] (emphasis added)

Moreover, the Universal Declaration of Human Rights proclaimed

> as a common standard of achievement for all peoples and all nations, to the end that every individual and every organ of society, keeping this Declaration constantly in mind, shall strive by *teaching and education to promote respect for these rights and freedoms* (. . .)[38] (emphasis added)

At the regional level, the African Charter on Human and Peoples' Rights, in its article 25, explicitly calls on African states to

> promote and ensure *through teaching, education and publication, the respect for the rights and freedoms contained in the present Charter* and to see to it that these freedoms and rights as well as corresponding obligations and duties are understood, (emphasis added)

In 1994, the General Assembly of the United Nations proclaimed the United Nations Decade for Human Rights Education (1996–2004), on recommendation of the World Conference on Human Rights (Vienna, June 1994).

The recognition of education as a major instrument to promote and enforce human rights is based on the conviction that we all have the right to know our rights—and it can only be enforced when we learn and understand about the human rights enshrined in national constitutions and in all international human rights instruments.

People are empowered to act when they learn about their human rights and can actively defend themselves from abuses, overcoming their lack of concern towards politics. In addition, imparting of knowledge and skills regarding human rights promotes

a. The strengthening of respect for human rights and fundamental freedoms;
b. The full development of the human personality and the sense of its dignity;
c. The promotion of understanding, tolerance, gender equality and friendship among all nations, indigenous peoples and racial, national, ethnic, religious, and linguistic groups;
d. The enabling of all persons to participate effectively in a free society;
e. The furtherance of the activities of the United Nations for the maintenance of peace.[39]

Empowerment through human rights education develops the individual's awareness of rights and obligations regarding his/her human condition and includes everyone in the citizenry; it charges people with the responsibility of claiming rights for themselves and others, as well as respecting those rights. People become aware of the difference individuals can make and the importance of joining efforts to do so. Additionally, human rights can become more tangible when related to people's own life experiences, which strengthens the power of these rights in the process of building a more equitable, just, and peaceful world.

The implementation of human rights education goes beyond inclusion in the schools' curricula, for it involves a whole commitment to human rights, from the training of teachers to a safe and healthy learning environment. Human rights education is not only a set of contents to be transmitted to learners, but also understandings of how and where it will be done. Schools' staff must be fully aware of human rights, which should be incorporated in all strategies, procedures, and activities developed and performed by them.

Finally, human rights education should be an integral part of the right to education,[40] both in formal and non-formal schooling.

Sex Education

Education on sexuality, relationships, and reproductive health is deeply connected with women's and girls' rights. The Convention on the Elimination of All Forms of Discrimination against Women (CEDAW) and the recommendations of the General Comments of the related Committee are clear on the importance of sex education.[41] Nevertheless, sexuality is inherent to human beings and men and women, boys and girls, every person should have the right to be educated on sexual health, and the Committee of the Rights of the Child states that

> Adequate measures to address HIV/AIDS can be undertaken only if the rights of children and adolescents are fully respected. The most relevant rights in this regard, in addition to those enumerated in paragraph 5 above, are the following: (. . .) the right to preventive health care, sex education and family planning education and services(. . .).[42]

Sex education is the process of acquiring knowledge and skills concerning sexual behaviour (which comprises sexual orientation, relationships, birth control, and disease prevention), empowering individuals to make decisions, assert their choices, and protect their physical, emotional, and moral integrity. As a result, individuals learn when and how to seek help and become better able to engage in healthier relationships, exert control over their own lives, and recognize other people's rights, cultural differences, and attitudes towards sexuality—mainly regarding sensitive issues such as sexual orientation, contraception methods, abortion, and gender roles.[43]

One could never emphasise enough the core importance of sex education to children—especially girls—with regards to HIV/AIDS prevention, family planning, and elimination of gender discrimination. The right to sex education should be realized with the inclusion of sex education in the curricula worldwide, despite large obstacles such as cultural, religious, and political factors which might tend to prevent schools and educational authorities from enforcing such education.

Education Paradigm Shift

Independently of the reasons, be they economic, social, or cultural, a major change in the pedagogical approach is necessary to deal with the current education crisis. Curriculum adaptation, special programs, acknowledgement of cultural peculiarities, and flexible school schedules are many of the potential solutions for such educational problems as large classes, uncaring and untrained teachers, passive teaching methods, inappropriate curriculum, inappropriate testing/student retention, and lack of parent involvement.

A *Manual on Rights-Based Education* has been developed as a result of collaboration between UNESCO Bangkok and the UN Special Rapporteur. Such an approach recognizes that human rights are interdependent and inter-related and seeks to protect and put them into effect. Human rights are the means, the ends, the mechanisms of evaluation, and the focal point of Rights-Based Education. The manual is based on international human rights law, aiming to bring human rights standards into educational practice, encompassing health, nutrition, safety, and protection from abuse and violence.

One of the issues addressed in the manual is the quality of education, which should be learner-centred and relevant to learners, as well as respectful to human rights, such as privacy, gender equality, freedom of expression, and the participation of learners in the education process.[44] This means that both content and pedagogical approach are crucial to quality of education.

Furthermore, the content should be related to real-life experiences and learners' cultural and social context, encouraging full participation of all parties involved, enforcing their fundamental rights of freedom of expression, access to information, privacy, and health, among others. The importance of education content has also been recognised by the Committee of the Rights of the Child.[45]

A propos, Freire had always stressed the need to change the traditional schooling system, which treats students as objects and contributes to the marginalization of minorities, as opposed to "liberatory" pedagogy, one that uses the dialogical method to facilitate the growth of humanization and empowerment[46] and enforces the principle of equality while respecting differences. The focus must be on education for equity, transformation, and inclusion of all individuals through the development of consciousness and critical thinking.

Freire has based his work on the belief in the power of education to change the world for the better, supporting freedom from oppression and inclusion of all individuals. In his book *Pedagogia da Autonomia* (Pedagogy for Autonomy), he enunciates the three pillar concepts of teaching:

1. there is no teaching without learning;
2. to teach is not to transmit knowledge; and
3. the process of education is a human peculiarity.[47]

Freire's pedagogy requires a whole new approach to the exercise of power over education; responsibility is to be shared between all parties involved (teachers, learners, those responsible for learners, and the community at large) from the curriculum planning to the process of learning. The dialogical process resulting herein comes about from the recognition of and respect for each individual's personal knowledge and skills, which enables all to participate equally in the organization and development of education.

Teachers and learners share equally the experience of learning through questioning, reflecting, and participating; as a result, this process contributes to the enforcement of infinitely diverse human potentials, instead of refuting, weakening, distorting, or repressing them.

Such a pedagogical approach builds up to the formation of critical consciousness and allows people to question the nature of their historical and social situation—to "read their world"—becoming more than a mere passive object to the information disseminated by others.[48]

The schooling system is not supposed to be limited to reproducing a dominant ideology, to teach a truth that is not true for all, fostering impossible dreams and hopes in the learners; but at the same time it must allow them to dream. It requires an affectionate—yet scientific—posture by the teacher.[49]

The role of the teacher is crucial, but s/he cannot be just an individual in the world, rather than an individual with the world and with other people, sharing the experience of being in "quest"—in a permanent process of questioning, changing, growing, learning, improving, and finding new directions.[50]

Teachers become educators when they get fully aware of the surrounding world's influence on every individual. And, most of all, they must be open to the reality of learners, get acquainted with their way of being, adhere to their right to be. Educators choose to change the world with learners.[51]

Being actively aware of the world, the teacher becomes better able to do more than just disciplining the process through which the world gets into the students, imitating the world, filling their empty vessels with chunks of knowledge.[52]

In an ever-increasing globalized world, learning processes must recognize and value differences; teachers must be prepared to deal with diversity in every level (cultural, social, economic, religious, ethnic, and linguistic) and schools must be prepared to cultivate a joyful environment to foster this get-together. Learning is to celebrate the communication and interaction between people.

Conclusion

The future of humankind relies on the fulfilment of the right to education: equality, freedom, dignity, equitable social and economic development, sustainable development, and peace are highly dependent on successful universal education policies.

Nevertheless, just providing universal formal schooling is not a guarantee of an educational system that prepares the individuals to be free. Although it is clear that a lot of work needs to be done until every individual is provided education worldwide, the process of learning can always be improved to achieve its goals of preparing people to participate actively and consciously in the society of which they are part. And education must be respectful of every individual's cultural background so that each person can make the most of it in their personal journey and in their interaction with others.

A rights-based approach to education requires respect for the human rights of all individuals involved in the learning process; it offers education as an entitlement, rather than as a privilege, and does not exempt any actor of the learning process from his/her responsibility for the full protection and fulfilment of any other fundamental right.

Such an approach to education takes place when learners are respected for their autonomy and dignity; moreover, they must be provided all things necessary for them to take part actively in the learning process and to develop their awareness of reality. They learn about their past, understand their present, and acknowledge their power to fight for their future.

Education requires dialogue and affection between teachers and learners. The learning process involves joy, beauty, affection, ethics, equality, mutual respect, and faith in a better world.

Notes

1. World Declaration on Education For All, Jomtien, 1990, article 6. Learning begins at birth. This calls for early childhood care and initial education. These can be provided through arrangements involving families, communities, or institutional programmes, as appropriate.

2. CRC General Comments General Comment no. 1: The Aims of Education, Article 29 (1).

3. According to Jung, individuation is "a process by which individual beings are being formed and differentiated . . . having as its goal the development of the individual personality" (Jung, C.W. 6: par. 767), bearing in mind that "As the individual is not just a single, separate being, but by his very existence presupposes a collective relationship, it follows that the process of individuation must lead to more intense and broader collective relationships and not to isolation." (CW 6, par. 768) "Individuation does not shut one out from the world, but gathers the world to itself." (CW 8, par. 432) quoted in Sharp, 1991.

4. Bowen, 2003.

5. Nowak, 2001:190.

6. Hodgson, 1998:8.

7. "Article 9: sect. 1st. Knowledge and learning generally diffused, through a community, being essential to the preservation of a free Government, and spreading the opportunities, and advantages of education through the various parts of the Country, (. . .) shall be and remain a fund for the exclusive purpose of promoting the interest of Literature, and the sciences, and for the support of seminaries and public schools.(. . .); sect. 2. It shall be the duty of the General assembly, as soon as circumstances will permit, to provide, by law, for a general system of education, ascending in a regular gradation, from township schools to a state university, wherein tuition shall be gratis, and equally open to all." As in http://www.in.gov/icpr/archives/constitution/1816.html#art9

8. Hodgson, 1998:8.

9. Nowak, 2001:192.

10. United Nations Charter, Preamble.

11. Education, Democracy and Human Rights in Swedish development co-operation, Swedish International Development Cooperation Agency, 2004: p. 17.

12. Nowak, 2001:196.

13. As in http://www.fact-index.com/t/th/three_generations_of_human_right8.html

14. Declaration on the Right to Development, adopted by the General Assembly in 1986.

15. World Education Report 2000:23.

16. Gomes Canotilho, 1998:434.

17. Dakar Framework for Action-Education For All: Meeting Our Collective Commitments Text adopted by the World Education Forum-Dakar, Senegal, 26–28 April 2000: 6. (. . .) it is unacceptable in the year 2000 that more than 113 million children have no access to primary education, 880 million adults are illiterate, gender discrimination continues to permeate education systems, and the quality of learning and the acquisition of human values and skills fall far short of the aspirations and needs of individuals and societies.(. . .)

18. World Education Report 2000:17.

19. J. Samofi; Education for What? Education for Whom? Guidelines for National Policy Reports in Education, UNESCO, Paris, 1994, p. 28. quoted in Special Raporteur's Annual Report 2004.

20. "Every person—child, youth, and adult—shall be able to benefit from educational opportunities designed to meet their basic learning needs. These needs comprise both essential learning tools (such as literacy, oral expression, numeracy, and problem

solving) and the basic learning content (such as knowledge, skills, values, and attitudes) required by human beings to be able to survive, to develop their full capacities, to live and work in dignity, to participate fully in development, to improve the quality of their lives, to make informed decisions, and to continue learning. . . ." (Jomtien Declaration, 1990: article 1)

21. World Education Report 2000:76.

22. Special Rapporteur Annual Report 2004, par. 15.

23. As seen in http://campus.northpark.edu/history/Koeller/ ModWorld/Development/neoliberalism.htm; website on longer on line.

24. Special Rapporteur Annual Report 2004, par. 8.

25. OXFAM Briefing Paper 3, "A Tax on Human Development", 2001:2.

26. Not surprisingly, social protection is one of the prevention measures of International Programme on the Elimination of Child Labour of the ILO, so that families do not have to rely on their children's workforce to pay for their living.

27. World Declaration on Education For All, Jomtien, 1990: Article 3 (3) The most urgent priority is to ensure access to, and improve the quality of, education for girls and women, and to remove every obstacle that hampers their active participation. All gender stereotyping in education should be eliminated.

28. A Fair Chance, Global Campaign for Education, April 2003: 2.

29. Ibid, p. 25.

30. Special Rapporteur Annual Report 2004, par. 32.

31. As seen in http://www.unesco.org/education/educnews/20_12_ 12/gender.htm; website on longer on line.

32. As seen in http://www.eenet.org.uk/theory_ practice/whatisit. shtml; website no longer on line.

33. World Declaration on Education For AU, Jomtien, 1990, Preamble: "More than 100 million children and countless adults fail to complete basic education programmes; millions more satisfy the attendance requirements but do not acquire essential knowledge and skills; (. . .)"

34. Freire, 2000:50–51.

35. A Fair Chance, Global Campaign for Education, April 2003: 24.

36. Dakar Framework for Action, par. 67: There is an urgent need to adopt effective strategies to identify and include the socially, culturally and economically excluded. This requires participatory analysis of exclusion at household, community and school levels, and the development of diverse, flexible, and innovative approaches to learning and an environment that fosters mutual respect and trust."

37. Charter of the United Nations, article 1(3).

38. Universal Declaration of Human Rights, proclamation.

39. Report of the United Nations High Commissioner for Human Rights on the implementation of the Plan of Action for the United Nations Decade for Human Rights Education, Appendix, par. 2.

40. UNESCO Executive Board 165th Session-Elements for an Overall Unesco Strategy on Human Rights, par. 31

41. CEDAW, Article 10(h): "Access to specific educational information to help to ensure the health and well-being of families, including information and advice on family planning." General Recommendations of the Committee, 21: "In order to make an informed decision about safe and reliable contraceptive measures, women must have information about contraceptive measures and their use, and guaranteed access to sex education and family planning services, as provided in article 10 (h) of the Convention." Recommendations for government action, par. 31: "States parties should also, in particular: (c) Prioritize the prevention of unwanted pregnancy through family planning and sex education."

42. Committee of the Rights of the Child, General Comments 3, par. 6.

43. As in http://www.avert.org/sexedu.htm

44. *Manual on Rights-Based Education*. Collaborative project between Katarina Tomasevski (UN. Special Rapporteur on the Right to Education) and UNESCO Asia and Pacific Regional Bureau for Education, Bangkok, Thailand.

45. General Comment no. 1 (on the article 29 [I]) "The Aims of Education", par. 3: "The child's right to education is not only a matter of access (CRC—art. 28) but also of content. (. . .)"

46. Freire, 1970: 43.

47. Freire, 1998.

48. Freire, 1970: 68.

49. Freire, 1998.

50. Freire, ibid.

51. Freire, ibid.

52. Freire, 1970: 36.

References

Bowen, James (2003), *A History of Western Education,* Vol. I–III, Routledge.

Canotilho, J.J. Gomes (1998), *Direito Constitucional e Teoria da Constituicão,* Almedina.

Freire, Paulo (1970), *Pedagogia do Oprimido,* Paz e Terra, versão.

Freire, Paulo (1997) *Pedagogia da Autonomia: Saberes necessarios à pratica educativa,* Paz e Terra, versão e-book.

Freire, Paulo (2000), *A Educaçao na Cidade.*Cortez, versao e-book.

Hodgson, Douglas (1998), *The Human Right to Education.* Ashgate.

Nowak, Manfred (2001). The Right to Education. In Asbjorn Eide, Catarina Krause, & Allan Rosas, *Economic, Social and Cultural Rights—A Textbook,* Martinus Nifhoff Publishers, pp. 189–211.

CAETANO PIMENTEL resides in Rio de Janeiro, Brazil. This article is based on a monograph he wrote for a post-graduation course on Human Rights and Democracy at the University of Coimbra, Coimbra, Portugal.

Knowing, Valuing, and Shaping One's Culture

A precursor to acknowledging, accepting, and respecting the culture of others

ELINOR L. BROWN

As children we are naturally curious, yet suspicious and apprehensive when placed in different or unfamiliar environments. As we encounter cultural differences, we generally rely on our subconscious frames of reference to analyze, compare, and make judgments about the value and validity of other cultures and endeavor to continuously reinforce our embedded beliefs and perceptions about self and others (Allport, 1979; Erickson, 1997; Goodenough, 1987). That's what makes us as humans resourceful, creative, and adaptable but at the same time fearful and intolerant of others.

However, with our growing global economic and political interdependence, we must prepare our teacher candidates and future workforce to be morally cognizant of, genuinely respectful toward, and effectively prepared to appropriately interact with the diverse cultures they will encounter in a global society.

Brown (2004a), Haberman (1996), Ladson-Billings (1994), and Pang (2001) indicate that, to be effective, educators must possess the multicultural knowledge, attitudes, and behaviors that appropriately respond to issues of student diversity and cross-cultural acceptance and validation. Further, Banks (1997/2001), Brown (2005a), and Gay (2000) espouse that classroom teachers must be prepared to recognize both hidden and overt biases within the educational system and advocate for equitable access to educational opportunity for all students.

Anderson (1990), Cushner et al. (2004), Howard (2002), and Zeichner and Hoeft (1996) state that equally important imperatives are that future teachers develop the skills and sensitivity to: become cultural brokers in their classrooms, embed global social justice paradigms in their curriculums, and facilitate the integration of equity and cross-cultural civility into the cognitive structures of their students' current and future selves.

However, studies conducted by Brown (2004b), Sleeter (2001), and Richardson (1996) found that most teacher candidates lack sufficient cross-cultural competence and sensitivity to appropriately address the complex needs of diverse student groups, and are less likely to be aware of the hidden biases within their school community or to acknowledge and build on the cultural capital that non-majority students bring to the classroom.

Brown (2005b), Gollnick and Chinn (2005), Howard (1999), and Sleeter (1995) indicate that to raise the cross-cultural cognizance and cultural diversity sensitivity of future teachers they must first be afforded the opportunity to objectively examine, reflectively clarify, and openly share the foundations of their own cultural frames of reference (e.g., class, ethnicity, gender, race, and religion). Further, this scrutiny should include the implicit and explicit shared beliefs, values, and behaviors of their own cultural groups, the subjective concepts of self in relationship to these groups, and the values and characteristics one is willing to share with those outside of one's groups (Allen & Labbo, 2001; Allport, 1979; Brown, 2004c).

Allport (1979), Bennett (2003), Erickson (1997), Gollnick and Chinn (2005), and Goodenough (1987) contend that cultural frames of reference are imprinted early in life and subconsciously continue to evolve over the lifespan. Banks (2001), Brown (2005b), and Howard (1999) indicate that these cultural lenses dictate our self-concepts and determine how we value, respect, accept, and interact with others both within and outside of our micro-cultures and how we define ourselves in relation to the majority culture. Hence, a precursor to developing strong cross-cultural competencies is knowing, valuing, and sharing both the subconscious and conscious cultures of self (Banks, 2001; Bennett, 2003; Brown, 2005a; Goodlad & Mantle-Bromley, 2004; Howard, 1999).

To raise self-awareness, teacher educators such as Allen and Labbo (2001), Banks (2001), Brown (2004a), and Sleeter (1996) often initiate cultural diversity training with self-examination activities that require participants to examine their own cultural underpinnings as a precursor to exploring the cultures of others. By developing activities that engage students in examining the subconscious foundations of their beliefs, perceptions, and behaviors and then facilitating peer debriefings on how this subjective foundation influences their conscious approach to cross-cultural interaction often stimulates cross-cultural discussions and fosters positive changes in cross-cultural attitudes and behaviors (Banks, 2001; Giroux & Simon, 1989; Zeilchner & Hoeft, 1996).

The purpose of this article is to share a unique strategy (the cultural puzzle) used in graduate, undergraduate, and secondary education to assist students in examining and sharing their cultural heritage to: (1) raise their level of self-awareness, (2) increase cross-cultural communication, (3) improve authentic cross-cultural knowledge, and (4) create a cohesive classroom community. Over the past six years, university students' reflective journals, on-line and in-class discussions, and course evaluations indicate that the knowledge gained from the cultural puzzle activity is instrumental in establishing a sense of community that supports them as they strengthen bridges across cultural borders and develop techniques toward becoming equitable multicultural decision-makers.

The Cultural Puzzle

University students are required to develop a puzzle depicting how they came to be the person that they are today. In other words, what, how, and by whom was their current persona shaped? To insure that each puzzle is a true reflection of the student's heritage and is not influenced by the instructor, there is no lecture or individual introduction on the first day of class. Instead, the first class consists of a course overview and a hands-on seminar on using Blackboard as a communication tool.

The instructions given for the puzzle assignment include: (1) each participant must conduct family interviews that include their current generation (e.g., siblings, cousins, extended family, foster family), at least two from the previous generation (e.g., parents, aunts/uncles, primary caregivers) and where possible two from at least two generations prior (e.g., grandparents, great grandparents, extended family, friends); (2) the cultural findings may be portrayed in any medium, form, or material they select; (3) students must share their puzzles in 3–4-minute self introductions during the following class; and (4) the assignment must be completed by class time the following week. These requirements provide a justifiable reason for questioning sometimes resistant family members about cultural traditions, encourage creativity and ownership in the process, promote and sustain a sense of class community and minimize student procrastination.

To assist in identifying the various micro-cultures that influence their cultural frames of reference, students are directed to two of the required texts used in the course: *Cultural Diversity in a Pluralistic Society* by D. Gollnick and P. Chinn (2000/2005) and *Cultural Diversity and Education: Foundations, Curriculum, and Teaching* by J. Banks (2001/2005). Students may use the categories found in these texts, add other micro-cultures, and delete or otherwise modify the categories.

Throughout the six years that the cultural puzzle has been a requirement, no student has produced a puzzle resembling how I envisioned the activity. See Figure 1 for my vision of a cultural puzzle. The shape and form of student puzzles usually

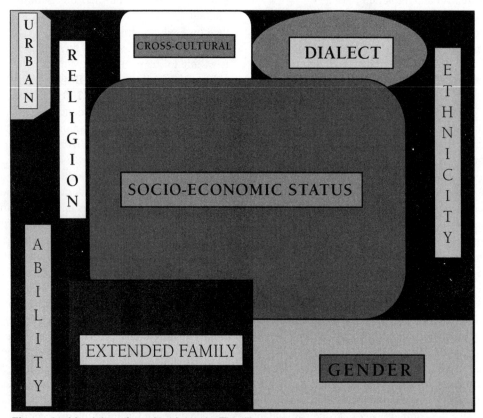

Figure 1 My vision of a cultural puzzle. This illustration is a photograph of a cultural puzzle created by Elinor L. Brown and her students.

represents something that has significance to their personal histories. Puzzles have been characterized as animals (e.g., cow, turtle, and rooster), plants (e.g., tree, flower, and garden) and objects (e.g., hammer, car, quilt, and crossword puzzle).

The creativity, commitment, and ingenuity of the students far exceed my expectations. A Hawaiian music major gave a power point presentation showing important people and places in Hawaiian life that influenced him (e.g., home, family members, and church). He narrated the presentation in the three languages prominent in his Hawaiian culture and used Hawaiian music in the background.

The interdependence of the four puzzle objectives is evident in reflective journals, online discussions, and in-class interactions. Students often connect their willingness to engage in cross-cultural discussions and activities with their increased awareness of self and classmates. Augmenting and sharing accurate cross-cultural knowledge is attributed to engaging in receptive cross-cultural dialogue. The increased level of awareness, sensitivity, and communication encourages the development of a supportive class community.

Raising Self-Awareness

The intent of the self-awareness objective is to: (1) facilitate an awareness that family structures and values are significant influences on self-concepts, cross-cultural relationships, aspirations, and world-views; (2) foster an understanding of the correlation between one's various micro-cultures (e.g., gender, religion, race, and social class) and how one perceives and interacts with others; and (3) explore the influence of the majority culture on one's concepts of self as a member of the dominant or non-dominant culture.

The process of developing and exploring this information is a valuable tool that I use throughout the course as a foundation and reference to assist students in understanding their attitudes and behaviors and in expanding their world-views to become more effective professionals, better citizens, and more attuned to our increasing global interdependence.

Increasing Cross-Cultural Communication

The purpose of the increasing cross-cultural communication objective is to: (1) augment student in-class participation in cross-cultural group discussions; (2) encourage students to collaborate with peers outside of their comfort zones; and (3) stimulate candid on-line discussions dealing with current issues.

By sharing cultural heritages through the puzzle activity participants illustrate how they developed their differing ways of understanding the world without feeling that their privacy is being invaded. As the class views and listens to each other they become sensitive to the customs, histories, struggles, and perceptions of peers and how these histories are related to their own. As students tell personal stories, others often find that first impressions are unreliable; the "inner" self is far more complex and revealing than "outsiders" can fathom and that it just may

be safe to share their personal views with peers outside of their cultural group.

The course uses Blackboard as an ongoing on-line discussion tool. Each student is required to participate in a minimum of one on-line discussion per week. Dialogues are initiated by the students and usually begin as a continuation of in-class discussions, a personal reflection on class activities, or with a topic on current diversity issues found in the media. Often students attach articles and links for classmates to read and respond to. After the first two weeks, I found that most students logged on daily and responded to the postings by addressing peers by name.

Improve Authentic Cross-Cultural Knowledge

The purpose of the improving authentic cross-cultural knowledge objective is to: (1) dispel cultural myths; (2) raise students' cross-cultural verbal and nonverbal communication skills; and (3) assist in developing culturally relevant teaching and classroom management strategies.

As the comfort level rises and students feel safe in the classroom environment, they begin to raise questions about their beliefs and search for information about the attitudes and behaviors of those outside of their cultural group. Throughout the semester students seek information and share personal experiences that were previously considered too sensitive to openly discuss across cultural borders (e.g., family and cultural traditions, discipline strategies for diverse students, religious canons, social issues, appropriate cross-cultural parent/ teacher contact, personal hair and skin care, student/teacher cross-cultural interactions, and understanding cross-cultural verbal and nonverbal cues).

Students use the on-line discussion board and in-class small group discussions to seek peer assistance in resolving issues that arise in their professional and personal lives, to debate current events, editorials, or social and political commentary, and seek to understand the underlying cultural reasoning behind different attitudes and behaviors.

Building a Cohensive Class Community

The objective of building class community is to: (1) develop a safe and supportive class environment; (2) foster open, respectful, and genuine in-class interaction across cultural borders; (3) encourage students to consider participating in cross-cultural group activities, discussions, and research projects; and (4) promote post-class student instituted congenial discussions on litigious topics.

As students enter class on the first day, I find that most sit in their comfort zones (with those that look like them, exhibit similar communication styles and speech patterns, and/or were reared in the same region). Surprisingly, gender is not a factor in how students initially group themselves. After the cultural puzzle presentations, many students realign themselves by sitting with classmates who share their interests and concerns rather than their physical characteristics and dialect. They are more respectful of each others' opinions, seek and provide authentic cross-cultural information, eagerly hold on-line and after-class discussions, and join in social activities together. Classmates become friends rather than just peers enrolled in the same course.

Prior to instituting the cultural puzzle activity, I assigned students to groups to insure cross-cultural interaction and diverse perspectives on research projects. After initiating the cultural puzzle activity, I find that students reach out to peers across cultural borders and form collaborative partnerships for field experiences and research projects on their own. They often seek out group partners based on their diverse perspectives, which make for well integrated groupings without instructor intervention.

In midpoint evaluations, most students indicate that the puzzle activity helped them become more sensitive to the perspectives of others, more open to engaging in cross-cultural activities, and eager to broaden their cross-cultural worldview by incorporating other perspectives into their own schemas. By semester's end, I find that most students reach a higher level of comfort in cross-cultural settings, exhibit a willingness to negotiate a middle ground on cross-cultural issues, and often encourage each other to engage in social justice activities in their communities and schools.

Because the goal of the cultural puzzle is different for secondary students, the timing of its introduction and presentation is reversed. The activity is presented as a culminating project to give students time to become familiar with the mentoring experience, comfortable with their mentors, and to develop cross-cultural allies and friends among their peers.

Secondary Students

In secondary education, the threefold intent of the cultural puzzle activity is to: (1) alleviate some of the stress, anxiety, and isolation felt by many non-majority and first-generation American students within their school environment; (2) raise student self-esteem; and (3) build a sense of belonging within the school community.

The secondary students are assigned the activity during the seventh week of a ten-week interaction with teacher candidate mentors in an urban high school. This gives the students time to establish a comfortable relationship with their mentors and to meet and socially interact with other mentees outside of their cultural groups.

The cultural puzzle is used as the culminating project to give the secondary students a sense of power and pride in determining how and to what degree they will share their histories and to demonstrate the value of the cultural capital that diverse secondary students bring to the school environment.

First-generation immigrant and refugee students are asked to develop puzzles sharing their memories of home and family, describing what they miss most, their perceptions of life in America, and their future dreams. Non-foreign-born students are asked to develop puzzles describing their families and communities, who and what has influenced them the most, and their future goals and desires. All students may ask their mentors for guidance but must complete the project on their own within the allotted two weeks.

As with the university students, each secondary student makes a formal presentation of the puzzle to their peers and mentors during a culminating brunch. However, to minimize the anxiety associated with speaking and sharing in front of adults and classmates, secondary students are not given presentation time constraints.

There are no restrictions on the size, shape, or form the students choose for their puzzles. I or their mentors provide materials when needed. Most secondary participants use pictures (e.g., family, friends, homes, neighborhoods, and countries) to share their histories. However, many refugee students arrive with no photographs and/or only remnant artifacts of the homes they left behind and families that have been scattered to other countries.

Some of these students are so traumatized by their experiences that they cannot share their histories, others cry during their presentations, and some express guilt about surviving where friends and family have perished. To assist refugee students who may not have strong English-language skills or who may falter during their presentations, friends or their mentor will stand with them to provide moral support and clarify or interpret where necessary. Many of the teacher candidate mentors are visably moved as they listen to these histories and observe the affect on both refugee students and American-born students.

The puzzles of both majority and non-dominant culture American-born mentees consistently show family and friends in positive situations (e.g., engaged in fun activities, "hanging out" in the neighborhood, or at family and community gatherings). Though some students have experienced trauma in their lives (e.g., death, illness, drugs, or violence), none choose to include it in their puzzles but may mention an incident during their presentation. However, if a favorite family member, friend, or pet has moved away or died they will include their picture.

Most puzzles also contain pictures of places the student has been or would like to visit, famous people perceived as role models and heroes, and careers they aspire to pursue. The following excerpts are from teacher candidate mentors' reflective journals immediately following secondary student presentations.

> "I can't imagine what some of these kids have had to endure. . . . some of their puzzles brought me to tears. No wonder they don't adjust as quickly as we think they should. Who cares about math when you still have nightmares about surviving one more day?"

> "I know some of these kids have never been out of the city and don't have the money to participate in stimulating summer activities . . . as I watched them tell their stories, I saw a wealth of rich and powerful family experiences that could be incorporated in my lessons."

> "The mentees showed me how magnificent life can be no matter where you fit on the economic scale. Also, no

matter what kids go through, the human spirit can thrive if we just take the time to nurture it."

"I was surprised as how the kids would help each other with their presentations when one got stuck with language, started to cry, or was afraid to present. Even though they were from different places and had different experiences . . . they showed great compassion for each other. We can learn a lot from kids."

"I marveled at the pride all of these kids have in their heritage and how surprised they were that we wanted them to share their cultures with us as we shared ours with them."

Conclusions

In conclusion, I would like to reflect on the research and practices of Banks (2001), Brown (2004a), Haberman (1996), Howard (1999), and Sleeter (1995) which indicate that developing self-examination activities such as the cultural puzzle will: (1) engage students in exploring the subconscious underpinnings of their beliefs, perceptions, and behaviors; (2) facilitate debriefings, peer discussions, and reflections on why these attitudes and behaviors influence their conscious approach to cross-cultural interaction; (3) enlighten participants on how their actions influence the behaviors and attitudes of others; and (4) lay the foundation for building cross-cultural competence and social justice advocacy in educators and students. Using the cultural puzzle as a self-examination tool:

1. Allows participants to scrutinize the subconscious roots of their perceptions, attitudes, and behaviors. This examination and recognition are precursors to acknowledging, accepting, and respecting the cultures of others;
2. Provides a safe venue to facilitate self-disclosure through the sharing of cultural heritages without the perception of invading one's privacy or making judgments about others. Participants only share what they want others to know;
3. Encourages relinquishment of the natural affinity to congregate and associate within the safety of one's own cultural group namely those that look and or speak alike;
4. Stimulates human curiosity about those outside of one's cultural frames of reference, facilitates the transmission of authentic cross-cultural knowledge, and broadens the world view of all participants; and
5. Affords an excellent segues into the deeper cross-cultural training necessary to prepare our students and educators for the interdependence of a global society.

References

Allport, G. W. (1979). *The nature of prejudice*, (25th ed.). Reading, MA: Addison-Wesley.

Allen, J., & Labbo, L. (2001). Giving it a second thought: Making culturally engaged teaching culturally engaging. *Language Arts (79)*1, 40–52.

Anderson, L. (1990). A rationale for global education. In K. A. Tye (Ed.), *Global education: From thought to action* (pp. 13–34). Arlington, VA: Association for Supervision and Curriculum Development.

Banks, C. M. (2001). Becoming a cross-cultural teacher. In C. F. Diaz (Ed.), *Multicultural education in the 21st century*, (pp. 171–183). New York: Addison-Wesley.

Banks, J. A. (1997). *Educating citizens in a multicultural society.* New York: Teachers College Press.

Banks, J. A. (2001) *Cultural diversity and education: Foundations, curriculum, and teaching* (4th ed.). Boston: Allyn & Bacon.

Bennett, C. (2003). *Comprehensive multicultural education: Theory and practice* (5th ed.). Needham Heights, MA: Allyn & Bacon.

Brown, E. L. (2004a). What precipitates change in cultural diversity awareness during a multicultural course: The message or the method? *Journal of Teacher Education, 55*(4), 325–340.

Brown, E. L. (2004b). The relationship of self-concepts to changes in cultural diversity awareness: Implications for urban teacher educators. *The Urban Review, 36*(2), 119–146.

Brown, E. L. (2004c). Overcoming the challenges of stand-alone multicultural courses: The possibilities of technology integration. *Journal of Technology in Teacher Education, 12*(4), 535–559.

Brown, E. L. (2005a). Service-learning in teacher education: Creative strategies for alternative routes to certification. *Equity & Excellence in Education, 38*(1), 61–74.

Brown, E. L. (2005b). Using photography to explore hidden realities and raise cross-cultural sensitivity in future teachers. *The Urban Review, 37*(2), 149–171.

Cushner, K., McClelland, A., & Safford, P. (2004). *Human development in education: An integrative approach* (4th ed.). New York: McGraw-Hill.

Erickson, F. (1997). Culture in society and in educational practices. In J. A. Banks & C. M. Banks (Eds.), *Multicultural education: Issues and perspectives,* (3rd ed.) (pp. 32–60). Needham Heights, MA: Allyn & Bacon.

Gay, G. (2000). *Culturally responsive teaching: Theory, research, and practice.* New York: Teacher's College Press.

Giroux, H., & Simon, R.(1989). *Popular culture: schooling and everyday life.* Granby, MA: Bergin & Garvey.

Gollnick, D., & Chinn, P. (2005). *Multicultural education in a pluralistic society,* (6th ed.).Upper Saddle River, NJ: Merrill Prentice Hall.

Goodenough, W. (1987). Multiculturalism as the normal human experience. In E. M. Eddy & W. L. Partridge (Eds.), *Applied anthropology in America,* (2nd Ed). New York: Columbia University Press.

Goodlad, J. I., Mantle-Bromley, C., & Goodlad, S. J. (2004). *Education for everyone: Agenda for education in a democracy.* San Francisco: Jossey-Bass.

Haberman, M. (1996). Selecting and preparing culturally competent teachers for urban schools. In J. Sikula, T. J. Buttery, & E. Guyton (Eds.), *Handbook of research on teacher education,* (pp.747–801). New York: Macmillan.

Howard, G. (1999). *We can't teach what we don't know: White teachers, multiracial schools.* New York: Teacher College Press.

Ladson-Billings, G. (1994). *The dreamkeepers: Successful teachers of African-American children.* New York: Jossey-Bass.

Pang, V. O. (2001). *Multicultural education: A caring-centered, reflective approach.* New York: McGraw-Hill.

Richardson, V. (1996). The role of attitude and beliefs in learning to teach, In J. Sikula, T. Buttery, & E. Guyton (Eds.), *Handbook of research on teacher education* (2nd ed.), New York: Macmillan, pp 102–119.

Sleeter, C. (1996). *Multicultural education as social activism.* Albany, NY: State University of New York Press.

Sleeter, C. (2001). Preparing teachers for culturally diverse schools: Research and the overwhelming presence of whiteness. *Journal of Teacher Education, 52*(2), 94–106.

Sleeter, C. E. (1995). White preservice students and multicultural education course work. In J. M. Larkin & C. E. Sleeter (Eds.), *Developing multicultural teacher education curriculum* (pp. 17–30). Albany, NY: State University of New York.

Zeilchner, K., & Hoeft, K. (1996). Teacher socialization for cultural diversity. In J. Sikula, T. J. Buttery, & E. Guyton (Eds.), *Handbook of research on teacher education* (2nd ed.) (pp. 525–547). New York: Macmillan.

ELINOR L. BROWN is an associate professor in the College of Education at the University of Kentucky, Lexington, Kentucky.

Beyond Promise: Autobiography and Multicultural Education

HONGYU WANG & TIANLONG YU

Introduction

In studying the politics of identity, we find that who we are is invariably related to who others are, as well as to whom we have been and want to become. (William F. Pinar, 2004, p. 30)

Autobiography is not an unequivocally empowering medium but a contradictory form of cultural politics that has both progressive and reactionary forms. (Wendy S. Hesford, 1999, p. xxiv)

Reading and writing autobiography as a pedagogical mode of engaging multicultural education is no longer new. We also adopt this strategy in our own respective teachings at two universities where students are predominantly White and (lower) middle-class women.

We each use two autobiographical works: one is the highly celebrated *I Know Why the Caged Bird Sings* by the renowned African-American poet and novelist Maya Angelou (2000/1975), which narrates an uplifting journey of a Black girl who rose above racism, sexism, and poverty to achieve her dream; the other is *Invisible Privilege: A Memoir about Race, Class, & Gender* by a Jewish, (upper) middle-class woman, Paula Rothenberg (2000), a noted scholar in women's studies and multicultural studies, who writes about her difficult journey of understanding White privilege and choosing to fight against social injustices and inequities.

These two books depict the lived experiences of two individuals who took on the task of fighting for social justice, albeit with distinctly different paths. The promise of using both books was to engage our students with their own identity politics as educators. Our experiences in teaching them, however, question such a promise because many students refused to read them in a way that would interrogate their own identities.

As Goodson (1998) points out, storytelling itself is not necessarily empowering but can be implicated in reproducing dominant discourses and structures. Reflecting upon our teaching stories, we intend to address the contradictions of using autobiography in multicultural education and envision new discourses for a transformative pedagogy.

Our adoption of an autobiographical approach in teaching multiculturalism was motivated by our efforts to go beyond the dominant approach to multicultural education, what James Banks (1991) would call a "contributions approach" or "heroes and holidays approach," which emphasizes teaching ethnic differences and cultural tolerance. While celebrating inclusion and stressing sensitivity training, such an approach fails to adequately analyze power relationships and leaves structural injustice and inequities unchallenged. Moreover, it is an essentialist model as it tends to define identities in static and fixed terms, failing to grasp the dynamic, complex, and changing nature of ethnic/racial/cultural identity. In addition, it tends to focus on making students aware of "others," not touching upon who they are as gendered, raced, and classed persons.

Disrupting such a promise, we shift our focus to the intersection between structure and person to examine identity issues: How is personal identity constructed socially, economically, and politically? Autobiography, when written and taught in such a way that the self is situated in social and cultural contexts, seems to be an excellent medium for engaging such work.

Ironically, our efforts to challenge the promise of the additive multicultural education approach through the focus on identity also leave us in an unsettling pedagogical process. Using autobiography to engage students with lived experiences turns out to be yet another promise with both possibilities and limitations. It is on this site of beyond double "promises" that we reflect, complicate, and re-situate multicultural pedagogy.

In this article, we not only reflect on our own teaching approaches, we also attempt to understand how teaching autobiographical works has influenced our own identities as teachers. Both of us are Chinese working at American universities as international faculty members. While one is male and the other is female, we also come from somewhat different theoretical backgrounds: Tianlong Yu is more embedded in critical pedagogy while Hongyu Wang takes more of a poststructuralist autobiographical approach. Despite these differences, we share a commitment to social justice and equity which requires both structural change and personal transformation.

In what follows, we start with each other's reflections on teaching two autobiographies, showing our respective paths and our struggles. These reflections are followed by a "conversation" in which we talk about our own subjectivity-in-making influenced by our teaching. We conclude this writing with an invitation of engaging autobiography in multicultural education as a difficult pedagogical task which destabilizes both teacher's and students' taken-for-granted worlds.

Reflections on Teaching

[Bakhtin] imagines the self as a conversation, often a struggle, of discrepant voices with each other, voices (and words) speaking from different positions and invested with different degrees and kinds of authority. (Gary Saul Morson & Caryl Emerson, 1990, p. 218)

Tianlong Yu's Reflection

In our first class meeting, my students spoke about their notions of multiculturalism and multicultural education. In the minds of many students, this class is about "culture." It is about multiple cultures, or ethnic differences. Isn't it? They were genuinely puzzled why a class on culture has to deal with issues of gender, class, or sexuality (it was relatively easier for them to understand that race should be an issue).

It did not take me long to sense how big the gap was between what I intended for the course and what my students expected from it (seemingly a common scenario experienced by teacher educators teaching multicultural education courses. For example, see Abidah and Teel, 2000). The additive approach is not only usually taught by instructors but also often expected by students.

In addition, the predominant job-preparation orientation of teacher education programs, especially in traditionally certification-oriented programs like the ones I teach in, is hardly helpful in developing an identity-based, critical, multicultural education approach. Obsessed with "content methods" or "teaching strategies" and viewing teacher education largely in terms of skills development and techniques training, students are seemingly not motivated to engage themselves in critical reflections on racism, sexism, and classism. The current emphasis on standards and high-stakes testing in national educational policy undoubtedly promotes this clinical orientation in teacher education and undermines the critical task of multicultural education.

Against this difficult context complicated by students' unwillingness and unpreparedness for the course issues, I struggled to construct a critical and affirming pedagogy with my students, one that, as Peter McLaren (2003) envisions, empowers us to tell stories, author meanings, and shape voices. A "working from within" (Pinar, 1994) approach was emphasized as I reminded my students in the beginning that this class is really not about our students; rather, it is about us as teachers. We must analyze and challenge our own perceptions, attitudes, and understandings as both persons and educators towards diversity issues, and improve our skills as practitioners accordingly. We are embarking on a journey to examine the formation of our own identities and engage in a conversation with others.

We first read Maya Angelou's *I Know Why the Caged Bird Sings*. Deeply moved by her unyielding struggle against all odds in a ruthlessly racist society and her eventual hard-earned triumph, I was surprised by the comment from one of my female students: "The book is just so-so: it doesn't meet my expecta-

tion. Nothing stands out." Before I could give any response, another gentleman added, "Black struggle, again. Haven't we heard enough?"

I was quickly thrown into a reality: Angelou's story is largely irrelevant to some of these White women and men. I naturally wondered if they had similar reactions upon reading any of the "Great Books" in the canon, such as those of Shakespeare or Hemingway, which indeed dominated their high school and university literature courses. Different readers may always have different understandings of the same book; yet, how does the issue of race play a role here? Or, does it play a role?

These students apparently felt uncomfortable, maybe offended, by the stories about the Black and White conflicts, the Black sufferings under White racism, and the Black struggles against social injustice. I didn't expect a uniform understanding of the book from all my students; yet, I wasn't prepared for the apathy and indifference some of the students showed, either. This early surprise reinforced my intention to give them another opportunity to listen to those stories, to read those people's lives.

As Maxine Greene (1997) states, "Learning to look through multiple perspectives, young people may be helped to build bridges among themselves; attending to a range of human stories, they may be provoked to heal and to transform" (p. 519). Understanding my students' lack of exposure and the resulting resistance to the multiple and different perspectives, I insisted that they read and re-read the story: No, we have *not* heard enough; in society at large and in education particularly, the voices of Black and other minority people are still largely silenced. We have a responsibility to listen.

Despite the resistance of some students, overall, the class's reaction to Angelou was positive. Most of the students (female, White, and lower middle class) were moved by the story. During the class discussion they showed their heartfelt sympathies with her sufferings and their admiration for her strengths and success. They saw being poor and being woman as the two largest barriers in Angelou's life journey and they were inspired by the fact that she triumphantly overcame both and achieved a fulfilling life.

Here, issues of gender and class loomed large. A humble woman struggling against gender bias and poverty, Angelou was identified and accepted as one of them; her life was celebrated and admired. She became their role model. Angelou's messages of dedication, hard work, faith, and perseverance found strong repercussions in my students.

I was pleased and puzzled at the same time. My students learned a lot from Angelou but also missed something important. They didn't (or refused to) see "color." They didn't (or refused to) see race. Yet, Angelou's being woman and being poor were inextricably tied to being Black. Being Black was an integral part of her identity. Race relations constituted the determining background of her personal struggle and White racism was essential in causing her suffering. Denying this critical context inevitably caused a partial and problematic understanding of her story.

My students' reading of Angelou echoes Christine Sleeter's (1993) findings about how White teachers construct race.

Descendants of European immigrants, White teachers could easily draw on their own family histories to understand how social mobility is achieved in North America. They themselves have attained upward mobility by earning college degrees and becoming teachers. Therefore, both family and personal experiences seem to clearly justify individual dedication and hard work, a message hailed by Angelou, and a "color-blind" approach to race relations.

Failing to see the unequal distribution of power and wealth among racial groups, White teachers unconscientiously adopt a psychological view to look at individual lives. Moreover, focusing on their own struggles in life, White teachers fail to recognize the injustice and inequalities racial minorities suffer and the privilege they, as Whites, are born with.

My students' selective acceptance and un-acceptance of certain characters soon reached another level. I was almost shocked by their overwhelming rejection of Paula Rothenberg's book. They were obviously taken by a Black woman's good spirit during hard reality, but turned off by a White woman's constant and explicit harsh criticism of sexism, class domination, and particularly White racism. Their resistance to her definition of racism as "the subordination of people of color by White people" (p. 172) is most significant.

Rothenberg (2001) talks to White people about racism thusly: "I believe that racism is a White problem and that White people have a special responsibility for undoing the damage that has been done in our name and to our advantage" (p. 2). Such a critique of White racism caused considerable frustration, guilt, and denial in my students. As one student wrote: "I would feel guilty for what they went through as a race. Her writing was so powerful it felt like my guilt would be justified because of the color of my skin."

This reflects a typical psychological reaction of my White students confronting the issue of racism. The challenge for them is to see "Whiteness" as a social construct, not a personal trait. They need to see racism as "institutionalized prejudice with a compelling and brutal history" (Rothenberg, 2001, p. 172). And they need to understand that we can possibly eliminate racism only when we start to view racism as a socio-cultural and structural problem (Loewen, 1999).

Viewing racism and other problems such as sexism and homophobia as individual/personal problems instead of social and cultural ills leads students to oppose ideas for social and structural reforms to address those problems, such as the affirmative action policy in college admissions. In objection to it, my students cried "reverse racism." They argued that affirmative action policies discriminate against men and Whites in the name of gender and race equality; that taking away men's and Whites' rights is taking a step back; and that a society must stop trying to correct one wrong with another.

These ideas are indeed well thought out, but the misconceptions and resistance are evident. We need to ask: Don't those who were oppressed and exploited for so long deserve a little more support now? When Blacks, women, and other minorities were the victims of rampant racism and sexism, when they suffered savage inequalities and brutal injustice, which were perpetuated by powerful Whites and males, who cried out for equality? Certainly not the powerful!

Only when their privileges were challenged, did the powerful begin to embrace equality and justice and cry foul. As Rothenberg (2001) argues convincingly, in order for the underprivileged to truly have an equal opportunity to participate in social affairs, it is necessary to give them preference for a time. And history has shown that it is possible to change the systems and rules that govern human lives and to alter power relations that perpetuate inequalities and injustices (pp.145–146).

It has been quite a struggle to teach and to learn. Resistance, yes; but students also are thinking and rethinking every idea they have been exposed to. My hope for the class is that we have posed some real challenges to ourselves, to the *status quo* in our lives. These challenges call our privileges into question, whether they be ethnic, racial, gendered, or classed, and inevitably question our self identities.

Hongyu Wang's Reflection

As Gilmore (1994) points out, both autobiography and postmodernism are concerned with the contested site of identity and subjectivity while postmodernism challenges any stable, essential notion of the self. Strongly influenced by post-structural theories, I use autobiography in my teaching as the site for complicating students' understandings of self and culture. Reading and writing autobiography can capture the complexity of a person's life in its lively depiction of multiple layers of human experiences, which shows a process of identity-in-making rather than a static picture of the self fixed in any social construction.

Race, gender, class, sexuality, or nationality as discourses and practices are fluid, and, while politically charged, are lived by a concrete person in complex social contexts. Autobiography, when embedded in broad cultural situations, is both intellectually challenging and emotionally appealing for critical self and communal reflections.

The combination of Paula Rothenberg's and Maya Angelou's books evolved from my teaching experiences. Since I teach at a state university and the majority of my students are White women, I hoped that Rothenberg's journey of racial and gendered consciousness could inform students' own journeys. She (2000) states, "I see my primary audience as other White people, and I see my task as using the privilege I am able to draw upon to get a hearing for things that are not always said" (p. 2). When I co-taught a doctoral seminar with a colleague on diversity and equity, I suggested this book for our class.

However, my imagined similarity between students' and Rothenberg's backgrounds did not produce any easy connection but provoked uncomfortable readings among students. Many students saw her as a 1960s radical who did not understand at all what life was really about. But as the class progressed, the book made much more sense and students returned to the book constantly, and quite a few of them reflected upon their initial resistance to "seeing" privileges in their own lives.

The book became the most enlightening text for some students in that class. One of our students mentioned that her struggles with this book were greatly helped by reading another book in another class—Maya Angelou's *I Know Why the Caged Bird Sings*—and it was the latter book that helped her to understand the notion of privilege. Reading her comments, I became excited about the promise of juxtaposing two books in my teachings, which, I thought, must be an ideal combination for students to approach the world through different angles of *both* self and other.

Now I have used both books for several semesters in our master's program and become more aware of the risks of autobiography despite its promise of engaging students with lived experiences. The relationship between self and other is such a complicated interplay that the privileged site of the self can be reinforced rather than interrogated through teaching autobiography.

I usually use Angelou's book first, hoping that a different world in which a Black girl's struggles and coming of age is narrated under the racist social contexts of her time could open up for students a world they may not be familiar with. Such an engagement with the other through the voice of the other is a necessary step to see the self differently. While leading them out to other people's worlds, I also intend to lead them back to understand the self through reading Rothenberg's book. After understanding others, one can re-enter the self with a fuller critical edge.

However, my arrangement is disrupted by many students' heartfelt celebration of Angelou's enchanting autobiography accompanied by their utter resistance to Rothenberg's radical encounter with privilege. In this simultaneous warm reception and angry rejection, individualism rather than cultural construction of selfhood is reinforced.

If Angelous could achieve so much with her strength, humor, and stigma, *despite* racism; if Rothenberg experienced so much privilege from her class and race but still whined about her gender, who would be sympathetic with a spoiled girl who kept complaining? What matters, after all, is one's ability to live one's own life, my students comment.

While reading these two books is required, writing autobiographical experiences is not required. Many students, though, provoked by the autobiographical prose, in their written responses to these two books, write autobiographically. Ironically, despite the dramatic differences between their backgrounds and Maya Angelou's, many of them wrote about their similarity to her.

While as women, we do share a lot of experiences cross culturally, what is disappointing to me is that Maya Angelou's racial otherness is assimilated into the sameness. An important aspect of her life is that it was heavily impacted by racism. However, although this shocked students on the one hand, it was marginalized in their eagerness to find similarities between different lives.

Such is the danger of empathy, a notion that both Jacques Derrida and Emmanuel Levinas urge us to go beyond in their calling for the respect for the otherness of the other. In the attempt to empathize with the other, an irreplaceable element of the unknown in the other is lost; in such an assimilation of the other into the self, the newness of the other disappears. Students quietly turned away from "the surprise of the other" (Edgerton, 1996) offered by a woman like Angelou who suffered from racism, leaving the privileged site of Whiteness disturbed a bit but unchanged.

For many mainstream American students, reading the successful stories of minority models is comforting; however, reading about the painful struggles of another person sharing White skin is unbearable. Rothenberg's assertion that "in the world in which I lived, human beings had no race—which is to say—they were White" (2000, p. 9) mirrors the lives many of my students have had as they grew up in predominantly White rural communities.

However, they quickly dismiss her struggle with her racial identity and fiercely refuse her claim that racism is a White problem which calls for White people to deal with it. Rothenberg's challenge is a challenge to the stability of their own sense of the self, a challenge which requires an element of "self-shattering" (Pinar, 2004) if it is confronted and answered.

I would like to argue—I usually do so in the class—that acknowledging others' suffering does not negate our own suffering but expands our ability to feel and connect. Acknowledging one's own privileged layer of the self does not negate our own goodness but challenges us to understand the impact of the self on other people's lives. While it is relatively easy to be sympathetic from a distance with another person who suffered a great deal in life, "to recognize oneself as implicated in the social forces that create the climate of obstacles the other must confront" (Boler, 1997, p. 263) is utterly painful. In this sense, multicultural education is not so much about Others (Banks, 1999) as it is about Self and the entangled relationship between self and other.

The differences in social class between Rothenberg and my students did play a role in their negative responses to the book, as they could not see how such a "White" woman, who enjoyed so much social-economic privilege, has anything to do with them. Just as students' alignment with Angelou's book is through (underprivileged) woman's eyes, my students' lower middle class status and rural background makes them refuse to see into the mirror of racial privilege. While their flight from confronting the issues of race needs to be disrupted, their experiences through their own gender and class need to be validated and respected.

While my intention to make students look into the mirror of both self and other failed, I also question my own pedagogical desire in this attempt: does not students' resistance show that multiplicity of identity and intersections of race, class, and gender makes the claim for social justice ambiguous? Their refusal to see the sameness in the mirror of Whiteness and their refusal to see the differences in the mirror of gender challenge the very notion of the "mirror," a notion that Jacques Derrida (1991) problematizes.

As Betty Bergland (1994) points out, the relationship between discourse and the subject is not an easy one: the efforts to search for "representative voices" (or images—in the metaphor of mirror) no longer can sustain the challenge of a postmodern subject which is not unitary or essentialist. There is no "one true story" (Miller, 2005) to tell. There is no one version of being White, or being Black.

Only in acknowledging the contradictory, multiple, and shifting site of identity can we make specific and contextualized modes of resistance possible (Foucault, 1978). After all, Angelou's and Rothenberg's stories have demonstrated the complexity and fluidity of identity. In this sense, the gap between the instructor's intention and students' own meaning-making in identifying and dis-identifying can be turned into a productive site in which both student and teacher reach beyond themselves to journey, together yet on different paths.

The complicated dynamics of self and other in teaching through autobiography in multicultural education is imbued with power relationships. While Wendy S. Hesford (1999) is concerned with how to turn this site into an empowering experience for marginalized students, I intend to address the circulation of power more from understanding the racially privileged students, as I believe they are also major transformative forces.

The difficulty in destabilizing one's long-cherished identity is also implicated in its fragility. Our work as multicultural educators is to be willing to lead students and ourselves to the limit so that transformation can happen at the moment when we are open to our own vulnerability. The very difficulty that students have experienced sometimes leads them to understand how their own identities have to be risked and renewed in order to engage social change.

In Bakhtin's (1984) terms, when polyphony is introduced into the process of conversing with the self, creativity in inventing selfhood can be released. Reading, writing, and teaching autobiography itself may not be empowering, but our pedagogical attention to the interaction between students and texts informs and further makes possible a transformative process of disrupting the *status quo* and leading to the creation of new subjectivities.

A Conversation on Teacher's Identity

When I do not know myself, I cannot know who my students are. I will see them through a glass darkly, in the shadows of my unexamined life—and when I cannot see them clearly, I cannot teach them well. (Parker Palmer, 1998, p. 2)

Teaching multicultural education through identity politics also puts educators' own subjectivity at the edge. Good autobiographies usually evoke strong responses from readers, whether positive or negative, or both. Mediating class discussions loaded by strong emotions, the teacher cannot engage such a pedagogical process without also working on her or his own feelings and identifications. As international faculty members, we struggle with making sense of our own lives in a cross-cultural and multicultural educational setting.

What follows is our conversation about how teaching makes us rethink our own national, gendered, social, and classed identities. This is an ongoing process that is always open to new ways of understanding, so we use the format of conversing to show the fluidity of identity construction. Engaging identity politics through autobiography, teachers may have to interrogate their own identities many times along the way.

Hongyu: Reading Mary Doll's book (1996) and her reflection on first being a nice girl and then being a nice teacher brings a revelation to me. What she describes about her encounter with an obnoxious male college student is also my imagined nightmare as I encounter "American maleness" in my own multicultural education classes.

> **Whenever we reached a disagreement over course issues, they drew a reference to the fact that I was different from them and they were aware that our difference lay mainly in the fact that I am Asian and they are White.**
>
> —Tianlong

I have never reached the point she did when she finally could not put up with him anymore and just blew up, but that is my ultimate fear. I am afraid that one day I will be just like her; after all the smiles, elusive answers, gentle questions to deflect students' aggression, I will suddenly release my frustrations right in front of every student and become, yes, a "bad" woman in the public eyes.

I have managed to slip through the hierarchical system in China by being a nice girl yet with excellent academic records, a cultural and gendered construction which supported my success in the public world. This success simultaneously reinforces (being nice) and disrupts (being intelligent) the gendered norm.

Teaching multicultural education, more than any other class, however, no longer allows me a space to be *both* nice *and* intelligent. My pedagogical, intellectual, and moral position of anti-racism, anti-(hetero)sexism, and anti-classism requires me to be assertive and to be comfortable with confrontations. Being nice no longer comes in handy. With the realization of my own niceness both socially and self-imposed, may I learn to allow the assertive and aggressive part of the self to come forward in a less violent way? What is your story, Tianlong? What have the experiences of teaching this class taught you about yourself?

Tianlong: Teaching this class made me more aware that being Asian is part of my identity. It is interesting for me to realize how students consistently saw me as a person and educator in terms of my racial and ethnic background even though they proclaimed that they held "color-blind" approaches to human relations. Whenever we reached a disagreement over course issues, they drew reference to the fact that I was different from them and they were aware that our difference lay mainly in the fact that I am Asian and they are White. They acknowledged that my being Asian had significantly affected my worldview and lifestyle; yet they were slow to understand how much they may also have been deeply situated in Whiteness.

What I did was to purposefully draw on my own ethnic background to parallel the stories of Angelou and Rothenberg and give students another chance to look at race and ethnicity as they are lived and to understand and challenge their (and my) own situated identities. Responding to the equal opportunity myth in America uncritically embraced by many of my students, I discussed my personal encounter with racial discrimination in the job market and how my struggle had affected my identity.

I told them a naming paradox I experienced. Exactly because of the racial discrimination I experienced and I was afraid would happen (I was aware of the University of Chicago and MIT study about how resumes with White-sounding names received more responses from prospective employers than those with same credentials but non-White names), at one time I wanted to change my Chinese name into an English one.

That was quite an agonizing experience as I was in a dilemma. I didn't want to give up the name my parents gave me and all of their expectations behind it; yet I didn't want my foreign name to turn people off in the job market and become an inhibiting factor in my new career and life in America. Sometimes I thought I should take an English name just to go with the established norms and rules in America (as many foreigners have already done here). That could be one way I show my respect for this culture I have embraced (I am sympathetic to many Americans who have tremendous difficulties pronouncing my Chinese name). On the other hand, however, I wondered how much I must sacrifice to be accepted into the mainstream and why I have to contribute to the stubborn mentality that undermines true inclusion and diversity.

I was compelled to recognize the existence of multiple identities and their contextual construction in my own life. I realized how much I need to *play* my identity *painfully* in a foreign place I yearn to call home. My naming dilemma put me in a struggle for visibility, acceptance, and inner balance and harmony as well. By the way, the reaction of my close American friends to my thought of name changing was most interesting. They strongly opposed the idea, saying that they accept me for who and what I am, but they seemed to ignore my struggle in a racist society where names still bear high stakes that influence individuals' lives.

As for today, I'm still undecided. While teaching multiculturalism, I have been compelled to tell my stories and live my struggles again and again. I am just hoping that along with this process, I am strengthening my self-knowledge about who I am and what kind of person I am becoming.

Hongyu: This is amazing! Names are an essential part of identity: how we name ourselves and how others name us influence the way we perceive the world and are perceived by others. Remember the story that Angelou tells about how her White boss refused to call her by her own name but made up a name for her? Her victory in getting her name back was hilarious for my students.

The invisibility of being an Asian has been a constant struggle for many people. Sometimes I wonder whether there is a gendered plot in such an invisibility which often implies inferiority. The images of Chinese men and many times Chinese-American men, in the popular fantasy of the American media, are usually "feminine," weak, not manly enough while on the other hand macho martial arts masters who are good at killing also appear, perhaps as an overcompensated image (Eng, 2001). Both are not really true to the everyday life of many Chinese men. Ironically, the best part of Chinese martial arts novels is about wisdom and how to achieve the balance of *yin* and *yang,* rather than the media portrayal of violence. Chinese men can be highly patriarchal in their quiet, reserved way, too.

With the feminization of Chinese men, the image of Chinese women is the ultimate weak sex, perhaps, to use William Pinar's (2004) *currere* analysis, a projection of a split, repudiated, denied element of the American self to achieve "true" manhood. While it is far from reality—the strength of Chinese women has sustained Chinese civilization (Wang, in press)—I do feel this projection from my students, especially in multicultural education classes.

While I am much less aggressive than my White women colleagues, students' anger with encountering difficult knowledge circulates more violently back to me, once in a while, in such a manner that I feel that they want to put me "back in my place." Do they also, perhaps more unconsciously, expect me to be the sweet, docile Chinese woman in teaching that is envisioned here in the United States?

Names are an essential part of identity: how we name ourselves and how others name us influence the way we perceive the world and are perceived by others.

—Hongyu

When we talk about pedagogical relationships, we usually pay attention to the influence of the teacher on the student in terms of power relationships. What intrigues me now is the question about what influences students can have on the teacher. Especially in multicultural education, more often than not, teachers come from minority backgrounds. Teaching has asked me to come to terms with what it means to be both a Chinese and a woman.

Tianlong: I agree with you and I believe my students have profoundly influenced me, personally and professionally. They are the active players in my subjectivity in the making as they have taught me as much as I have taught them. As stated earlier, I came to teach this class with a clear social justice orientation. Like you, I also define myself as an anti-racist, anti-(hetero)sexist, and anti-classist educator, and I believed my positions and stances regarding these critical issues are non-negotiable. After teaching this class, I am still firm about my beliefs, but I also have begun to wonder if anything is really non-negotiable and if social justice itself is constructed.

Teaching this course has pushed me to investigate my own life journey, my politics, and my orientations as an educator. I have realized how my international journey from China to the U.S. has particularly made me aware of social inequalities and injustice and how this awareness has caused both insights and constraints in my thinking. Born and raised in a remote rural area, I experienced firsthand the effects of poverty. I learned, first, to accept and then to challenge the scarcity of our material life and developed a consciousness of social classes.

Such consciousness has colored my overall approach to education. Focusing on class division and the resulting social inequities, I tend to adopt a structural analysis and dismiss the psychological view that explains individual success or failure. My students once used me as an example to support the popular conservative theory that individual motivation and effort are what matters to succeed in a free land of equal opportunity.

As an Asian, born poor, having overcome many barriers during a long cross-cultural journey to become a professional in highly competitive academia, I apparently served as a "model minority." I furiously rejected this ostensibly positive label. With the total rejection, however, I also left aside a balanced analysis of the dynamic and complex relations between individual and society. After reading and especially listening to students' positive responses to Angelou's story, I now realize how important it is to respect and encourage personal dedication and hard work in an adverse social environment. Human resilience, strengths, and faith, as Angelou and many others have demonstrated, are indeed what support individuals struggling for social justice and equity.

Moreover, I have come to understand how my "situatedness" as a teacher has affected my teaching. I used to take for granted this part of my identity and subconsciously looked at my students through this fixed lens. I think that is why I often became frustrated while teaching. When I begin to challenge my own politics and resistance, I understand my students' better. And a willingness to understand students in turn helps me continue to look into myself.

No one is freed from particular conditioning. We are all individuals, "individuals who are part of classes, are gendered, raced, have assumed specific choices in their sexuality, profess specific religious creeds, beliefs, and understandings" (McLaren & Torres, 1998, p. 198). And as teacher educators, we must understand, as Maxine Greene (1992) does, "the teacher as questioner, as beginner, someone caught in wonderment and uncertainty, reaching beyond to choose and know. . . . Teacher's renewal is equally, wonderfully incomplete; there is always, always more" (p.viii).

With this new understanding and appreciation in mind, I realize that the renewal, for both students and the teacher, is forever an ongoing process.

An Incomplete Conclusion

Indeed, it is an ongoing process. We intend to challenge the dominant approach multicultural education through shifting the pedagogical focus to the issue of identity, which is situated between self and culture. Yet our teachings tell us that using autobiography as a way of engaging multicultural education at a deeper level than the superficial additive approach does not necessarily fulfill its promise.

Pedagogical efforts must be made to lead students into the complex interaction between social structure and individual identity and between self and other so that both personal and social transformation can possibly be achieved. In the process, we have also shown how we shifted our own positions to meet our students without compromising our shared commitment to social justice, equity, and democratization of both self and culture. Our collaboration on this writing itself is a process of accepting and working with our differences between each other while enhancing our mutual understanding.

As May Paomay Tung (2000) insightfully points out, "to write about the interactions of individual lives and their cultural background is like trying to find a beginning and an end of a sphere: There is none" (p. 2). Teaching is like that too. Our entrance points may not be the same, as Tianlong Yu focuses more on the structure due to his critical pedagogy orientation while Hongyu Wang focuses more on the person due to her poststructural autobiographical orientation.

However we do not stay at one point on the spectrum but move towards the complicated interaction in the middle. As we converse, talk, and learn from each other, we come to realize that perhaps there is no definite beginning or end. Wherever one starts, as long as the interactive dynamics between person and structure and between self and other can be *kept* instead of abandoned, one is open to the creative potential of an intertwining, evolving, and transforming process engaging both self and culture.

This process of teaching, conversing, and writing does not offer any resolution or formula for teaching multicultural education, as we have learned that there is no discourse or practice inherently liberatory or empowering, but our pedagogical desires, discourses, and practices are complicated along the way to reach new possibilities. So this essay offers a provocation and an invitation for multicultural educators to be on the path of going beyond any promise to open up alternative paths. Let the conclusion of this essay circle back to our ongoing journey. . . .

References

Abidah, J. & Teel, M. K. (2000). *Because of the kids: Facing racial and cultural differences in urban schools.* New York: Teachers College Press.

Angelou, M. (1991). *I know why the caged bird sings.* New York: Random House.

Bakhtin, M. M. (1984). *Problems of Dostoevsky's poetics.* Trans. from Russian by Caryl Emerson. Minneapolis, MN: University of Minnesota Press.

Banks, J. A. (1991). *Teaching strategies for ethnic studies* (5th ed.). Boston: Allyn & Bacon.

Banks, J. A. (1999). *Introduction to multicultural education* (3rd ed.). Boston: Allyn & Bacon.

Bergland, B. (1994). Postmodernism and the autobiographical subject: Reconstructing the "other." In K. Ashley, L. Gilmore & G. Peters (Eds.), *Autobiography and postmodernism* (pp. 130–166). Amherst, MA: The University of Massachusetts Press.

Boler, M. (1997). The risk of empathy: Interrogating multiculturalism's gaze. *Cultural Studies, 11*(2), 253–273.

Derrida, J. (1991). From "Psyche: Inventions of the Other." In P. Kamuf (Ed.), *A Derrida reader: Between the blinds* (pp. 200–220). New York: Columbia University Press.

Doll, M. (1996). *To the lighthouse and back: Writings on teaching and living.* New York: Peter Lang.

Edgerton, S. H. (1996). *Translating the curriculum: Multiculturalism into cultural studies.* New York: Routledge.

Eng, D. L. (2001). *Racial castration: Managing masculinity in Asian America.* Durham, NC: Duke University Press.

Foucault, M. (1978). *The history of sexuality* (Vol. 1). New York; Vintage Books.

Gilmore, L. (1994). The mark of autobiography: Postmodernism, autobiography, and genre. In K. Ashley, L. Gilmore & G. Peters (Eds.), *Autobiography and postmodernism* (pp. 3–18). Amherst, MA: The University of Massachusetts Press.

Goodson, I. F. (1998). Storying the self: Life politics and the study of the teacher's life and work. In William F. Pinar (Ed.), *Curriculum: Toward new identities* (pp. 3–20). New York: Garland.

Greene, M. (1992). Foreword. In A.G. Rud Jr. & W.P. Oldenorf (Eds.), *A place for teacher renewal* (pp. vii–ix). New York: Teachers College Press.

Greene, M. (1997). The passions of pluralism: Multiculturalism and the expanding community. In S. Cahn (Ed.) *Classic and contemporary readings in the philosophy of education* (pp. 510–521). New York: McGraw-Hill.

Hesford, W. S. (1999). *Framing identities: Autobiography and the politics of pedagogy.* Minneapolis, MN: University of Minnesota Press.

Loewen, J. (1995). *Lies my teacher told me: Everything your American history textbook got wrong.* New York: Simon & Schuster.

McLaren, P. (2003). *Life in schools.* (4th ed.). New York: Allyn & Bacon.

McLaren, P. & Torres, C. A. (1998). Voicing from the margins: The politics and passion of pluralism in the work of Maxine Greene. In W. C. Ayers & J. L. Miller (Eds.), *A light in dark times: Maxine Greene and the unfinished conversation* (pp.190–203). New York: Teachers College Press.

Miller, J. (2005). *Sounds of silence breaking: Women, autobiography, and curriculum.* New York: Peter Lang.

Morson, G. S., & Emerson, C. (1990). *Mikhail Bakhtin: Creation of a prosaics.* Stanford, CA: Stanford University Press.

Palmer, P. (1998). *The courage to teach.* San Francisco: Jossey-Bass.

Pinar, W. F. (1994). *Autobiography, politics, and sexuality.* New York: Peter Lang.

Pinar, W. F. (2004). *What is curriculum theory?* Mahwah, NJ: Lawrence Erlbaum.

Rothenberg, P. (2000). *Invisible privilege: A memoir about race, class, and gender.* Lawrence, KS: The University Press of Kansas.

Sleeter, C. (1993). How White teachers construct race. In C. McCarthy & W. Crichlow (Eds.), *Race, identity, and representation in education* (pp. 157–171). New York: Routledge.

Tung, M. (2000). *Chinese Americans and their immigrant parents.* New York: The Haworth Clinical Practice.

Wang, H. The strength of the feminine, lyrics of Chinese women's self, and the power of education. In C. Eppert & H. Wang (Eds.), *Cross cultural studies in curriculum: Eastern thought, educational insights.* Mahwah, NJ: Lawrence Erlbaum.

HONGYU WANG is an assistant professor in the School of Teaching and Curriculum Leadership at Oklahoma State University, Stillwater, Oklahoma, and **TIANLONG YU** is an assistant professor in the Department of Education at D'Youville College, Buffalo, New York.

Expanding Appreciation for "Others" among European-American Pre-Teacher Populations

CAROLYN SLEMENS WARD

History

During the four and one-half years that I have taught social foundations and multicultural education for aspiring teachers and special education teachers at the Western Illinois University-Quad Cities campus, the class has evolved from being a hodge-podge of required content that maintained little student accountability and provided questionable attitude-changing experiences to a class where a significant majority of students express positive expansion in knowledge, understanding, tolerance, and appreciation of cultural diversity as evidenced by survey results. The improvement of the class followed much soul searching, sleepless nights, risk taking, failures, tenacity, continuous reading, and research.

The Western Illinois University-Quad Cities campus is located in an urban area with surrounding suburbs, and many of the students travel long distances from small town and rural communities. Although the urban area is ethnically diverse, the teacher education program is comprised of a predominantly European-American student population. My classes usually include one African-American at the most, perhaps two or three Mexican-Americans, with the remaining students of European-American background.

I find that when first entering the multicultural education classroom, many Quad City students who are already overloaded, working part-time, parenting, and who may exhibit poor time-management skills, view the sixteen-week, three-hour course as just another hoop to jump through in order to obtain a teaching certificate. By the end of the course, anonymous survey results along with student comments indicate that a significant majority of students' understandings and attitudes regarding ethnic and cultural diversity issues have expanded and improved.

Objectives

Our nation's teachers play a key role in alleviating or exacerbating educational inequality across our nation. Oftentimes this educational inequality is based on ethnicity, class, and gender as well as additional cultural factors. It is essential that teacher education programs include courses that address multicultural issues with the goal of developing true respect for those who are different than one's self.

At the start of my social foundations and multicultural education class, students are informed that some may discover that teaching is not for them. A teacher fulfills too important a role in a child's life to not be an encourager, a respecter of all students, an empowering agent, a cultural mediator, and a holder of high expectations for every student in his/her classroom. Teachers may be masters of their subject areas while at the same time do irreparable harm to some of their students through ignorance of various cultural backgrounds or an outright disrespect for those who are different from themselves.

In order to gain respect for all others, pre-service teachers. need to first understand what culture is; research their own cultural backgrounds and how individual cultural backgrounds influence the way one judges others; realize why we need multicultural education in our schools through an examination of the educational, economic, political, and social inequities in our society; and be exposed to the true history of the United States—warts and all. How has this country historically treated and presently treat people from various cultural and ethnic groups? What does this say about the present as well as past macro-culture of this nation? What are the elements that comprise our macro-culture?

With the aforementioned background, issues of racism, classism, sexism, homophobia, ableism, and misunderstanding of language minority students are more easily understood. Upon successful completion of the course, the student is able to:

- Demonstrate an understanding of multicultural education and the role of culture in the educational process.
- Develop a greater appreciation and understanding of individual differences represented in the social foundations and multicultural education classroom and how individual perspectives have been influenced by various cultural backgrounds.

- Describe (based on valid and reliable research) current demographic, economic, social, cultural, and political trends impacting U.S. society and schooling.
- Identify the impact of historical, contemporary, and future issues of diversity in the educational process based on valid and reliable research, i.e., race, ethnicity, social class, gender, sexual orientation, ability, and language.
- Improve the ability to think logically, critically, and in an integrated manner in terms of analyzing the need for educational reform in order to meet the needs of a diverse learning community.
- Formulate plausible curriculum and delivery strategies to address the diverse needs of students.
- Demonstrate a realization regarding the efficacy of teachers in making a positive difference in individual lives as well as in an inequitable society—a social reconstructionist approach to multicultural education. (Sleeter & Grant, 1999)

Specific Activities

One focus of the course is a required eight-week journalizing field experience of tutoring/mentoring those who are at risk of failing academically, socially, and/or emotionally. Students are involved with several Title I schools in the area as well as agencies/organizations such as the Boys and Girls Club, the Martin Luther King, Jr. Community Center, and additional after school programs for children and adults. Students are encouraged to widen their life experiences by working with others who are significantly different from themselves whether it be in terms of social class, ethnicity, ability, etc.

Another course requirement is to attend a school board meeting and write a brief summary. Students are provided information about school boards and are encouraged to notice if the board truly represents the diversity found in the school-community. Many times, attending these meetings proves to be revealing regarding community power structures and the role of the school-community concerning important school district decisions.

Finally, pedagogical methods are introduced and discussed through empowering and cooperative group projects that address multicultural issues under the following topics:

- Human relations approaches to teaching,
- Student empowering strategies,
- Critical thinking strategies,
- Cooperative learning strategies,
- Classroom management strategies concerning diverse student populations, and
- Multicultural education curricula for K–12 classrooms.

Students develop peer evaluation criteria for the group presentations and then evaluate each presentation accordingly, while the presentations are also evaluated by the instructor on pre-established criteria.

Instructional methods and materials for the course are varied with a high level of student-accountability through multiple and varied assessments along with ongoing dialogue in the classroom as well as through a WebCT3 site that includes a student dialogue box with optional anonymity. For example, one assignment is to report about a relevant current event while another is to create a personal cultural collage to share with other class members.

There are also a variety of experiential exercises such as small cooperative group illustrations of children growing up in various socio-economic classes and then surmising what the life-chances for these children are in our society (Ward, 2002). Finally, several guest speakers sharing their various cultural experiences in the U.S. add reality, interest, and excitement to the course.

An additional objective for the course is to develop a sense of community within the multicultural education classroom. I find myself more of a facilitator than an instructor at times—facilitating discussions and reactions to several powerful video presentations concerning racism, learning disabilities, and sexual orientation as well as other topics. A touch of humor as well as patience and not taking oneself too seriously always help here. The small group projects that research and demonstrate various teaching methods for multicultural education also aid in developing this sense of community, as I ensure that project groups are as culturally and ethnically diverse as possible.

Many students find that working in culturally diverse groups in presenting research projects is empowering and is the highlight of the course; others cite the eight-week journalizing field experience of tutoring/mentoring students who are at risk of failing academically, socially, and/or emotionally as the most enlightening course experience; while others mention the many discussions concerning various cultural issues as the most meaningful. The variety and multiplicity of learning activities, assignments, and assessments are essential for college/university classrooms comprising students who demonstrate a variety of learning styles and multiple intelligences, even though the classes may *appear* to be rather homogenous. Because of the variety, almost all students excel with several assignments, activities, and assessments.

Along with the variety of assignments and assessments, students are provided with clear assignment criteria in order to lessen confusion and promote equal treatment that is expected from students. This does not mean that I am not available to provide extra help for individual students—serving as coach at times. Additionally, because the four tests administered throughout the semester are in essay format, students are encouraged to retake tests in order to improve their scores. The objective is for students to learn and reflect upon the presented material—not to "catch" students failing.

Supporting Data

While attempting to determine whether or not student access to an anonymous dialogue box through a WebCT3 site was a positive factor in expanding knowledge, understanding, and boundaries of tolerance and appreciation of various cultural issues, I found that over a period of two semesters teaching two multicultural education classes per semester, the smaller classes which had no access to the anonymous dialogue box rated their knowledge, understanding, and expanding boundaries of tolerance and appreciation of cultural issues somewhat higher than the larger classes which *had* access to the anonymous dialogue box. The more intense sense of community within the smaller classes as well as increased time for instructor conversations with individual students may have given the edge to smaller class size over having anonymous dialogue access. The statements that were rated at the end of the semester from 0, low, to 5, high, for each category on the anonymous survey were:

1. "I feel that I have increased my *understanding and knowledge* about the following: racism, gender, class, sexual orientation, ability, bilingual education, U.S. culture." With n=86, the mean percent for the highest rating of 5 was as follows for each category: racism 63%, gender 48%, class 50%, sexual orientation 51%, ability 53%, bilingual education 75%, and U.S. culture 57%. (One to three students in each of the four classes selected a 0–2 rating for some categories.)

2. "I feel that my boundaries of *tolerance and appreciation* have been expanded regarding individuals coming from the following (different from mine) backgrounds." The mean percent for the highest rating of 5 was as follows for each category: race/ethnicity 78%, gender 61%, class 67%, sexual orientation 69%, ability 65%, language 72%. (One to two students in each of the four classes selected a 0–2 rating for some categories.)

The higher mean percent rating for the categories of bilingual education and language may have been influenced by the fact that this topic was the last addressed in the semester, or it may have been that class members actually had little knowledge and appreciation concerning limited English proficient (LEP) students and methods to address their needs.

Student comments were positive as written on student evaluation forms, especially for the most recent two years. Positive comments include:

> "What I liked best about this course was the respect that was established between *all* people."

> "I very much appreciated the community aspect of the class. I enjoyed coming to each session and seeing other points of view."

> "I really enjoyed this class, even though it forced me to realize I'm not as open minded as I thought".

> "What I liked best about this class is that it opened my eyes to the prejudice within myself and engrained in our society."

Comments such as these encourage me to continue taking risks and to continuously learn and improve myself as a multicultural educator and role model in order to make a positive difference in the world of education and, thus, in our society.

References

Sleeter, C. & Grant, C. (1999). *Making choices for multicultural education: Five approaches to race, class, and gender* (3rd ed.). Upper Saddle River, NJ: Merrill/Prentice Hall.

Ward, C. (2002). Preparing K–12 teachers to teach for social justice: An experiential exercise with a focus on inequality and life-chances based on socio-economic status, *Multicultural Education, 9:*4, 22–24.

CAROLYN SLEMENS WARD is an associate professor in the department of Educational and Interdisciplinary Studies at Western Illinois University-Quad Cities, Moline, Illinois.

Whose World Is This?

JAYNE R. BEILKE

Whose world is this?
The world is yours, the world is yours
It's mine, it's mine, it's mine
Whose world is this?
Nas (1994)

Introduction

As defined by critical theorists, critical multicultural education requires the development of a critical consciousness (*conscientization*). The elements of critical consciousness include dialogue, problem-posing, and the exploration of generative themes such as race, class, and gender. The formation of a partnership between university students and a community nonprofit, youth-serving agency, can be a powerful catalyst in the development of critical multicultural consciousness.

This article describes an on-going partnership between university secondary education majors in a multicultural education class and the local Boys and Girls Club. It draws upon student reflective journals to illustrate the process of developing critical multicultural consciousness and the potential for praxis (change).

Muncie Boys and Girls Club

The Muncie Boys and Girls Club is located in Industry, one of Muncie's two historically Black neighborhoods. Industry neighborhood was the site of the Ball Brothers glass factories that produced canning jars during the Progressive Era. In 1886, the discovery of natural gas deposits drew the industrialist Ball Brothers from New York to Muncie and ushered in glass manufacturing throughout east-central Indiana.

Shortly after the turn of the 20th century, the natural gas deposits were exhausted due to the lack of conservation (Lynd and Lynd, 1929). Manufacturing firms relocated, but a town of 20,000 inhabitants had been established, due in large part to streams of southern blacks and Appalachian whites who had been drawn to Muncie by the prospect of jobs.

Travelling from Ball State University to the Club, one passes Munsyana Homes, Muncie's oldest housing projects, which were built in 1941. Munsyana Homes are two-story drab lime-green and beige rectangular cinder block buildings that occupy several city blocks. Despite the outward appearance of order

and containment, the Homes are the scene of heavy drug trafficking and related crime. Nearby is a liquor store whose owner once won the city's "Outstanding Business of the Year" award. Abandoned convenience stores, a thriving blood plasma center, small businesses, storefront churches and the abandoned relics of the glass factories all mix together in Industry.

The Muncie Boys and Girls Club is housed in a brick building built in 1951. The original windows were removed long ago to prevent theft and vandalism. There is no visible tagging (graffiti) anywhere on the Club facility, which is a sign that neighborhood gangs recognize it as neutral space. It has a large gymnasium, a recreation room filled with pool tables, an arts and crafts room, a small kitchen, a lounge with a television set and sofas, and an education room. It serves 170 inner city children and youth each day ranging from 5 to 17 years of age. Representative of the city's persistent residential segregation, most of the African American members of the Club live in the black neighborhoods while poor whites live in Shedtown.

University students who grew up and live in Muncie call the Southside "the low end." Although the majority of the Club's clients are African American, an increasing number identify themselves as "other" or biracial. The common denominator, however, is not race, but social class. The Club's members represent families of lower socioeconomic status who populate the city's working class. At the elementary school next door, the entire student body qualifies for the federal free or reduced lunch program.

A membership to the Boys and Girls Club costs one dollar a month, but "scholarships" are readily available for children who cannot afford it. The purpose of the membership fee is to encourage commitment—a sense of belonging—rather than to provide monetary support for the Club, which is supported by the United Way and private donations. Club staff members are all too aware that children join gangs for just that reason—to belong. During its busiest period, after school until 6:00 PM, the Club can be a chaotic place, as evidenced by one student's first impression:

Amy*: In a way the Club looked worse than I had imagined. Children were screaming and shouting for no reason. I tried talking to the kids and asking them their names and what they did there. Two of the four kids I talked to just blew me off. The other two kind of talked to me, but in a very loud, obnoxious manner to the point where I couldn't understand them very well. I was stunned by the constant noise and opening and slamming of doors.

The Boys and Girls Club is an example of non-formal education (NFE), defined (after Philip Coombs) as "any organized, systematic educational activity outside the framework of the formal [school] system designed to provide selective types of learning to particular subgroups in the population, adults as well as children" (Paulston & LeRoy, 1982, 336—7). NFE is perhaps most closely associated with literacy programs in countries such as Nicaragua (Arnove, 1986) and Brazil and Guinea-Bissau (Freire, 1978).

The national Boys and Girls Club curriculum consists of the following program areas: athletics, education, gang and drug prevention, good citizenship, and survival skills (e.g. cooking). Local chapters are allowed to customize the curriculum to fit their needs.

Towards Critical Multicultural Consciousness through Community Engagement

Planned activities can last anywhere from 20 minutes to an hour. Participation in recreation is held out as a reward for completing homework. Although they do not typically hold teaching licensure, staff members function as a combination of teacher, social worker, and mentor. They are united by their commitment to working with underserved youth and are more often than not familiar with the territory. They know, for example, that mobility plays a large role in the lives of children from lower socioeconomic families. Such families may move frequently in an attempt to avoid the rent collector, Child Protective Services, or an abusive spouse. For many children, the Club provides a stable environment for a few hours a week.

University Teaching Majors

While talking with a resident of the Whiteley neighborhood, she referred to the university as "out there." Puzzled, I said, "You speak of it as though it were another world." She responded emphatically, "it *is* another world!" Located a scant two miles northwest of the Club, the university is named for the aforementioned Ball Brothers who, in 1918, purchased a failing normal school and infused it with capital. Ball State University is now a comprehensive university with a student population of 18,500.

Although teaching majors no longer dominate the university, they remain integral to its institutional mission. The majority of education majors come from rural communities within a 90-mile radius of the university. They are often first generation college students who graduated from high schools with homogenous white, middleclass populations. For many of them, the sheer size of the university itself is an eye-opening experience.

Secondary education (junior high, middle school, high school) majors who are preparing to be junior high, middle school, and high school teachers are required to take one course

in multicultural education. Informal profiles constructed by the students at the beginning of the course reveal that they identify themselves as middleclass, Christian, and small town (sometimes rural). Consistent with their belief that whiteness is normative, these students do not identify themselves racially; while African American and Asian students always do so.

Most of the students prefer country and Christian contemporary music. A few white and black students also listen to rap music and gospel. When asked what they would change about public education if they had the power, they initially have no suggestions. It has, after all, worked for them—they are part of the 30 per cent of high school students who attend postsecondary institutions.

Critical Multicultural Education

The conceptual framework of critical theory is derived from the works of Paolo Freire, Henry Giroux, Peter McLaren, and others. Brazilian educator Paolo Freire contributed the concept of *conscientization,* or "the process in which [people] achieve a deepening awareness both of the sociocultural reality that shapes their lives and of their capacity to transform that reality" (Freire, 1985, footnote 2, p. 93). In order to achieve that reality, one must first locate—or perceive clearly (objectively)—his/her place (role) in that reality. In the process of interrogating one's sociopolitical reality, one becomes progressively more critical of it. One also begins to recognize his/her role as a change agent.

According to Freire, then, this agency allows people not only to critically name the world, but also to *change* it (Freire, 1982). Critical theorists believe that we inhabit "a world rife with contradictions and asymmetries of power and privilege" (McLaren, 1994, 175). This world is both constructed by and acted upon by its inhabitants, who are bound by class, race, and gender interests. It follows that the world they create is then necessarily racist, classist, and gendered.

The critical educator employs a dialectical approach. That is, s/he recognizes that the problems of society are part of the interconnectedness between society and the individual. In other words, the critical educator blames neither the "victim" nor the system, but sees clearly his/her role as creator, actor, and acted upon, within the larger society. The critical educator searches for the larger social, economic, and political implications of seemingly isolated phenomena (McLaren, 1994). For example, the public school curriculum ostensibly prepares students for meaningful work, citizenship, and socialization. But in a larger sense it also plays a powerful role in social reproduction, or the perpetuation of the class system.

One of the most insidious forms of social reproduction—and a frequent target of critical theorists—is tracking. Beginning in elementary school, students are "sorted" on the basis of test scores. By the time they reach high school, they are tracked into a constellation of vocational education, tech prep, or college preparatory courses. Although this is done in the name of efficiency, critical theorists would argue that it acts to maintain a working class and to produce a relatively small leadership class.

Building upon critical theory, Peter McLaren has defined critical multiculturalism as a perspective from which "representations of race, class and gender are understood as the result of large social struggles over signs and meanings" (McLaren, 2000, 221). "Power signs" are words that evoke strong images such as "Black," "poor," "welfare mothers," and "homeless." People who fall into these categories are viewed monolithically. They also serve as reference points upon which social and school policies are predicated. Persons so signified are objectified and marginalized by the dominant society. An example of this marginalization is the racializing of standardized test scores in an attempt to link ethnicity to intelligence.

According to McLaren, the application of critical theory to multiculturalism invokes this central question: "How do we develop an understanding of difference that avoids an essentializing of Otherness?" (McLaren, 1994, 286). Multicultural education courses often denigrate "the Other" as someone who needs to be acted upon—to be assimilated into the dominant society (Delpit, 1995). This is apt to occur in multicultural education courses with a service learning component where critical theory is not well integrated into the field placement and reinforced dialogically (Rosenberger, 2001). In her research on service learning, Marilynne Boyle-Baise has identified three paradigms—charity, civic education, and community building—each with its own goals and outcomes (Boyle-Baise, 2002).

It is not surprising that research reveals that pre-service teachers are most likely to belong to the first category. After all, they often cite the desire "to make a difference" as one of their reasons for choosing education as a profession. In its most benign form, the charity impulse translates into "good deeds." At its worst, it perpetuates whiteness, middle class status and Christianity as normative. Rather than "making a difference," critical theory requires students to think differently about their world.

Critical Pedagogy

The first task of developing a critical multicultural perspective is to see oneself more objectively by "unpacking" power, privilege, and racial identity. Community engagement can be a powerful pedagogical force in that process. But in order to develop a critical consciousness, critical theory must be inextricably integrated with the community agency field experience. Course materials and class discussions must reinforce and explicate the phenomena encountered in the field. In order for students to deconstruct their world, faculty must make conscious pedagogical choices.

I chose the following books as texts: Jonathan Kozol's *Savage Inequalities,* Alex Kotlowitz' *There Are No Children Here,* and Gregory H. Williams' *Life on the Color Line.* The sophomores in my university class still use high school, rather than the university, as a reference point. Kozol's portraits of under-resourced schools with their powerful imagery of sewage flowing into classrooms and football fields without goalposts are a jarring contrast to the schools attended by my students. Students often mistake the wealthy schools described by Kozol as private—rather than public—schools.

Kotlowitz' book is a documentary of two boys (Pharaoh and Lafeyette) growing up in the Henry Horner housing projects in Chicago. Although it is less than four hours away from Muncie, most of my students have never been to Chicago. This book introduces them to the world of the urban poor. Pharaoh, in particular, is a sympathetic character whose sweetness stands in stark contrast to his life in the projects. But along with chronicling drive-by shootings and the death of Lafeyette's best friend, the book celebrates the resilience of the boys (who belong to the Boys Club[1]) and their mother, LaJoe.

In his memoir of growing up as an impoverished light-skinned black in Muncie during the 1950s, Williams' book describes the city's racial divisiveness. Williams and his brother were brought to Muncie from Virginia, where his father passed for white until personal and economic misfortune left him penniless. Williams attended the elementary school next to the Club and played basketball at the Club. A story of poverty as much as racism, it underscores the persistence of residential and economic segregation in Muncie. In addition to the books, the course materials include other relevant print materials and videos about race, class, oppression and power.

According to Freire, the elements of critical pedagogy include dialogue, problem-posing, and generative themes. Dialogical communication allows for liberation by providing "individual and collective possibilities for reflection and action" (McLaren, 1994, 307). It calls for a balance to be struck between the more or less empowered parties. By communicating in an authentic way—*truly* relating—students are able to participate in the decisions made in the class.

Dialogical communication can produce honest, authentic debate among students over issues such as bilingual education, affirmative action, and welfare policies. Beyond the classroom, a key element of dialogue is accomplished through reflective journals. Each week, students reflect on a topic related to the required readings. The Club allows for the application of theory to practice. Through e-mail, the classroom dialogue can be extended and problems posed.

Problem-posing education allows students and teachers to investigate universal or, after Freire, "generative" themes. Power signs and representations prevent us from seeing clearly. By problemitizing the world, however, students are given a critical lens through which to view the world—a lens unblurred by class, race, or gender constructs. Community engagement creates the opportunity in which problemitizing can occur. For example:

Rachel: They asked us to design a mural for the new Keystone Club room, so we thought we would have a go at it. We were supposed to come up with something that would represent teenaged kids, and that would give the room some life. After an hour of brainstorming we had come up with a good idea. We had planned to do squares of bright color on the wall with black silhouettes of kids doing different things such as playing games, watching TV, hanging out with friends, and so on. But when we told the director, she said, "but what if the kids think these are all black kids, and there is some kind of meaning behind this?" We had not thought of that at all, and truthfully I was a little embarrassed. So we made a few adjustments, with the help of one of the Keystone Kids, and the end result came out pretty cool.

Like many non-profit agencies in 2002, the Club struggled financially. Both corporate and individual donations declined as the lingering result of the attack on the World Trade Towers and the economic recession (Lewis, 2002). In the wake of 9/11, people sent donations to New York City rather than to local agencies. Potentially more devastating, the economic recession accounted for shortfalls for virtually all non-profit organizations from animal shelters to soup kitchens.

Rachel: When we got to the Club, once again the money was not there for them to go out and buy the paints needed.

Luckily, Ms Hampton [education director] remembered that they had some paints they were going to use a few years ago to paint a rainbow on the wall of the art room. So we rummaged around and found those. Thankfully the paints were all in good enough shape that they were still usable.

Now that I think about it, I realize how much money the organizations I was involved with my whole life had. I cannot remember a time that we did not get something because the money was not there. Anytime that I need something I just go out and buy it but after visiting the Boys and Girls club last Saturday I realized that they do not have that option.

A prime generative theme addressed by critical multicultural education is that of racial identity. In order to deconstruct race, a certain de-centering of one's identity must first occur. Several developmental theories of racial identity, which view race as a social and psychologically constructed process, have been advanced. Janet Helms (1990) defines racial identity as "a sense of group or collective identity based on one's perception that he or she shares common racial heritage with a particular racial group" (p. 3). Understanding the sociocultural construct of race is crucial to developing a critical perspective.

As discussed earlier in this article, white students rarely see themselves in terms of racial identity. While they are quick to point out that they are middleclass, they do not identify themselves as white. For that reason, it is important to first define one's white cultural identity before moving on to a nonracist white identity. The ability to see oneself as the Other is an example of disintegration, where one begins to experience dissonance about one's racial identity:

Amy: Last week a perfect display of who the "other" was occurred. Directly quoting a child as I walked into the Club, he said, "shit, you are the whitest person I ever seen, you about as white as this piece of wood." If you might have guessed the piece of wood was a very light beige/flesh color. I hesitated and didn't know how to respond so I didn't say much. The whole point of integrating this quote into my journal is because I strongly believe it defines me as being the "other" at the Club.

Liz: The Club definitely influenced my view on being Hispanic. For a long time I was embarrassed by it, and later on I didn't even think about being Hispanic either way because I was with white people all of the time. The kids at the club helped remind me that I do look different, and they helped me see how beneficial my appearance and being a minority will be.

In Peggy McIntosh' (1989) brief but classic article "White Privilege: Unpacking the Invisible Knapsack," she lists unearned assets which can be found in a metaphorical knapsack of privilege. Examples range from the assurance that "I can if I wish arrange to be in the company of people of my race most of the time" to "I can choose blemish cover or bandages in 'flesh' color and have them more or less match my skin." University students generally interpret the word "privilege" as a trapping of the upper class. By interrogating the meaning of privilege (i.e., something that is taken for granted) students find examples of privilege writ small:

Destiny: One thing that stuck in my head was when this little girl asked me what I had in my mouth. I said it was a retainer and she said, "oh, did you ever have braces?" I told her yes and she said, "My dentist told me and my momma I needed braces but she say she can't afford them." That made me really think about how some of these kids are deprived of certain things.

By deconstructing class privilege, students not only begin to see themselves more clearly, but can also recognize strengths and resilience in Club members. By the age of 8, Jerry was already the primary caregiver for his younger sisters, while his mother worked. He often bullied some of the smaller Club members as well as my university students.

But Jerry's complexity became evident over the course of the semester. When a new, white child showed up at the Club, Jerry became his protector. In return, the child's grateful parents asked Jerry to accompany them on a trip to Washington DC the following summer. While on the trip, the Club's loudspeaker squawked out the message that Jerry had called to "tell everyone hello."

Spending time with Jerry allowed my students to recognize his belligerence as a form of resistance to victimization (Allport, 1954). During a tutoring session, he threatened to "knock those glasses right off your face" if my student wouldn't provide him with the correct answers. Gently refusing to do so, the student noticed that Jerry had tears in his eyes as he patiently continued to help him with his composition. Other students also began to "see" him more clearly:

Richard: It was quite a surprise to get to the Boys and Girls Club and find that their Fall Festival was scheduled that day. Enter Jerry. He's black and I think he's in junior high. Jerry asked me if the kids were playing, and I said they didn't have tickets. He proceeded to cover for those kids. He had a dozen or so tickets, and he used them paying for other kids to play musical chairs.

Jerry was my interesting event at the Festival. I didn't get the opportunity to talk with him much, but I can see something in him. I see a person who's being like a big brother to some of the kids. I see someone willing to do things for others. I see someone who may very well turn out to be a community-oriented person, serving his home (wherever that may be in the future).

Under Construction: Pedagogy to Praxis

The process of conscientization is not developmental; one does not take orderly, discrete steps from problem-posing or dialogue to praxis. Rather, it is a holistic process in which all elements are interconnected and occur as integrated parts of the whole. Critical pedagogy through community engagement can effectively foster dialogue and problem-solving but praxis is more difficult to achieve.

Freire defines praxis as being "reflection and action upon the world in order to transform it" (Freire, 1982, 36). The goal of praxis is liberatory—the achievement of a more just and equitable world for all inhabitants. One of its prerequisites is the evidence of humanization of the Other through the formation of authentic relationships. In a university multicultural education course bounded by time constraints and frequency of student contact, it is difficult to achieve the kind of cognitive dissonance that produces praxis. Nevertheless, like privilege, praxis writ small does occur through the establishment of authentic relationships:

Mike: I am starting to get more comfortable because I have been getting to know the kids better, and vice versa. I have learned that just helping a kid do math problems or look up words can be rather cold and impersonal. It is still satisfying to help them do these things, but sometimes it seems like a one way experience. When it's over, the satisfaction seems to fade quickly unless I have made a personal connection with the kid. In the future, I am going to try to think of each interaction with kids (or anyone else for that matter) as a shared experience and consciously look for ways to develop relationships.

To "consciously look for ways" signals the intentionality that Freire says is necessary for action. In Mike's case, the passive act of tutoring a student by using drill sheets and vocabulary practice is in itself not satisfactory. By creating an authentic relationship, both parties can learn something from each other and precipitate action:

Jason: My most enduring image of the Boys/Girls Club was witnessing, through the different ages of the children, a cruel assembly line of poverty, oppression, and ignorance turning innocent, happy and hopeful children into delinquent, angry and hopeless children. I remember a young little boy, innocently and comfortably grabbing my hand, holding it with a smile, as he led me to find him a basketball. As well, I remember a boy, only a few years older than the former one, who angrily threw a basketball down and walked off court cursing over something so trivial he probably forgot it by the end of the day. If I had

the power, I would end the process of tracking students in schools.

To summarize, I advance the following definition of critical multicultural consciousness through engagement: *Critical multicultural consciousness through community engagement is predicated on the formation of a mutually beneficial partnership between educational entities (formal or nonformal) for the purpose of conscientization. The process is guided by critical pedagogy (including dialogue, problem-posing, and generative themes) and the hopeful possibility of praxis (social action).* Within these wide boundaries, critical multicultural consciousness affords pre-service teachers the opportunity to interrogate and deconstruct their world-view.

As a process, critical multicultural consciousness is neither paradigmatic nor developmental. It does, however, require a certain redefinition of authority, a coherent integration between theory and practice so that each informs the other, a commitment to the formation of authentic relationships, and recognition of transformation writ small.

Conclusion: Beyond the Scholarship of Engagement

With the publication of *Scholarship Reconsidered*, Ernest L. Boyer challenged the traditional role of faculty as being removed from their communities. He recommended a reconnection between scholarship and community that would ultimately provide "service" for the common good. In the calls for service that emanated in reaction to the "Me Decade" of the 1980s (notably, Putnam, 1995), Boyer's book was a clarion call to university faculty to reconnect with communities and engage through the scholarship of discovery, integration, application, integration, and teaching (Boyer, 1990).

According to Boyer's paradigm, the scholarship of discovery focuses on research or the production of knowledge. The scholarship of integration is an endorsement of generalization rather than specialization. The scholarship of application speaks directly to service: i.e., using knowledge for the "common good." And the scholarship of teaching urges faculty to find creative ways to transmit knowledge to students. Boyer's paradigm of the scholarship of engagement, however, raises troubling questions about the role of faculty, the constituency of "community," and the meaning of "the common good" itself. University faculty provide solutions with little input from stakeholders. In fact, university faculty stand apart from both community agents and students.

When Boyer speaks of community, he is referring to a community of scholars rather than endorsing an equitable, mutually beneficial, partnership between community agencies and universities. When advocating a team approach to problem solving, he is referring to a team of scholars working together.

This is no less true in regards to the scholarship of teaching, where faculty are urged to be creative and inspired, but retain their hierarchical role in the academy. But in order to support community engagement in a critical sense—and to approach critical consciousness—the authority role of faculty must be redefined. At the very least, the scholarship of teaching must become more facilitative than didactic.

Boyer envisions the scholarship of engagement as providing the solutions to environmental, educational, political, social, and "other" problems: "Other problems" are defined as those that "require more carefully crafted study and, indeed, solutions that rely not only on new knowledge, but on integration, too" (Boyer, 1990, 77). But Boyer's idea of the common good is hegemonic. Social problems are not problemitized, and solutions are perceived as corrections to aberrations of the status quo. Essentially, Boyer sees the world as one that is acted upon by elites.

Collaborations between educational institutions and community agencies have become ubiquitous over the last decade. The literature related to community service learning and multicultural education is steadily growing. Within that larger discourse, critical theory has much to offer theorists and practitioners.

Grounded in critical theory, critical multicultural consciousness mandates no less, however, than a reconceptualization of the scholarship of engagement. It challenges scholars to go beyond Boyer's emphasis on the intellect to include Freire's emphasis on the heart (humanism). The addition of a critical component to the scholarship of engagement will not only allow scholars, practitioners, and students to problemitize the field of community service learning itself, but, in the spirit of Freire, to change it.

Notes

1. The Boys Club became the Boys and Girls Club in 1990.

*pseudonyms are used unless permission has been given.

References

Allport, G. W. (1954). *The nature of prejudice.* Reading, MA: Addison-Wesley.

Arnove, R. F. (1986). *Education and revolution in Nicaragua.* New York: Praeger Publishers.

Boyer, E. L. (1990). *Scholarship reconsidered: Priorities of the professoriate.* Washington, DC: Carnegie Foundation for the Advancement of Teaching.

Boyle-Baise, M. (2002). *Multicultural service learning: Educating teachers in diverse communities.* New York: Teachers College Press.

Delpit, L. (1995). Education in a multicultural society. In *Other people's children: Cultural conflict in the classroom.* New York: The New Press.

Freire, P. (1978). *Pedagogy in process: The letters to Guinea-Bissau.* New York: Seabury Press.

Freire, P. (1982). *Pedagogy of the oppressed.* New York: Continnum (original work published 1970).

Freire, P. (1985). *The politics of education.* New York: Bergin & Garvey.

Helms, J., (ed.). (1990). *Black and white racial identity: Theory, research, and practice.* Westport, CT: Greenwood.

Kotlowitz, A. (1991). *There are no children here: The story of two boys growing up in the other America.* New York: Anchor Books.

Kozol, J. (1991). *Savage inequalities: Children in America's schools.* New York: Harper Perennial.

Lewis, N. (2002). Charitable giving slides. *Chronicle of Philanthropy: 27.*

Lynd, R. (1929). *Middletown: A study in modern American culture.* New York: Harcourt Brace & Company.

MacIntosh, P. (1989). White privilege: Unpacking the invisible knapsack. *Peace and Freedom* July/August: 10–12.

McLaren, Peter. (1994). *Life in schools: An introduction to critical pedagogy in the foundations of education.* 2nd ed. White Plains, NY: Longman.

McLaren, Peter. (2000). White terror and oppositional agency: Towards a critical multiculturalism. In Duarte, E. M. & S. Smith, eds. *Foundational perspectives in multicultural education* (213–240). New York: Longman.

Nas (Nasir Jones). (1994). The world is yours. *Illmatic.* Sony Music Entertainment, Inc. Manufactured by Columbia Records. New York. Executive producers Faith N. & M. C. Serch.

Paulston, R. G. & LeRoy, G. (1982). Nonformal education and change from below. In Altbach, P. G., R. F. Arnove, & G. P. Kelly, eds. *Comparative education.* New York: MacMillan.

Putnam, R. D. 1995. Bowling alone. *Journal of Democracy 9:* 65–78.

Rosenberger, C. (2000). Beyond empathy: Developing critical consciousness through service learning. In O'Grady, C. R., (ed.), *Integrating service learning and multicultural education in colleges and universities* (23–43). Mahwah, NJ: Lawrence Erlbaum Associates.

Williams, G. H. (1995). *Life on the color line: the true story of a White boy who discovered he was Black.* New York: Dutton (Penguin Group USA).

JAYNE R. BEILKE is an associate professor in the Department of Educational Studies of Teachers College at Ball State University, Muncie, Indiana.

UNIT 4

Identity and Personal Development: A Multicultural Focus

Unit Selections

Key Points to Consider

- Why should an educator be sensitive to cultural identity?

- What should children learn about the cultural heritages and values of other children in their schools?

- How do social class differences relate to misunderstandings among students from different social positions in a community?

- How are cultural stereotypes damaging to students?

- What challenges do minority students encounter that majority students in a desegregated school do not encounter?

- What difficulties have Arab and Muslim Americans faced since September 11, 2001? How can teachers help?

Student Web Site

www.mhcls.com/online

Internet References

Further information regarding these Web sites may be found in this book's preface or online.

Ethics Updates/Lawrence Hinman
http://ethics.acusd.edu

Kathy Schrock's Guide for Educators
http://school.discovery.com/schrockguide/

Let 100 Flowers Bloom/Kristen Nicholson-Nelson
http://teacher.scholastic.com/professional/assessment/100flowers.htm

The National Academy for Child Development
http://www.nacd.org

People are impacted by many social forces as they interact with others in the process of forming themselves as individuals. Multicultural education can help students as well as teachers to identify those social forces that affect their personal development.

The development of each person's unique concept of self (the development of one's identity as a person) is the most important developmental learning task that any of us undertake. The preschool, elementary, and secondary school years are ones in which each of us learns critically important cognitive and affective strategies for defining ourselves, others, and the world. Multicultural education seeks to help people develop intellectual and emotional responses to other people that will be accepting and empathic. There has been much psychological and psychiatric research over the past few decades on the differences between prejudiced and tolerant (accepting) personalities. One opportunity educators have as they work with students in school settings is to provide good examples of accepting, tolerant behavior and to help students develop positive, affirmative views of themselves and others. Gordon A. Allport, in his classic book *The Nature of Prejudice,* commented in his chapter on "The Tolerant Personality" that we could be "doubly sure" that early instruction and practice in accepting diversity is important in directing a child toward becoming a tolerant person. Thus, we take up the topic of personal identity development in this unit.

As educators we need to see the interconnections among such factors as gender, social class, position in society, racial or ethnic heritage, and the primary cultural values that inform the way people see the world and themselves. We need to be sensitive to their visions of who they are and of how things are in the world. We need to "see our clients whole." It is important for teachers to set positive examples of acceptance, open-mindedness, empathy, compassion, and concern for the well-being of each student.

We need to help students to understand themselves, to define their strengths and their concerns, and to empower them to encounter their own personal social reality critically. This is a task each person must learn to do in childhood and adolescence in order to empower themselves to interpret and evaluate their own experience. This task can be integrated and effectively achieved within the intellectual mission of the school. One way to do this is to encourage students to critically interpret and evaluate the texts that they read and to discuss issues in class openly and actively. Each student needs to be able to explore the boundaries of his or her intellectual strengths and weaknesses and to explore the social boundaries encountered in school and out of school.

Multicultural education is intended for and needed by all students in order for them to develop sensitivity to the many varying heritages and backgrounds that make up the United States and Canada and to forge their own conception of who they are as people. Why should only one cultural heritage be thoroughly taught while all others are essentially ignored in elementary and secondary school years in a pluralistic national social environment, the demographics of which are changing so dramatically? Cultural values are of primary importance in the process of a person's conceptualization of him- or herself. This unit's articles explore various models of human interaction and the psychosocial foundations for the formation of knowledge bases of students. How students form social groups in culturally integrated school settings is explored along with the

Digital Vision/PunchStock

behavioral differences among members of "loose-knit" and "tight-knit" social groups in desegregated school settings. The ways in which students define themselves and their possibilities as they move across or are trapped within their perceived social boundaries in school and community settings are explored. How educators can better utilize the knowledge bases of minority cultural families in assisting minority students to achieve better social integration into mainstream school settings is also examined. The importance of educators trying to establish more effective communications linkages between students' family and cultural environments is further examined. The multiple social roles students frequently have to play, both in and out of school, are another phenomenon in personality development that receives analysis in these essays.

Students live in a hierarchy of social contexts in which their racial, cultural, gender, and social class backgrounds, and the degree of their personal identification with each of these factors, influence their important choices and decisions regarding their own identity. Some of the research on how teachers can achieve more effective intercultural socialization is also considered. One of the questions being studied in desegregated school settings concerns the circumstances in which higher rates of intercultural friendship develop. How do we get all cultural group members to learn each other's cultural heritages? Helping students to learn from the cultural perspectives of other groups so that all students might better comprehend alternative, diverse definitions of their social environments is one of the tasks of multicultural education. Another purpose of multicultural education programming is to teach tolerant, accepting attitudes toward others of differing cultural backgrounds. Allport and several other major psychiatrists and social psychologists of past decades have taught us that prejudice and tolerance (acceptance) are learned behaviors. We can learn to be accepting, caring, compassionate persons. Educators are not powerless in the face of the prejudiced view many students bring to school from their homes.

The essays in this unit are relevant to courses in educational policy studies and leadership, cultural foundations of education, sociology or anthropology of education, history and philosophy of education, and curriculum theory and construction, among others.

A Developing Identity
Hispanics in the United States

Immigrant civic integration is an integral part of the Corporation's focus on strengthening U.S. democracy. In this essay, Roberto Suro, director of the Pew Hispanic Center, addresses how Hispanics—both those newly arrived in the U.S. and those who have been citizens for generations— are both impacting and being influenced by American society.

ROBERTO SURO

The U.S. Census Bureau tells us that in 2004 there were 40,459,196 people in the United States who identified themselves as "Hispanic or Latino." Which is it, then, "Hispanic" or "Latino," or both? The *Los Angeles Times* sticks to "Latino." The U.S. Office of Management and Budget (OMB), the arbiter of such things for the federal government, debated the matter and decided not to pick one or the other so as not to offend anyone. The confusion, and occasional controversy, over the name is just symbolic of a much larger question to which there is no simple answer: who are these people? Indeed, you have to ask: are they, in fact, a single people with a common identity, a common bond or common goals? This is important to know because that population number reported by the U.S. Census Bureau is big already, and growing fast. Forty million folks is enough that if they started pulling in the same direction all at once, they could probably change the nation's course—socially, culturally, perhaps even politically one day.

What direction would that be? It is certainly not linguistic. Hispanics are not going to make the United States into a Spanish-speaking country because nearly a quarter of this population speaks little or no Spanish at all, according to the Census, and more than a third say they speak English very well. So, it's not language. Moreover, Hispanics do not share a common race, ethnicity or ancestry, which are the usual ways to identify a population group. They can be black or white, of indigenous origins or not, and their cultural heritages are quite diverse.

The official definition from the OMB relies on national origins, saying the term "Hispanic or Latino" refers to people who trace their descent from Mexico, Puerto Rico, Cuba, Central and South America and other Spanish cultures. That's a pretty broad description because it encompasses immigrants who have just arrived in the United States from those regions as well as those who trace their ancestry in America back many generations. More significantly, the idea of a Hispanic or Latino people comprising many nationalities is not a very strong concept in those regions; not as strong, certainly, as individual national identities. The notion that people from all these places are bound together by an overarching group identity exists more powerfully now in the United States than in Latin America. So, whether the label is Hispanic or Latino, the "label on the label" says *Made in the USA*. In other words, we are dealing with a uniquely American phenomenon: even if it is based on national origins rooted elsewhere, the group identity for many Hispanics is created in the United States. To understand where this population change may be taking us as a nation, we have to look close to home, not abroad.

'Whatever the meaning of "Hispanic" or "Latino"—and I am going to use these terms interchangeably in this essay— it is not one that is artificial or imposed. If you ask people a question like, "Are you of Hispanic or Latino origin?" a good many respond affirmatively. That is how the U.S. Census gets a population count. You can ask the question in several different ways with many different kinds of surveys, and the size of the group and its basic characteristics turn out to be more or less the same. At the most basic level, then, the Latino/Hispanic "yes" is a matter of self-identification. And if more than 40 million people self-identify as Latino or Hispanic, then this sense of group membership is something large and significant on the nation's landscape.

I could argue on the basis of sound evidence that the growth of the Hispanic population is as important a demographic development today as the inception of the Baby Boom was sixty years ago. But if you press me on what makes someone a Hispanic or a Latino, my responses start getting fuzzy after self-identification, and I am not being coy in saying that. I have been watching and writing about Hispanics for thirty years, and I answer "yes" for myself when asked, but the more I learn, the less I know for certain about identity. What are the boundaries of this group? What binds us together? What are we saying to each other and to everyone else when we assert this self-identification?

Models of Identity

The search for answers, as best I can tell, has to start with two admissions: first, when it comes to Hispanics, let's acknowledge that we are watching a work in progress. Second, let's accept that we need new ways of talking about group identity because the old ones don't work very well with this population.

On the first point, the population statistics leave no doubt: the number of Hispanics doubled between 1970 and 1990 and has nearly doubled again since 1990. No population can grow that fast without changing, particularly when immigration is driving much of the growth. About four-of-every-ten Hispanics are foreign born, and among those newcomers, well more than half have arrived in the U.S. since 1990. Those numbers represent a lot of people who are still very much in the process of adjusting to new lives in a new place. And the transition will last beyond their lifetimes. High fertility rates among immigrants is the other propellant of population growth. Another three-in-ten Hispanics are the native-born children of foreign-born parents. This is the second generation, and these young people—whose median age is less than thirteen—are adapting what they inherit from their parents and what they learn outside their homes to fit their own needs. Altogether, then, about 70 percent of the Hispanic population is involved in a process of fundamental cultural transition at some stage or another. Some trajectories are becoming evident, but the final results are still very much in doubt. Hispanics are a people in motion, so we must accept the uncertainty they bring with them and be patient. Understanding their impact on American society could take a while. It could take decades.

The next step—the second admission I am suggesting—involves our historical models of group identity. There are two—minority group and ethnic group—and neither works very well with Hispanics. The first is based on the African American experience: the majority—the mainstream of society—identifies a minority group on the basis of race or by other markers that have served as grounds for unjust exclusion. The excluded group, in turn, asserts collective bonds as it seeks redress of grievances. And in the case of African Americans, even after fifty years of political and economic gains, the group is still often defined, and often defines itself, as being outsiders whose status in American society is still uncertain. The ethnic group model is based on the experience of the Irish, the Italians and other European immigrants. They began as outsiders, even outcasts, with a distinct identity based on national origins. Over time, however, through a process of assimilation and absorption, they gained acceptance to the mainstream and their group identities faded. In effect, they became white.

Even if you believe that history likes repetition, there is no good reason to assume that Latinos will march down either of these roads. Hispanics do not share an obvious common marker like skin color that sets them apart, and they have not begun their journey through American society from a common and tragic starting point, such as slavery. Perhaps this helps to explain why society has not imposed an identity on Latinos as rigidly or as pejoratively as it did on blacks, and why Latino identity does not derive from a collective experience such as resistance to persecution. Indeed, many Latinos are immigrants who have come to this country seeing it as a land of opportunity and have succeeded in realizing their aspirations. On the other hand, Latinos are also not entirely an immigrant population that has been invited into the mainstream. Important segments of the Hispanic population have lived aspects of the minority-group experience. These Latinos have a history as victims of discrimination, and they have created institutions as well as a political identity that developed out of a civil rights struggle. Moreover, about half of the Latino foreign-born population is in the United States without legal authorization and most have no avenue for becoming fully incorporated into the country's national life no matter how much they assimilate. So the Hispanic experience intertwines enough aspects of both the minority and ethnic group models that neither model alone suffices.

The notion that Hispanics from different countries are bound together by an overarching group identity exists more powerfully now in the United States than in Latin America. So, whether the label is Hispanic or Latino, the 'label on the label' says _Made in the USA_.

The Latino experience in the U.S. is not going to be exactly like that of blacks or Italians or other minorities: it is going to be something else. Whatever Hispanic identity ends up being, to understand it, we're going to have to open up our thinking about race and ethnicity and about the ways that group identities take shape. We are seeing something new unfolding before our eyes, but the phenomenon is far enough along that we can look back and see where it started and how certain trajectories have begun to take shape.

Many Different Perceptions

Over the course of several years I have worked on a variety of public opinion surveys of the Hispanic population, and this research tells us that Latino identities are fairly fluid and that their view of the United States is expansive. This means, for example, that most Hispanics see no conflict between learning English and continuing to speak Spanish, between learning

American ways and retaining a Latin culture. They see the United States as desirable, and admirable in many ways in comparison to their countries of origin except on one point: they believe that moral values and family ties are stronger in Latin America than here. But most importantly, they see the United States as a nation that embraces many cultures and not as a place that tries to impose a single national type.

The same fluidity is apparent in the ways that Latinos see themselves. In a 2002 survey, the Pew Hispanic Center asked a large national sample of Hispanics about the terms they use to identify themselves so we could determine which terms they favored most. We gave them three choices: American, Hispanic or Latino, or their country of origin and asked which term they used first or if there was only one term they preferred. The responses varied sharply between immigrants and those born in the United States. More than two-thirds of the immigrants favored their country of origin, saying they were most likely to identify themselves with terms like, "Mexican," "Cuban" or "Dominican." That is not surprising; after all, they were referring to the countries where they were born and raised. Only a small share of the immigrants (6 percent) called themselves "American." Meanwhile, about half of native-born Latinos preferred "American," while a substantial number (29 percent) also primarily identified themselves by their country of origin.

The most curious finding involved the terms "Hispanic" and "Latino" because they were not very popular. The group label was preferred by no more than one-quarter of either the immigrants or the native born. It's not that they are hostile to the idea of an overarching Latino identity encompassing the whole of the Hispanic population, but that identity is not at the forefront of their thoughts. "Hispanic" and "Latino" are not the first terms they reach for when they want to tell you who they are, at least when they have other choices that reflect national identities.

This sense of fragmentation along national lines was evident elsewhere in the same poll, the 2002 National Survey of Latinos, which my organization conducted in partnership with the Kaiser Family Foundation. An overwhelming 85 percent of respondents said that Latinos from different countries have separate and distinct cultures rather than sharing one Hispanic or Latino culture. In a similar vein, respondents were about evenly divided over whether or not Hispanics from different countries were working together to achieve common political aims. But it would be a mistake to dismiss all tendencies toward group identity just because that notion seems to lose out in competition with individual national identities.

When Hispanics are asked about how others perceive them, you find a different story. In that 2002 survey and others, Latinos by large majorities—as high as eight-out-of-ten—say Hispanics as a whole are the victims of discrimination. Near majorities—four-out-of-ten—say that discrimination is a major problem preventing Latinos from succeeding in this country. Three-out-of-ten say that they, personally, have experienced discrimination or that someone close to them has been discriminated against in the last five years. From within the group, the Hispanic/Latino identity may seem weak, but members of the group clearly feel that the rest of society sees that identity

forcefully. Ethnic or racial identities can often arise from two sources: what members of a group feel that they share in common and the roles imposed on them or projected on them by the majority. Given the nature of American society today and the characteristics of the Latino population, this is a particularly fluid mix.

Latino leaders and institutions have used the tools developed by African Americans and benefited from the same types of legislation and court decisions in seeking redress of grievances.

Then again, the Latino population is itself a complex intermingling of people whose families have been here for generations, who have come here from Latin America and who are the children of immigrants. As I noted before, about 70 percent of this population is made up of immigrants and their children—the people who to some degree are involved in a process of assimilation. This reality is reflected in Latinos' views on many different matters, not just the nature of group identity. Perhaps the best way to track this process of assimilation is to look at the languages that Hispanics speak: English, Spanish and the mix of both. Many different kinds of public opinion surveys on different subjects have shown broad and consistent differences between Latinos who speak only Spanish, most often recently arrived immigrants, and those who speak only English, most typically those with long family histories in the United States. And there is often a range of views among bilinguals. In surveys conducted by the Pew Hispanic Center, this pattern has emerged on subjects ranging from the acceptability of divorce, to the chances of success in the Iraq war, to the quality of education in U.S. public schools.

Take the issue of abortion, for example, which we have asked about in several surveys. Large numbers of Latinos who speak and read only Spanish find abortion unacceptable—nearly 90 percent in some polls. Bilingual Hispanics are also disapproving but less overwhelmingly, by about 75 percent. Among those who speak and read only English, a bit more than half find abortion morally unacceptable, which is close to the split you find in the non-Hispanic population. Consider something that is less of a hot-button issue, and you get the same result: in the 2002 survey, for instance, we asked whether it is better for children to live in their parents' home until they get married. Among the Spanish dominant, 95 percent agreed. Among the bilinguals, 75 percent said yes. And with the English speakers, 52 percent agreed, which was just a bit higher than what we found with non-Latinos.

On a great variety of matters, therefore, it seems that immigrant Spanish-speaking Latinos hold distinctive views, while the native-born English speakers hold views that are roughly similar to the American population as a whole. And this result is reflected in attitudes about more than just social issues. In that same 2002 survey, we asked about fatalism—a sense very common among the poor in Latin America that they are not in control of their own destinies. Among Latinos who speak only Spanish, 59 percent agreed with the statement, "It doesn't do any good to plan for the future because you don't have any control over it." Among Latinos who speak only English, a scant 24 percent agreed with that statement. Bilingual Hispanics were in-between, at 31 percent. Only 17 percent of non-Latinos agreed that they have no control over their futures. On this very simple but very basic measure of how individuals see their fates, as on a great many other issues, the shift to English produces a remarkably clear shift in attitudes.

What I've concluded from looking at a variety of surveys is that exposure to American ways through the acquisition of English produces absorption of those ways. Certainly, not every aspect of the American experience gets adopted, but enough does to show that a significant process of assimilation is taking place: people change when they come to the United States and the change accelerates when a great big doorway into their hearts and minds is opened by language.

An Ongoing Process of Change

Language is something we know a lot about because it is a very tangible, testable marker and because there is a great deal of data on it from the Census, from big government household surveys that are carried out regularly, as well as the kinds of public opinion polls that we conduct at the Pew Hispanic Center. The data from all these sources is very consistent. For example, about three-quarters of foreign-born Latinos, the first generation, speaks only Spanish and the rest of the immigrants are bilingual to some extent. The second generation—the children of immigrants—are about evenly divided between English speakers and bilinguals, with almost none reaching adulthood speaking only Spanish. And, among Hispanics of longer tenure in the U.S.—those born here, of American-born parents—more than three-quarters speak only English and the rest are bilingual to some extent, though often their Spanish is weak. So we know for certain that a transition to English is taking place across generations with a lot of bilingualism along the way.

In addition to linguistic adaptations, the survey data I referenced before indicates that a process of change is underway in the Latino population as immigrants and their offspring adopt a variety of values typical of the American public at large. The language data tell us that this process moves along gradually, but steadily. The demographic data show that Latino population growth is constantly being fed by people coming in at the beginning of the process—recent immigrants and their children. Thus, even though a great deal of assimilation is taking place, it can seem that nothing is happening, that Latinos are not changing or even that they are resistant to change, because the Spanish-speaking population is constantly being refreshed by new arrivals. Indeed, for the past decade or so, immigrants early in the assimilation process have accounted for a majority of Hispanic adults, and so it will be for the foreseeable future. In my view, then, these realities reinforce the notion that Latinos are a people in transition, a people in the process of becoming something new.

Suppose then, that by some act of magic—because that's what it would take—not one more Latino immigrant entered the United States. How would the American Hispanic population evolve as a segment of U.S. society if no more newcomers arrived?

One possibility is that differences would wash away and Latinos would become fluent in English, improve their economic status and simply become a lot like everyone else in a couple of generations. In this regard, some commentators have already heralded the glorious return of the melting pot. Give it time, they advise, and Latinos will simply be melded into the white mainstream just as the European immigrants were a century ago. Embracing this view wholeheartedly, however, requires believing two things: that today's newcomers are basically the same as those of the past and that the United States has not changed in a hundred years. Both are debatable propositions. I would argue, as I indicated earlier, that the contemporary context offers much better clues as to the direction of Hispanic trajectories than the historical models.

Think back again to the 1970s, the time when the current wave of Latino immigration and population growth got underway. In retrospect, it is evident that the United States was then in the middle of an era of profound change. The old industrial manufacturing base of the American economy was withering away, to be replaced by the new service sector. A fundamental element of the nation's social structure was being transformed as women gained new status in the home, at work and in the public arena. Finally, the growth of the Hispanic population also coincided with the maturing of the civil rights era.

All of these changes had their start before the Latino population began to grow, and Latinos were, at most, minor players in the initial phases of these transformations. They certainly did not play causal roles. But now, as we move through the first decades of the 21st century, the effects of those transformations are still being absorbed by the nation even as Hispanics become much more numerous. Latinos, then, are like the character who appears peripheral in the first act of a play and then takes center stage midway through the second. By virtue of their population size, however, the Latino population will be a protagonist with a major role to play in the third act, now unfolding.

Consider, for example, the changes wrought by the civil rights era. The main expansion of the Latino population occurred after the United States, in the middle of the 20th century, fundamentally reassessed the way it perceives people who are not part of the white majority and how it manages relations between those groups and the majority. That upheaval, and the new social structures it created, now condition the way in which newly arrived Latino immigrants and their children see themselves and are seen by others. In this regard, their experience is fundamentally different than that of the European immigrants who arrived in the U.S. and underwent an assimilation process prior to the civil rights era.

A key to understanding this difference is recalling that there was, in fact, a Hispanic population in the U.S. when the civil rights era began and that it took part in the upheaval. Led primarily by native-born Mexican Americans, Latino organizations fought against discrimination that had been imposed on them both by law and custom, especially in Texas. An entire generation of Latino leaders and institutions used the tools developed by African Americans and benefited from the same types of legislation and court decisions in seeking redress of grievances. Those leaders and institutions were well established in Hispanic communities when the population began to grow through immigration in the 1970s. And, perhaps more significantly, Hispanics had been recognized in both judicial decisions and legal statutes as members of what many would describe as part of the newly recognized post-1960s social structure: the minority group.

So, everyone added to the Hispanic population automatically becomes part of a group that is formally defined as a people apart, a people with a shared identity, a people who had suffered inferior status and still might need protection from prejudice. Regardless of whether they are rich or poor, regardless of whether they come from a Caribbean capital or an Andean village, all of these people are categorized together under the label "Hispanic or Latino." This inevitably means that the process of assimilation for today's immigrants and their offspring will be very different than it was during the late 19th and early 20th century era of trans-Atlantic migration.

By law, the undocumented are prohibited from working, from receiving most public services and from ever seeking citizenship, yet they readily find employment, albeit in the lower reaches of the labor force, and are essentially free to live here as long as they like.

Prejudice in many forms certainly existed a hundred years ago, and many immigrants certainly suffered from it. One important response to this experience was to organize socially, politically and religiously, as national groups; that is as Italians, Irish, or Jews for example. Out of necessity, many of the European immigrant groups actually strengthened their ethnic bonds and identities in the first stages of the assimilation process because organizing as national groups was often the most effective way of getting established in this country.

The United States is, arguably, a more tolerant place today than it was a hundred years ago, and the mechanisms for asserting group identities are different, as well. Immigrants from Latin America still often organize themselves as national groups, but the host society offers them an alternative in the form of an Hispanic identity, which overarches national differences. Indeed, U.S. institutions and legal regulations formally recognize and favor group identity far more than national origins. For example, there are about 700,000 people of Guatemalan origin living in the U.S., according to the Census. That is a pretty small group, and one that does not enjoy any particular recognition. As a Hispanic or Latino, however, each of those individuals becomes part of a formally recognized minority group—and the nation's largest minority group, at that. Assertion of this iden-

tity, which does not exist in Guatemala, actually brings with it some stature and protection. The family of a recently arrived immigrant from Guatemala will have no connection to the experience of a Mexican-American who lived in South Texas in the 1950s, but their process of assimilation to this country will be highly conditioned by the great social changes put in place because of those Latinos who played a small part in the civil rights era. As a result, the trajectory from Guatemala to America now leads through this peculiar condition that we, as a society, label as Hispanic or Latino. Assimilation has never been simple or direct, but today, the avenues by which old identities fade and new ones are developed seem particularly complex, fluid and varied.

It may be tempting at times to expect, or hope, that Latinos at the beginning of the 21st century will follow the same pathways as European immigrants did at the beginning of the 20th. But the circumstances surrounding the two groups are hugely different and, as time goes on, those differences are only likely to grow.

During most of the last great era of immigration, the United States operated something very close to an open-door policy for those who came across the Atlantic. Asians were systematically excluded on racial grounds, but the only Europeans denied entry were those judged to be carrying disease or likely to become public charges. Although many thousands were quarantined and sent home from Ellis Island, those allowed to land were, in time—though sometimes after much turmoil—enfolded into the nation's civic life. All had the right to seek citizenship, eventually. Today, the United States, however unintentionally, operates a two-tier immigration system. Some are allowed into the country legally, with a well-defined set of rights and obligations and most are granted the right to remain permanently and become citizens after a number of years. Many others, however, enter the country illegally. Despite laws and enforcement efforts to the contrary, their presence is tolerated, at least tacitly. Evidence of this fact is that best estimates suggest the population of unauthorized immigrants has grown to more than 11 million people, and that once beyond the border region, they face little risk of apprehension. By law, the undocumented are prohibited from working, from receiving most public services and from ever seeking citizenship, yet they readily find employment, albeit in the lower reaches of the labor force, and are essentially free to live here as long as they like.

By any measure, this is a sizeable population and arguably, the only one that is now systematically excluded from full participation in society. There are now more illegal migrants living in the United States than there were blacks living under Jim Crow in the states of the old Confederacy at the time of the *Brown v. Board of Education* decision in 1954—and this cohort represents a sizeable portion of the Hispanic population. About one-out-of-every-five Latinos is undocumented, including about one-half of all foreign-born Hispanics. Nearly one-out-of-every-three Latinos lives in a family with at least one undocumented relative. And, for the past several years, the number of unauthorized immigrants has exceeded the legal flow. Thus, illegality has become one of the defining characteristics of the Latino population.

While it would be easy to overstate the potential leverage represented by the size of the Latino population, their numbers—and standing as America's largest minority group—are already too big to ignore.

Though drastically different than the kind of discrimination suffered by African Americans or Mexican Americans prior to the civil rights era, because it is a status that is chosen rather than imposed, being undocumented is a marker of exclusion and marginalization. It is the basis for an identity as a people apart. No matter to what extent an illegal immigrant learns English and adopts American ways, he or she faces an insuperable barrier to full inclusion and participation in American society. And then again—though it may seem an unlikely prospect—a single act of Congress could simply erase that barrier.

The New Dividing Lines

Immigration status is a new boundary line, one that confronts Latinos like no other group and that is likely, over time, to condition the ways that newcomers are incorporated into American society, or not. But at the same time, the "old" boundary lines of race and ethnicity are also undergoing change because the United States is a fundamentally different place than when either African Americans or the immigrants of the trans-Atlantic era were forming group identities. In both those cases, there was a dividing line drawn sharply through American society. On one side sat a white majority that set societal, political and cultural norms, and those norms were overwhelmingly Anglo-Saxon, Christian and male. Now, women, blacks, Jews and all kinds of other folks are involved in defining American norms, there are several different kinds of dividing lines and they are blurry in places and sometimes even zigzag. Immigrants today, like immigrants before, are busy absorbing American ways; the difference is that nowadays there are many more ways to be an American, many more accepted flavors and variations. The Latino immigrant influx arrived as the United States was in the process of establishing a more diverse vision of itself. The process seems irreversible but is not finished, nor is it fully codified or digested. Latino immigrants and their offspring are adapting to a United States that is already immersed in a process of transformation that may be further impacted by the Latino immigrants themselves. This is a demographic coincidence that may well be of profound historical impact.

For example, in the 1970s, as the Baby Boomers became adults, they put off having children; many never did and many had just one or two. In the same decade, as noted earlier, the influx of immigrants from Latin America, especially Mexico, began to grow. These two trends, entirely unrelated in their origins, gathered momentum across decades and produced effects that continue to reverberate throughout American society: the first created a dearth of people while the second resulted in an abundance. Without this confluence—meaning, absent Hispanic immigration and high fertility rates—the United States might

well begin to resemble nations such as Italy or Japan, which have quickly aging populations that are also shrinking in size. When the Boomers retire, Hispanics will be there to fill out the workforce. Thus, the significance of Latino population growth has to be measured not just by the sheer size of their numbers but against what is happening with the rest of the population.

While Latinos make up 14 percent of the total population, they account for 21 percent of all children under the age of 10. Look at another key segment of the population: young adults. Between 2000 and 2005, the number of non-Hispanic whites between the ages of 20 and 35 declined by nearly 800,000. Meanwhile, the number of Latinos in that age range increased by more than 1.7 million. The Latino population is not only growing fast, it is accelerating while the rest of the population is getting older and hardly growing at all. That context enormously leverages the significance of the Hispanic numbers. The fact that Latinos are the only population in the United States that can be cited as fast growing not only defines their size but also helps to highlight their place in American society, bestowing a particular degree of status, as well.

While it would be easy to overstate the potential leverage represented by the size of the Latino population, their numbers—and standing as America's largest minority group—are already too big to ignore. Employers, marketers and politicians increasingly seek out Latinos as workers, consumers and voters. This attention may be self-serving, but it is attention nonetheless, and probably ripe for future spin. Latinos are the rare group whose position in society is defined less by who they have been than by who they will become.

In the public policy arena, the size and projected growth of the Hispanic population has already had a notable impact. The banking industry, for example, was so concerned about keeping immigrant Latinos as a potential source of new consumers that it successfully lobbied the Bush Administration to block Congressional efforts to keep undocumented immigrants from opening bank accounts. Indeed, concerns over the future political clout of the Hispanic population have acted as a brake on a variety of efforts to adopt restrictive immigration policies. And, when the Supreme Court decided in 2004 to preserve affirmative action in university admissions, one of the rationales was the growing size of the minority population in the coming years. This perception of demographic significance is not going to resolve all of the hardships or remove all of the barriers faced by Latinos but it is widespread enough in the majority society that the position of Latinos today is more positive than that of blacks in the 1970s or Italians, for example, in the 1920s. Group identities are powerfully shaped by the majority, and in this case, demography is a critical factor. Moreover, Latinos themselves absorb some of this sentiment, generating a feeling of demographic pride, even demographic triumphalism, at times.

The picture I've tried to paint in this essay is not one of a racial minority group cordoned off from the rest of society. Nor is it the picture of an immigrant ethnic group at the gates waiting for admission into a society that will absorb it and wash away its differences. As I noted earlier, this phenomenon is something different than we have seen before. Latino/Hispanics comprise a group with an identity that sets them apart, but not permanently. The boundaries that define the group are shifting and they are permeable, which is characteristic of a society that values homogeneity of purpose but also embraces cultural, religious and ethnic diversity. Still, the societal contradictions faced by Latinos abound: for example, they intermarry with a freedom unimaginable for blacks fifty years ago, one signal of the ongoing assimilation process, and yet, at the same time, a large Latino cohort—the undocumented—live in the shadow of the law. It is unlikely that this range of experiences will narrow any time soon.

So what conclusions can we reach after considering the many factors impacting the lives that Latinos/Hispanics live in the U.S. today? Surely at least one thing is clear: the Latino/Hispanic identity is one that allows for multiple and varied expressions. Latinos have arrived on the scene as American notions of identity continue to evolve and they have brought with them the kind of identities that may be well suited to the moment. The result, the combination of the two—a nation with less rigid boundaries and a people with a more fluid identity—will undoubtedly change both the host society and the newcomers. In the past, the United States has tended to either reinforce group differences or negate them, but now it seems headed into a future where it will do neither. Instead, the prospects are for a society that sometimes embraces, even celebrates, some aspects of group identities while at the same time fuses people of different sorts together in pursuit of common purposes and goals. It is an uncertain and potentially confusing prospect—but promising, as well—and one that has only just begun to unfold.

Now, which is it, "Latino" or "Hispanic?" The answer is that "Hispanic" is the preferred choice of about a third of the group and is most popular in Texas and Florida. "Latino" is preferred by a bit more than a tenth, mostly in California and New York. But the majority has no preference and will use both. How could it be otherwise in 21st century America?

ROBERTO SURO is director of the Pew Hispanic Center, a Washington, D.C.-based research organization. The Center was founded in July 2001 with support from the Pew Charitable Trusts. A former journalist, Suro has 30 years of experience writing on Hispanic issues and immigration. He is author of *Strangers Among Us: Latino Lives in a Changing America,* (Vintage) as well as numerous reports, articles and other publications about the growth of the Latino population. During his career in journalism Suro worked for *TIME* Magazine, *The New York Times, The Washington Post* and other publications.

From *Carnegie Reporter,* Spring 2006, pp. 22–31. Copyright © 2006 by Carnegie Corporation of New York. Reprinted by permission. www.carnegie.org

Making Connections with the Past

(Un)Masking African American history at a neighborhood community center

Gary Stiler and Lisa Allen

Introduction

As educators, we generally focus on promising practices that emerge from traditional classroom settings. Remediation, derived from scientifically-based research, is typically viewed as a treatment to be applied in public school settings in order to improve academic achievement.

But are we overlooking other sources of creative and compelling curricula, forms of data, and inspirational pedagogy? Are we ignoring community-based initiatives and successful strategies used in non-traditional settings? Do community centers and neighborhood day care programs have anything to teach us about improving the academic achievement of all students?

This article describes one such setting and program that has much to offer. Our work at the Carver Community Center demonstrates that non-traditional community organizations also ascribe to high academic standards and use curricula in ways that enhance self esteem and promote academic achievement.

Overview

The Carver Community Center in Evansville, Indiana, uses an academic enrichment program to support neighborhood students. The curriculum involves children in learning about African-American literary traditions and folk art. The Center's work is based on the premise that African-American children need to encounter the reality of history as in integral part of the curriculum; not as a superficial add-on.

During the after-school program described here, students constructed replicas of indigenous art from inexpensive and commonly found materials. The ecology of learning during this 3-month activity was rich in music, storytelling, and creativity. Elementary students participated in informal pre- and post-activity discussions that indicated an increased level of awareness about African-American history.

It is our intent to describe the setting in which this project occurred, an overview of supporting literature, the method and materials used to engage K–6 students in the process of discovery, and an illustration of the effects of this project on participant learning.

The Setting

The Carver Center is located in an African-American neighborhood in downtown Evansville. It has a 30 year tradition of serving a segregated, low income, intergenerational community. The Center provides an early childhood program, a K–12 after-school enrichment program, and serves a vibrant senior citizen component.

The after-school program serves approximately 60 neighborhood children each day, primarily as an after-school alternative. Ninety percent of the families served fall below the 30th percentile in income. Ninety-two percent of the children served at the Center come from single parent households.

While programs stress academic enrichment activities, the Center also offers an afternoon meal, content-area tutoring, homework assistance, and drug, alcohol, and tobacco awareness programs. The staff works with elementary, middle school, and high school students on music, science, computer, and art projects. Enrichment activities generally focus on language arts, social studies, and math and science, but in the fall of each year an Afrocentric curriculum involves students in the construction of exhibits for the Children's African-American History Museum.

The Children's Museum began 5 years ago as an alternative to the more traditional, and adult-oriented African-American Museum several blocks away. Since then, the after-school program has involved children in the design and construction of exhibits. The annual process begins as staff chooses an annual theme, and the children begin learning about and working on exhibits.

These activities begin early in the fall semester prior to the opening of the Museum in February during Black History Month. Past themes have included African Americans in Sports, Music, Art and Literature. The 2004 Museum theme was "A Timeline of African-American History."

In subsequent sections of this article we describe how K–6 children, in the after-school enrichment program, designed and constructed exhibit materials for the 2004 edition of the Museum. Our intent is to illustrate one example of an Afrocentric curriculum and describe its effect on participant awareness of African-American history. The objective here is to describe an example of our work at the Carver Center, and to illustrate the challenges and successes associated with teaching about American History from a perspective that has been neglected and marginalized in mainstream curricula.

The Case for Afrocentric Curricula

The effects of traditional instructional materials and the media have served to increase awareness among educators about the need for a discerning, Afrocentric curriculum that acknowledges racial identity and the interplay of historical perspectives. Banks (2001) laid the foundation for transformative curriculum change. He described four approaches to the creation of multicultural curricula. Bank's model ranges from the standard contributions and additive approaches, to those seeking to truly transformative curricula.

The development of racial identity among young African-American children has much to do with how minorities are depicted in the media. In this regard, Hooks (1996), Bogle (2001) and Entman and Rojecki (2001) describe the effects of media misrepresentation upon society and upon the perceptions of individuals. Tatum (2003) and Beachum and McCray (2004) discuss the negative effects of popular media on racial identity.

These indications promote a need to pre-empt the effects of media driven imagery with media literacy education. Such approaches would stress the interpretation of media messages rather than passive reception. Entman and Rojecki (2004) assert the need for educators to promote the development of racial identity and positive values. One approach to this recommendation is to use an Afrocentric curriculum that raises important questions about American history that are unlikely to be discussed at any depth in a traditional classroom setting.

Much of the support for Afrocentric curricula lies in research relating to identity development. Dubois (1903) first articulated the dual nature of Blacks in America and the inherent psychological confusion caused by conflicting identities. Cross and Fhagen-Smith (2001), and Tatum (2003) suggested that the emerging self-images of African-American children are saturated with racial stereotypes and media images that promote negative self-esteem. Asante (1991) asserted that the frame of reference inherent in standard curricula needs to be shifted, in order to more fully represent other perspectives. According to Asante, such a shift will promote self-esteem and the development of positive identities among African American children.

Gay (2000) stressed the power of culturally responsive curricula. She identified the essential characteristics of curricula as validating, comprehensive, multidimensional, empowering, transformative, and emancipatory. Smith, Atkins, and Connell (2003) suggested that increased levels of academic achievement may be indicated by enhanced racial-ethnic pride in the context of a supportive family, school, and community environment. In terms of application, Hudson, Stratton, Thomas, and Vukson (2004) cited examples of culturally responsive Afrocentric curricula. These curricula have had a positive effect on students in those critical areas of self-esteem and academic performance (Pollard & Ajirotutu, 2000; Potts, 2003; Watson & Smitherman, 1997).

Learning about African-American History at the Carver Center

As an early childhood specialist at the Carver Center, Lisa Allen understands what the literature implies, and recognized that her students needed to know more about their heritage. She has a strong belief that theory needs to be applied in the classroom in order to achieve desirable and measurable outcomes.

Lisa explains that she can see the effects of greater awareness about origins and culture in her students. She says that she knows that it is beneficial for them to explore their African traditions and to talk about slavery, life as a slave, and escape. She also relates that, "in knowing about their ancestry, my students can better understand prejudice and the Civil Rights Movement." She believes that teaching about African-American history is a very important part of her job.

In an effort to promote this form of culturally responsive pedagogy, Ms. Allen and her staff developed an annual curriculum on African-American history. Each year, they select a different theme for the fall semester. The curriculum unit lasts for approximately three months and annually involves from 20 to 50, kindergarten through 6th grade students. Their goal is to prepare students for Black History Month and to involve them in the design and assembly of exhibits and displays for the Children's African-American History Museum at the Carver Center.

As After-School Program Leader, Ms. Allen's intent is to offer opportunities through which her students can explore the deeper connections between past and present. She utilizes an interdisciplinary strategy that integrates history, art, mathematics, language arts, and science.

Her intent during the 2004 project cycle was to make connections among the artistic traditions of Africa—from the deep south of the eighteenth century, through the eras of reconstruction and segregation. She used storytelling, music, and multimedia art as her medium of instruction. Her planned outcome was to engage her K–6 students in the reconstruction of indigenous African and African-American artifacts. These included masks, necklaces, effigies, dwellings, quilts, and printed fabrics.

Storytelling and Dialogue

Beginning with the premise that a deeper appreciation of cultural artifacts may be discovered through dialogue, Ms. Allen lead her students through daily discussions about African-American history and the artistic, symbolic, and religious nature of artifacts that the students would make. The beginning of each session would be prompted by Ms. Allen as she assumed her role as storyteller. The students would gather around Ms. Allen as she began her story. She used selections from *The River Jordan* (Burke & Croy, 1999), *Hidden in Plain View* (Tobin & Dobard, 2000), *The Watsons go to Birmingham* (Curtis, 1995), *Sojourner Truth* (McKissack & McKissack, 1992), *One More River to Cross* (Haskins, 1992), *Underground Railroad* (National Park

Service, 1998), *Escape to Freedom* (Davis, 1989), *Lyle Station, Indiana: Yesterday and Today* (Evansville Office of Development, 1984), *Lest We Forget* (Maia, 1997), and stories from *The Riverside Anthology of the African American Literary Tradition* (Hill, 1997).

Under the backdrop of traditional African music, Ms. Allen read to her students, asked them questions, and recorded their answers on poster paper. The posters were retained and used to help students recall important discussions during the course of the project. As a storyteller, Ms. Allen made a conscious attempt to integrate themes that stressed the importance of community, scholarship, and continuity.

Reconstructing African-American Artifacts

The children worked to assemble artifacts connected to the stories they heard and talked about. They made paper maché masks, yarn effigies, fiber dwellings, glass necklaces, or cotton quilts. As the children prepared to begin assembling artifacts, they were assigned to groups and given instructions on how to design and assemble a specific artifact. They were permitted to visit other groups to learn what each was making, but returned to their own work group to complete the assigned artifact.

Children were guided through the construction phase of the project by adult leaders. Photographs and drawings were used as examples of finished artifacts, but variations were permitted and encouraged. Adults intervened, as needed, when construction tasks exceeded the abilities of the children.

Assessment: Building Artifacts and Building Knowledge

Ms. Allen often referred to the project's overarching objectives in discussions with students. During the three-month project period, she used formal question and answer sessions to consolidate learning and to answer emerging questions. Ms. Allen reiterated key objectives and probed for deeper awareness among the children about the following overarching questions:

Why is it important to know Black history?
What can we do to learn more about Black history?
How can the study of Black history be extended beyond Black History Month?

Eighteen (18) students participated in the initial discussion regarding the meaning of African-American history. Children's' responses to these questions varied. However, they generally indicated limited awareness about African-American history and a lack of fluency regarding specific details. Answers also included higher level responses from several children that indicated varying degrees of prior knowledge.

Ms. Allen explained that the students who responded with more knowledgeable answers, were children who had been at the center for several years and who had previously participated in the project. The newcomers, she said, generally knew very little about African American history.

As the project ended, 14 students of the original 18 participated in the post-exposure question and answer session. Students were asked the question that began their project orientation early in the fall semester—*What is Black History*? Their responses indicated an increased awareness about the nature of African-American history and a greater fluency with regard to details and context. Table 1 illustrates a comparison of children's conceptions about African-American history before and after participating in the three-month project.

During the post-exposure debriefing session, students were able to name key figures and engage in peer-to-peer discussions about the meaning of the masks, effigies, fabric design, and jewelry. Student responses illustrated an awareness of and familiarity with individuals involved in the civil rights movement. They also offered more knowledgeable descriptions about civil rights and African-American history. Examples of student responses during the final discussion include the following responses to the question "What is Black History?":

> People like Martin Luther King Jr. and Harriet Tubman who try to help people get out of slavery and they couldn't do anything about it. (Taryn , 4th grade)

> Black History Month is . . . when Black people start to think about African Americans and what they did for us in the past. (Jwan, 5th grade)

> Black history was a point in time when millions of people were taken from their families and put into a ship and stacked on top of each other. The people sailed on a ship for a long time until they reached America. Dead bodies were thrown into the ocean and sharks would swim by the ship. No one knows how many people were thrown overboard. The slaves were sold for money in the new world on plantations and worked really hard. Harriett Tubman and others escaped on the underground railway. (Joi, 4th grade)

Throughout the unit, student ideas and their emerging opinions were noted with affirmation by the staff of the Carver Center. The children's imaginative ideas and adaptations to the artifacts were welcomed. The children made up stories about African families and how they lived as they constructed models of dwellings from raffia and styrofoam bowls. While assembling the artifacts, they speculated about what it was like to be captured and transported across the ocean in ships.

They also talked about the South, what it was like to be a slave, and the conditions that slaves lived in. They generated ideas about how to escape from slavery and what it must have been like to cross the Ohio River. They talked about how to locate safe-houses for escaped slaves from messages that were woven into quilts.

Discovering Words and Interpreting Meanings

During the course of the project the staff discovered that their use of terminology warranted examination. Ms. Allen and her staff discussed their unconscious acceptance of words used to describe items that the children learned about and assembled.

Table 1 Comparison of Student Responses to "What is Black History?" Pre-Exposure and Post-Exposure to an African-American History Unit

Pre-Exposure (n = 18)		Post-Exposure (n = 14)	
Charles—K	Black forest	Charles—K	When Black people get to think what they didn't think before
Jadrain—K	Black people	Jadrain—K	Slavery
Jonathan—1st grade	Black animals	Jonathan—1st grade	When Black people celebrate Black history
Issiah—1st grade	When white people got into the apartments and buildings and black people had to stay offbuses and all that kind of the stuff like Martin Luther King changed all the rules	Issiah—1st grade	The other Black people visited other people
Malik—2nd grade	Black cat	Malik—2nd grade	Black enemies
Corliss—4th grade	When people get to celebrate the people that died, like slaves	Corliss—4th grade	When we talk about slavery in the past and thankful we don't have slavery anymore
Marcus—5th grade	When Black history came like all the Black people come together and celebrate	Marcus—5th grade	Martin Luther King and Harriet Tubman thought of the underground railway and Rosa Parks didn't give up her seat—King tried to let freedom ring

Specifically, the words *hut* and *doll* were examined with regard to their denigrating connotations.

In reconstructing traditional West African dwellings, it became apparent that traditional structures were much more than mere grass huts. They exemplified a type of architecture that perfectly suited the unique environmental conditions of sub-Sahara Africa.

The use of the word *doll* was also examined. The yarn figures that children made had important symbolic and religious meanings that were trivialized by referring to them as ordinary dolls. Consequently, Ms. Allen used the word *effigies* to describe these important figures; her staff decided that the terms *dwellings* or *houses* appropriately describes traditional architecture.

These discussions and realizations had a transformative effect upon the adult participants. Conversations indicated they realized a need to more closely examine the words they used for hidden connotations about subordination and stereotypes. Through their discussions they gained insight into how value-laden words can be used to trivialize the accomplishments of oppressed minorities.

Ms. Allen related that she had not previously thought about the impact certain words have upon children's images of African American history. As a result of this heightened awareness, she said that she now selects stories and words with a higher degree of sensitivity.

Implications and Conclusions

The use of Afrocentric traditions as classroom exercises has implications beyond the commonplace foods, fun and festivals approach described by Ladson-Billings (1994). This proj-

ect gave both participants and staff insight into elements of African American history that they had not previously encountered. It served to move curricula used at the Carver Center beyond what Banks (1999) described as the additive or contributions approach to multicultural education. In effect, the dialogue, storytelling and construction of artifacts had a transformative effect upon both staff and K–6 participants.

Anecdotal evidence suggests that the curriculum had academic impacts beyond the Carver Center. Program Director Lisa Allen related conversations with several parents, as well as with teachers from neighborhood elementary schools. She related conversations with parents where they described their child's increased interest and ability to talk about African-American traditions at home. She also reported that several teachers related incidents where students from the Carver Center were able to enhance classroom discussions with their knowledge about Africa and African-American traditions and history.

The study of African-American traditions and artifacts at the Carver Center was embedded in context. The curriculum exposed children to academic instruction in the form of multimedia presentations that incorporated traditional African stories, music, African-American storytelling, and hands-on assembly for an extended period of time. In effect, students were immersed in an Afrocentric curriculum at the Carver Center, rather than merely being exposed to one.

The former experience, as described by Banks (1999), is characterized by the study of ethnic contributions as an extension of the standard curriculum and does not immerse students in the same intensity of study. In the case presented here, evidence of the effect of immersion over an extended period of time indicates that K–6 participants were able to interpret events and artifacts in a way that engendered a deeper level of respect for and understanding of their cultural heritage

Ms. Allen relates that she believes that her students see themselves in the stories that she tells them. She relates that they see the many choices that they now have, as compared to those few choices that their ancestors had. She says that they now listen to traditional African music and know much more about what was happening as the drums beat.

References

Asante, M. (1991). The afrocentric idea in education. *Journal of Negro Education, 60*(2), 170–180.

Banks, J. A. (1999). *An introduction to multicultural education* (2nd ed.). Boston: Allyn and Bacon.

Banks, J. A. (2001). *Cultural diversity and education: Foundations, curriculum, and teaching.* Boston: Allyn & Bacon.

Beachum, F. D., & McCray, C. R. (2004, September 14).Cultural collision in urban schools. *Current Issues in Education, 7*(5). Retrieved May 27, 2005, from http://cie.ed.asu.edu/volume7/number5/

Bogle, D. (2001). *Toms, coons, mulattoes, mammies & bucks: An interpretive history of blacks in american films* (4th ed.). New York: Continuum.

Burke, H. R. & Croy, D. (1999). *The river Jordan.* Marietta, OH: Watershed Books.

Cross, W., & Fhagen-Smith, P. (2001). Patterns of African-American identity development: A life-span perspective. In C. Wijeyesinghe & B. Jackson, III (Eds)., *New perspectives on racial identity development:A theoretical and practical anthology* (pp. 243–270). New York: New York University Press

Curtis, C. P. (1995). *The watsonsgo to birmingham.* New York: Delacorte Press.

Davis, O. (1989).*Escape to freedom.* New York: Viking Press.

DuBois, W.E.B. (1903). *The souls of black folk.* Boston: Bedford/St. Martin's.

Entman, R. & Rojecki, A. (2000) The black image in the white mind: Media and race in America. Chicago: University of Chicago Press.

Evansville Office of Development (1984). *Lyle station, Indiana: Yesterday and today.* Evansville, IN: Office of Development, Indiana State University-Evansville.

Gay, G. (2000). *Culturally responsive teaching: Theory, research, and practice.* New York: Teachers College Press.

Haskins, J. (1992).*One more river to cross.* New York: Scholastic.

Hill, P. L. (Ed.) (1997). *The riverside anthology of the African American literary tradition.* Boston: Houghton Mifflin

Hooks, B. (1996). *Reel to real: Race, sex and class at the movies.* London, UK: Routledge.

Hudson, D., Stratton, L., Thomas, D., & Vukson B. (2004). *Fostering growth and strengthening assets: School based violence prevention programs in African-American communities.* Retrieved November 22, 2004, from http://www.sph.umich.edu/jvpc/training/injury/studentpresentations/A-C%20schools.pdf

Ladson-Billings, G. (1994). Educating for diversity: What we can learn from multicultural education research. *Educational Leadership, 51*(8)22–27.

Maia, V. T. (1997). *Lest We Forget: The passage from Africa to slavery and emancipation.* New York: Crown.

McKissack, P. and McKissack, F. (1992). *Sojourner truth: A voice for freedom.* New York: Scholastic.

National Park Service (1998). *Underground railroad.* Official National Park Handbook, No. 156, Division of Publications, Washington, DC: U.S. Department of the Interior.

Potts, R. G. (2003). Emancipatory education versus school-based prevention in African-American communities. *American Journal of Community Psychology, 31*(1/2), 173–83.

Pollard, D. & Ajirotutu, C. (2000). *African-centered schooling in theory and practice.* Westport, CT: Bergin & Garvey.

Smith, E. P., Atkins, J., & Connell, C. M. (2003). Family, school, and community factors and relationships to racial-ethnic attitudes and academic achievement. *American Journal of Community Psychology, 32*(1/2), 159.

Tatum, B. D. (2003). *Why are all the black kids sitting together in the cafeteria?: and other conversations about race.* New York: Basic Books.

Tobin, J. L. & Dobard, R. G. (2000). *Hidden in plain view.* New York: Anchor Books.

Watson, C. & Smitherman, G. (1997). *Educating African-American males: Detroit's Malcolm X Academy solution.* Chicago: Third World Press.

GARY STILER is an assistant professor in the School of Education at the University of Redlands, Redlands, California, and **LISA ALLEN** is the program director at the Carver Community Center, Evansville, Indiana.

Affirming Identity in Multilingual Classrooms

By welcoming a student's home language into the classroom, schools actively engage English language learners in literacy.

JIM CUMMINS, VICKI BISMILLA, PATRICIA CHOW, SARAH COHEN, FRANCES GIAMPAPA, LISA LEONI, PERMINDER SANDHU, AND PADMA SASTRI

In *How People Learn,* Bransford, Brown, and Cocking (2000) synthesized research regarding the optimal conditions that foster learning; a follow-up volume edited by Donovan and Bransford (2005) examines the application of these learning principles to teaching history, mathematics, and science. Bransford and colleagues emphasize the following three conditions for effective learning: engaging prior understandings and background knowledge, integrating factual knowledge with conceptual frameworks by encouraging deep understanding, and supporting students in taking active control over the learning process.

Any instructional intervention that claims scientific credibility should reflect these principles, which are particularly important when it comes to English language learners. Prior knowledge refers not only to information or skills previously acquired in formal instruction but also to the totality of the experiences that have shaped the learner's identity and cognitive functioning. In classrooms with students from linguistically diverse backgrounds, instruction should explicitly activate this knowledge.

Knowledge is more than just the ability to remember. Deeper levels of understanding enable students to transfer knowledge from one context to another. Moreover, when students take ownership of their learning—when they invest their identities in learning outcomes—active learning takes place. Numerous research studies have shown that scripted, transmission-oriented pedagogy, which tends to be both superficial and passive, fails to build on English language learners' pre-existing cultural and linguistic knowledge (Warschauer, Knobel, & Stone, 2004).

Pre-existing knowledge for English language learners is encoded in their home languages. Consequently, educators should explicitly teach in a way that fosters transfer of concepts and skills from the student's home language to English. Research clearly shows the potential for this kind of cross-language transfer in school contexts that support biliteracy development (Cummins, 2001; Reyes, 2001). It is hard to argue that we are teaching the whole child when school policy dictates that students leave their language and culture at the schoolhouse door.

It is hard to argue that we are teaching the whole child when school policy dictates that students leave their language and culture at the schoolhouse door.

Embracing Differences

Sidra's experiences as an English language learner illustrate some of these concerns. Two years after she emigrated from Pakistan with her family, she described her early days as a 5th grader in a Canadian school:

> I was new, and I didn't know English. I could only say little sentences. I wore cultural clothes, and people usually judge a new person by their looks. If they see the clothes that I am wearing are not like their clothes, they will just think that I'm not one of them. If we had any partner activities, no one will pick me as their partner. I felt really, really left out. Kids also made fun of me because I looked different, and I couldn't speak English properly.

Sidra highlights themes that are notably absent from the "scientifically proven" prescriptions of No Child Left Behind (NCLB). She talks about the struggle to express herself, not just linguistically, but also culturally. Her "cultural clothes" are an expression of an identity that her peers have rejected, causing her to feel "really, really left out." But Sidra also had caring teachers who welcomed her into school. As she explained,

> I was the only person in grade 5 who wore cultural clothes. The teachers liked what I wore. They tried to talk to me

and ask me questions. I liked telling teachers about my culture and religion. It made me feel more comfortable and welcome.

Sidra's experiences show that human relationships are important in children's adjustment to schooling; engagement in learning, particularly for English language learners, is fueled as much by affect as by cognition. Despite her still-limited access to academic English, she writes extensively because she has a lot to share, and she knows that her teacher, Lisa Leoni, is genuinely interested in her experiences and insights. Sidra's account also illustrates the opportunity—and the responsibility—that teachers have to create environments that affirm the identities of English language learners, thereby increasing the confidence with which these students engage in language and literacy activities.

One Size Does Not Fit All

Affect, identity, respect, and human relationships: These constructs have not been evident in the radical education reforms ushered in by NCLB, which supposedly are based on scientific research. Numerous commentators have critiqued the scientific basis and instructional consequences of these policies (Allington, 2004; Garan, 2001; Krashen, 2004). Several false assumptions underlying these reforms apply specifically to English language learners:

- Students' home language is, at best, irrelevant. At worst, it is an impediment to literacy development and academic success.
- The cultural knowledge and linguistic abilities that English language learners bring to school have little instructional relevance.
- Instruction to develop English literacy should focus only on English literacy.
- Students can learn only what teachers explicitly teach.
- Culturally and linguistically diverse parents, whose English may be limited, do not have the language skills to contribute to their children's literacy development.

These assumptions, common before NCLB, have now become entrenched as a result of the ubiquity of high-stakes testing and the mandate for systematic and explicit phonics instruction from kindergarten through 6th grade (Lyon & Chhabra, 2004). Yet they violate the scientific consensus about how people learn (Bransford et al., 2000). They also reduce the opportunities for literacy engagement within the classroom (Guthrie, 2004). Finally, they are refuted by empirical data on literacy development among English language learners, which show that students' home language proficiency at time of arrival in an English-speaking country is the strongest predictor of English academic development (Thomas & Collier, 2002).

We present an alternative set of principles for promoting academic engagement among English language learners, which we draw from Early and colleagues' research project in Canada (2002). Central to our argument are two interrelated propositions:

- English language learners' cultural knowledge and language abilities in their home language are important resources in enabling academic engagement; and

- English language learners will engage academically to the extent that instruction affirms their identities and enables them to invest their identities in learning.

The Dual Language Identity Text

Teaching for cross-language transfer and literacy engagement can be problematic for teachers when multiple languages are represented in the classroom, none of which the teacher may know. One approach that we have been exploring in several schools in Canada's Greater Toronto area involves *identity texts*. These products, which can be written, spoken, visual, musical, dramatic, or multimodal combinations, are positive statements that students make about themselves.

Identity texts differ from more standard school assignments in both the process and the product. The assignment is cognitively challenging, but students can choose their topics. They decide how they will carry out the project and are encouraged to use the full repertoire of their talents in doing so.

For example, when she was in 7th grade—and less than a year after arriving in Canada—Madiha coauthored a 20-page English-Urdu dual language book titled *The New Country*. Together with her friends, Kanta and Sulmana, also originally from Pakistan, she wrote about "how hard it was to leave our country and come to a new country." Kanta and Sulmana were reasonably fluent in English because they had arrived in Toronto several years before, in 4th grade. Madiha, however, was in the early stages of English language acquisition.

The students collaborated on this project in the context of a unit on migration that integrated social studies, language, and ESL curriculum expectations. They researched and wrote the story over the course of several weeks, sharing their experiences and language skills. Madiha spoke little English but was fluent in Urdu; Sulmana was fluent and literate in both Urdu and English; Kanta, who was fluent in Punjabi and English, had mostly learned Urdu in Toronto. The girls discussed their ideas primarily in Urdu but wrote the initial draft of their story in English. Sulmana served as scribe for both languages.

In a "normal" classroom, Madiha's minimal knowledge of English would have severely limited her ability to participate in a 7th grade social studies unit. She certainly would not have been in a position to communicate extensively in English about her experiences, ideas, and insights. When the social structure of the classroom changed in simple ways, however, Madiha could express herself in ways that few English language learners experience in school. Her home language, in which all her experience prior to immigration was encoded, became once again a tool for learning. She contributed her ideas and experiences to the story, participated in discussions about how to translate vocabulary and expressions from Urdu to English and from English to Urdu, and shared in the affirmation that all three students experienced when they published their story.

Students can create identity texts on any topic relevant to their lives or of interest to them. Sometimes teachers will suggest topics or ways of carrying out the project; in other cases, students will generate topics themselves and decide what form the projects will take. Because these projects require substantial time to complete, it is useful to aim for cross-curricular integration. That way, the project can meet standards in several different content areas. For example, students might research the social history of their communities through document analysis and interviews with community members. Such a project would integrate curricular standards in language arts, social studies, and technology.

Because students *want* to do the work in the first place, they generally treasure the product they have created and wish to share it with those they care about. This usually doesn't happen with worksheets, regardless of how accurately the student completes them. The worksheet has no life beyond its immediate function, whereas the identity text lives on for a considerable time, either in tangible form, as in a book, or as a digital text on the Web.

Language in the Classroom

Thornwood Public School, a K–5 school in the Peel District School Board in Toronto, Canada, pioneered the process of the dual language identity text (Chow & Cummins, 2003; Schecter & Cummins, 2003). As is common in many urban public schools in Canada, students in Thornwood speak more than 40 different home languages, with no one language dominating. Patricia Chow's 1st and 2nd grade students created stories initially in English, the language of school instruction, because most of the primary students had not yet learned to read or write in their home languages. Students illustrated their stories and then worked with various people—parents, older students literate in their home languages, or teachers who spoke their languages—to translate these stories into the students' home languages. The school created the Dual Language Showcase Web site (http://thornwood. peelschools.org/Dual) to enable students to share their bilingual stories over the Internet with parents, relatives, and friends, both in Canada and in the students' countries of origin. With identity texts, audience becomes a powerful source of validation for the student.

As the Thornwood Dual Language Showcase project has evolved, dual language books have become a potent tool to support the integration of newcomers and English language learners. Students write initial drafts of stories in whichever language they choose, usually in their stronger language. Thus, newcomer students can write in their home language and demonstrate not only their literacy skills but also their ideas and feelings, giving full play to their imaginations. The image of newcomer students, in both their own eyes and in the eyes of others, changes dramatically when these students express themselves in this way within the school curriculum.

When none of the teachers or class members speaks the language of a particular newcomer student, the school explores contacts with community members or board-employed community liaison personnel or involves older students from the same language background whose English is more fluent. High school students from various language backgrounds receive credit for their involvement as community service work. Consequently, dual language texts have become a catalyst for fruitful forms of school-community engagement.

At Floradale Public School, another highly multilingual school in the Peel District School Board, teacher-librarian Padma Sastri has integrated both student-created and commercial dual language books into all aspects of library functioning. She prominently displays student-created dual language books near the library entrance, welcomes parents into the library to read books to students in their native languages, and encourages students to check out dual language books to take home to read with their families.

When students gather around her for the day's lesson in the library, Sastri enlists students to read a given story out loud in English. She also encourages various students to retell the story afterward in their home language. Said one observer,

> I listen amazed as one by one the students retell the story in Urdu, Turkish, Vietnamese, Chinese, Gujerati, Tamil, Korean, and Arabic. The other students in the class appear to be equally entranced, although neither I nor they understand most of the languages being used. It is captivating to hear the same story repeated in different languages with new or sometimes the same gestures to express a change in action.

By welcoming a student's home language, schools facilitate the flow of knowledge, ideas, and feelings between home and school and across languages.

Elementary school teacher Perminder Sandhu integrated discussions about students' language and culture into the curriculum of her 4th grade class in Coppard Glen Public School of Toronto's York Region District School Board. Students wrote about their languages, discussed the importance of continuing to speak their languages, and worked in pairs to create dual language or multilingual books, often with the help of their parents. One of Sandhu's students writes about his engagement with literacy and popular culture outside the school. Jagdeep, who is fluent in Punjabi, Hindi, and English, illustrates the importance of connecting, both cognitively and affectively, with students' prior experience:

> I love Punjabi stories. They're so exciting. When it comes to Hindi movies, I just can't stop watching them! They are very funny, and the problems are very sophisticated. It makes me proud of my cultural background.

For Sandhu, acknowledging and actively promoting students' linguistic and cultural capital is not simply a matter of activating students' prior knowledge—she fuses these practices in a pedagogy of respect. Sandhu explains,

> It informs my practice through and through. It runs in the bloodstream of my classroom. It's all about relationships, how we validate students' identities, how they accept their own identities. That ethos is fundamentally important—it's not an add-on. It takes less than two extra minutes of my time to get students to see the humanity of another human being at a most basic level. Because once they begin to see their own and one another's vulnerabilities, inhibitions, and realities, they connect.

Aims of Education

The job of an educator is to teach students to see vitality in themselves.

—Joseph Campbell

The pedagogical orientation illustrated in the examples above differs from many schools' current policies and practice in two major respects. First, the teacher acknowledges that the language in which English language learners' prior experience is encoded is an important resource for learning. Consequently, instruction explicitly aims for transfer of knowledge and skills across languages. Second, instruction communicates respect for students' languages and cultures and encourages students to engage with literacy and invest their identities in the learning process.

The Heart of Schooling

Educators, individually and collectively, always have choices. They can choose to go beyond curricular guidelines and mandates. They can meet curricular expectations and standards in ways that acknowledge and respect students' prior knowledge. They can engage English language learners in powerful literacy practices, such as creating identity texts. Identity texts also encourage collaboration among teachers, parents, and students. By including parents in the process, these practices affirm the funds of knowledge available in the community.

When we talk about the *whole child,* let us not forget the *whole teacher.* The process of identity negotiation is reciprocal. As teachers open up identity options for students, they also define their own identities. The teachers who supported and appreciated Sidra in her struggles to express herself and belong in her new school were also expressing what being educators meant to them. They saw Sidra not as a "limited-English-proficient" student but as a young person with intelligence, emotions, aspirations, and talents. They created classrooms that enabled her to express her identity.

Although NCLB has reinforced the bleak pedagogical landscapes that exist in many urban school systems, it *has* reinserted the achievement of English language learners and low-income students into policy discussions. Schools cannot meet adequate yearly progress goals without improving these students' achievement. Schools can achieve this goal much more effectively when they take into account identity investment as a core component of learning.

Many teachers understand intuitively that human relationships are at the heart of schooling. Student achievement will increase significantly only when this insight permeates all levels of education policymaking.

References

Allington, R. L. (2004). Setting the record straight. *Educational Leadership, 61*(6), 22–25.

Bransford, J. D., Brown, A. L., & Cocking, R. R. (2000). *How people learn: Brain, mind, experience, and school.* Washington, DC: National Academy Press.

Chow, P., & Cummins, J. (2003). Valuing multilingual and multicultural approaches to learning. In S. R. Schecter & J. Cummins (Eds.), *Multilingual education in practice: Using diversity as a resource* (pp. 32–61). Portsmouth, NH: Heinemann.

Cummins, J. (2001). *Negotiating identities: Education for empowerment in a diverse society* (2nd ed.). Los Angeles: California Association for Bilingual Education.

Donovan, M. S., & Bransford, J. D. (Eds.). (2005). *How students learn: History, mathematics, and science in the classroom.* Washington, DC: National Academy Press.

Early, M., et al. (2002). *From literacy to multiliteracies: Designing learning environments for knowledge generation within the new economy.* Proposal funded by the Social Sciences and Humanities Research Council of Canada.

Garan, E. M. (2001). What does the report of the National Reading Panel really tell us about teaching phonics? *Language Arts, 79*(1), 61–70.

Guthrie, J. T. (2004). Teaching for literacy engagement. *Journal of Literacy Research, 36,* 1–30.

Krashen, S. D. (2004). False claims about literacy development. *Educational Leadership, 61*(6), 18–21.

Lyon, G. R., & Chhabra, V. (2004). The science of reading research. *Educational Leadership, 61*(6), 12–17.

Reyes, M. L. (2001). Unleashing possibilities: Biliteracy in the primary grades. In M. L. Reyes & J. Halcón (Eds.), *The best for our children: Critical perspectives on literacy for Latino students* (pp. 96–121). New York: Teachers College Press.

Schecter, S., & Cummins, J. (Eds.). (2003). *Multilingual education in practice: Using diversity as a resource.* Portsmouth, NH: Heinemann.

Thomas, W. P., & Collier, V. P. (2002). *A national study of school effectiveness for language minority students' long-term academic achievement.* Santa Cruz, CA: Center for Research on Education, Diversity and Excellence, University of California–Santa Cruz.

Warschauer, M., Knobel, M., & Stone, L. (2004). Technology and equity in schooling: Deconstructing the digital divide. *Educational Policy, 18*(4), 562–588.

JIM CUMMINS (jcummins@oise.utoronto.ca) is a Professor in the Department of Curriculum, Teaching, and Learning at the Ontario Institute of Studies in Education, University of Toronto (OISE/UofT). **FRANCES GIAMPAPA** is a Postdoctoral Fellow and **SARAH COHEN** is a PhD student in the Department of Curriculum, Teaching, and Learning at OISE/UofT. **VICKI BISMILLA** is the Superintendent of Equity and **LISA LEONI** and **PERMINDER SANDHU** are elementary school teachers in the York Region District School Board. **PATRICIA CHOW** and **PADMA SASTRI** are elementary school teachers in the Peel District School Board.

Authors' note—The research reported in this paper was carried out with funding (2002–2005) from the Social Sciences and Humanities Research Council of Canada. To view student and teacher work as well as relevant research, visit www.multiliteracies.ca.

Myths and Stereotypes about Native Americans

Most non-Indians don't know a great deal about the first peoples of the Americas, Mr. Fleming avers. But what's worse is that much of what they do "know" is wrong.

WALTER C. FLEMING

When it comes to Americans' knowledge about Native American[1] culture and history, one might say there are two types of people—those who know nothing about Natives and those who know less than that. That's not exactly true, but most Americans are not very familiar with the first peoples of the Americas. Though some might argue that it is wholly unnecessary to have any knowledge about Native peoples, most would probably agree that some exposure to Native perspectives is a good thing for students. And Americans probably believe that it is the responsibility of the public education system to provide that exposure.

Because many people have such a limited knowledge of Indians, we are, arguably, among the most misunderstood ethnic groups in the United States. Native Americans are also among the most isolated groups. Thus the knowledge that most people have about Indians does not come from direct experience. What people know is limited by their sources of information—and, unfortunately, much of the information about Indians is derived from popular culture.

Even in areas where the concentration of Native peoples is high—say, in the West—most people do not know very much about the history and culture of the first citizens of their region. Even if non-Indians are familiar with Indians, the impressions they have of Native people can be quite negative. In fact, in states like Montana, the expression "familiarity breeds contempt" is descriptive of the tensions between Native and non-Native people.

Stereotyping is a poor substitute for getting to know individuals at a more intimate, meaningful level. By relying on stereotypes to describe Native Americans, whites come to believe that Indians are drunks, get free money from the government, and are made wealthy from casino revenue. Or they may believe that Indians are at one with nature, deeply religious, and wise in the ways of spirituality.

I do not intend to dispel all of the stereotypes or address all of the many myths about Native peoples; instead, I'd like to offer my perspective on the most important considerations that teachers and others might keep in mind when assessing curriculum, developing lesson plans, or teaching Indian children. Many of these myths may seem ridiculous, even silly, but each one is encountered by Native people on an almost daily basis.

Myth 1. Native Americans prefer to be called Native Americans. One of the most significant conversations with students seems to be the most basic. The first question people often ask me, as a Native person, is, "What do you want to be called?" Often, this is asked in the interest of political correctness, but as often it is a sincere question. There are several choices—including "Native American," "American Indian," and "Native"—and good arguments for, or against, using any one of these.

"Native American" seems to be the preference in academic circles. In my own writing or lectures, I am accustomed to using "Native American" in reference to the first peoples of this country (although in conversation I'm more likely to use "American Indian" or "Indian"). I am unapologetic in my use of these terms and don't find it necessary to spend lots of time (save in this article) explaining to others why I do, or do not, use one term or another.

"American Indian" and the shortened version, "Indian," have long been the subject of debate. Some Natives point out that the term "Indian" is an unhappy legacy of Christopher Columbus' so-called discovery and that the term is, therefore, a legacy of the subsequent colonization of the lands of the Native peoples of the Americas.

In Canada, the term most widely used to describe aboriginal people is "Native." Again, as with "Native American," one can argue that we are all *natives* of our respective countries of affiliation.

This discussion does not have any resolution. We, as Native people, are quite schizophrenic about it ourselves. In my own case, I'm likely to use Native, Native American, Indian, and American Indian quite interchangeably, sometimes even in the same sentence.

But all of these terms have one thing in common. They imply that there is some meaning to be derived from the term of choice, whatever that might be. For example, the terms "American Indian jewelry" or "Native American religion" in reality do not convey much information about more than 500 cultural beliefs or practices. Does "European" suggest a common history, culture, or desire? Does "Asian" mean that all those rich traditions can be so easily described?

As much as possible, I try to use tribal names, when known. Thus Squanto and Massasoit were Wampanoag leaders, and Sitting Bull was Hunkpapa Lakota. Though they can be referred to as "Indian" leaders, common sense suggests that these individuals had little in common.

Educators speak often about "teachable moments." Perhaps the discussion about what terms to use in reference to Native peoples can be part of a wider discussion about identity in America. Certainly, there are common points about the use of terms like Hispanic, Asian Americans, African Americans, and so on that can be productive in trying to understand this creature called "American."

Myth 2. Indians get special privileges. One stereotype strongly held in Indian Country[2] by non-Indians is that Indians receive special privileges that other American citizens do not. The 7 June 2006 electronic edition of the *Findlay* (Ohio) *Courier* shared this editorial opinion:

It's long been apparent that the laws granting Native American tribes sovereign nation status were a huge mistake. Rather than improving the lives of native people, the laws have created a state of dependency in which the tribes are neither truly sovereign nor fully a part of the larger nation. They are essentially wards of the federal government. They receive some special privileges designed to advance their welfare or maintain their native culture, but for the most part, the laws have made dependent victims of people who should have been integrated into the larger culture.

The editorial concluded, "We've foolishly allowed the Native Americans special tribal privileges, which has benefited neither them nor the nation as a whole."[3]

The *Courier* editorial did not describe what those "special tribal privileges" might be. But from long experience, I can surmise that the writer meant education, medical care, and money, all for free. Moreover, many believe that Native peoples do not pay taxes.

The reality is more complicated, and these assertions are based upon half-truths. Suppose it is true that Natives receive financial support for education. According to recent data, 63% of all undergraduate students in the United States received financial aid in the form of scholarships, grants, subsidized loans, and work/study.[4] The majority of these students are, in fact, non-Indians. Yet no one claims that these non-Indian students are getting a "free education."

Native students qualify for these same sources of funding. They may receive scholarships from their tribes or, as low-income students, qualify for federal Pell Grants. Some states offer fee waivers to Native students, but they also offer similar waivers to medical students, war orphans, senior citizens, dependents of prisoners of war, National Merit Scholarship semifinalists, and so on. The public seems to accept the propriety of granting waivers to children of Vietnam veterans but calls Indian fee waivers "special privileges." It is understandable then that many Natives consider the protests about these so-called special privileges to be based on race.

Those who are concerned about "special privileges" do not understand the nature of the relationship between Native tribes and the American federal government. Tribes signed treaties with the federal government that grant certain rights in exchange for the cession of land. Therefore, many of these "privileges" are considered treaty obligations. In the many treaties that tribes signed with the federal government were provisions that the government would provide education and health care to the tribes in exchange for the millions of acres of tribal lands. So education and health care have been "bought and paid for" by Native ancestors.

Some tribal members are indeed exempt from some taxes. The reason is logical and legal. Federal reservations are not part of the states in which they reside. Therefore, some American Indians who live and work on a reservation do not pay state taxes. But they pay other taxes, such as federal income taxes.

Myth 3. American Indians are a dying race. I met someone once who asked about my racial identity. I replied, "I'm a member of the Kickapoo tribe." He exclaimed, "I thought they were all dead!" This would certainly be news to my 1,600 fellow tribal members, but it does illustrate that many believe in the myth of the "vanishing red man." There is a well-known bronze sculpture titled "End of the Trail," by James Earle Fraser (circa 1918), which shows a dispirited warrior astride an equally dejected war pony. He seems threatened by extinction. At the time of the creation of the sculpture, population estimates for Native peoples showed that the American Indian population was, indeed, on the decline. Census data for the year 1900 enumerated approximately 237,000 Native Americans, Eskimo, and Aleut peoples, thought to be the nadir since 1820.[5]

As of 1 July 2003, the estimated number of people who were American Indians and Alaska Natives or American Indian and Alaska Native in combination with one or more other races was approximately 4.4 million.[6] This is hardly a sign of a dying race.

Myth 4. American Indians are easily identifiable. In truth, not all American Indians fit the physical stereotype. Not all are dark skinned (and none actually have red skin) with high cheekbones and black hair tied up in braids. Some Indian people are blond-haired and blue-eyed. Some have the features of African Americans.

An Indian child in the classroom may, by appearance, look like all the others. It is best not to make assumptions about ethnic identity solely from outward appearance. Even if the child is Native, he or she is first an individual.

Myth 5. All American Indians live on a reservation. According to the U.S. Census Bureau, 538,300 American Indians and Alaska Natives, alone or in combination with one or more other races, live on reservations or other trust lands.[7] This also includes those who live on historic Native lands in Oklahoma and state reservation lands. In all, 57% of American Indians and Alaska Natives live in metropolitan areas.

It is true, however, that in some states in the West—like Montana, South Dakota, Arizona, New Mexico, and Utah—the majority of Native people do live on or near an Indian reservation.

Myth 6. Native people intuitively know their culture and history. Native children are not born with an intimate knowledge of their heritage. That may seem silly to say, but teachers sometimes assume that a Native child in the classroom is the gateway to indigenous information. Our children must learn their native language as well as the stories, cultural practices, and ideals of their people just as we, their parents, learned them.

Sadly, some Native children know nothing of their tribal cultures, for a variety of reasons. Some come from families in which the parents are members of different tribes. Some parents do not know their own cultures because they were products of the boarding school system that discouraged traditional customs and traditions.[8]

A well-intended teacher may call on a Native child to supply information about Indian culture or history. The teacher may feel that giving the child center stage will enhance his or her self-confidence. Yet the teacher may be acting on invalid assumptions. First, the child may not know his or her own language, history, or heritage.[9] Second, some tribes value discretion and the non-disclosure of some aspects of tribal life. Third, some Native students feel that they cannot speak for anyone other than themselves. And, finally, traditional cultures sometimes teach that a child should not attempt to "outshine" his or her peers. So it's best not to put a Native child on the spot.[10]

Myth 7. American Indians feel honored by Indian mascots. There are elementary and secondary schools, colleges, and universities that have adopted Indian mascots, nicknames, and symbols. A number of these schools have come under scrutiny in their communities, and nationally, because many Native people and organizations say these portrayals are offensive and demeaning. More troubling is that many people do not understand why Indian people find these characterizations offensive.

The arguments about mascots and nicknames cannot be resolved here. However, it is important to understand the issues. The obvious offenders use offensive images of Native people, such as the Cleveland Indians caricature, Chief Wahoo, which many will recognize as a buck-toothed, fire-engine-red-skinned figure with a huge nose and grin to match.

The Cleveland baseball organization contends that Chief Wahoo is meant to be a tribute to Louis Francis Sockalexis, a member of the Penobscot tribe who was the first American Indian to play professional baseball. The club insists that Chief Wahoo is only a caricature and is not meant to degrade Indian people. Yet this caricature, in its present form, is insulting to Native Americans. Sadly, many will not reach that conclusion simply by looking at the logo in question.

Because it is difficult for non-Indians to understand the Native perspective on this issue, activists have had to rely on non-Indians' familiarity with and sensitivities to other ethnic cultures. One particularly effective cartoon shows four team logos. One is the Cleveland Indians logo; the others are logos for the fictional Cleveland Asians, Cleveland Africans, and Cleveland Hispanics. Each shows a cartoon figure grinning, literally from ear to ear, with enormous nose and teeth.[11] There would be no question that African Americans, Hispanics, and people of Asian descent would find these logos extremely objectionable. So why, in the face of obvious objections from Native people and their assertion that they do not feel "honored," is this symbol allowed to represent the Cleveland baseball team? Most commonly, the defense of the logo is that it's a cartoon, not a "real" Indian. Others support Chief Wahoo in defiance of what they believe is political correctness gone too far. Finally, there's the rationalization that "my best friend's cousin's brother-in-law is one-fourth Cherokee, and he doesn't think there's anything wrong with Chief Wahoo."

Some Natives find the names Cleveland Indians and Washington Redskins to be likewise objectionable. Certainly, no African American would want to play for a team called the "Cleveland Sambos."

Moving Beyond Stereotypes

Stereotypes, some believe, have a basis in reality. They can be a product of oversimplification, exaggeration, or generalization. Their harm is that they define an individual by attributes ascribed to the group as a whole. So the stereotype that American Indians are doomed to become alcoholics obviously colors one's impression of the many who do not drink alcohol at all.[12] So, too, the stereotype of all American Indians as "spiritual"—even though this may be perceived as a positive image—does not encompass the beliefs or practices of all individuals.

The challenge for educators is how we get beyond stereotyping. The answers are complex but must surely include more than adding a sidebar to a social studies text or including a Native American unit around Thanksgiving.

John Watts has suggested the following "best practices" for those teaching Native students at the college level.[13] They are also applicable to teachers of Indian people at any level.

- Practice personal warmth plus high expectations.
- Respect cultural differences.
- Learn the cultural resources of your students.
- Develop multiple instructional approaches.
- Be aware of the ways you ask questions.
- Remember that some students do not like to be "spotlighted" in front of a group.
- Be aware of proximity preferences—how close is comfortable?

Such suggestions are common sense. There are many excellent resources for educating children about stereotyping, but the key is awareness.[14] Learning about other cultures, their histories, and their beliefs gives students a basis for judgment that goes beyond generalizations.

Notes

1. The terms Native American, American Indian, Indian, Native, and so on are used interchangeably and refer to aboriginal peoples of the United States and their descendants.

2. In legal terms, "Indian Country" refers to Indian reservations, Indian communities, and Indian allotments (U.S. Code, Title 18, Part I, Chapter 53, § 1151). In general usage, it refers to reservations, regions, states, and communities where there is a significant Native population.

3. "*Courier* Editorials: Sovereignty," *Findlay* (Ohio) *Courier,* 7 June 2006, www.thecourier.com/templates/opinion/editorials/editorials.asp.

4. "Demographic and Financial Aid Data for the U.S. and Minnesota," Minnesota Office of Higher Education, retrieved 21 June 2006 from www.ohe.state.mn.us.

5. Walter C. Fleming, *The Complete Idiot's Guide to Native American History* (New York: Alpha Books, 2003), p. 290.

6. "American Indians and Alaska Natives Number 4.4 Million," International Information Programs, U.S. Department of State, retrieved 10 July 2006 from http://usinfo.state.gov.

7. Ibid.

8. Captain Richard C. Pratt, founder of the Indian Boarding School System, encapsulated the ideals of that educational philosophy when he said, "A great general has said that the only good Indian is a dead one, and that high sanction of his destruction has been an enormous factor in promoting Indian massacres. In a sense, I agree with the sentiment, but only in this: that all the Indian there is in the race should be dead. Kill the Indian in him, and save the man."

9. Native languages are in jeopardy. The U.S. Census Bureau reports that 71.8% of all American Indians and Alaska Natives speak only English at home. See "We the People: American Indians and Alaska Natives in the United States," CENSR-28, February 2006, http://www.census.gov.

10. For more on dealing with Indian children in the classroom, see John Watts, "Native American Students," Teaching Learning Committee, Montana State University, Bozeman, 2003, www.montana.edu/teachlearn/Papers (click on "culteralsens.html").

11. For a downloadable representation of the cartoon, see www.bluecorncomics.com/pics/auth.gif.

12. Sherman Alexie (Spokane/Coeur d'Alene) notes that, though the alcoholism rate among Native Americans is higher than in the general population, more Indians do not drink at all than in the general population (The Writer's Voice Community Reading, Billings, Montana, 1 November 1994).

13. John Watts, op. cit.

14. Recommended sources that offer discussion, tips, and curriculum ideas on stereotyping include: Office of the Superintendent of Public Instruction, *The Indian in the Classroom: Readings for the Teacher with Indian Students* (Helena: Montana Department of Education, 1972); Devon A. Mihesuah, *American Indians: Stereotypes and Realities* (Atlanta: Clarity Press, 1996); and Council on Interracial Books for Children, "Stereotyping of Native Americans," Native Nevada Classroom, University of Nevada, Reno, www.unr.edu/nnap/NT/i-8_9.htm.

WALTER C. FLEMING (Kickapoo) is a professor and head of the Department of Native American Studies at Montana State University, Bozeman, and author of *The Complete Idiot's Guide to Native American History* (Alpha, 2003).

Transcending Spaces: Exploring Identity in a Rural American Middle School

A university professor and an eighth-grade teacher collaborated to help middle school students think critically about race, class, and gender. Jean Ketter and Diana Buter describe the materials and activities they developed for a unit on exploring identity. They also critique the effectiveness of the unit in changing students' attitudes.

Jean Ketter and Diana Buter

Small Town People

We would like you to know

We are not all farmers

And we don't all stay in one place.

We do not all chew on

Straw.

We don't all walk five miles to school.

Although most of these characteristics are developed in small towns.

We would like you to know

Not all of us dream of fancy cars and houses.

We don't all have families of twelve.

We don't all sit by highways,

And watch cars go by.

We don't know everybody's name.

Most of us just dream of a nice family.

We would like you to know

We don't all raise hogs.

We don't all run around in baggy overalls.

Although farming is an important

Industry in Iowa.

A group of eighth-grade language arts students modeled this poem after Ana Castillo's "We Would Like You to Know" in response to an assignment in the unit Exploring Identity that was taught a few weeks after September 11, 2001.

We taught this unit because we believe thinking critically about race, class, and gender is particularly important with our white, rural students, who have had limited exposure to other cultures and ethnic groups except for what they have seen on television or in movies. In this unit, Diana, an experienced middle school language arts and reading teacher, and Jean, an associate professor of education, hoped to help students challenge mainstream media's depictions of people of color and other marginalized groups. As Gay argues, too often such groups are portrayed "as victims, servants to society, passive participants, second-class citizens, and imperfect imitations of European, Anglo male models (167). Also, we wanted students to understand how inequity is institutionalized in our country and thus cannot be overcome solely through individual effort or resolve.

We hoped to provide students with literary experiences that would help them connect with characters whose lives and experiences differed vastly from theirs and to see how their own race, class, and gender shaped their understanding of the world. Despite challenges, we discovered that a focus on critically reading multicultural literature helped students bridge their experiential gaps. Students can think and read critically about race, class, and gender at this age, but they need support through modeling, guided practice, and a choice of accessible literature.

Community and School Background

Hometown Middle School[1] is located in a central Iowa agricultural community with a population of 9,105. Hometown is the home of Iowa College, a nationally recognized liberal arts college, and Hometown Regional Medical Center, a major medical facility serving Hometown and surrounding communities. Hometown is located at least an hour from any sizable metropolitan area and is among the 55.4 percent of Iowa schools classified as rural ("Navigating"). The school system enrolls 1,769 students, and the middle school enrollment (grades 5–8) is 550.

Ninety-four percent of the student body and 99 percent of the faculty, staff, and administration are white. Approximately 28 percent of the district's students are bused to attendance centers from outside the city limits; 24 percent of the students receive free or reduced-fee lunches (Hometown School District).

Classroom Contexts

The eighth-grade language arts classes in which the Exploring Identity unit was implemented met daily for a ninety-minute block made up of two forty-two minute periods, one devoted to reading and the other to writing. This schedule allowed for flexibility in scheduling class activities within the block. Classes averaged twenty-two to twenty-five students.

Diana's approach to teaching is to begin building relationships with her students from the first day of class by modeling the respect toward her students that she expects in return. Prior to the beginning of the unit, Diana had worked to establish with her classes an atmosphere of mutual trust and respect in which students listened to and valued one another's ideas. Students were used to writing about and discussing literature using openended, divergent questions (what Diana called "fat" questions). Students were not accustomed to looking to the teacher for the definitive answer to discussion questions. They frequently reacted to assigned literature selections using written response and often worked in small peer groups to discuss and interpret literature.

Despite challenges, we discovered that a focus on critically reading multicultural literature helped students bridge their experiential gaps.

Jean and Diana had worked together as college supervisor and cooperating teacher and were participating in a reading group focused on young adult literature by and about people of color. Jean and her colleague Cynthia Lewis had begun the reading group for teachers as a research project aimed at looking at how best to approach teaching multicultural literature with predominantly white students in a rural setting (see Lewis, Ketter, and Fabos; Ketter and Lewis). These book-group discussions spurred Jean and Diana to test some of the ideas they had developed about teaching multicultural literature in their setting.

Diana and the students shared a common background and experiences. This homogeneity created a sense of familiarity and continuity in the classroom, and it also encouraged students to see their experiences as "normal" and universal. Because students felt comfortable with one another, they were open to the idea of exploring the lives and experiences of persons significantly different from them, and they shared a common frame of reference from which to launch the exploration. But this common frame was too easily perceived as the natural way to see the world; students drew on their perceptions to judge or understand others.

Planning the Unit

We believed that young adult literature could help students connect to characters with unfamiliar experiences and unlearn stereotypes created from lack of experience. We knew one challenge we faced was to encourage reading with an empathetic ear and eye, so we designed experiences that we thought would help students bridge the gaps between their lives and those of the characters.

A related challenge was to ensure that students neither trivialized nor exoticized the experiences of the characters. We saw how encouraging students to connect their experiences with characters of color could lead them to see their experiences as equivalent to those they read about. As Rosenberg warns against in "Underground Discourses: Exploring Whiteness in Teacher Education," we did not want our students to create parallels between their own and characters' lives that "obscure[d] the ways that racist domination impacts on the lives of marginalized groups" (83). Although Rosenberg refers to teacher educators, her caution applies equally well to students. We wanted to challenge a tendency to perceive characters who lived in any inner city, did not speak English as their first language, or did not live with married parents as not quite normal—or perhaps as not really "American."

Thus, we planned the unit in four stages to lead students from understanding and empathizing with others to questioning their assumptions about what is natural or normal. We believe that students who had read the texts and engaged in critical discussions would enlarge their vision of an "ideal" America, one that would include people all colors and ethnic origins, who spoke a variety of languages, and who came from a variety of social backgrounds.

Implementing the Unit

We presented students with the following goals on the first day of the unit:

1. You will examine the ways in which you are a unique individual.
2. You will deepen your understanding of how your identify affects the way you read and understand literature.
3. You will ask and answer specific questions about literature that will help you see literature in a more sophisticated way.
4. You will have an opportunity to step into the identity of another person—perhaps a person who is very "different" from you.
5. You will have an opportunity to create a clear vision of what you would like the "perfect" America to be.

Connecting with the Literature

In the first activity, we asked students to list all the characteristics they believed made up their identities. Then, using an overhead and several different colored pens, we recorded in a circle all the characteristics or factors they contributed. After we had included everything that students thought made up a person's identity, we erased from the circle any aspects of identity students believed they control, such as attitude, interests, and so forth. The remaining characteristics were those aspects of identity over which a person has no control, and we hoped to discover that these are the very things upon which we tend to base stereotypes. This discussion also provided an opportunity to talk about concepts of class, race, and gender.

At the end of the period, we asked students to write about a time they had been stereotyped unfairly or had stereotyped others unfairly. We decided to present our own reflection paragraphs as models. Jean wrote about a time she had made an unfair judgment based on a racial stereotype, and Diana wrote about being stereotyped because of her age.

To help students empathize with those who face racism and to see how race shapes one's perspective, we compared an excerpt from the memoir *Warriors Don't Cry* with a parallel clip from *Crisis at Central High,* an HBO movie. The memoir recounts the experiences of Melba Pattillo Beals, one of the "Little Rock Nine" who elected to be the first African Americans to integrate Central High in Little Rock, Arkansas. The excerpt describes how the African American students were verbally threatened, physically assaulted, and generally mistreated by teachers and students. After discussing the excerpt, we showed the film segment of the same event from the white assistant principal's point of view, a much less disturbing depiction of events than the excerpt presented. The discussion focused on three questions: (1) How does the perspective of the author affect how one tells a story? (2) How did the author's and filmmaker's purposes differ? (3) How do the students' identities affect the way they read the story or view the video? Students were shocked by the treatment the Little Rock Nine received, and students had no trouble grasping that the different narrative perspectives altered how the story was told. Perhaps because they did not understand how such treatment was typical for African Americans, some also seemed unable to empathize with the African American students, instead responding to their mistreatment with indignation at the students' passivity. They argued that Beals should have "fought back" or stood up to the white teachers and students. It was very difficult for these students to imagine how years of discrimination might alter one's consciousness or how fighting back might have resulted in physical and psychic injury.

After discussing the excerpt, we showed the film segment of the same event from the white assistant principal's point of view, a much less disturbing depiction of events than the excerpt presented.

In the next activity, student groups composed poems modeled after Ana Castillo's "We Would Like You to Know," writing from the perspective of a group who had been stereotyped or misrepresented. First we read aloud and discussed Castillo's poem, modeling the critical questions we planned to use with students during the unit. In our discussion, students raised some issues that were current in Iowa, such as some people's misperception that Mexican workers in the meatpacking plants were stealing jobs from whites.

After discussing the poem, students wrote their "We Would Like You to Know" poems in small groups. We were troubled when students wanted to write about marginalized groups they knew little about, such as Muslims or African Americans, because sometimes their poems came close to reinforcing stereotypes rather than challenging them. We do see some value in having students imagine they are experiencing the injustices less-privileged groups in society may experience, but again, we worry about what sort of comparisons students are making. Because students are only occupying that imagined place temporarily and because they do not fully understand what that experience is like, we worry that we might lead them to conclude that escaping racism and overcoming the barriers it presents are a simple matter of individual will. As Boler warns, helping students develop empathy for such experiences can be dangerous if it is nothing more than a "harmonious experience of reversibility and the pleasure of identification" (qtd. in Rosenberg 83).

In discussion based on the students' questions, we continued to challenge stereotypes students might have held.

Practicing Critical Reading

Next, students practiced using critical questions (see fig. 1). Before we read aloud "An Hour with Abuelo," a short story told from the point of view of an adolescent boy who is cajoled into visiting his grandfather at the nursing home (Cofer), we discussed a list of critical questions to use with the story and assigned pairs of students a question from the list to consider as they listened to the story. In discussion after the reading, students heard how others responded to the questions, asked questions about the questions themselves, and practiced new ways of thinking about literature that emphasized decentering their experience.

We next assigned a variety of young adult texts and asked students to formulate critical questions. In discussion based on the students' questions, we continued to challenge stereotypes students might have held. For example, we read the stories of three very different African American young women from *Sugar in the Raw* (Carroll). One young woman had grown up in San Francisco with professional parents. Another had grown up in a working-class, mixed-race neighborhood and had attended public schools. The third had attended a private religious school on the East Coast. Every author in the text was responding to a similar set of questions, which made it easier for us to discuss comparisons and contrasts among the three young women. We discussed the many ways the young women

Figure 1. Focus Question Models

Below are ten questions that will serve as models for you as you write your own questions about what we read. Since you will be doing this several times, vary the questions you ask. I do not want you to use the same questions every time, so keep track of which ones you have tried and try not to repeat them.

1. What do you know or can you guess about the narrator of this story? What is his or her gender, ethnicity, age, background? What sort of person do you think he or she is? What evidence do you find in the story to help you answer this question?
2. How does the identity of the narrator (race, class, gender, age, ethnicity, etc.) affect how he or she tells the story? Explain by giving examples.
3. To whom is the narrator telling the story? In other words, who might be the ideal audience for this story, and why do you think so?
4. Do you think the narrator has you in mind as someone he or she would want to tell this story to? Why or why not? If yes, how does that affect your reading of the story? If you don't think you are in the intended audience or feel the author isn't speaking to you, how does that affect your understanding of the story?
5. How do you think the author of this story wants you to feel about particular characters or events? How does the author achieve this end? What statements or events do you find in the story that promote a certain view or suggest that you should feel a certain way about something or someone?
6. How would this story be different if the narrator's identity were different? What specific things might change in the poem or story and how would they change?
7. What aspects of your identity affect the way you read this story? How do aspects of your identity affect your reading?
8. What incidents, viewpoints, or opinions are left out of the story? Why do you think the author may have left out certain viewpoints or information? What do you think these other perspectives or voices might add to the story?
9. Do you think the story gives a fair view of the events? Why or why not?
10. What has the author assumed are natural or good ways of acting? Do you agree or disagree with the author's messages about how we should behave or should be, and how does your agreement or disagreement with these messages affect how you read the story or poem?

Adapted from Simpson (120).

---

were similar—in their experience of racism, their preoccupation with skin color, and their confidence about being successful. But we also discovered how different these young women were and how knowing their race did not help us predict very much about them. Choosing middle-class young women with well-educated and professional parents worked against some of the stereotypes white students might hold about African American young adults.

We were not always able to predict how students would respond to a particular text, and students' reactions to Nikki Giovanni's "Nikki-Rosa" surprised us. Several students responded negatively to the last lines of the poem, where Giovanni predicts that people will "probably talk about my hard childhood/and never understand that/all the while I was quite happy" (207). We found several students misread or ignored the message of Giovanni's poem. In their written responses, they described her childhood as abnormal or deprived, exactly the image Giovanni was trying to challenge. For many of the students, the narrator seemed unnecessarily angry about how white people envisioned her childhood. One student in our discussion went so far as to call the narrator a "brat."

Not all of the students had this response. When we began to discuss more generally what the poem revealed to us as readers, students were able to list the stereotypical ways inner-city life was depicted. Two students did counter the stereotype by referring to their own experiences, which allowed us to reinforce the point that personal experiences can affect the reading and interpretation of a text. However, we who teach in rural, predominantly white schools must anticipate resistance from students who may not be accustomed to reading literature that challenges notions of white identity and privilege.

Peer Teaching Using Critical Questions

We began phase three of the unit by instructing small groups of students to prepare to lead discussion on a poem, many of which came from the anthology *Unsettling America* (Gillan and Gillan). As with all the reading, students wrote responses to questions they posed about the text. The next day, students met in their small groups to share responses to the poems and to plan discussion of the poem by selecting the focus questions they wanted to explore with the class.

To lead the discussion, each of the groups first read their poem aloud and shared their interpretations. They then asked their selected questions. We were impressed by how seriously students took the task of leading discussion and with the level and depth of student participation. Students' responses to the poems were sensitive and capable. "Translating Grandfather's House" (Vega), about a child being doubted by a teacher based on a stereotype, brought out some of the strongest reactions because many students vividly remembered teachers who they felt had misjudged or discounted them.

Envisioning an Ideal America

Students next constructed a collage. To begin, they wrote a reflection paragraph on what an ideal America would be. Students considered what they thought was already ideal or desirable about our country and what could be improved. They discussed their reflections in small groups and completed a chart listing the symbols they would use to represent the qualities they had agreed were desirable or needed improvement. All ideas were to be included on the chart and in the collage.

The process of making the collages was more important than the product itself. We were impressed with some of the discussions occurring in the small groups; other discussions revealed the limits of students' understanding. For example, many students wanted to express the concept of freedom of religion on their collages, and several set about doing so by making a cross. When Jean asked them what other religious symbols might encompass the different religions practiced in this country, students seemed surprised. Since we were teaching this unit soon after September 11, we thought it was important to remind students that Americans are also Jewish, Muslim, Buddhist, Sikh, and so forth, but it was clear that students wanted to include freedom of religion to express their support for school prayer and not to express the value of religious pluralism.

Since we were teaching this unit soon after September 11, we thought it was important to remind students that Americans are also Jewish, Muslim, Buddhist, Sikh, and so forth, but it was clear that students wanted to include freedom of religion to express their support for school prayer and not to express the value of religious pluralism.

Each of the collages was unique and several showed careful thought in design. Students depicted their desire for freedom of religion, freedom from crime, freedom from pollution, and freedom from discrimination. Most included the need for more tolerance of difference, but most resisted making their collages about only race or ethnicity. Many expressed the idea that racism and discrimination are less prevalent than in the past, but most acknowledged that progress was still to be made, which was gratifying.

Challenging Notions

We are still troubled by questions raised during the teaching of this unit. Is it possible to challenge rural, white middle schoolers' notions about whiteness and raise their awareness of white privilege using critical reading as a tool? Is it possible for a group of white eighth-grade students to transcend their perceptions of what is natural and normal in the world as they read literature about people with different perceptions? We certainly believe these things are possible, but we also believe more time and energy must be devoted to these goals in all language arts classrooms, K–12.

We think we made some progress with some students, but two weeks in one year of their schooling will not go far in changing the way students read and the way they see themselves in the world, particularly if these students' other reading experiences do not lead them to recognize the privilege of being seen as an individual or to challenge the use of whiteness

as a measure of what is normal or natural. Diana will continue to pursue these goals throughout the curriculum with her students, but many teachers do not see these goals as central to their teaching.

We also believe that creating classrooms where students read literature in a culturally critical way is crucial but may not be enough. For example, we read one student's final reflection on an "Ideal America" in which she suggests that America needs a "class for racist people" with both concern and hope. The idea that racism can be eliminated by a class or rehabilitation echoes the philosophies that define multicultural pedagogy as exposure to multicultural literature rather than as a critical reading of *all* texts, including the students' lives. We had hoped that students would come to see how pervasive racism is and how most of us subtly or not so subtly aid its persistence. These students, however, continued to see racism as something individual people acted on rather than as part of the fabric of our institutions. At least this student's quote shows an awareness of racism as abnormal and as resulting from ignorance. In the past, we have heard students voice the idea that racism is simply a part of the human condition and, consequently, unavoidable. At least this student hopes for change and realizes that education could be a tool in eliminating racism, and we agree with her. We believe that the unjust practices that continue to plague the United States should be challenged in every classroom—rural, suburban, and urban—and we believe education for all students should include critical experiences that bring them to recognize and to take effective action against the injustices that scar our national psyche.

We think we made some progress with some students, but two weeks in one year of their schooling will not go far in changing the way students read and the way they see themselves in the world, particularly if these students' other reading experiences do not lead them to recognize the privilege of being seen as an individual or to challenge the use of whiteness as a measure of what is normal or natural.

Note

1. All place names and student names are pseudonyms.

Works Cited

Beals, Melba Pattillo. *Warriors Don't Cry: A Searing Memoir of the Battle to Integrate Little Rock's Central High.* New York: Pocket, 1994.

Carroll, Rebecca, ed. *Sugar in the Raw: Voices of Young Black Girls in America.* New York: Three Rivers, 1997.

Castillo, Ana. "We Would Like You to Know." *Cool Salsa: Bilingual Poems on Growing Up Latino in the United States.* Ed. Lori M. Carlson. New York: Fawcett Juniper, 1994. 113–15.

Cofer, Judith Ortiz. "An Hour with Abuelo." *An Island Like You: Stories of the Barrio.* New York: Orchard, 1995. 66–71.

Crisis at Central High. Dir. Lamont Johnson. HBO, 1981.

Gay, Geneva. "Mirror Images on Common Issues: Parallels between Multicultural Education and Critical Pedagogy." *Multicultural Education, Critical Pedagogy, and the Politics of Difference.* Ed. Christine E. Sleeter and Peter L. McLaren. New York: State U of New York P, 1995. 155–89.

Gillan, Maria Mazziotti, and Jennifer Gillan, eds. *Unsettling America: An Anthology of Contemporary Multicultural Poetry.* New York: Viking, 1994.

Giovanni, Nikki. "Nikki-Rosa." *Unsettling America: An Anthology of Contemporary Multicultural Poetry.* Ed. Maria Mazziotti Gillan and Jennifer Gillan. New York: Viking, 1994. 206–07.

Ketter, Jean, and Cynthia Lewis. "Already Reading Texts and Concexts: Multicultural Literature in a Predominantly White Rural Community." *Theory into Practice* 40.3 (2001): 175–84.

Lewis, Cynthia, Jean Ketter, and Bettina Fabos. "Reading Race in a Rural Context." *The International Journal of Qualitative Studies in Education* 14.3 (2001): 317–50.

"Navigating Resources for Rural Schools: Tables and Figures." National Center for Education Statistics. 2000. 2 Mar. 2004 (http://nces.ed.gov/surveys/ruraled/data/WhatsRuralSummary.asp).

Rosenberg, Pearl M. "Underground Discourses: Exploring Whiteness in Teacher Education." *Off White: Readings on Race, Power, and Society.* Ed. Michelle Fine, Lois Weis, Linda C. Powell, and L. Mun Wong. New York: Routledge, 1997. 79–89.

Simpson, Anne. "Critical Questions: Whose Questions?" *The Reading Teacher* 50.2 (996): 118–27.

Vega, E. J. "Translating Grandfather's House." *Cool Salsa: Bilingual Poems on Growing Up Latino in the United States.* Ed. Lori M. Carlson. New York: Fawcett Juniper, 1994. 5–6.

JEAN KETTER teaches courses in educational foundations and in the theories and methods of English and foreign language instruction at Grinnell College. Her research focuses on the sociocultural aspects of multicultural literature instruction and on the political and pedagogical implications of high-stakes reading and writing assessments. email: Ketter@grinnell.edu. **DIANA BUTER** has taught English for twenty-one years in both high school and middle school. She spent the 2003–04 school year visiting schools around the state of Iowa as the 2003–04 Iowa Teacher of the Year. email: dbuter@grinnell.k12.ia.us.

From *English Journal,* 93: 6, July 2004, pp. 47–53. Copyright © 2004 by National Council of Teachers of English. Reprinted by permission.

UNIT 5

Curriculum and Instruction in Multicultural Perspective

Unit Selections

Key Points to Consider

- How should teachers and students deal with xenophobic reactions when they occur?

- What are the similarities and distinctions between a "culture" and an "ethnic group?"

- Why is it effective to integrate multicultural curriculum content into all aspects of a school curriculum?

- What are the varying ways in which multicultural education is defined? Which model of multicultural education do you prefer?

- What is the rationale for the existence of the multicultural educational effort in the elementary and secondary schools? Should all students be exposed to it? Why or why not?

- Why is literacy education such a hotly debated topic in education?

Student Web Site

www.mhcls.com/online

Internet References

Further information regarding these Web sites may be found in this book's preface or online.

American Indian Science and Engineering Society
   http://www.aises.org
Child Welfare League of America
   http://www.cwla.org
STANDARDS: An International Journal of Multicultural Studies
   http://www.colorado.edu/journals/standards/

Curriculum and instruction includes all concerns relative to subject matter to be taught and all pedagogical theory relating to methods of instruction. All pedagogical theory is based on some philosophical assumptions relating to what is worth knowing and what actions are good. Every school curriculum is the product of specific choices among those available. Since classroom teachers are the "delivery systems" for a curriculum, along with whatever texts are used, teachers have the opportunity to interpret and add their own insights regarding the curricula they teach.

It is in the area of curriculum and instruction in the elementary and secondary schools, as well as in teacher education curricula, that a fundamental transformation must occur to sensitize all young people, including those living in isolated rural and small town communities, to the multicultural reality of our national civilization. There are several different approaches to multicultural educational programming in the schools. This area of study has developed steadily, in stages, since the events of the 1960s, 1970s, and 1980s forced a reassessment of our sense of social justice. There are programs in some school systems that merely include the study of the minority cultural groups living in their particular area, and this is often done through isolated, elective courses or units in required courses that students must take. This is not the approach to multicultural education that most current leaders in the field favor. Today, most experienced multicultural educators favor a more inclusive approach to the subject—the infusion of multicultural themes into the entire life of the school and all possible course content. Such an inclusive approach to multicultural education seeks to help students and teachers to develop a sense of social consciousness. This sense, coupled with a more global and integrated conception of our social reality, will empower them to make more critical assessments than have been made in the past about such distinctions as the disparity between public democratic rhetoric and the reality of some social groups, which still have not been accepted into society's mainstream.

An important focus of multicultural education is that a democratic nation has a moral responsibility to see that minority ethnic, cultural, or religious groups are not isolated or marginalized in the social life of the nation. The educational institutions of a nation tend to be the primary places where children and young adults learn about their national history, literature, and scientific achievement. Multicultural educational content is necessary in all American schools because students, even in the most culturally isolated rural and small-town settings, do learn opinions and beliefs about ethnic, cultural, and religious groups other than their own. What students learn in the informal social relations of their home communities about other social groups is often factually misleading or incorrect. This is how our past heritage of racism and negative stereotypes of differing social groups evolved. There has been much progress in the area of civil rights, but there has also been resurgent racism and intercultural misunderstanding. School is the one place children and adolescents go each day where it is possible for them to learn an objective

Patrick Clark/Getty Images

view of the culturally pluralistic national heritage that is both their present and future social reality. All communities are linked in some way to the culturally pluralistic social reality of the nation. When students leave high school to go into military service, attend college, or attempt careers in other parts of the nation in the corporate sector, government, or the arts, they will encounter a multicultural world very different from their often isolated local community or cultural group.

Becoming a multicultural person is a process that any dedicated teacher should be willing to pursue. We need to help students of all cultural heritages to become effective citizens of our national communities. Xenophobia and cultural prejudice have no proper place in any truly democratic national community. The English language is not in trouble. We are in trouble only if we cannot live up to our self-proclaimed heritage as a "nation of immigrants." We must remember our national heritage. We must also remember that our forefathers acquired the lands of Native Americans, 34 percent of the territory of Mexico in 1848, and the island of Puerto Rico in 1898. With those acquisitions came responsibilities that we cannot avoid if we are a morally conscious people. All Americans deserve a fair representation of their respective cultural voices.

Teachers should help their students to recognize and respect ethnic and cultural diversity and to value the ways in which it enhances and enriches the quality of our civilization. Children and adolescents should also be made aware that each of them has the right to choose how fully to identify with his or her own ethnic or cultural group.

The essays in this unit reflect a wide variety of perspectives on how to broaden the multicultural effort in our schools. The authors seek to incorporate more intercultural and global content and experiences into the main body of curriculum and instruction. Educators will find that, taken together, these essays provide a very sound basis for understanding what multicultural curriculum and instruction should be about. They are relevant to coursework in curriculum and instruction, curriculum theory and construction, educational policy studies and leadership, history and philosophy of education, and cultural foundations of education.

As Diversity Grows, So Must We

Schools that experience rapid demographic shifts can meet the challenge by implementing five phases of professional development.

GARY R. HOWARD

Many school districts nationwide are experiencing rapid growth in the number of students of color, culturally and linguistically diverse students, and students from low-income families. From my work with education leaders in some of these diversity-enhanced school districts, I know they are places of vibrant opportunity—places that call us to meaningful and exciting work. In these "welcome-to-America" schools, the global community shows up in our classrooms every day, inviting us—even requiring us—to grow as we learn from and with our students and their families.

The Need for Growth

All is not well, however, in these rapidly transitioning schools. Some teachers, administrators, and parents view their schools' increasing diversity as a problem rather than an opportunity. For example, in a school district on the West Coast where the number of Latino students has quadrupled in the past 10 years, a teacher recently asked me, "Why are they sending these kids to our school?" In another district outside New York City—where the student population was once predominantly rich, white, and Jewish but is now about 90 percent low-income kids of color, mostly from the Caribbean and Latin America—a principal remarked in one workshop, "These kids don't value education, and their parents aren't helping either. They don't seem to care about their children's future." In a school district near Minneapolis with a rapidly increasing black population, a white parent remarked, "Students who are coming here now don't have much respect for authority That's why we have so many discipline problems."

Diversity-enhanced schools are places of vibrant opportunity—places that call us as educators to meaningful and exciting work.

Other educators and parents, although less negative, still feel uneasy about their schools' new demographics. In a high school outside Washington, D.C., where the Latino immigrant population is increasing rapidly, a teacher told me that he was disappointed in himself for not feeling comfortable engaging his students in a discussion of immigration issues, a hot topic in the community in spring 2006. "I knew the kids needed to talk, but I just couldn't go there." And a black teacher who taught French successfully for many years in predominantly white suburban schools told me recently, "When I first found myself teaching classes of mostly black kids, I went home frustrated every night because I knew I wasn't getting through to them, and they were giving me a hard time. It only started getting better when I finally figured out that I had to reexamine everything I was doing."

This teacher has it right. As educators in rapidly transitioning schools, we need to reexamine everything we're doing. Continuing with business as usual will mean failure or mediocrity for too many of our students, as the data related to racial, cultural, linguistic, and economic achievement gaps demonstrate (National Center for Education Statistics, 2005). Rapidly changing demographics demand that we engage in a vigorous, ongoing, and systemic process of professional development to prepare all educators in the school to function effectively in a highly diverse environment.

Many education leaders in diversity-enhanced schools are moving beyond blame and befuddlement and working to transform themselves and their schools to serve all their students well. From observing and collaborating with them, I have learned that this transformative work proceeds best in five phases: (1) building trust, (2) engaging personal culture, (3) confronting issues of social dominance and social justice, (4) transforming instructional practices, and (5) engaging the entire school community

Phase 1: Building Trust

Ninety percent of U.S. public school teachers are white; most grew up and attended school in middle-class, English-speaking, predominantly white communities and received their teacher preparation in predominantly white colleges and universities (Gay, Dingus, Jackson, 2003). Thus, many white educators simply have not acquired the experiential and education background that would prepare them for the growing diversity of their students (Ladson-Billings, 2002; Vavrus, 2002).

The first priority in the trust phase is to acknowledge this challenge in a positive, inclusive, and honest way. School leaders should base initial discussions on the following assumptions:

- Inequities in diverse schools are not, for the most part, a function of intentional discrimination.
- Educators of *all* racial and cultural groups need to develop new competencies and pedagogies to successfully engage our changing populations.
- White teachers have their own cultural connections and unique personal narratives that are legitimate aspects of the overall mix of school diversity

School leaders should also model for their colleagues inclusive and nonjudgmental discussion, reflection, and engagement strategies that teachers can use to establish positive learning communities in their classrooms.

For example, school leaders in the Apple Valley Unified School District in Southern California, where racial, cultural, and linguistic diversity is rapidly increasing, have invested considerable time and resources in creating a climate of openness and trust. They recently implemented four days of intensive work with teams from each school, including principals, teacher leaders, union representatives, parents, clergy, business leaders, and community activists from the NAACP and other organizations.

One essential outcome in this initial phase of the conversation is to establish that racial, cultural, and economic differences are real—and that they make a difference in education outcomes. Said one Apple Valley participant, "I have become aware that the issue of race needs to be dealt with, not minimized." Said another, "I need to move beyond being color-blind." A second key outcome is to establish the need for a personal and professional journey toward greater awareness. As an Apple Valley educator noted, "There were a lot of different stories and viewpoints shared at this inservice, but the one thing we can agree on is that everyone needs to improve in certain areas." A third key outcome in the trust phase is to demonstrate that difficult topics can be discussed in an environment that is honest, safe, and productive. One Apple Valley teacher commented, "We were able to talk about all of the issues and not worry about being politically correct."

Through this work, Apple Valley educators and community leaders established a climate of constructive collaboration that can be directed toward addressing the district's new challenges. From the perspective of the school superintendent, "This is a conversation our community is not used to having, so we had to build a positive climate before moving to the harder questions of action."

Phase 2: Engaging Personal Culture

Change has to start with educators before it can realistically begin to take place with students. The central aim of the second phase of the work is building educators' *cultural competence*—

their ability to form authentic and effective relationships across differences.

Young people, particularly those from historically marginalized groups, have sensitive antennae for authenticity. I recently asked a group of racially and culturally diverse high school students to name the teachers in their school who really cared about them, respected them, and enjoyed getting to know them as people. Forty students pooling their answers could name only 10 teachers from a faculty of 120, which may be one reason this high school has a 50 percent dropout rate for students of color.

Aronson and Steele's (2005) work on stereotype threat demonstrates that intellectual performance, rather than being a fixed and constant quality, is quite fragile and can vary greatly depending on the social and interpersonal context of learning. In repeated studies, these researchers found that three factors have a major effect on students' motivation and performance: their feelings of belonging, their trust in the people around them, and their belief that teachers value their intellectual competence. This research suggests that the capacity of adults in the school to form trusting relationships with and supportive learning environments for their students can greatly influence achievement outcomes.

Leaders in the Metropolitan School District of Lawrence Township, outside Indianapolis, have taken this perspective seriously. Clear data showed gaps among ethnic groups in achievement, participation in higher-level courses, discipline referrals, and dropout rates. In response, district teachers and administrators engaged in a vigorous and ongoing process of self-examination and personal growth related to cultural competence.

Central-office and building administrators started with themselves. Along with selected teachers from each school, they engaged in a multiyear program of shared reading, reflective conversations, professional development activities, and joint planning to increase their own and their colleagues' levels of cultural competence. They studied and practiced Margaret Wheatley's (2002) principles of conversation, with particular emphasis on her admonitions to expect things to be messy and to be willing to be disturbed. They designed their own Socratic seminars using chapters from *We Can't Teach What We Don't Know* (Howard, 2006) and used the stages of personal identity development model from that book as a foundation for ongoing reflective conversations about their own journeys toward cultural competence.

As this work among leaders began to be applied in various school buildings, one principal observed, "We are talking about things that we were afraid to talk about before—like our own prejudices and the biases in some of our curriculum materials." In another school, educators' discussions led to a decision to move parent-teacher conferences out of the school building and into the apartment complexes where their black and Latino students live.

Phase 3: Confronting Social Dominance and Social Justice

When we look at school outcome data, the history of racism, classism, and exclusion in the United States stares us in the face. Systems of privilege and preference often create enclaves of exclusivity in schools, in which certain demographic groups are served well while others languish in failure or mediocrity. As diversity grows in rapidly transitioning school districts, demographic gaps become increasingly apparent.

Educators of *all* racial and cultural groups need to develop new competencies and pedagogies to successfully engage our changing populations.

In phase three, educators directly confront the current and historical inequities that affect education. The central purpose of this phase is to construct a compelling narrative of social justice that will inform, inspire, and sustain educators in their work, without falling into the rhetoric of shame and blame. School leaders and teachers engage in a lively conversation about race, class, gender, sexual orientation, immigration, and other dimensions of diversity and social dominance. David Koyama, principal of a diversity-enhanced elementary school outside Seattle, said, "One of my most important functions as a school leader is to transform political jargon like 'no child left behind' into a moral imperative that inspires teachers to work toward justice, not mere compliance."

Unraveling social dominance takes courage—the kind of courage shown by the central office and school leadership team in the Roseville Area School District outside the twin cities of Minneapolis and St. Paul. Roseville is in the midst of a rapid demographic shift. As we approached this phase of the work, I asked Roseville leaders to examine how issues of privilege, power, and dominance might be functioning in their schools to shape educators' assumptions and beliefs about students and create inequitable outcomes.

One of the workshop activities engaged participants in a forced-choice simulation requiring them to choose which aspects of their identity they would give up or deny for the sake of personal survival in a hostile environment. Choosing from such identities as race, ethnicity, language, religion, values, and vocation, many white educators were quick to give up race. Among the Roseville administrative team, which is 95 percent white, the one white principal who chose to keep his racial identity during the simulation said during the debriefing discussion, "I seriously challenge my white colleagues who so easily gave up their race. I think if we are honest with ourselves, few would choose to lose the privilege and power that come with being white in the United States."

As an outgrowth of the authentic and sometimes contentious conversations that emerged from this and other activities, several core leaders and the superintendent identified a need to craft a strong Equity Vision statement for the district. The Equity Vision now headlines all opening-of-school events each year and is publicly displayed in district offices and schools. It reads,

> Roseville Area Schools is committed to ensuring an equitable and respectful educational experience for every student, family, and staff member, regardless of race,

gender, sexual orientation, socioeconomic status, ability, home or first language, religion, national origin, or age.

As a result of the increased consciousness about issues of dominance and social justice, several schools have formed Equity Teams of teachers and students, and an Equity Parent Group has begun to meet. The district is looking seriously at how many students from dominant and subordinate groups are in its gifted and AP classes and is conscientiously working for more balance.

Like Roseville, other diversity-enhanced districts must establish clear public markers that unambiguously state, "This is who we are, this is what we believe, and this is what we will do." Any approach to school reform that does not honestly engage issues of power, privilege, and social dominance is naive, ungrounded in history, and unlikely to yield the deep changes needed to make schools more inclusive and equitable.

Phase 4: Transforming Instructional Practices

In this phase, schools assess and, where necessary, transform the way they carry out instruction to become more responsive to diversity. For teachers, this means examining pedagogy and curriculum, as well as expectations and interaction patterns with students. It means looking honestly at outcome data and creating new strategies designed to serve the students whom current instruction is not reaching. For school leaders, this often means facing the limits of their own knowledge and skills and becoming colearners with teachers to find ways to transform classroom practices.

In Loudoun County Public Schools, outside Washington, D.C., teachers and school leaders are taking this work seriously. One of the fastest-growing school systems in the United States, Loudoun County is experiencing rapid increases in racial, cultural, linguistic, and economic diversity on its eastern edge, closer to the city, while remaining more monocultural to the west. Six of Loudoun's most diverse schools have formed leadership teams to promote the following essential elements of culturally responsive teaching (CRT):

- Forming authentic and caring relationships with students.
- Using curriculum that honors each student's culture and life experience.
- Shifting instructional strategies to meet the diverse learning needs of students.
- Communicating respect for each student's intelligence.
- Holding consistent and high expectations for all learners. (Gay, 2000; Ladson-Billings, 1994; McKinley, 2005; Shade, Kelly, & Oberg, 1997)

CRT teams vary in size and membership but usually include principals, assistant principals, counselors, lead teachers, specialists, and, in some cases, parents. In addition to engaging deeply in the phases outlined above, these teams have begun to work with their broader school faculties to transform instruction. At Loudoun County's Sugarland Elementary, teacher members of the CRT team have designed student-based action research projects. They selected individual students from their most academically challenged demographic groups and then used the principles of CRT to plan new interventions to engage these students and track their progress.

As educators in rapidly transitioning schools, we need to reexamine everything we're doing.

In one action research project, a 5th grade teacher focused on a Latino student, an English language learner who "couldn't put two sentences together, let alone write the five-paragraph essay that is required to pass our 5th grade assessment." The teacher's first reaction was to ask, "How was this student allowed to slip by all these years without learning anything beyond 2nd grade writing skills?" When the teacher launched her CRT project, however, her perspective became more proactive. She realized that she couldn't just deliver the 5th grade curriculum—she had to meet this student where he was. She built a personal connection with the student, learned about his family culture and interests (a fascination with monkeys was a major access point), and used this relationship to reinforce his academic development. The student responded to her high expectations and passed his 5th grade writing assessment. And after missing its No Child Left Behind compliance goals in past years, Sugarland recently achieved adequate yearly progress for all subgroups in its highly diverse student population.

This phase requires a crucial paradigm shift, in which teachers and other school professionals stop blaming students and their families for gaps in academic achievement. Instead of pointing fingers, educators in Loudoun schools are placing their energies where they will have the most impact—in changing their *own* attitudes, beliefs, expectations, and practices. I frequently ask teachers and school leaders, "Of all the many factors that determine school success for our students, where can we as educators have the most influence?" After educators participate in the work outlined here, the answer is always, "Changing ourselves."

Phase 5: Engaging the Entire School Community

Changing demographics have profound implications for all levels and functions of the school system. To create welcoming and equitable learning environments for diverse students and their families, school leaders must engage the entire school community.

Leaders in the East Ramapo Central School District in New York State have committed themselves to just such a system-wide initiative. The school district, which lies across the Tappan Zee Bridge from New York City, has experienced a dramatic shift in student population in the past 15 years as low-income Haitian, Jamaican, Dominican, Latino, and black families from the city have moved into the community and middle-class white families have, unfortunately but predictably, fled to private schools or other less diverse districts.

In the midst of this demographic revolution, East Ramapo's broad-based diversity initiative has engaged all groups and constituencies in the school district community, not just teachers and administrators. For example, the district has provided workshops to help classified employees acknowledge their powerful role in setting a welcoming tone and creating an inclusive climate for students, parents, and colleagues in school offices, lunchrooms, hallways, and on the playground. For bus drivers, this work has meant gaining cultural competence skills for managing their immense safety responsibilities while communicating clearly and compassionately across many languages and cultures on their buses.

In one session that I led with school secretaries, we worked through their confusion and frustration related to all the diverse languages being spoken in the school offices and, in some cases, their feelings of anger and resentment about the demographic changes that had taken place in "their" schools. Asked what they learned from the session, participants commented, "I saw the frustration people can have, especially if they are from another country." "We all basically have the same feelings about family, pride in our culture, and the importance of getting along." "I learned from white people that they can also sometimes feel like a minority." In addition to these sessions, East Ramapo has created learning opportunities for school board members, parents, students, counselors, and special education classroom assistants. The district has convened regular community forums focusing on student achievement and creating conversations across many diverse cultures. White parents who have kept their children in the public schools because they see the value of diversity in their education have been significant participants in these conversations.

As a result of East Ramapo's efforts, the achievement gaps in test scores along ethnic and economic lines have significantly narrowed. In the six years since the district consciously began implementing the professional development model discussed here, the pass rate for black and Hispanic students combined on the New York State elementary language arts test increased from 43 percent in 2000 to 54 percent in 2006; on the math test, the pass rate increased from 40 percent to 61 percent. During that same period, the gap between black and Hispanic students (combined) and white and Asian students (combined) decreased by 6 percentage points in language arts and 23 percentage points in math. The achievement gap between low-income elementary students and the general population decreased by 10 points in language arts and 6 points in math—results that are particularly impressive, given that the proportion of economically disadvantaged students grew from 51 percent in 2000 to 72 percent in 2006.

A Journey Toward Awareness

Professional development for creating inclusive, equitable, and excellent schools is a long-term process. The school districts described here are at various stages in the process. Everyone involved would agree that the work is messier and more complex than can be communicated in this brief overview. However, one central leadership commitment is clear in all of these rapidly transitioning districts: When diversity comes to town, we are all challenged to grow.

References

Aronson, J., & Steele, C. M. (2005). Stereotypes and the fragility of human competence, motivation, and self-concept. In C. Dweck & E. Elliot (Eds.), *Handbook of competence and motivation* (pp. 436–456). New York: Guilford.

Gay, G. (2000). *Culturally responsive teaching: Theory, research, and practice.* New York: Teachers College Press.

Gay, G., Dingus, J. E., & Jackson, C. W. (2003, July). *The presence and performance of teachers of color in the profession.* Unpublished report prepared for the National Collaborative on Diversity in the Teaching Force, Washington, DC.

Howard, G. (2006). *We can't teach what we don't know: White teachers in multiracial schools* (2nd ed.). New York: Teachers College Press.

Ladson-Billings, G. (1994). *The dreamkeepers: Successful teachers of African American students.* San Francisco: Jossey-Bass.

Ladson-Billings, G. (2002). *Crossing over to Canaan: The journey of new teachers in diverse classrooms.* San Francisco: Jossey-Bass.

McKinley, J. H. (2005, March). *Culturally responsive teaching and learning.* Paper presented at the Annual State Conference of the Washington Alliance of Black School Educators, Bellevue, WA.

National Center for Education Statistics. (2005). *The nation's report card.* Washington, DC: Author.

Shade, B. J., Kelly, C., & Oberg, M. (1997). *Creating culturally responsive classrooms.* Washington, DC: American Psychological Association.

Vavrus, M. (2002). *Transforming the multiculrural education of teachers: Theory, research and practice.* New York: Teachers College Press.

Wheatley, M. (2002). *Turning to one another: Simple conversations to restore hope to the future.* San Francisco: Barrett-Koehler.

GARY R. HOWARD is Founder and President of the REACH Center for Multicultural Education in Seattle (www.reachctr.org); 206-634-2073; garyhoward@earthlink.net. He is the author of *We Can't Teach What We Don't Know: White Teachers, Multiracial Schools* (Teachers College Press, 2nd ed., 2006).

Arts in the Classroom

"La Llave" (The Key) to Awareness, Community Relations, and Parental Involvement

Margarita Machado-Casas
University of North Carolina at Chapel Hill

As a teacher and a person of color, I am committed to social justice, equity, and meaningful teaching that takes students' cultural heritage into consideration in the workplace. Yet this is not easy in American schools. When entering the classroom we are expected to act as if we are blind to the social-economic issues our students struggle with daily. We are expected to teach only academic subjects and not deal with what school really is about—an extension of home and preparation for real life situations that are more complex than just dealing with character education. When in the classroom we are trained to be authoritative beings that control through "regimentation," "depositing," and "manipulation." As teachers we become our students' oppressors (Freire, 1970, p. 107). Being and acting as teacher the oppressor is harmful for all students but particularly for immigrants who on top of having to learn a new language, and a new educational system, have to suppress their cultural being,—all they have known in order to fit into American schools.

I was born in Nicaragua, from which seven in my family and I fled to Panama escaping from war and an oppressive government. We lived in Panama for five and a half years before political instability caused turmoil in that country as well. Having experienced this oppression before, my father courageously opted to bring the family to the United States. I arrived in California at the age of 14. Knowing less than basic English I was enrolled in a middle school in Fullerton, California, where I was placed in an ESL (Sheltered English class). My initial school experience was devastating. I not only did not know the language enough to communicate my thoughts and feelings in an understandable manner, but I was also having to re-learn school and the behaviors one is to display when in school. For example, back in both Nicaragua and Panama, students were expected to have an opinion and to express it without raising their hands.

As a child in the U.S., I was often the translator, the bridge between my parents and schools, the one person who in the process of translating became responsible for getting the message across properly. My parents were never invited to school events and were too busy working to get involved. Schools did nothing to encourage parental involvement of immigrant parents. As a student my experience, life, language, and family were ignored. I was being told in school that "Yo" (me) was not good enough for this society, and I had to change. This sudden alienation became an everyday event; one that persisted throughout my school years. I felt culturally and cognitively abused, "Whether urbane or harsh, cultural invasion is thus always an act of violence against the persons of the invaded culture, who lose their originality or face the threat of losing it" (Freire, p. 133).

Being successful in our current educational system means being able to acculturate to the dominant culture (Credit Nieto, 1999, pg. 75), and, now with accountability, demands it means being able to successfully pass a test. When I came into the country as an immigrant child, I remember the struggles I went through, I was invisible, my "real" life experiences were ignored. In my case, I came to see "real" life experiences as those we live daily, e.g., encounters with strangers, family members, friends, and community members that make us happy and/or sad. I also saw real life in our homes and school, where we saw, touched, smelled, and used our other senses. Reality, to me, included reactions with and from others; looks we are given and names we are called; pains, struggles, faces that make sad; actions, mannerism that make us who we are; love, interactions with others; what we eat; what we dance to; the languages we speak; and the way we act and think in the world. I would have been better prepared to deal with these struggles if I had had a school environment where school was an extension of home, real life, a place where acculturation was not the goal, but rather self-exploration, critical thinking, and exposure to real life situations to bring about "concientization" (Freire, 1970, p. 140) to promote action. Creating this kind of environment would have allowed me to break the current mold of thinking and begin to create new ways of thinking. As a teacher, I wanted my students to have what I did not. In my own classroom I wanted to create new ways of thinking that addressed students' different life situations. I began thinking about what I had that I could use. I realized the starting points were the classroom and myself.

I wanted the classroom to be an open-safe-respectful environment where all cultures, races, and ethnic differences were celebrated and promoted and where the home culture and school experience came together in significant ways. I learned this was revolutionary, "Revolution is achieved with neither verbalism or activism, but rather with praxis, that is, with reflection and action directed at the structures to be transformed" (Freire, p. 107). I began to organize my classroom into a community that was very much connected with home and real life situations. I wanted to make real life social justice issues accessible, visible, and practiced. Yet, I was in need of the "La llave" [the key] that would enable all this, and arts integration became "mi llave" [my key].

What constitutes arts? I define arts by not just a drawing, song, dance, but rather by those everyday experiences that lead us to thinking, questioning, talking, communicating with others, communicating our feelings, doing, hurting, loving, but most importantly feeling and voice/expression. Why the arts? We are surrounded by arts. We breathe them, live them, touch them, and experience the arts daily, both consciously and unconsciously. From the time we are born we are invaded with artistic gestures that portray love, affection, beauty, pain, suffering, and everyday life: "Experiences in the arts richly augment our ordinary life experiences and by doing so, often lead us to tactical understanding of the deeper meaning of our existence, our culture, and our world" (Fisher & McDonald, 2002, p. 1). Through the "arts," students and parents in my classroom began cooperating with their children. This, in turn, created reflection and action in both the classroom and community. Arts created a praxis that allowed students and parents to engage in dialogue and to get involved in school and acting.

Thinking about Being the Teacher

The teacher is a sociocultural mediator when she or he "becomes the link between the child's sociocultural experiences at home and school. That is the teacher becomes the sociocultural, sociohistorical mediator of important formal and informal knowledge about the culture and society in which children develop" (Diaz & Flores, 2000). Therefore, taking the role of a teacher as a sociocultural mediator involves making connections with students and those who impact student's lives. Teachers have the power to bring students and parents into a three-way relationship I call *sociocultural triangulation* (See Figure 1).

Sociocultural triangulation assumes all three are equal and equally responsible to promote a child's progress. The role of the teacher in this triangulation process is to start the communication between student, parent or guardian and teacher that will promote sociocultural acceptance and inclusion in the classroom. The role of the teacher in this case is redefined and restructured to give up control in order to allow dialogue, thinking, and reflection to occur, "If the true commitment to the people, involving transformation of the reality by which they are oppressed, required a theory of transforming action, this theory cannot fail to assign the people a fundamental role in the transformation process" (Freire, p. 108).

In this article I describe how arts integration enabled me to develop such triangulation that resulted in shifting of the roles of the parties involved. Further, I will explain the ways in which organized art activities helped create a classroom environment where relationships between student and parents or guardians evolved in order to promote individuality, cultural inclusion, "conscientization," and equity. By utilizing arts as the "llave" [key] we began to create a cultural platform between a diverse classroom and an equally diverse community. In order to illuminate this, I will explore three areas I organized to achieve these goals: my classroom, my teachings, and community connections. Along with arts integration these three connections (which also lead to sociocultural triangulation) were essential to the creation of a new platform that connected the community and school in a new way of thinking about learning through the arts.

The Classroom

My classroom was a 4th grade two-way immersion classroom in which instruction in the fourth grade was provided in both English and Spanish. Fifty percent of the time instruction was provided in English and fifty percent of the time in Spanish. Half of the students were minorities, mostly Latino/a and Chicano/a, and the other half of the class was White or other ethnicities. The class was considerably from a low socioeconomic background as well as considerably diverse. Class diversity was represented

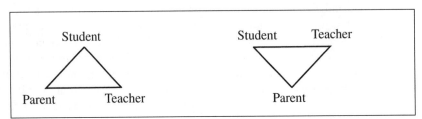

Figure 1 Sociocultural triangulation[*]

[*]This triangulation can be initiated by anyone and no one is the head or controller of this process.

both economically and socially. Parents' occupations ranged from housewives, "campesinos" [farm workers], factory workers, teachers, and professionals working for the government.

When walking into the classroom one would immediately notice how the classroom was divided into different sections or walls. Looking south was the children's international diversity wall, which included pictures of children from around the world. Each picture was enlarged and it included a narrative written by the child or an adult about that child's experience. This wall was of great success in the classroom. Both students and parents enjoyed looking at the pictures and reading the narratives. Still on the south side of the wall, immediately after that wall was a calendar wall, which was in both English and Spanish and more pictures and narratives of children from all over the world. North of the international diversity wall was the social studies wall that presented issues related to subjects being studied in class. The wall contained writing samples of all children. East of the room was the creative wall, this wall was initially designed to give children the opportunity to post drawings, but after I began the sociocultural triangulation process through arts it became the most important wall in the classroom—one both students and parents helped design and maintain.

The classroom was not solely mine, but instead a more collective community space where students, parents, guardians, and I were responsible to make sure the classroom was running smoothly. Before the school year started I contacted all parents via telephone or correspondence. I introduced myself and told them a little bit about my life; this gave parents the opportunity to get to know my life experiences and me. I then proceeded to tell parents that there was an "open door" policy, and that they were welcomed and encouraged to come to volunteer in the classroom. I invited them over to the classroom prior to school starting. Many came and we talked about what they saw as the struggles their children have had, frustrations they have had, and ways in which I could help them both. At this time I informed parents that I was going to be calling them every Friday to give them updates and reports of how the classroom was going. They seemed both shocked, and doubtful; I later found out that the majority of them did not think I was going to be actually calling them every Friday.

As I came from a working class family, I am aware of parents' busy schedules as well as the necessity to sometimes carry more than one job to sustain a family. To that end, I explained to parents that *how* they are involved with their child's schooling is more important than the *amount* of involvement. I wanted parents to be able to express their experiences with their children and me (optional). I wanted parents to begin dialogue, to talk to their children about their struggles when they bring an issue home, to ask their children about school, to share their qualities (those things they are good at), whatever they might be, and most importantly to talk and reflect with them. Some parents expressed concerns that they "Did not have anything they were good at, many of us are just housewives or factory workers, 'campesinos' (farm workers)." I reiterated that everyone has something they are good at and that I was sure that if I asked their children what their parents or guardians were good

at they could tell me in a second. I reinforced the concept that children appreciate any interaction with parents; and the most important interaction was one that started dialogue and reflection. I explained to parents that I was committed to doing all that was in my power to inform parents and guardians of what we were doing in class, that I saw them as colleagues, so input given to me was appreciated and encouraged. By being including and welcoming, parents and guardians and students began to feel comfortable around the classroom, with me, and with other students. They began to trust me and the classroom environment.

As I wanted my classroom to be an extension of home, of real life experiences, I needed a way for parents to participate. Moreover, I wanted this participation to be something that was special and not something that would merely help the teacher with her tasks. It seemed to me that one way to accomplish this was to build a partnership with parents through arts. I began to do this by assigning creative projects to students that involved math, social studies, language arts, and arts. The assignments consisted of students going home and finding things around the classroom and/or neighborhood that had to do with school activities. The goal was for students and parents to look around their world, their reality and find beauty and art within it. For example, when we discussed geometric shapes in the classroom I asked students to go home and with parental or guardian help they were to find an object that would match the shapes we were studying. If they could not find one like it, they had to select objects that when connected to others, created that shape. It was a project that everyone seemed to enjoy. One student could not find the shape of a trapezoid, so his father helped him create one with old car parts. Along with the parent, the student sketched each part of the car where it was taken from and explained the process of figuring out what parts would fit together to create a trapezoid. The student also talked about the process of how the metal was bent, welded, and put together. The student brought it to class to share his invention along with an explanation of how he did it. I used that moment to explain to students that arts does not only involve drawing and coloring but also creating new things out of old ones; arts involves everyday experiences and objects that surround us.

My Teaching

Arts have been one of my favorite tools in the classroom. It was a great source of release when I was a child, as it was through the arts I that was able to express many emotions, feelings, and thoughts. For this reason, I felt that including arts in the classroom and in my lessons was imperative. Initially, arts were used in the classroom as a way to express or retell what students were writing or working on. As in the trapezoid example mentioned above, this was very superficial, and it did not require much critical thinking. I began thinking about my intentions and what art expression meant to me while growing up as an immigrant. With that in mind, I began to think about my goal and about changing my role as a teacher. My goal was to promote critical thinking, a sense of commonality, transcendence of time, connection with real life situations, and recognition of power structures that affected characters in the past and that are still affecting many today. After I had a vision of what could be achieved and my role as the sociocultural mediator, I began to think about ways in which I could utilize the arts to raise awareness, promote critical thinking, equity, and social justice. I had my work cut out for me!

Children are always really excited to read about others' experiences, lives, and struggles. Therefore, I chose several biographies and gave students a summary of the biographies that included some of the accomplishments of the characters. I asked the class to choose one biography and write why they wanted to read that particular biography. Students then took the biographies home and shared with their parents the choices they had. Many children returned to class with their favorites and their parents' favorites. Students were also instructed to draw a picture that predicted events which they thought were going to take place in the story; they were to do this with only the information I provided for them. Some parents wrote their favorites on a piece a paper along with the reasons why they liked that particular biography. Some parents wrote it in Spanish and others in English. This allowed them to be included regardless of the language they spoke. I explained to students that I asked them to come up with reasons as to why we should read these biographies in order for them to begin to think about social-political and cultural issues they and their parents are interested in. I then asked for volunteers to discuss their prediction drawings. They were to explain what it was and why they chose those colors, background, and the meaning behind the scene. This became a wonderful artistic activity and experience given that every student had a different interpretation of each of the stories, and therefore colors, background, and scene were and had different meaning. The three biographies they chose were Frida Kahlo, Anne Frank, and Biddy Mason. Frida Kahlo was read in English, Anne Frank in Spanish, and Biddy Mason in Spanish. We began by reading Anne Frank. To save space here, I will only discuss Anne Frank.

The story of Anne Frank is a book that is filled with socio-political issues. First, we began the unit by reading the book and talking about Germany during that time. I provided the class with historical information about Hitler, the Jewish community, and Germany. None of these historical facts included pictures of Hitler. They were then asked to create a portrait of Germany during those times. The portrait was to include the feeling, struggles, and emotions students thought were being felt by either Germans, Jews, or Hitler. Many drew either a picture of Hitler or included Hitler in their portraits; surprisingly enough almost all but two students drew Hitler with blond hair and blue eyes. When asked to share their portraits with the class many expressed that Hitler was blond with blue eyes because he liked people who were "like him, blond with blue eyes." Here students began to make a connection to their own life experiences, their feeling comfortable or liking people who were like them. So, if Hitler liked people who were blond with blue eyes, then he must be blond and have blue eyes. When they all finished presenting their portraits, I showed them several pictures of Hitler. They were all shocked

to find out that Hitler was not blond, nor did he have blue eyes. I also told them that Hitler's mother was Jewish. And they suddenly began to think. Their eyes were wide open; they were in deep thought. We talked about why it was more acceptable for Hitler to be blond with blue eyes than for him to have dark hair and brown eyes. I got responses such as, "If he was just like the Jews, brown hair, and dark eyes, then why did he dislike them?" "He must not like himself." "I know some people who are mean to many who are like them; like Latinos hurting Latinos."

We talked about what life was about during that time, and what it was to be a young woman without the opportunity to experience "la vida" (life). This conversation about Anne Frank was happening in the classroom and at home. I asked parents to begin a portrait of the Anne Frank story at home. I explained to them that as the story proceeded they were to add something to the portrait. I felt this was a great opportunity to get parents involved and share their experiences their "vida" (life). I asked parents to share how their experiences were similar to those of Anne Frank. Hence, together with their children, many parents worked on the Anne Frank portrait. As the story proceeded they were to add whatever from Anne's life or their life they thought was important to the portrait.

Although this story was one that touched them, they were still responding superficially to the story. I wanted them to feel like the key person in the story, to put their feet in Anne Frank's shoes. Therefore, I asked them to literally take their shoes off and to share them with the person next to them and to put each other's shoes on. I too had to exchange shoes with a student. They were all really excited about doing this. I moved the desks, dimmed the lights, and had students close their eyes. I began playing German classical music and we all began to "walk in someone else's shoes." I asked the class to think about their feelings, emotions, to imagine being a teenager during the holocaust and not being able to enjoy life fully, to imagine being imprisoned, trapped, and scared because of persecution. After the exercise was completed, they were quiet, and some raised their hands. They shared how it felt to imagine being someone else. Many talked about being powerless or "sin poder," frightened, trapped, and caged "como un animal." This activity provided students with a more creative way of looking at the arts. It was the arts that involved movement, sense of one's place, and thinking about others while being here. For fourth graders this was a unique way of feeling the arts—seeing beauty, pain, and otherness.

I asked them to think about the way they felt and to portray their feelings in any way they wanted to. They could do this by singing, acting, drawing, or creating a mini-book. Two created sketches, one sang, and the rest created portraits of what they experienced while being in someone else's shoes. One child drew a portrait of Anne as a girl crying, in one corner was the Star of David and on the other side were armed forces. The side of the face that had armed forces was white with blue eyes and blond hair and the side with the Star of David was brown with black eyes and dark hair. Bars imprisoned the girl, and a tear was coming out of her eye. In the writing description, it said, "The

Hitler army wants her to be white, blond with blue eyes, but she has black hair and dark eyes, and that is why she is in a prison; the attic of that home. Anne was an amazing girl who was proud of who she was and who wrote those letters to let us know what not to do and to take people like they are." One child performed a sketch that connected her own personal experiences with those of Anne Frank. The sketch was a moving and sad story of her grandmother and her family running away from Mexico, away from the threat of being killed. This skit created an interesting conversation between the entire class. Children began to talk about oppression, ethnicity, race, power, powerlessness, discrimination, racism, genocide, social political implications, survival, and what it means to us now. Since many of them did not know the terminology, they only expressed themselves through experiences and examples. As they were giving me examples I began to provide them with the terms that described that particular situation. For example, Hitler killed thousands of people and this is called genocide. We talked about color and preconceived notions many have about a particular race because of the color of their skin. Another student began to sing about class differences, which lead us to talk about privilege and poverty. Many students could relate to this given that many had felt mistreatment because of their social class.

They all had wonderful examples of artistic expressions; their feelings and reactions showed they understood how struggle is painful regardless of when it happens. With this activity, it did not matter if you could draw, sing, or dance. Any form of artistic expression was accepted; it became the universal language of acceptance. Arts became a universal voice that was open and accessible to all.

Community

As parents began to get involved and informed about what was going on in the classroom, other family members became involved as well. Many parents were immigrants and their migration experiences as well as their struggles with a life in a new country had valuable lessons for their children. Being an immigrant whose experiences were ignored, I reiterated to parents that their experiences were valuable and appreciated. Parents became involved in helping to create portraits, giving children ideas, and sharing their own stories. They were dialoguing, communicating, and reflecting on their experiences together. Students began sharing their family stories with the class to find out that many of our stories were similar.

I noticed that children were really interested in other children's stories, in their own family stories, and the way each child expressed their stories through the use the art. Because I was aware that "men and women . . . [are] beings who cannot be truly human apart from communication, for they are essentially communicative creatures" and that "to impede communication is to reduce men to the status of 'things'" (Freire, p. 109), I decided to invite parents, grandparents, guardians, uncles, friends and anyone who wanted to share their struggles, motivations, purpose, moments of feeling powerless, and the

sources of their strengths to participate. Parents were encouraged to create or do something artistic with their children to bring them to class and also present with their son or daughter. I announced this activity a month or two in advance just as I began to make home visits. During home visits we began to share life experiences, anecdotes, and stories. I asked parents, guardians, grandparents, and other family members if they would be willing to share their stories and argued it was important for them to tell children their "whys." Most importantly, I wanted them to share the "whys" for their being in this country and what their motivations and hopes were. In addition, they were asked to share what the lack of opportunities and struggles were that motivated them to flee their own countries. Visiting with them at home and calling parents every Friday worked well and helped me schedule the first couple of presentations. Prior to parents presenting, I sent a bulletin home that included some of the portraits students had created along with a brief description of what we were doing in class. In the bulletin I invited parents to come in and observe other parents' presentations, and I told them I was going to provide snacks and drinks for students and parents.

More than half of the parents showed up that afternoon to hear the presentations. They brought multi-ethnic foods and drinks. One even brought "taquitos" for the entire class. Since it was my idea to do this, I decided to begin the presentations. I talked to the class about coming to the United States, learning the language, and the struggles my parents overcame in this country. I told them about my going to college and trying to be a good teacher who promotes social justice. I showed pictures of my country, my family, and sang for the class. An immigrant mother who had only been in the United States for three years gave the second presentation. She had been a teacher in Mexico and was a factory worker here. She had two jobs and the father of the family had three jobs. The mother and son had created a collage of pictures and portraits that illustrated their story. The son introduced his mother. "This is 'mi Jefa' (my boss or mother), and she is going to share our story with you. Please listen to her; she does not know English, but I will tell you what she is telling and our teacher will help me if need help." The mother began to share that they were a middle class family in Mexico; they owned a house, two cows, and at least three-dozen chickens. The animals enabled them to survive while growing up. She got up every morning to work on the farm, went to school, and then came back after school to work some more. She loved books and really wanted to be a teacher; so she begged her parents to let her go to school. They agreed but only if she continued helping with the animals on the farm. When she started attending university, she took a bus for two hours to get to classes everyday. After graduation, her father became ill. Since she could not support the farm with her salary, and they lost everything. She and her husband were the only two working. She was making less than fifty dollars a month, and her husband made even less. They were really struggling. She said that she wanted her children to go to college and have a better life.

So, they came to this country hoping to be able to do better here. Indeed she had hoped she could teach here. She was shocked when she found out that her degree was worth nothing here and her skills were not appreciated. She decided to place her children in the dual immersion program my class was part of because she wanted to be able to communicate with the teacher. But most importantly she wanted her children to maintain their language. They shared the collage they had created and the portraits of "el ranchito" they had in Mexico. The mother shared that she was not a very artistic person, but creating a collage gave her a new way to look at art. She called it "el arte de mis recuerdos" [the art of my memories]. The son then proceeded to talk about why it was so important for him to go to school. He said, "I need to go to school so that I can buy 'mi jefa un ranchito.'"

Third, an Anglo family of three (mother, father, and son) presented. They spoke only English so their son translated into Spanish. They brought a song to share with the class. Both parents were professionals who lived in an upper middle class neighborhood. They wanted their children to be in the two-way immersion program because they wanted their children to be culturally well rounded, not racist, and to speak a second language. They shared with the class that in their neighborhood there are not any minorities, and they thought it was important for their children to experience being with other children. They also mentioned that three generations before their parents came from Germany not knowing the language and struggling like many of the parents and guardians who are in the class. They also brought black and white pictures of their family in Germany and talked about how excited they were to have children who are bilingual when they are not. They then began to sing a song they sang at home, as a family. This family song had become the way to connect past with present, to maintain their history and to keep their ancestors alive.

These community meetings became the high points of the school year. They became events where the parents and guardians shared their culinary arts and a time for us to learn about foods and experiences from different parts of the world. The classroom became a larger community that consisted of students, teacher, and family members. It was a community in which everyday diversity, differences, struggles, achievements, and pains were shared and respected. Many of the students and parents had known each other only briefly and did not even know that they had so much in common. Some became good friends and started talking on the phone. Others just began to understand many of the struggles others parents had gone through. Others collaborated in creating arts projects with other families who had similar experiences or who were neighbors. Some parents united to bring issues pertaining to them and their children to school officials and school board meetings. They began to have voice. These meetings continued throughout the year as a way to share what is so natural if explored: artistic expression.

Conclusion

Being a teacher of color means being a political being (Apple, 1990). Yet, "la llave," a key, is needed to invite parents and guardians into the education of their students. The arts became a means to begin dialogue where students and parents and guardians could communicate, express themselves, and connect their personal experiences. Arts became an expression of their lives, a way to see the world, and a way to understand different points of view. Through the arts they expressed their desires and needs. They also came to see school differently. Their children were engaged in their real lives as actors and critics.

Students were not just making pictures. Rather they began to experience differences of opinions through arts. They began to explore their own beliefs and those beliefs of their parents and guardians. They began to think critically about the sociopolitical implications mentioned in Anne Frank and other biographies, and how these implications apply to them today. Students began to recognize the difficulties of walking in other people's shoes and found the arts as a way to accomplish this. Art also was used to make writing more interesting, fun, and to make it theirs: to own it.

Arts also became the way for parents to communicate with their children, to talk, to share, to work together, to get to know each other. Parents also learned about each other's families and the reasons why they were in a two-way immersion program and, for some, in this country. It gave students the opportunity to feel proud of their cultural heritage, their family, and their classmates. It provided all of us with a community where social justice, critical thinking, respect, and consciousness were valued. It provided parents, students and me, the teacher, with a process of critical pedagogy. This process was discovery oriented and used the arts as a way of looking at differences. An arts pedagogy was used as a platform to provide a safe method and space for different groups to express traditions and perspectives, to articulate social injustices, to ultimately dialogue, think, reflect and act. Parents and students empowered themselves through their artistic expression. The arts are "La llave" [the key] that teachers can use to create a classroom where all children and their parents and guardians are accepted, respected, and seen as powerful political beings.

References

Diaz, E., & Flores, B. (2000). Teacher as sociocultural mediator: Teaching to the potential. In M. de la cruz Reyes & J. Halcon (Eds.), *Best for Latino children: Critical literacy perspectives*. New York: Teachers College Press.

Fisher, D. & McDonald, N. (2002). *Developing arts-loving readers: Top 10 questions teachers are asking about integrated arts education*. Maryland: Scarecrow Press.

Freire, P. (1970). *Pedagogy of the oppressed*. New York: Seabury.

Nieto, S. (1999). *The light in their eyes: Creating multicultural learning communities*. New York: Teachers College Press.

Rewriting "Goldilocks" in the Urban, Multicultural Elementary School

To teach narrative structure in a meaningful way, a teacher and a researcher experimented with multiliteracies and new technology in an urban elementary school.

HEATHER LOTHERINGTON AND SANDRA CHOW

At Joyce Public School (JPS) in the greater Toronto area of Ontario, Canada, we have been engaged in exploratory research with the overarching aim of observing, creating, understanding, and documenting multiliteracies in action—21st-century literacies that engage multiculturalism, multilingualism, and multimodalism in complex interplay. The project discussed in this article was a pilot study for a methodology for creating digital narratives, a flexible way to introduce narrative structure to a population of culturally diverse, urban elementary school children. Though the project is still experimental, the results of our study are provocative and instructive.

Our goal was to update the traditional children's story "Goldilocks and the Three Bears" using new technologies. The update was focused on culture. Whereas traditional children's literature in the Western canon relies on versions set in print by famous European authors such as Hans Christian Andersen and the Brothers Grimm, the stories themselves often traveled to Europe and then on to North America through and from other cultures. We wanted the children to learn what a story is and to retell a traditional story from their perspectives grounded in contemporary reality, so that the story would become more inclusive of their worlds. Over the course of a year, children in the primary grades learned the basic narrative of "Goldilocks and the Three Bears," then created versions that were more accessible and meaningful to them. This is the story of Goldilocks's extreme makeover.

Once Upon a Time . . .

In 2003, I (Heather Lotherington, first author) spent a sabbatical year in and around JPS in an effort to understand what literacy acquisition constituted for urban, multicultural, and multilingual children who were learning to communicate effectively in a sophisticated media-saturated society with a language and cultural framework not native to most of them. The project began in response to researchers' calls for the revision of traditional literacy curricula in our multiliteracies era (Cope & Kalantzis, 2000a; Lankshear & Knobel, 2003; New London Group, 1996; Snyder, 2002).

One of the most enjoyable parts of each week was my regular reading to children in Sandra Chow's (second author's) kindergarten class. These one-on-one story readings were directed to children who lacked experience with English or narratives, because of their cultural, social, or economic circumstances. My volunteer reading was in response to the principal's casual observation that many incoming schoolchildren lacked the exposure to stories that was expected from preschool socialization in Canada. The weekly readings took place in the library corner of the classroom during the free activity period and I read to children selected by the teacher. Eventually as I became recognized as "the story lady," children ventured over independently to pick stories for me to read.

The children I read to included a trio of Cantonese-speaking girls who liked to make modeling clay pizza together and were leery about being separated, a boy of Caribbean cultural background who had little idea of stories or books, and a number of other children who were new to Canada and in the process of acquiring English. I always asked them to choose their stories from the bookstand in the library corner. By far, the highest demand was for "Goldilocks and the Three Bears."

The story of "Goldilocks and the Three Bears" was familiar to the children because Sandra had engaged them in a diagnostic assessment task using this story at the beginning of the year, in which the children had been flooded with many experiences of a single story to build a narrative knowledge base. The story had been read numerous times in class, and then each child had retold it individually on video, so the teacher was able to assess the children's comprehension of story shape as well as their language development. Still, I wondered why Goldilocks appeared to be the runaway favorite, given the choices available in the class library. I knew that many of these children lacked preschool exposure to stories, so it was possible that they simply didn't know many other stories. But what was the particular attraction to Goldilocks?

There were no blond children in the class—indeed there were very few in the whole school. The story would make little sense to urban children who probably have never encountered bears, a cottage in the woods, or, indeed, porridge. The idea of a child wandering around alone would be preposterous to inner-city children brought up under strict parental vigilance. Furthermore, the story resolution of Goldilocks jumping out a window would be seen as certain death from the perspective of these high-rise dwellers. So what drew them to this story?

One teacher at the school suggested that breaking-and-entering was something the children could relate to. Wondering whether this was indeed a possible real-life link to the narrative, I proposed a project to rewrite "Goldilocks," using the digital resources of the school, to make her story more inclusive of children's contemporary urban reality.

Educational Context

The Toronto District School Board (TDSB) is the largest in Canada and one of the largest in North America (TDSB, n.d., ¶ 1). The population of children attending JPS is typical of elementary schools in the TDSB: Recently, 62% of the students spoke a language other than English at home.

JPS is located in the northwestern part of the city, surrounded by light industry. Most of the students' families are new to the country, and the majority live in a cluster of high-rise apartment buildings where approximately 4,000 people are living. The community is marked as culturally and linguistically rich, though economically poor; it is clearly lacking in the cultural capital (Bourdieu, 1991) assumed for school success in the provincial curriculum, where literacy and language learning are highly dependent on knowledge of the English language and Canadian culture.

Canada is an officially multicultural country, but the benefits of multiculturalism and multilingualism are not considered in the provincial school system where high-stakes mandatory testing equates literacy with knowledge of the English language. The system envisions culture through an Anglo-Canadian historical lens, resulting in a provincial Canadian version of Hirsch's (1987) limited notion of American monocultural literacy (Lotherington, 2004). In order to prepare students for these tests, schools treat students' language and cultural diversity as a problem rather than a resource (Ruiz, 1984), something to be fixed through English as a second language classes.

To provide social equilibrium for incoming children whose cultural and linguistic backgrounds are not consonant with the agenda of provincial test measures, JPS has introduced a platform of technologically enhanced learning. Children learn everything from story reading to music composing in a digitally enhanced environment. JPS been recognized as an innovator in uses of educational technology (Granger, Morbey,

Lotherington, Owston, & Wideman, 2002), and honored with numerous citations and awards. As such, the school is an ideal laboratory for the creation and study of digital narratives.

21st-Century Literacies

Our digital narratives project is theoretically grounded in an evolving theory of *multiliteracies*, a concept developed by the New London Group a decade ago (1996) in a provocative reconceptualization of literacy:

> "Multiliteracies"—a word we chose because it describes two important arguments we might have with the emerging cultural, institutional, and global order. The first argument engages with the multiplicity of communications channels and media; the second with the increasing salience of cultural and linguistic diversity. (Cope & Kalantzis, 2000b, p. 5)

Turbill (2002) hypothesized that we have entered "the age of multiliteracies" in which "[m]eaning making . . . involves being able to 'read' not only print text but also color, sound, movement, and visual representations." Multiliteracies in action are being widely researched and reported (see Alvermann, 2002; Hawisher & Selfe, 2000; Kist, 2005; Lankshear & Knobel, 2003; Snyder, 2002) although research tends to focus on adolescents and the majority of studies address social rather than school-based literacies.

Kist (2005) overviewed multiliteracies projects at six schools in Canada and the United States, focusing generally on high school work. However, he included a grade 6 video teaching project at a middle school in an affluent suburb of Chicago that folds language arts puppet plays into screenwriting. As he noted, "[o]ne of the main characteristics of these classrooms was allowing students to use multiple forms of representation on a daily basis" (p. 130).

Healy and Dooley (2002) reported on children in grades 1 and 2 in two schools in Brisbane, Australia, who created Power-Point presentations and played video games to learn mathematical and language concepts, engaging emergent multiliteracies. The researchers pointed out that their work on multiliteracies addressed a "current paucity of research on teacher relations with children during literacy education in the first years of schooling" (p. 12).

Lotherington et al. (2001) described two elementary schools in inner-city Toronto neighborhoods in which interactive learning spaces for multiple literacies were created by literally knocking down dividing walls. Novel collaborative opportunities arose for teachers, students, and media center staff in their reconfigured spaces, which affected traditional learning and teaching roles and promoted collaborative projects.

Websites inviting children to enter into narratives using interactive cyberediting tools, such as the interactive history of Altoona, Pennsylvania, at http://aahs.aasdcat.com/9a/default. htm (Strangman, 2002); and the internationally collaborative stories without words (http://members.chello.nl/hesselink/) are further inspiring examples of digital narratives that support our exploratory project.

We set out to find a way to transform traditional storybooks into more fluid, individualized digital retellings, evoking the creative license of traditional oral storytelling to tailor retellings to the audience at hand. This engages what Ong (1982) described decades ago as "the 'secondary orality' of present-day high-technology culture, in which a new orality is sustained by telephone, radio, television, and other electronic devices that depend for their existence and functioning on writing and print" (p. 11). I wanted to work with the teachers and the children to co-create a process for inviting the incipient reader into the narrative—that is, to engage readers as writers with the agency to rework a well-known story. I also wanted to find a way to update the traditional fairy tales and folklore that provide the bedrock of early childhood reading experiences to make them more consistent with contemporary multicultural society.

As Warschauer (1999) pointed out, contemporary literacies interpret the world using current textual processes and products (p. 13). The children attending JPS were using postmodern literacy resources—screens, keyboards, and software—enabling text shaping and illustration making to reframe time-tested Eurocentric stories, such as "Goldilocks and the Three Bears." As it turned out, we had much to learn from the children's sense of culture.

Researching Goldilocks

Nations, like narratives, lose their origins in the myths of time and only fully realize their horizons in the mind's eye. (Bhabha, 1990, p. 1)

The principal and most teachers were open to the idea of rewriting "Goldilocks" as a novel way of teaching narrative development in the primary years, an approach in concert with reader-response instruction, which views reading as a dynamic process engaging children in a transactional, aesthetic, and emotional relationship with the text (Broad, 2002). However, one teacher was resistant to the idea of character revision, making the case that the story was a classic that had stood the test of time and didn't need to be altered just because society had changed. This teacher was, herself, a member of a cultural minority; she felt that Goldilocks was a piece of Canadian socialization for her that shouldn't be tampered with.

Concerned about spurious assumptions as to Goldilocks's origins and curious as to the story's roots, I booked an appointment at the Osborne Collection of Early Children's Books, in the Toronto Public Library, to see the original handwritten and illustrated manuscript of *The Story of the Three Bears* (Mure, 1967/1831), which had been discovered in 1949 in the original bequest from the English librarian Edgar Osborne. Curiously, then, Goldilocks could indeed claim to be a part of Canadian culture, in that she had immigrated in manuscript form to the Toronto Public Library.

I tracked the evolution of *The Story of the Three Bears* in British and American literary publications through the 19th and into the early 20th century. Goldilocks had had a circuitous becoming! In the original Scottish cautionary folktale from which the narrative is theorized to have evolved, Goldilocks was a she-fox who enters the lair of three bears and is eaten for her transgression (Bettelheim, 1976). The vixen is reinterpreted as a vindictive old woman living in an English manor in the print debut of the story handwritten by Miss Eleanor Mure for her nephew's fourth birthday (Mure, 1967/1831). By the mid-19th century, Goldilocks has been transformed into a mischievous little girl named Silver Locks (Anonymous, 1856), though she doesn't yet have blond hair or the name to match. She becomes a blond later in the century, but does not emerge consistently as Goldilocks until the early 20th century (Lotherington, 2005).

The resistant teacher's objections to modernizing Goldilocks were thus considered and researched. "The Three Bears" in fact did have a curious and unexpected literary tie with Canada, but Goldilocks as the protagonist of the folk tale had been fabricated. First the vixen had been anthropomorphized, then made younger and fairer as the 19th century rolled into the 20th, becoming cemented in our cultural consciousness as a little blonde girl through the agency of print. As Ong (1982) pointed out, "[t]hough words are grounded in oral speech, writing tyrannically locks them into a visual field forever" (p. 12). It was time to give Goldilocks a 21st-century makeover.

Rewriting Goldilocks

With approval from the principal, and ethical clearance and funding assistance from the Social Sciences and Humanities Research Council of Canada, a number of teachers agreed to try out the experimental rewriting project the following year to see whether it proved to be a viable means of teaching narrative structure. Rewriting Goldilocks: Emergent Transliteracies was organized as a participatory action-research project in which each teacher tried out what he or she thought would work in the classroom in response to discussions of understanding contemporary multiliteracies, teaching narrative structure, engaging the emergent reader, and experimenting with digital text forms. The project was exploratory in nature, situated in qualitative rather than quantitative inquiry. Our aims were to figure out how to teach narratives using digital resources so that children could write their cultural realities into the story.

We met for in-school and after-school sharing sessions where we brainstormed ideas about how to structure and implement a digital rewriting of the story of "Goldilocks and the Three Bears." Though most teachers saw the project through, it was Sandra Chow who persevered to create the first collection of digitally rendered rewritings of "Goldilocks and the Three Bears." Her story is told here.

Teaching Narrative Structure

I (Sandra) decided to try out the Goldilocks rewriting experiment in the grade 2 class I taught that year. At the beginning of the school year, I requested that our school purchase a number of versions of the story of "Goldilocks and the Three Bears," including traditional and contemporary versions, so that I could familiarize children with the basic narrative. I read the various versions of the prototypical "Goldilocks and the Three Bears" story (e.g., versions written by Byron Barton, 1999, and Paul

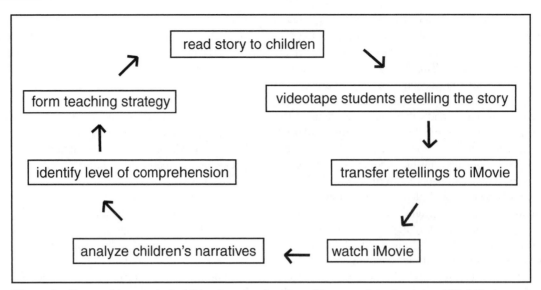

Figure 1 Researching grade 2 children's understanding of the narrative structure of "Goldilocks and the Three Bears."

Galdone, 1979) to my class many times so that they would become very familiar with the story. I then asked the students to retell the story in their journals. Following this, I introduced a story map so the students were able to grasp the various elements of the story more clearly. My hope was that establishing a solid understanding of the story would allow students to manipulate the story into their own version. Figure 1 summarizes the teaching preparation for the story rewriting process.

Story retellings in the early primary grades are extended forms of talk. I wanted to know whether each child could retell a simple story with a recognizable beginning, middle, and end. Could the child use descriptive language and incorporate a literary style with phrases such as "once upon a time . . ." and "happily ever after"? Did the child understand the impact of environment on the story, or the ways in which a character acts?

Next, we read stories by authors who wrote quirkier versions of the three bears story (e.g., *Somebody and the Three Blairs* by Marilyn Tolhurst, 1994; *Santa and the Three Bears* by Dominic Catalano, 2000; *Abuelo and the Three Bears* by Jerry Tello and Ana Lopez Escriva, 1997). Students began to see how the main elements of a story (e.g., setting, characters,

ending) could be altered slightly, while maintaining identifiable patterns and key themes, so that the story was individually "retold." I began highlighting the various parts of a story in my teaching: characters, setting, plot problem, and solution (see Table 1).

As we learned about these basic elements in "Goldilocks and the Three Bears," the students were asked to change the characters, setting, and ending to create their "own" three bears story. Students incorporated multiple literacy modalities, including technology (Wiggleworks software by Scholastic for a base story; digital pictures), group work (poster of the story setting), visual arts (diorama construction), writing, and drama (a puppet show) in order to enhance their learning of these key story elements. Their final product was an individual version of the story with their own unique settings, characters, and endings produced digitally on hypercards—slides that include a text box, illustration, and sound (using HyperStudio, a multimedia authoring tool for project-based learning by Knowledge Adventure). Their stories were then printed in book form as a Father's Day present (see http://schools.tdsb.on.ca/joyce/main/gold ilocks/index.htm for selected children's stories).

Table 1 Instructions for Writing an Individualized Three Bears Story

1. Introduction	Start with: Once upon a time . . . , One day . . . , One morning . . . , or One afternoon. . . .
	Create a setting (time and place).
2. Talk about your main character	Describe the character's physical appearance.
	Describe the character's personality.
3. Plot: What happens in the story?	The problems: Goldilocks goes into and around the house uninvited.
	The solutions: The bears come home, see what has happened, and find Goldilocks.
4. Choose an ending	Goldilocks runs away.
	Goldilocks stays for supper.

Table 2 Technical Support for Children's Story Retelling

Classroom Activity	Technology Support
Small group analysis of setting based on *Abuelo and the Three Bears* (Jerry Tello, Ana Lopez Escriva), Wiggleworks (Scholastic) program. Students were assigned a specific setting in the story and asked to describe it fully through pictures and words.	Wiggleworks (Scholastic) *read* and *read aloud* functions Digital photography
Math/science investigation of the house of the three bears. Students were asked to construct, using various building materials (e.g., pattern blocks, multilink cubes), the house of the three bears.	Digital photography
Wiggleworks used to make a plan (picture and words) of students' self-selected setting for their own Goldilocks story.	Wiggleworks *write* function
Individual student dioramas of their self-selected setting for their own Goldilocks story.	Digital photography
Students create puppets of the characters they will be using in their own Goldilocks story, and plan out an oral version of their story first.	Digital photography
Creation of rewritten Goldilocks stories in digital format with illustrations.	HyperStudio

Teaching With Technology

Teaching with technology is a unique strength of our school, which has received national designation in Canada as a technologically innovative school. I have found that using technology in the classroom enhances learning, improves efficiency and flexibility, and increases student motivation. Our class has a digital camera, a laptop computer with a projector and screen, and a number of individual computers. Our school has a mobile computer lab and a library lab with a digital white board. Table 2 outlines the technology incorporated in stages of rewriting Goldilocks.

We continue to experiment with technological creativity in the rewritten stories. I (Sandra) am trying out narrating the children's rewritten stories with their voices; animating the stories using HyperStudio; dramatizing the story, then videotaping and digitizing children's dramatizations using iMovie (Apple application for creating movies); incorporating morphing software to morph students as authors into their stories; and translating words into other languages.

Reading Goldilocks from the Inside Out

Texts can represent all sorts of different adjustments to orality-literacy polarities. (Ong, 1982, p. 157)

What did we learn? The children clearly enjoyed writing their own versions of "Goldilocks and the Three Bears," and subsequent classes have loudly applauded the HyperStudio versions

Sandra's grade 2 children wrote in our pilot year. But there was much to think about.

Listening to a teacher remark on the courage of a young child to color the face outlined on his screen brown—something she would never have had the bravado to try when she was in school as a minority student, I (Heather) had hopes of finding Goldilocks reborn as Dreadlocks. From grade 1 came a lovely depiction of Bradylocks, a little dark-skinned girl with large black braids (see Figure 2), but she was the exception. Classroom teachers informed me that children lived in a digital sphere: Culture for them was YTV (a Canadian children's television network), Pokémon, and Yu-Gi-Oh. They were right. Children's revisions of Goldilocks were far more complex than anything I had imagined, evoking intertextual references to digital and pop culture, and taking Goldilocks into outer space.

The revised protagonists showed the benefits of Sandra's detailed work on character development. Goldilocks took on a number of diverse identities in the children's rewritten tales: mermaid, vampire, dog, bird, shark, and space explorer. In these stories, she (or he or it) invades the homes of ghosts, aliens, kittens, fish, and witches, but the quintessential three of traditional tales is maintained (Bettelheim, 1976).

In my imagining, a revised Goldilocks mirrored the children's urban, multicultural reality: She would not be a little, fair-haired girl; the bears would be raccoons or skunks or squirrels—accessible city creatures—and the cottage in the woods would be an urban dwelling. Given that porridge was an unfamiliar food to most children, I hoped for more recognizable foods that would be healthy choices. Indeed, children were quite adventurous, and foods experienced by the rewritten protagonists included

Once upon a time there was a girl named Bradylocks and her mother sent her out to buy some buttyfull clothes.
On the way home she found something strange.

Figure 2 Bradylocks

fishfood (for Goldilocks rewritten as a mermaid), ice cream, rice pudding, pizza, soup, pie, and carrots. In one marvelous extraterrestrial adventure, the alien asks: "Who's been eating my slime?" Even this seemed to be an improvement on porridge.

The children exceeded my expectations by far. In the best stories, Goldilocks is delineated in terms of personality, rather than superficially redrawn. In one little girl's bold rewrite, the protagonist is Sharky, a classic bully (see Figure 3), who invades the home of three goldfish and takes for himself not the baby goldfish's food, chair, and bed, but papa's. When he is discovered sleeping in papa's bed by the three goldfish, the story is resolved dramatically (see Figure 4): Sharky simply eats the three goldfish and lives happily ever after!

Goldilocks is transformed by another student into a robber "who is evil, dumb, and stinky," though really he's just hungry; the bears figure this out and offer him some of the soup he sneaked in to eat. A little boy recreates Goldilocks as a space explorer who is imagined not as a vandal but as an adventurer. A little girl sees Goldilocks as neglected, just looking for some comfort in life, a characterization eerily similar to the very first commercial version of the traditional tale: *Story of the Three Bears,* published in 1837 by Robert Southey, featuring an old beggar woman as the protagonist (Lotherington, 2005). In the child's version, Goldilocks is found sleeping in baby bear's bed by bears who are smiling, and who provide a peaceful and parentally generous resolution to her invasion of their privacy

(see Figure 5): Goldilocks is fed and accompanied home, where she does her homework. A year later, baby bear visits her for a sleepover. Goldilocks is seen as a child who is fundamentally good but who needs attention and direction, which the bears supply.

Goldilocks—Before and After

The survival of narrative does not depend on its ability to adapt itself to new media; narrative has been around so long that it has little to fear from computers. Rather it is the future of new media as a form of entertainment that depends on their ability to develop their own forms of narrativity. (Ryan, 2004, p. 356)

The narratives in this pilot project were written and drawn in HyperStudio software, then printed in book version for Father's Day when the children took them home and read them to their parents. They also showed their parents the dioramas of the settings of their stories. At present the stories are linear, in concert with trying to teach the concept of narratives to grade 2.

We are now in the second year of trials for our rewritten stories and it is clear that the current year's grade 2 class loves the hypertext "Goldilocks" stories their predecessors created. This year, the class is rewriting "The Little Red Hen," who calls for help in sowing and harvesting grain to make bread, and is

Figure 3 Sharky the bully

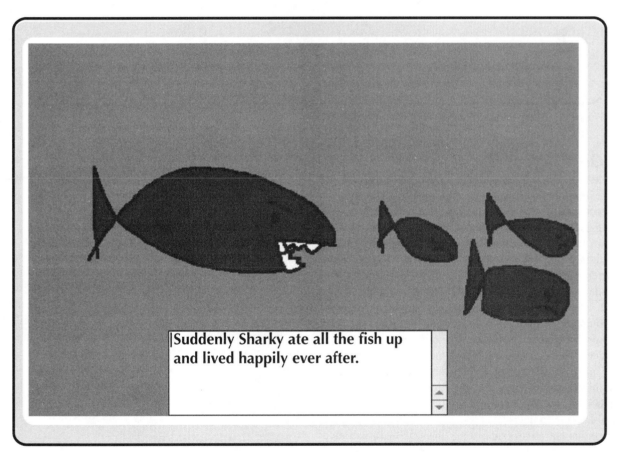

Figure 4 Story ending: Sharky lives happily ever after

answered by lazy barnyard animals who do not wish to help in the process of making bread but are happy to eat the finished loaf. These rewritten protagonists are making foods such as hot dogs, macaroni, and birthday cake; in castles, hospitals, deserts, and under the sea; with gargoyles, princesses, tigers, and jellyfish—though, of course, not all in the same story. They are augmenting expressive modalities from paper to screen with drama, video, and digital animation.

Figure 5 Story ending: Friendly bears find Goldilocks

Was Our Project Successful?

The process and results of our rewriting to update the 20th-century textual characterization of Goldilocks to a 21st-century digital protagonist was successful on many fronts, but not always in the ways anticipated. The project was truly multi-modal, incorporating art, drama (puppetry), text, and hypertext. The children's digital narratives were engagingly novel retold tales—exemplary postmodern picture books (Anstey, 2002). The products were multicultural, though not in the way I had expected. It is clear that expectations of contemporary multi-cultural literature require much fine-tuning to include the very digital world we were endeavoring to bring into the process and product. These children envision their cultural worlds as plugged into pop culture; their ideas about culture are more heavily influenced by television than by the physical world around them.

Our aims were to devise and test a pedagogical process for creating digital narratives that had the power to teach narrative structure within a multiliteracies paradigm in the primary grades. We sought to produce meaningful and directed pedagogical possibilities, not quantifiable results. Our process had to provide a route for children to learn narrative structure and to be authors of their own narrative versions. This, in effect, was the test.

The children in Sandra's grade 2 class acquired a thorough understanding of narrative structure through intimate knowledge of the traditional story "Goldilocks and the Three Bears."

They were able to retell the story, not solely in the original version—a useful measure of comprehension—but creatively as a work from their own individual cultural perspectives. This was a much more sophisticated literacy task, especially for 7- and 8-year-olds!

The project helped us in our ongoing quest for ways to approach curricular literacy instruction within a paradigm of multiliteracies. The children interlaced old and new literacies, moving from paper to screen with ease and flexibility and, in the process, were transformed from passive emergent readers external to the text culturally, linguistically, and intellectually, to authors working inside their own text versions. In this way, they took ownership of their literacy acquisition by learning to write their own worlds into the stories told by others (Freire, 1970/1998). They did this multimodally by using the digital media that are native to 21st-century children. They are teaching us how to create a pedagogy of multiliteracies.

References

Alvermann, D.E. (Ed.). (2002). *Adolescents and literacies in a digital world.* New York: Peter Lang.

Anonymous. (1856). *The three bears.* London: Routledge.

Anstey, M. (2002). "It's not all black and white": Postmodern picture books and new literacies. *Journal of Adolescent & Adult Literacy, 45,* 444–457.

Bettelheim, B. (1976). *The uses of enchantment: The meaning and importance of fairy tales.* New York: Alfred A. Knopf.

Bhabha, H.K. (1990). Introduction: Narrating the nation. In H.K. Bhabha (Ed.), *Nation and narration* (pp. 1–7). London: Routledge.

Bourdieu, P. (1991). *Language and symbolic power.* Cambridge, MA: Harvard University Press.

Broad, K. (2002). Reader response instruction for emergent readers. In M. Hunsberger & G. Labercane (Eds.), *Making meaning in the response-based classroom* (pp. 13–29). Boston: Allyn & Bacon.

Cope, B., & Kalantzis, M. (Eds.). (2000a). *Multiliteracies: Literacy learning and the design of social futures.* London: Routledge.

Cope, B., & Kalantzis, M. (2000b). Introduction. Multiliteracies: The beginnings of an idea. In B. Cope & M. Kalantzis (Eds.), *Multiliteracies: Literacy learning and the design of social futures* (pp. 3–8). London: Routledge.

Freire, P. (1998). *Pedagogy of the oppressed* (M.B. Ramos, Trans.). New York: Continuum. (Original work published 1970)

Granger, C., Morbey, M.L., Lotherington, H., Owston, R., & Wideman, H. (2002). Canada: Factors contributing to teachers' successful implementation of information technology. *Journal of Computer Assisted Learning, 18,* 480–488.

Hawisher, G.E., & Selfe, C.L. (Eds.). (2000). *Global literacies and the world-wide web.* London: Routledge.

Healy, A., & Dooley, K. (2002, December). *Digital reading pedagogy for novice readers.* Paper presented at the annual Meeting of the Australian Association for Research in Education, Brisbane. (ERIC Document Reproduction Service No. ED 473959; http://www.eric.ed.gov/contentdelivery/servlet/ERICServlet?accno=ED473959)

Hirsch, E.D., Jr. (1987). *Cultural literacy: What every American needs to know.* Boston: Houghton Mifflin.

Kist, W. (2005). *New literacies in action: Teaching and learning in multiple media.* New York: Teachers College Press.

Lankshear, C., & Knobel, M. (2003). *New literacies: Changing knowledge and classroom learning.* Buckingham, England; Philadelphia: Open University Press.

Lotherington, H. (2004). Emergent metaliteracies: What the Xbox has to offer the EQAO. *Linguistics and Education, 14,* 305–319.

Lotherington, H. (2005). Writing postmodern fairy tales at Main Street School: Digital narratives and evolving transliteracies. *McGill Journal of Education, 40*(1), 109–119.

Lotherington, H., Morbey, M.L., Granger, C., & Doan, L. (2001). Tearing down the walls: New literacies and new horizons in the elementary school. In B. Barrell (Ed.), *Technology, teaching and learning: Issues in the integration of technology* (pp. 131–161). Calgary, AB: Detselig.

Mure, E. (1967). *The story of the three bears.* Toronto: Oxford University Press. (Original work published 1831)

New London Group. (1996). A pedagogy of multiliteracies: Designing social factors. *Harvard Educational Review, 66,* 60–92.

Ong, W.J. (1982). *Orality and literacy: The technologizing of the word.* London: Routledge.

Ruiz, R. (1984). Orientations in language planning. *NABE Journal, 8*(2), 15–34.

Ryan, M.-L. (2004). Will new media produce new narratives? In M.-L. Ryan (Ed.), *Narrative across media: The languages of storytelling* (pp. 337–359). Lincoln: University of Nebraska Press.

Snyder, I. (Ed.). (2002). *Silicon literacies: Communication, innovation and education in the electronic age.* London: Routledge.

Southey, R. (1837). *Story of the three bears.* Oxford, England: Oxford University Press.

Strangman, N. (2002, October). Using technology to take young readers on a digital journey to the past. *Reading Online, 6*(3). Retrieved July 5, 2006, from http://www/readingonline.org/articles/art_index.asp?HREF=voices/huschak/index.html

Toronto District School Board (n.d.) *About us.* Retrieved July 5, 2006, from http://www.tdsb.on.ca/_site/ViewItem.asp?siteid=133&menuid=529&pageid=413

Turbill, J. (2002, February). The four ages of reading philosophy and pedagogy: A framework for examining theory and practice. *Reading Online, 5*(6). Retrieved June 15, 2006, from http://www.readingonline.org/international/inter_index.asp?HREF=turbill4/index.html

Warschauer, M. (1999). *Electronic literacies: Language, culture and power in online education.* Mahwah, NJ: Erlbaum.

Children's Literature Cited

Barton, B. (1999). *The three bears.* New York: HarperCollins.

Catalano, D. (2000). *Santa and the three bears.* Honesdale, PA: Boyds Mills Press.

Galdone, P. (1979). *The three bears.* New York: Clarion Books.

Tello, J., & Escriva, A.L. (1997). *Abuelo and the three bears.* New York: Scholastic.

Tolhurst, M. (1994). *Somebody and the three Blairs.* New York: Scholastic.

LOTHERINGTON teaches at York University (4700 Keele Street, Toronto, ON M3J 1P3, Canada). E-mail hlotherington@edu.yorku.ca. CHOW teaches at Joyce Public School in Toronto.

From *The Reading Teacher,* by Heather Lotherington and Sandra Chow, Vol. 60, no. 3, November 2006, pp. 242–252. Copyright © 2006 by The International Reading Association. Reprinted by permission. www.reading.org

Assessing English Language Learners' Content Knowledge in Middle School Classrooms

This We Believe *Characteristics*

- Assessment and evaluation programs that promote quality learning
- High expectations for every member of the learning community
- Multiple learning and teaching approaches that respond to their diversity

N. ELENI PAPPAMIHIEL AND FLORIN MIHAI

The number of English Language Learners (ELLs) in U.S. public schools increased more than 45% between the 1997–1998 school year and 2003 (Padolsky, 2004). Given this trend, middle school teachers are seeing more and more ELLs in their classrooms, but a significant number of these teachers feel either unprepared or underprepared to work with non-native speakers of English (Lewis, Parsad, Carey, Bartfai, Farris, & Smerdon 1999; President's Advisory Commission on Educational Excellence for Hispanic Americans, 2000). The purpose of this article is to highlight ways in which middle school content area teachers can more effectively assess ELLs in their classrooms.

In the following pages, five questions are posed to guide middle school content teachers in making adaptations and accommodations when using traditional classroom tests. The objective of these adaptations is to create a more valid and reliable assessment picture. We hope to show that teachers do not need to create completely different tests for ELLs in all instances, but rather, they can adapt current classroom assessment instruments to accommodate the linguistic and cultural needs of ELLs until they are able to fully participate in classroom assessment without adaptation. While we acknowledge that there are many types of alternative assessments, such as performance and portfolio assessments, that are effective with ELLs, this article is designed to assist regular middle school classroom teachers when these other types of assessment are not feasible or available. Our hope is that middle school teachers will use a combination of adapted traditional assessments and effective alternative assessments with ELLs.

Assessing English Language Learners

"For a non-native speaker of English . . . every test given in English becomes, in part, a language or literacy test." (American Psycho-

logical Association, 1999, p. 73). Moreover, we know that bilingual individuals vary greatly in their academic use of language, making language background an important consideration in any testing situation (President's Advisory Commission on Educational Excellence for Hispanic Americans, 2000). Yet, some teachers do not consider testing adaptations and accommodations "fair" to their native speakers of English, emphasizing that any testing changes would alter the testing environment. However, for linguistically diverse students, any test given in English automatically constitutes an unequal testing environment when compared to that of a native speaker of English. When teachers acknowledge the need for testing adaptations and accommodations, it is often difficult to find information to guide them.

Much of the current literature concerning the assessment of ELLs is focused on the assessment of language proficiency. So, when middle school teachers look for resources about the assessment of ELLs, they may find a vast amount of information on how to effectively assess how well an ELL speaks, reads, or writes in English, but it is more difficult to find effective strategies to use when assessing ELLs' content knowledge. While it is critical to understand ELLs' English language proficiency to assess their content proficiency, this type of proficiency assessment is not the central evaluation task that concerns most content area teachers. In other words, a science teacher would certainly care to know the ELL's language proficiency but would be more concerned about assessing the specific science content that student had mastered.

Information available for application to content area classrooms most often relates to various instructional strategies rather than testing strategies. To help make the determination about mastery of content objectives more valid, we suggest that teachers answer five questions. These questions do not constitute an exhaustive inventory but rather are intended to provide a starting point for content area teachers who are seeking to make their classroom tests and quizzes more valid. The five questions are listed below:

1. Do I know my students' English language proficiencies?
2. Have I designed a test that mirrors classroom objectives, strategies, and activities?
3. Have I made use of all relevant and available visuals and graphics?
4. Have I incorporated true accommodations to level the playing field for my ELLs?
5. Have I created a clear scoring rubric that will allow me to provide culturally sensitive and useful feedback?

These five questions reflect major aspects of assessment and help provide a clearer, more holistic picture of an ELL's abilities, strengths, and weaknesses. They account for English proficiency, the reduction of language requirements, the use of non-linguistic cues as adaptations, appropriate accommodations, and appropriate feedback. In the following paragraphs, each will be outlined with links to research, classroom practice, and examples.

Do I Know My Students' English Proficiency Levels?

Embedded within this question are a variety of characteristics that go beyond an ELL's ability to form grammatically correct sentences in English. Acknowledging the fact that English proficiency is a complex concept can help many teachers adapt their tests to meet that proficiency. According to Canale and Swain (1979), among others, English proficiency can be viewed within the concept of communicative competence. This type of competence posits that English proficiency is not limited to grammatical competence, but also includes sociolinguistic, strategic, and discourse competence. Hence, when making adaptations for ELLs' competence in English, it is important to look at their ability to understand the culture embedded in the language, repair breakdowns in communication, and engage in appropriate conversations in addition to forming grammatically correct sentences.

Moreover, understanding where an ELL falls in terms of English language proficiency means making not only curricular adaptations and accommodations for them but also designing such adaptations for assessment purposes. Perhaps Ernst-Slavin, Moore, and Maloney (2002) provided the most comprehensive information to help teachers match English language proficiency with strategies and adaptations (see Figure 1). Ernst-Slavin and associates have provided specific strategies that are intended to enhance students' emerging abilities and help them overcome linguistics deficits. For example, at the *early production* level Ernst-Slavin has recommended that questions only require a yes/no or either/or response. Furthermore, they write that effective strategies would include retellings, oral readings, and some written practice. Whereas, at the *speech emergence* level, ELLs have relatively good social English skills and are becoming more familiar with academic English structures. An ELL at this level would be relatively comfortable with open-ended questions and descriptions. Knowing these characteristics of a student's English language proficiency, a ninth grade science teacher could adapt test questions so that more open-ended questions are posed. In addition, this same teacher could accommodate an ELL at this level by providing a glossary of useful terms and fill-in-the-blank paragraphs that would allow the student to focus on expressing content mastery rather than linguistic advances. An example of an extreme linguistic burden can be seen in the following ninth grade word problem taken from the practice items for the Florida Comprehensive Assessment Test (FCAT, n.d.) mathematics section. Students were asked to calculate volume.

> An engineer is designing a metal gasket for a spacecraft. The gasket has the shape of a cylinder with a cylindrical hole through the center. The diameter of the gasket is 9 centimeters, and its height is 4 centimeters. The diameter of the hole is 3 centimeters. What is the volume of metal, in cubic centimeters, that is required to make the gasket?

While an unlabeled diagram of the cylinder with the hole is provided, the vocabulary of the problem itself, (gasket, spacecraft, cylindrical, etc.) can make this problem impossible for an ELL to solve. To an ELL at the early production level (assuming that he/she has mastered such vocabulary as "shape," "diameter," "volume," and "cylinder"), this problem may very well have read like this:

> An ____ is designing a metal ____ for a ____. The ____ has the shape of a cylinder with a hole through the center. The diameter of the ____ is 9 centimeters, and its height is 4 centimeters. The diameter of the hole is 3 centimeters. What is the volume of ____, in ____ centimeters, that is required to make the ____?

Even though the necessary information to solve the problem still exists in the item, it is inaccessible for this ELL. By simplifying the word problem and labeling the diagram (Figure 2) with the appropriate vocabulary that has been learned and reinforced in class, the teacher could assess this student's mastery of the concept of volume by reducing the linguistic burden of the math assessment. It is important to note that, although the language of the problem has been changed, the concept being assessed has not been altered. With some word simplification, this word problem may change to read as illustrated in Figure 2.

Language simplification, repetition of frequently used phrases, and peer/teacher-aid can help ELLs respond to content questions within their linguistic boundaries.

By knowing and working within ELLs' English language proficiencies, a teacher is able to more validly and reliably determine their mastery of content rather than making this expression of knowledge dependent upon their limited mastery of the English language. Language simplification, repetition of frequently used phrases, and a peer/teacher-aid can help ELLs respond to content questions within their linguistic boundaries. Trusted peers and teachers can provide scaffolded language support, especially at the beginning stages of language acquisition and in instances where classroom concepts are text driven, as in a social studies classroom (Egbert & Simich-Dudgeon, 2001). It is essential that a content area teacher know not only what ELLs can do on their own, but also what they are capable of with appropriate linguistic aid (e.g., graphic organizers, tables, glossaries). This type of assessment can also help content area teachers determine what other types of adaptations and accommodations are necessary as ELLs progress through the stages of language development.

Modified objectives reduce the linguistic burden on the ELL without reducing the cognitive demand of the objective.

Figure 1 Stages of Language Development and Cultural Adaptation

Stage I: Preproduction

Linguistic Considerations: Student . . .	Cultural Considerations	Suggestions for Teachers	Questioning Techniques: Appropriate Questions Include . . .	Effective Activities
• Communicates with gestures, actions, and verbal formulas • Is building receptive vocabulary • Is recycling learning language practice • Benefits from listening comprehension activities	• Silent period	• Create a stress-free environment • Provide support and encouragement • Avoid asking direct questions	• Find the . . . • Point to . . . • Put the ____ next to the ____. • Do you have the ____? • Who did ____? • What is his/her name? • What is this (concrete object)? • Who is he/she? • Who has the ____?	• Face-to-face conversation • Simple demonstrated directions • Participation in art/music/PE • Puzzles/games, real objects/manipulatives • Picture books • Encouraging drawing

Stage II: Early Production

• Intuitively understands that English is a system • Labels and categorizes • Encounters native language interference • Uses one- and two-word responses and chunks of language • Can say, "I don't understand."	• Adaptation fatigue	• Monitor error correction • Use anticipation guides • Use list of key terms for previewing • Use audiotapes of readings and lectures • Use graphic organizers	• Questions that require a yes/no answer • Questions that ask either/or	• Low-level questions • Retelling a story • Picture books with simple texts • Simple written responses • Copying words and sentences • Recipes • Oral reading • Written practice

Stage III: Speech Emergence

• Uses language purposefully • Produces complete sentences	• Tension between assimilation and acculturation • Recovering from previous frustration and fatigue	• Use frequent comprehension checks • Design lessons focusing on concepts • Introduce expanded vocabulary • Use models, charts, maps, and timelines	• Open ended questions; why or how questions • Specific questions • How is it that ____? • Tell me about ____.	• Demonstrations • Simple oral presentations • Answering higher level questions • Hands-on activities • Small group work • Word sound symbol production • Simple writing • Computer lessons play and role-playing • Choral reading

Stage IV: Intermediate Fluency

• Can produce connected narrative • Can use reading and writing incorporated into lesson • Can write answers to higher level questions • Can resolve conflicts verbally	• Cultural adjustment	• Validate students' languages and cultures	• What would you recommend or suggest? • How do you think this story will end? • What is the story about? • What is your opinion on this? • Describe/compare and contrast • How are these the same or different? • What would happen if ____? • Which do you prefer? Why?	• Content/subject explanations • Paragraph writing • Reading for information in content areas • Summaries, outlines, book reports • Explanations of new ideas/concepts • Workbooks, worksheets, and tests • Lecture discussions • Literary analysis of plot, character, setting • Simple report writing

Source: Table 2 in Ernst–Slavit, G. Moore, M.A., & Maloney, C.D. (2002, October). Changing Lives: Teaching English and litereature to ESL students. *Journal of Adolescent & Adult Literacy, 46*(2), 116–131. Reprinted with permission of the International Reading Association.

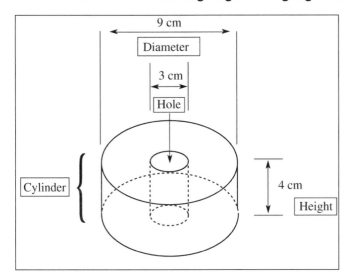

Figure 2 Example of labeling with language simplification. A cylinder has a diameter of 9 centimeters, and its height is 4 centimeters. There is a hole in the middle of the cylinder. The diameter of the hole is 3 centimeters. You want to fill the cylinder with water. What is the volume of water that is required to fill the cylinder in cubic centimeters (cm^3)?

An example of such an assessment may include a short answer response item on a social studies test that would normally be answered with a short essay written by the student. More specifically, when a social studies teacher is focusing on consumerism and wants to assess students' ability to comparison shop, he may ask students to answer the following question.

> You want to buy a new jacket. The Pistons jacket is almost twice the price of a similar jacket sold by Macy's. Do you buy the expensive Pistons jacket or the Macy's brand? Why?

This short answer question can be broken down into a series of simplified questions that scaffold the ELL's response in a manner that allows the teacher to determine exactly where the student's comprehension may be compromised. Another method of scaffolding the item would be to have students complete a graphic organizer. Examples of each of these methods are given in Figure 3.

Have I Designed a Test That Mirrors Classroom Objectives, Strategies, and Activities?

A clear statement of objectives is necessary for any assessment of student achievement (Genessee & Upshur, 1996). Ideally, before any testing takes place, content area teachers have already adapted classroom objectives and activities according to their ELLs' language proficiency. For example, a science teacher may have the following class objective for her middle school earth science class, "Students will be able to accurately define the words 'gravity,' 'erosion,' and 'deposition' and give examples of each." For an ELL at an early production level, she may have adapted this objective to, "Student is able to accurately identify pictorial examples of *gravity, erosion,* and *deposition* and provide two- to three-word descriptions." The test designed to assess the ELL student's mastery of this information should reflect the adapted objec-

SPEECH EMERGENCE

You want to buy a jacket. There is one jacket that cost $200. It is expensive because it has the name of a famous sports team on it. There is another jacket that is made by the store that costs $50. This jacket does not have the name of the sports team on it. Both jackets are made of wool and have a silk liner.

1. What is the cost of each jacket?

    Sports Jacket _____ Store Jacket _____

2. Are the two jackets of the same quality?

    Yes _____ No _____

3. Which one would you buy?

4. Why?

EARLY PRODUCTION

You want to buy a jacket. There is one jacket that costs $200. It is expensive because it has the name of a famous sports team on it. There is another jacket that is made by the store that costs $50. This jacket does not have the name of the sports team on it. Both jackets are made of wool and have silk liners.

1. Compare the two jackets.

    Sports Jacket _____ Store Jacket _____

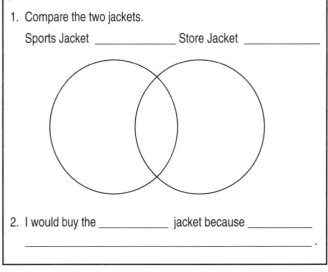

2. I would buy the _____ jacket because _____
    _____ .

Figure 3 Comparison Shopping

tive. While it is not recommended that teachers consistently create completely different learning objectives for their ELLs, all instructional objectives should fit each ELL's level of English language proficiency. As tests should be direct reflections of classroom objectives, so should adapted classroom objectives be assessed using adapted tests. In the example, the science teacher would not ask her early production ELL to write a complete definition as she might her native English speakers, but rather, the ELL would engage in an application activity similar to classroom activities that make use of visuals and short two- to three-word phrases. Modified objectives reduce the linguistic burden on the ELL without reducing the cognitive demand of the objective.

In classrooms this understanding of criteria also indicates an equally clear understanding of test task. In other words, teachers should not introduce a new task to ELLs on test day; all test tasks should reflect activities that have already been introduced in an instructional setting multiple times. This type of transparency and established routine is critical so that ELLs are assessed on their knowledge of content not their knowledge of how to do the activity. For example, some ELLs may consider a short answer response to be as brief as three to four words, whereas many American teachers might consider a short answer task to be the equivalent of at least one paragraph. If ELLs are only asked to produce short answer responses on tests, they may not demonstrate full mastery of content because their understanding of the task is different from that of the teacher.

Have I Made Use of All Relevant and Available Visuals and Graphics?

When working with most ELLs at any level of English language proficiency, visuals and graphic organizers are essential tools. However, many teachers do not use many visuals or graphics on their tests, relying on students' prior knowledge and memory to aid them in responding to questions. Teachers should use the same visuals and graphic organizers on tests that were used in classroom instruction to help reduce the language requirements of content tests. Moreover, visuals and graphics should appear in similar positions on tests as they have in classroom activities. For example, if pictures are placed immediately beside a complex passage to aid understanding, then that same picture should be placed in a similar position on the test relating to that passage. Also, if a Venn diagram is used in a classroom activity, the teacher should not switch to a T-diagram on a test to compare two objects or concepts.

ELLs who are more advanced in their English proficiency can help teachers with visuals. Case (2002) wrote that in science classes, ELLs themselves can create pictures and visuals to supplement their answers on classroom tests that require higher order thinking skills. This type of response enables the ELL student to provide another avenue of communication that is not linguistically dependent. Additionally, Case found that ELLs were more successful when allowed to supplement their test responses with quotes from their own past journals, allowing them to demonstrate mastery of a concept by finding exactly the right quote without having the burden of reproducing English sentences under test conditions that may have taken them a long time to create originally.

In math classes, word problems are especially difficult for ELLs due to the extreme linguistic demands of these types of problems. Celedon-Pattichis (2004) found that middle school ELLs had extreme difficulty distinguishing "natural language" from mathematical language, resulting in students confusing numbers that appeared as natural language (e.g., size 7 dress or number 2 can of peas) in the word problem with mathematical language that related to the actual calculation needed. She emphasized that teachers spend time initially reading for understanding, which is often not done at test time. Therefore, word problems should be written in such a way that the ELL student can process the language and mathematics aspects of the problem in a reasonable amount of time. Lee, Silverman, & Montoya (2002) recommended that young ELLs be encouraged to create diagrams and other types of drawings when responding to word problems on tests (Figure 4). In these problems, students have been asked to "draw" math problems to provide a visual check of their comprehension. By having ELLs create their own visuals, teachers can be sure that they are understanding the problem itself as well as applying the appropriate mathematical process.

Figure 4   Pictorial responses to mathematics problems

Accommodations are not meant to give ELLs an edge over native English speaking students but rather to help eliminate the linguistic burden placed on non-native speakers of English.

Have I Incorporated True Accommodations to Level the Playing Field for My ELLs?

According to Butler and Stevens (1997) the most commonly used accommodations for ELLs include bilingual dictionaries, extended time, alternative setting, simplification of directions, test modifications (e.g., translation, visual supports, additional examples), and procedural modifications (e.g., breaks during testing, reading aloud of questions, oral directions in the native language). In most cases, these accommodations are used on large-scale assessments, but results from studies of their use can inform classroom testing by providing classroom teachers with a more realistic picture of what constitutes a true testing accommodation. Some of these accommodations are more feasible than others, and some, such as direct translation, should be avoided altogether under most conditions.

Abedi, Hofstetter, and Lord (2004) wrote that a true accommodation can, "level the playing field for English learners, without giving them an advantage over students who are not receiving accommodated assessments. . . . Ideally, an assessment accommodation should yield an interaction effect, where the accommodation improves the performance of English language learners but not the performance of native English speakers." (p.6) In other words, accommodations are not meant to give ELLs an edge over native English speaking students but rather to help eliminate the linguistic burden placed on non-native speakers of English.

For classroom tests, we can recommend the following accommodations that reduce the linguistic burden for ELLs while still retaining the responsibility of content mastery. Teachers can reduce idiomatic and slang expressions as well as phrasal verbs (e.g., to run over to, to run into, to run out of) that may be confusing. While many teachers allow ELLs to use bilingual dictionaries on tests, glossaries and customized dictionaries have been shown to be more effective (Abedi & Hejri, 2004). Since a bilingual dictionary is not content or context specific, it will provide all possible translations of a word. The common English word "go" had 20 definitions just in its intransitive sense. Adding the transitive sense leaves a student with nine more possibilities. However, a glossed text would define "go" within the boundaries of the particular context of that text. For example, in the sentence "This shirt goes with this tie," the word "go" would be glossed at the margin as "to be compatible with."

A popular large-scale test accommodation is extended time. Often ELLs are given as much time as needed, provided that they can complete a particular section or portion of the test within one school day. However, classroom teachers who are limited by bell schedules and physical constraints within the classroom cannot easily make use of this popular accommodation. So, instead of giving ELLs extra time in class, take-home tests can be given or ELLs can be given a test with a reduced number of items that correspond to the same constructs and objectives on the full version.

With the increasing popularity of the Internet, translations of text have become easier; however, research has found at least three major problems. First, rarely are identical translations possible. Word difficulty and procedures do not have a one-to-one correspondence in all languages (Figueroa, 1990). Secondly, if the language of instruction has been English, it is unlikely that the ELL student will be familiar with the content in his or her native language. For example, if our intrepid math teacher wants to translate the previously cited word problem to Spanish, she may use the term "junta de culata" for the English term "gasket," but if the ELL student from Mexico has only studied that concept in English it is unlikely he or she will know the word in Spanish since it may not be part of that student's social vernacular. Unless ELLs are taught content bilingually, they should not be expected to demonstrate knowledge learned in English in their native language.

The third, and related, difficulty with translation is that ELLs may or may not be literate in their native language. Testing in Haitian-Creole will only be considered valid if Haitian students can read and write at an appropriate level in that language.

Have I Created a Clear Scoring Rubric That Will Allow Me to Provide Culturally Sensitive and Useful Feedback?

Shepard (2000) wrote, "Students must have a clear understanding of the criteria by which their work will be assessed" (p. 11). Rubrics are an essential part of the assessment process and allow teachers to be sure "a score or grade was based on actual student performance rather than some idiosyncratic or indefensible application of the scoring criteria" (O'Malley & Pierce, 1996, p.20). In addition, and especially for ELLs, shared rubrics allow teachers to show students exactly what will be expected of them on tests and other assessments. This increased transparency can help to reduce test anxiety and act as a study guide for ELLs. For teachers of ELLs, rubrics give them a further opportunity to critically examine the English demands of a given test. Finally, specific rubrics tied to instructional objectives can help ensure consistency throughout the entire teaching-testing cycle (Brown, 2004).

Rubrics for ELLs should take into consideration their level of English proficiency in addition to teacher expectations in relation to content mastery. For example, if teachers develop rubrics of accomplishment that include "approaches standard" and "exceeds standard" definitions as well as "meets standard," they can track student progress in content and language mastery. This feedback cycle can help teachers individualize intervention procedures that can provide positive washback on the instructional process. For example, in a middle school social studies class in which students are asked to compare and contrast immigration patterns in the U.S. and Canada, teachers can create rubrics that identify several key indicators and levels of accomplishment (Figure 5).

In this rubric indicator, the teacher can now see evidence of content mastery approaching, meeting, or exceeding standard and can view language progress.

With regard to culturally sensitive feedback, content area teachers should provide feedback that is clear, concise, and understandable as well as culturally appropriate. It does little good to spend time providing feedback that will be either misunderstood or disregarded by an ELL student who does not understand the cultural context of that feedback.

If the language of instruction has been English, it is unlikely that the ELL student will be familiar with the content in his or her native language.

Figure 5 Rubric Element for Assessing Understanding of Immigration Patterns

Indicator	Approaches Expectations	Meets Expectations	Exceeds Expectations
Identification of specific problems	Student identifies immigration patterns in both countries but does not provide comparison or contrast information	Student identifies immigration patterns in both countries providing at least one point of similarity and difference for each pattern	Student identifies immigration patterns in both countries, provides more than one point of similarity and differences, citing possible reasons for each

Scarcella (1992) provided some situations where miscommunication regarding feedback may take place. The first of these involves the role of feedback provided by students. As many teachers are aware, it is not unusual for ELLs to feign understanding so that they do not draw unwanted attention to themselves in class. Hence, content area teachers should question culturally appropriate "signals" (e.g., nodding) that indicate that ELLs are paying attention and understanding. In addition, teachers need to ensure that ELLs are aware of what they view as paying attention and demonstrating understanding. Some cultures consider eye contact to be very disrespectful, but it is thought to be an indicator of attention in many U.S. classrooms.

Scarcella went on to note six other areas of possible misunderstanding.

1. What constitutes criticism or compliments for that student?
2. How does that student view or value error correction? How is peer feedback treated in the classroom?
3. How does this student request clarification? How would these requests be interpreted by a teacher?
4. How does this student feel about being singled out (spotlighted) in class?
5. How does the teacher use questions to check comprehension? How would these questions be interpreted by the student?
6. How are pauses and wait time interpreted by the student and the teacher? How fast does the student need to respond to a question?

These areas of potential miscommunication are often easily circumvented by simply asking the students themselves. Because many teachers and ELLs have not consciously thought about these classroom aspects before, they do not realize misunderstanding is even possible until a conflict occurs. By establishing guidelines ahead of time, teachers can help ensure that their feedback is being processed in a useful manner. For example, if ELLs come from cultures in which display questions are not often asked (e.g., "What time is it?" asked while the teacher is looking at the clock), the ELLs may become offended thinking that the teacher is insulting them. Additionally, if ELLs come from cultures that value thoughtful consideration of a question before a response is expected, the relatively short wait time allowed in U.S. classrooms will be confusing and send conflicting signals. The ELL students may think that the teacher must not value their answers if the teacher does not allow enough time to ponder it. If the teacher does not feel comfortable talking directly to the ELL, often other students from that same cultural group can provide important insights.

Error correction is often a controversial topic. How much and how often should ELLs be corrected in class? Because ELLs are going through a variety of stages of language acquisition (Ernst-Slavin, Moore, & Maloney, 2002), it is generally considered inappropriate to constantly correct an ELL's English. Modeling correct usage and grammatical structure are thought to be more helpful in the long run. However, not all cultures view indirect correction as valuable (Scarcella, 1992). Ran (2001) found that Chinese parents were disappointed when they met with teachers because the teachers did not provide enough critical feedback concerning their children. On the other hand, the teachers felt that the parents did not appreciate their supportive tone that highlighted their children's strengths and progress despite their ongoing limitations in the language.

In sum, rubrics can provide teachers with focused, clear direction in providing culturally sensitive feedback to students who may or may not fully understand the academic culture they find themselves in. This transparency and stability can help both groups—teachers and students—move through murky waters.

Conclusions

We have outlined several questions that content area teachers can ask themselves when preparing classroom assessments and tests for ELLs. The questions themselves are designed to move teachers who have not received extensive training in teaching English as a second language through a series of stages from test development to feedback and correction. However, we do not want to further complicate the assessment process by insinuating that these questions will solve every problem and challenge that teachers face when working with ELLs.

Classroom assessment is, by far, a more complex issue than we have time and space to address. To more effectively address this complexity, in these final paragraphs we would like to encourage content area teachers to use multiple assessment points when working with ELLs. We are optimistic that teachers will use not only formal tests but also informal assessments such as running records and journals to assess the content mastery of their ELLs. Even more so, we hope that content area teachers will make extensive use of portfolios and performance types of assessments in combination with more traditional classroom tests adapted to gain a fuller, more holistic, picture of ELLs' abilities in both the English language and in content areas.

Finally, we have not touched on the topic of large-scale assessment with ELLs. This highly controversial topic has, and will continue to be, a much-debated issue in all schools as accountability at the state and federal levels becomes more dependent on the scores of special populations of students, like English Language Learners. As mentioned previously, our hope is that assessment of ELLs becomes more of a process of developing a holistic picture of students' abilities and needs based on their growth over time and the development of higher order thinking skills in another language.

References

Abedi, J., & Hejri, F. (2004). Accommodations for students with limited English proficiency in the National Assessment of Educational Progress. *Applied Measurement in Education, 17,* 371–392.

Abedi, J., Hofstetter, C. H., & Lord, C. (2004). Assessment accommodations for English Language Learners: Implications for policy-based empirical research. *Review of Educational Research, 74*(1), 1–28.

American Psychological Association. (1999) *Standards for educational and psychological testing.* Washington, DC: American Psychological Association.

Brown, H. D. (2004). *Language assessment: Principles and classroom practices.* New York: Pearson Education.

Butler, F. A., & Stevens, R. (1997). *Accommodation strategies for English language learners on large-scale assessments: Student characteristics and other considerations* (CSE Tech. Rep. No. 448). Los Angeles: University of California, National Center for Research on Evaluation, Standards, and Student Testing.

Canale, M., & Swain, M. (1979). *Communicative approaches to second language teaching and testing.* Ontario, Canada: Ontario Department of Education. (ERIC Document Reproduction Service No. ED187152)

Case, R. E. (2002). The intersection of language, education, and content: Science instruction for ESL students. *The Clearing House, 76*(2), 71–74.

Celedon-Pattichis, S. (2004). Alternative secondary mathematics programs for migrant students: Cultural and linguistic considerations. In C. Salinas & M. E. Franquiz (Eds.), *Scholars in the field: The challenges of migrant education* (pp. 195–208). Charleston, WV: ERIC.

Egbert, J., & Simich-Dudgeon, C. (2001). Providing support for non-native learners of English in the social studies classroom. *The Social Studies, 92*(1), 22–25.

Ernst-Slavit, G., Moore, M., & Maloney, C. (2002). Changing lives: Teaching English and literature to ESL students. *Journal of Adolescent & Adult Literacy, 46*(2), 116–131.

Figueroa, R. (1990). Assessment of linguistic minority group children. In C. Reynolds & R. Kamphaus (Eds.), *Handbook of psychological and educational assessment of children: Intelligence and achievement* (pp. 671–696). New York: The Guilford Press.

Florida Comprehensive Assessment Test. (n.d.) Retrieved March 3, 2005, from http://www.firn.edu/doe/sas/fcat/fcatit02.htm

Genessee, F., & Upshur, J. A. (1996). *Classroom-based evaluation in second language education.* Cambridge, UK: Cambridge University Press.

Lee, F. Y., Silverman, F. L., & Montoya, P. (2002). Assessing the math performance of young ESL students. *Principal, 81*(3), 29–31.

Lewis, L., Parsad, B., Carey, N., Bartfai, N., Farris, E., & Smerdon, B. (1999). *Teacher quality: A report on the preparation and qualifications of public school teachers. Statistical Analysis Report.* Washington, DC: National Center for Educational Statistics. (NCES No. 1999080)

O'Malley, J. M., & Pierce, L. V. (1996). *Authentic assessment for English language language learners: Practical approaches for teachers.* Menlo Park, CA: Addison-Wesley.

Padolsky, D. (2004). *How many school-aged English language learners (ELLs) are there in the U.S.?* National Clearinghouse for English Language Acquisition. Retrieved March 3, 2005, from http://www.ncela.gwu.edu/expert/faq/01leps.htm

President's Advisory Commission on Educational Excellence for Hispanic Americans. (2000, September). *Creating the will: Hispanics achieving educational excellence.* Washington, DC: Author. (ERIC Document Reproduction Service No. ED 441652)

Ran, A. (2001). Traveling on parallel tracks: Chinese parents and English teachers. *Educational Research, 43,* 311–328.

Scarcella, R. (1992). Providing culturally sensitive feedback. In P. A. Richard-Amato & M. A. Snow (Eds.), *The multicultural classroom: Readings for content area teachers* (pp. 126–142). Menlo Park, CA: Addison-Wesley.

Shepard, L. A. (2000). The role of assessment in a learning culture. *Educational Researcher, 29*(7), 4–14.

N. Eleni Pappamihiel is an assistant professor in the multilingual/mulitcultural education program in the Dept. of Middle and Secondary Education, Florida State University, Tallahassee. E-mail: pappamih@coe.fsu.edu. **Florin Mihai** is an assistant professor of middle and secondary education at Florida State University, Tallahasse. E-mail: fmm5810@mailer.fsu.edu.

Promoting School Achievement among American Indian Students throughout the School Years

As American Indian children develop, they gain social awareness and their cultural identity becomes stronger; thus, they become more cognizant of the cultural disconnect between their non-Indian school and their Indian culture.

KRISTIN POWERS

American Indian students as a population are not achieving high academic standards. For example, only 57 percent of American Indians who took the 8th-grade National Assessment of Educational Progress reading test in 2003 scored at or above the basic level, and only 16 percent scored at or above the proficient reading level (versus 83 percent and 41 percent, respectively, of white students) (National Center for Education Statistics, 2004). Yet school failure appears to be acquired rather than inherent at the onset of schooling. Many researchers have reported that American Indian children function at an average range academically until the 4th grade; by 10th grade, however, they are, on average, three years behind their non-Native peers (Hornett, 1990; Rampaul, Singh, & Didyk, 1984; Safran, Safran, & Pirozak, 1994). The reasons for this "crossover" effect are not clear, although a combination of school, family, and student characteristics most likely is at work.

Underachievement among Native students often is attributed to culturally incongruent school settings. At school, many American Indian students must negotiate unfamiliar discipline, instruction and evaluation methods, rules for forming interpersonal relationships, and curricula that diverge from those promoted by their family, tribe, and community (Chrisjohn, Towson, & Peters, 1988; Lomawaima, 1995; Snipp, 1995). If cultural differences between home and school are the source of academic failure among American Indian students, the decline in achievement would suggest that these differences widen as youth age. Elementary curricula and instructional methods may be more aligned to Native cultural values (e.g., cooperation, thematic or holistic learning, oral recital) than those in the later grades. Hornett (1990) suggests that developmental changes within the child contribute to the cultural gap. He argued that as

American Indian children develop, they gain social awareness and their cultural identity becomes stronger; thus, they become more cognizant of the cultural disconnect between their non-Indian school and their Indian culture. The challenge, therefore, is determining how to bridge the cultural gap while maintaining high standards and promoting a positive climate for school learning.

The Research Project

Extant survey data collected from 240 urban American Indian youth (primarily Ojibwa, Lakota, and Dakota) from two large urban Midwestern cities, ages 9 to 18, were examined to identify educational variables that were negatively correlated with students' age (Geenen, 1998). Fifty-eight survey items were combined into 11 scales that measured 10 educational variables (e.g., student achievement, home-school collaboration, and achievement motivation) and the respondents' affiliation with their Native culture.

A negative correlation between age and student achievement ($r = -.379$; $p \le .001$), as measured by self-reported grades and overall achievement, was found, which supports the "crossover" effect. Similarly, American Indian students' school attendance and participation were negatively correlated with age ($r = -.248$; $p \le .001$). Thus, older American Indian students were less likely than younger American Indian students to report passing grades, consistent attendance, and high levels of engagement with school activities—all important indicators of educational attainment and success.

The hypothesis that declining student achievement is associated with increasing discontinuity between the culture of the school and home was not supported by these data. Neither the respondents' affiliation with their Native culture (e.g., how important Indian values are, speaking a tribal language in the home, participation in traditional activities and rituals) nor the extent to which their school embraced Native culture (e.g., teaching Indian cultural values, history, stories, and tribal languages at school; attending school with other Native youth) was correlated with age. While this study is very preliminary and based only on cross-sectional survey data, it does suggest that the crossover effect is not simply a result of cultural discontinuity. Some of the educational factors that were negatively correlated to age may deserve greater attention as school personnel attempt to combat underachievement among older American Indian students. These efforts are described next.

Student Achievement Motivation

Like non-Native students, American Indian students' achievement motivation is central to their academic achievement and persistence in school (McInerney & Swisher, 1995). McInerney and Swisher hypothesized that the presence of achievement motivation may indicate that American Indian students have successfully negotiated the cultural discontinuity of the school by adopting some of the mainstream strategies for school success without feeling that they have abandoned their cultural heritage. Conversely, the absence of a desire to achieve, attend, and participate in school may be symptomatic of what Ogbu (1981) described as the demand to develop alternative competencies. Faced with a long history of racial discrimination, some American Indian adolescents may discredit the importance of school and develop alternative competencies and motivations that are in opposition to school values.

In the present study, student achievement motivation, as measured by such items as "I try to do my best at school" and "It is important to me to be proud of my school work," was negatively correlated with student age ($r = -.169$; $p = .009$). This suggests that American Indian students may become less motivated to do well in school as they age. Therefore, primary, elementary, and secondary teachers should strive to provide engaging instruction for their American Indian students by adhering to universal principles of effective instruction while incorporating native culture and content into the curriculum (Powers, in press). Culture-based educational programs, such as the Kamehameha Early Education Program (KEEP) (Goldenberg & Gallimore, 1989) or the inquiry-based Rough Rock program (McCarthy, Wallace, Lynch, & Benally, 1991), which incorporate Native themes, languages, and Elders in the content and delivery of instruction, may serve as viable models for keeping American Indian students academically motivated. Efforts to increase student achievement motivation also should be directed at decreasing remediation. Repeated exposure to remedial activities that lack a cognitive and a cultural emphasis is likely to deplete students' desire to commit to academic tasks.

Teacher Expectations

Some evidence suggests that teacher expectations for American Indian students' success declines as the students progress through the grades (Rampaul, Singh, & Didyk, 1984). In the present study, students were asked whether they thought their school work was too easy, too hard, or just right; whether people at their school expect them to do well; and whether the adults at their school encourage them to do the best that they can. The American Indian students' responses to this teacher expectation scale were not correlated with age, suggesting that youth of all ages in this sample reported similarly about teacher expectations. Ideally, this finding would indicate that teachers maintain high and attainable expectations for their American Indian students across the various grades. Yet, failure to find a statistically significant correlation between teachers' expectations and age may also be due to either insufficient sample size or indicate low teacher expectations across the age groups. Teachers of American Indian students should constantly ask themselves: "Am I holding my American Indian students to the same rigorous standards that I expect from my other students?" Again, an overreliance on remediation activities rather than in-depth, inquiry-based instructional activities should be a signal to teachers to reconsider their expectations for American Indian students.

Teacher Supportiveness

American Indian students' ability to access the social capital of school personnel also may be compromised by their divergent cultural competencies. Plank's (1994) in-depth study of Navajo reservation school teachers illustrates how intercultural communication differences impede social bonding between teachers and students. For example, an experienced teacher of Navajo students stated:

> If I'm walking with . . . a Navajo, we may not say anything, and they are comfortable with that. Me, on the one (sic) hand, I feel like I should be saying something (Plank, 1994, p. 8).

Teachers may misread American Indian students as being uninterested in developing a relationship with them, or as overly shy, rude, or immature; this misperception is likely to impede the formation of interpersonal relationships between school staff and Indian students (Hornett, 1990; Kasten, 1992; Plank, 1994). A lack of interpersonal relationships with school personnel puts American Indian students at a disadvantage because those social bonds are critical to fostering a sense of belonging to school that leads to students' confidence in their own academic abilities and the availability of educators to provide academic support (Finn, 1989; Goodenow, 1993). Corner (1984) has observed that "when the school staff fail to permit positive attachment and identification, attachment and identification take place in a negative way" (p. 327). Interviews conducted with American Indian dropouts suggest that de-identification with school personnel and the norms of the school is a part of the drop-out process (Dehyle, 1992). The cross-over effect in American Indian student achievement may be the result of declines in school staff accessibility and supportiveness as American Indian students develop.

In the present study, teacher supportiveness was negatively correlated with student age ($r = -.183$, $p = .004$), which suggests that older youth found their teachers to be less available and supportive than younger youth. Items on this scale include: "Do you get along with your teachers?" "Has a teacher gotten to know you really well?" "Would you turn to a teacher for help if you were depressed?" These results raise the possibility that improved interpersonal relationships with teachers may help middle childhood and adolescent students remain committed to school. Teachers' and students' relationships will be strengthened through meaningful mentoring, extracurricular, and community-based programs, such as the American Indian Reservation Project, in which student teachers provide "academic tutoring, companionship and role modeling" while boarding with their Navajo students (Stachowski, 1998).

Family Involvement

Parents' presence and participation at school may buffer American Indian students from declining teacher expectations, supportiveness, and accessibility by promoting greater cultural consistency within academic programs and by offering additional academic assistance. Parental involvement is critical to assisting American Indian students in negotiating the mainstream culture of public school (Friedel, 1999). Surprisingly, older American Indian students did not report lower rates of parental involvement in school than younger students in the present study. It is possible that the attempts made by the districts in this study to incorporate Native culture into the curricula and instruction fostered greater parental involvement. For example, most of the respondents indicated that they had learned about Indian culture (86 percent) and Indian legends (75 percent) at school.

A lack of interpersonal relationships with school personnel puts American Indian students at a disadvantage, because those social bonds are critical to fostering a sense of belonging to school that leads to students' confidence in their own academic abilities.

Including Native American culture in the curriculum design and instruction may entice American Indian parents to remain involved in home-school collaborations as their children develop; yet, some American Indian parents may need assistance in helping their older youth meet academic demands. Historically low rates of educational attainment among American Indians make it more likely that American Indian parents lack the content skills necessary to assist their children as the curriculum becomes more advanced. For example, a study of over a thousand 5th- and 6th-grade students found American Indians to be twice as likely as African American or Anglo students to report that they had no one to ask for help on their mathematics homework (Mather, 1997).

Safe and Drug-free Schools

Older students in this study reported the occurrence of much more fighting and alcohol and drug use than did younger students. Urban American Indian youth may experience even greater risks associated with violence and alcohol and drug use than their rural or reservation dwelling peers because they have lost the support of extended kin who often assist in mentoring and disciplining adolescents (Machamer & Gruber, 1998). Parental involvement and a sense of belonging to the culture and norms of the school protect adolescents from deviant and potentially harmful behaviors such as alcohol, tobacco, and other drug (ATOD) use (Hawkins, Guo, Hill, Battin-Pearson, & Abbott, 2001). Rather than embracing "zero tolerance" policies, which Watts and Erevelles (2004) argue give "schools new ways to justify the expulsion, exclusion, shaming and labeling of students who need professional help rather than punishment" (p. 281), schools should improve parental involvement and students' sense of belonging to the culture and norms of the school in order to protect American Indian adolescents from school violence and ATOD use (Hawkins et al., 2001).

Implications for School Personnel

Teachers should consider, first and foremost, strengthening their interpersonal connections with their American Indian students. Strong relationships between students and teachers promote a sense of belonging, freedom to take academic risks, and investment in academic learning (i.e., academic motivation), and may help American Indian students negotiate cultural discontinuities between school and home. Teacher training on Native cultural competencies is a positive step toward increasing teachers' understanding and commitment to forming positive relationships with their students. School-wide anti-bullying, anger management, and substance abuse programs also may curb declines in student achievement. Finally, school-wide screenings may be effective in identifying American Indian students before underachievement becomes entrenched. An individualized intervention plan for American Indian students when they begin to fall behind in achievement or attendance should be implemented, monitored, and revised until the desired outcomes are achieved. This plan should be based on ecological assessments that consider developmental imperatives and individual assets (e.g., native cultural affiliation, parent support for learning) and vulnerabilities (e.g., insufficient teacher support, violence, and ATOD use at school) in selecting from among various intervention options.

Achievement data on sub-populations of students, such as American Indian students, should be examined regularly for signs of underperformance at each grade level. However, school personnel should understand that not all American Indian students identify with their Native culture in the same way. Cultural differences exist within and among the different tribes; thus, some students, particularly urban students who are three or four generations removed from their tribal homeland, may identify more with the mainstream culture of their school than with their Native culture. Accordingly, addressing cultural discontinuity may or may not improve achievement among older American Indian students. However, sufficient access to meaningful learning opportunities, supportive teachers, and safe schools is likely to propagate school success.

References

Chrisjohn, R., Towson, S., & Peters, M. (1988). Indian achievement in school: Adaptation to hostile environments. In J. W. Berry, S. H. Irvine, & E. B. Hunt (Eds.), *Indigenous cognition: Functioning in cultural context* (pp. 257–283). Dordrecht, The Netherlands: Marinus Nijhoff.

Comer, J. P. (1984). Home-school relationships as they affect the academic success of children. *Education and Urban Society, 16*(3), 323–337.

Dehyle, D. (1992). Constructing failure and maintaining cultural identity: Navajo and Ute school leavers. *Journal of American Indian Education, 31*(2), 24–47.

Finn, J. D. (1989). Withdrawing from school. *Review of Educational Research, 59*(2), 117–142.

Friedel, T. L. (1999). The role of Aboriginal parents in public education: Barriers to change in an urban setting. *Canadian Journal of Native Education, 23*(2), 139–157.

Geenen, K. (1998). *A model of school learning for American Indian Youth* (Doctoral dissertation, University of Minnesota, Minneapolis, 1998). Retrieved August 30, 2004, from Digital Dissertation at www.lib.umi.com/dissertations/.

Goldenberg, C., & Gallimore, R. (1989). Teaching California's diverse student population: The common ground between educational and cultural research. *California Public Schools Forum, 3*, 41–56.

Goodenow, C. (1993). The psychological sense of school membership among adolescents: Scale development and educational correlates. *Psychology in the Schools, 30*(1), 79–90.

Hawkins, J. D., Guo, J., Hill, K. G., Battin-Pearson, S., & Abbott, R. D. (2001). Long-term effects of the Seattle Social Development intervention on school bonding trajectories. *Applied Developmental Science, 5*(4), 225–236.

Hornett, D. M. (1990). Elementary-age tasks, cultural identity, and the academic performance of young American Indian children. *Action in Teacher Education, 12*(3), 43–49.

Kasten, W. C. (1992). Bridging the horizon: American Indian beliefs and whole language learning. *Anthropology, and Education Quarterly, 23*, 108–119.

Lomawaima, K. T. (1995). Educating Native Americans. In J. A. Banks & C. A. M. Banks (Eds.), *The handbook of research on multicultural education* (pp. 331–345). New York: Macmillan.

Machamer, A. M., & Gruber, E. (1998). Secondary school, family and educational risk: Comparing American Indian adolescents and their peers. *Journal of Educational Research, 91*(6), 357–370.

Mather, J. R. C. (1997). How do American Indian fifth and sixth graders perceive mathematics and the mathematics classroom? *Journal of American Indian Education, 36*(2), 39–48.

McCarthy, T. L., Wallace, S., Lynch, R. H., & Benally, A. (1991). Classroom inquiry and Navajo learning styles: A call for reassessment. *Anthropology and Education Quarterly, 22*(1), 42–59.

McInerney, D. M., & Swisher, K. G. (1995). Exploring Navajo motivation in school settings. *Journal of American Indian Education, 36*(3), 28–51.

National Center for Education Statistics. (2003). *Percentage of students, by reading achievement level and race/ethnicity, grade 4: 1992–2003.* Retrieved August 25, 2004, from http://nces.ed.gov/nationsreportcard/reading/results2003/natachieve-re-g4.asp

Ogbu, J. (1981). Origins of human competence: A cultural-ecological perspective. *Child Development, 52*, 413–429.

Plank, G. A. (1994). What silence means for educators of American Indian children. *Journal of American Indian Education, 34*(1), 3–19.

Powers, K. (in press). An exploratory study of cultural identify and culture-based educational programs for urban American Indian students. *Urban Education.*

Rampaul, W. E., Singh, M., & Didyk, J. (1984). The relationship between academic achievement, self-concept, creativity, and teacher expectations among Native children in a northern Manitoba school. *The Alberta Journal of Educational Research, 30*(3), 213–225.

Safran, S. P., Safran, J. S., & Pirozak, E. (1994). Native American youth: Meeting their needs in a multicultural society. *Journal of Humanistic Education and Development, 33*(2), 50–57.

Snipp, C. M. (1995). American Indian Studies. In J. A. Banks & C. A. McGee Banks (Eds.), *Handbook of research on multicultural education* (pp. 245–258). New York: Macmillan.

Stachowski, L. L. (1998). Student teachers' efforts to promote self-esteem in Navajo pupils. *The Educational Forum, 62*, 341–346.

Watts, I. E., & Erevelles, N. (2004). These deadly times: Reconceptualizing school violence by using critical race theory and disability studies. *American Educational Research Journal, 41*(2), 271–299.

KRISTIN POWERS is Assistant Professor, College of Education, California State University Long Beach.

From *Childhood Education*, International Focus Issue, 2005, pp. 338–342. Copyright © 2005 by the Association for Childhood Education International. Reprinted by permission of Kristin Powers and the Association for Childhood Education International.

Family and Consumer Sciences Delivers Middle School Multicultural Education

This We Believe *Characteristics*

- Multiple learning and teaching approaches that respond to their diversity
- Curriculum that is relevant, challenging, integrative, and exploratory
- Students and teachers engaged in active learning
- An inviting, supportive, and safe environment
- School-wide efforts and policies that foster health, wellness, and safety

BARBARA A. CLAUSS

Vive la difference! This expression is often used to suggest that the differences between males and females are to be appreciated, yet it means so much more! Human diversity, in *all* its forms, deserves to be acknowledged and respected. Indeed, the multiplicity of the population of the United States calls for all people to demonstrate respect for differences through appropriate interpersonal skills. However, we are not born valuing individual and group differences or knowing how to interact effectively with a variety of people in school, in the workplace, and in the community. Fortunately, we can *learn* it through multicultural education, and an excellent setting is middle school family and consumer sciences.

Why Multicultural Education?

The goal of multicultural education is to teach the knowledge, skills, and attitudes *all* students will need to survive and function effectively in the future (Banks, 2002). It is based on the core values of acknowledging and prizing cultural diversity, respecting universal human rights, supporting human dignity, taking responsibility for a world community, and revering the earth.

Student outcomes of multicultural education include multicultural competence, which is comprised of the development of knowledge, perception, critical thinking, and behavior from multiple perspectives. It emphasizes understanding diversity and effective functioning in a diverse, global society (Bennett, 2003). The core values relate to all people, regardless of culture, ethnicity, social class, religion, gender, age, or abilities.

Effective communication is key to multicultural competence. Through interaction, we gain insight beyond our personal experiences and become more aware of the influence of our own cultures on our perspectives (Banks, 2002; Bennett, 2003).

The development of multicultural competence is essential for effective functioning in a global society. Nevertheless, the standards movement in education, with its focus on achievement of competencies in language arts, math, science, and social studies, has made it less likely that multicultural competence is promoted in school curricula. Consequently, multicultural education has been limited to superficial applications in which a culture's music, art, literature, food, dress, and housing are noted in social studies, language arts, or fine arts.

Sadly, such cursory acknowledgment of cultures distorts and degrades their complex, dynamic nature. As a result, students fail to grasp the essence of cultural diversity and the associated competencies. Few of them leave school with the knowledge, skills, and attitudes to function effectively in work, community, and personal realms (Carnegie Council on Adolescent Development, 1989).

Given the increasing diversity of the population of the United States, future adults must have greater skill at interacting with a variety of people in family, school, work, and community settings. It is imperative that students gain multicultural competence before they leave school, and the most appropriate level to embark on this process is middle school.

Why Middle School?

Since young adolescents' attitudes and beliefs are very malleable, the prime setting for multicultural education is middle school (Manning, 1999/2000). During the age span from 10 to 15 years, youth tend to focus on developing a sense of self, forming cultural identities, enlarging their social sphere beyond the family, establishing close friendships with others, forming opinions about others, and developing a sense of fairness and justness. This transitional phase is a critical period during which information and positive experiences with others can leave lasting impressions. Family and consumer sciences (FACS) is well prepared to be that favorable influence.

Why Family and Consumer Sciences?

FACS teachers are in a particularly appropriate position to foster in their students a greater understanding of cultures, respect for individual and group differences, and ability to develop essential interpersonal skills (Clausell, 1998; Greenwood, Darling, & Hansen-Gandy, 1997). A closer look reveals that FACS teachers impart the knowledge, facilitate the skills, and encourage the attitudes that *all* students will need to survive and function effectively in the future. In other words, they teach multicultural education.

Corresponding Philosophies

Philosophically, FACS and multicultural education share many ideals. The Vision Statement of the Family and Consumer Sciences Education Division (FACSED) of the Association for Career and Technical Education (ACTE) (1994) affirmed that "Family and Consumer Sciences Education empowers individuals and families across the life span to manage the challenges of living and working in a diverse global society. Our unique focus is on families, work, and their interrelationships" (ACTE, 1994). With a firm belief in cultivating well-being, citizenship, effective functioning, and appreciation of human worth, FACS is an inherently appropriate context for multicultural education.

For example, while studying a unit on family relationships, students may focus on strategies to manage the challenges of living and working in the 21st century. In addition to outlining the practices of families in dominant American culture (i.e., white, middle-class, professional), students can examine family forms and the function of family members in other cultures, within and outside the U.S. In doing so, they learn that there are adaptive functions to various family forms, such as three-generation or communal households. One measurable student outcome of this learning experience is ability to analyze family management strategies in response to demands of employment, with an emphasis on the flexibility of various cultural responses.

FACS Curriculum: Standards

The National Standards for Family and Consumer Sciences Education (FACSE) (National Association of State Administrators of Family and Consumer Sciences Education [NASAFACS], 1998) outlined comprehensive content standards and recommended FACS core concepts and student competencies to guide planning, implementation, and assessment. Of particular relevance are the standards pertaining to family, interpersonal relationships, and human development. They share a focus on respecting diversity and examining factors that influence self-concept, perceptions of others, values, and interpersonal relationships.

For example, a concept found in the standards is "global influences on today's families." To gain a historical perspective, middle school students can research management strategies developed by families during World War II, when many men were in the military and many women joined the workforce. Students can compare

and contrast those experiences to the family management strategies employed by contemporary military families. While students would find differences based on the economic, social, and political climates and technological development, they would also find similarities in some resources families use, such as tangible social support. A measurable student outcome of this learning experience is ability to compare and contrast military family management during wartime.

Applied Nature of FACS Education

FACS is a multidisciplinary field, drawing on physical and social sciences, mathematics, art, humanities, and philosophy (East, 1980). The applied nature of FACS in middle school brings abstract concepts from its root disciplines into daily life and makes them meaningful and useful in the here and now.

> **The applied nature of FACS in the middle school brings abstract concepts from its root disciplines into daily life and makes them meaningful.**

For example, the concept "stereotype" may be addressed in social studies, but it is in a FACS class where the concept assumes personal relevance in a lesson on barriers to effective interpersonal relationships. Perhaps middle school students participate in a perspective-taking activity in which they are assigned to a cultural group with which they do not identify. Group members discuss the stereotypes of their assigned culture that they have heard or themselves believe. Next, they assume the position of a member of the cultural group and prepare a list of things they wish people would stop saying about them and doing to them. Then, they list the things they wish people would say and do instead. After sharing their ideas with the class, students reflect on the impact of their belief in stereotypes on their relationships with classmates. One measurable student outcome for this learning experience is ability to analyze and evaluate stereotypes. Students' attitudes may also be affected; one student outcome reflecting affective development is ability to become aware of the negative impact stereotypes can have on relationships. Not only can students explain the concept and give examples of it, they can feel its impact personally, by "walking in another's shoes."

FACS Curriculum: Processes

The applied nature of FACS relates not only to the immediate relevance of the factual information, but the use of specific actions. The explosion of information and innovation in the 21st century combined with diversity of lived experience makes teaching all pertinent content impossible (Costa & Liebmann, 1997). That is why the National Standards for FACSE include process questions that pertain to thinking, communication, leadership, and management (NASAFACS, 1998). The emphasis is not on a single, correct answer (Fox, 1997), but on processes, or the "how" of learning (Costa & Liebmann, 1997). Four primary processes undergird FACS education and are apparent in every facet of the curriculum.

Thinking. The National Standards for FACSE emphasize intentional and goal-directed thinking that is both critical and creative.

Critical thinking involves methodical examination of perspectives to determine assumptions and values, opinions and facts. While critical thinking is systematic and analytical, creative thinking is novel—a departure from a critique of what is known to valuing unusual, original perspectives (NASAFACS, 1998). Problems of daily life may be analyzed and evaluated systematically; creative thinking is useful for understanding others and carrying out social action.

For example, students read a critical incident—a situation requiring a decision to be made. Incidents are considered critical if the wrong decision were to be made there would be serious consequences; yet there is no obvious, correct decision (Pederson, 2004). Perhaps an African American high school student has been invited to speak at an assembly of primarily white, middle class elementary school students, most of whom have never known an African American child or adult. She was asked to address racism, the progress made in combating it, and steps that have yet to be taken. She has been asked to speak on behalf of African Americans across the United States. She must decide what to do.

FACS students can analyze the critical incident to determine the issues involved and possible courses of action to be followed by the high school student. An essential piece of this learning experience is predicting consequences of behavior; hence a measurable student outcome is ability to choose a course of action based on careful consideration of the issues and consequences.

Communication. Communication is critical to multicultural education, as it is the mechanism through which individuals and groups exchange views and mediate conflict (NASAFACS, 1998). "Communication is the transmission or interchange of thoughts, feelings, opinions, and information between a sender and a receiver" (NASAFACS, p. 18). It involves not only speaking and listening, but nonverbal interchanges, as well. Reading and writing are also important forms of communication in personal, academic, and workforce contexts.

FACS students learn how to listen actively, paraphrase senders' messages, and express their own beliefs, feelings, and experiences effectively through "I" messages. These skills are developed through practice and role-playing. Yet, there are other facets of communication that are key to multicultural education.

For example, not only are there differences in communication styles and dialects from one country to another, there are differences from one state to another and from one region to another within a state. Since not many middle school students have had the opportunity to travel extensively within the United States, a good activity for expanding their perceptions of communication styles involves viewing and listening to a video in which age-mates from different locations in the U.S. engage in casual conversation about the same topic. Each segment of the video isolates a single location.

During the video, students paraphrase the message they perceive and note unique, unfamiliar, or indistinguishable words or sounds, as well as novel nonverbal communication. At the end of each segment, students summarize the conversation. Referring to a script of each segment, the teacher can clarify or correct students' perceptions, while explaining origins of unfamiliar words. Students describe the impact of each group's communication style on their own understanding of the conversation and their overall perception of the group. Finally, students discuss the impact of their own communication styles on people from other geographic locations or cultural groups. One measurable student outcome of this learning experience is ability to project the impact of regional and cultural differences in communication on accuracy of message transmission. Students will also become aware of subtle and obvious features of communication style by regional or cultural group.

Leadership. Leadership processes include managing, facilitating, negotiating, encouraging, and participating, as well as directing. "Leaders tell, sell, participate, and delegate, using different strategies at different times and with different group members in order to involve and encourage everyone toward achieving the shared vision" (NASAFACS, 1998, p. 19). Effective leadership empowers all group members to make decisions, act, and contribute to group cohesiveness. It is fundamental to social action in the workplace, community, and personal domains. Working in groups with assigned roles and responsibilities, students realize that every classmate contributes to learning.

For example, a group of five middle school students choose to create a wildflower garden on the school campus as their service-learning project. Each one is assigned a role—project manager, secretary/treasurer, fund raiser, landscape architect, or planting/maintenance manager. Each student is responsible for performing specialized tasks and engaging the other group members in supporting roles to complete the work (e.g., the landscape architect is responsible for designing the garden plot, but will rely on other group members for suggestions and feedback).

As the project is being completed, the group members assess progress according to such criteria as adherence to the time line, adherence to the budget, perceptions of each other's ability to fulfill responsibilities, and so on. When the project is complete, students assess the product according to criteria, such as relationship of actual product to planned product, or more specific criteria, such as consistency of the finished product with the architect's plan. Two of the many possible measurable student outcomes of this experience are ability to delegate responsibility effectively and ability to evaluate process and product.

Management. Management is a broad, often complex concept involving many specific processes such as goal-setting, planning, decision-making/problem solving, implementing, and evaluating. These processes are used by individuals and families to meet their needs and satisfy their wants (NASAFACS, 1998). Management entails three types of action that are essential to the practical problems approach (NASAFACS, 1998).

> **While technical action is based on objective information, interpretive action relies on interaction with others to share ideas and understand others' perspectives.**

Technical action pertains to knowledge, facts, and manipulative skills. It can be seen as a response to the question "What?" For example, students take technical action to contrast characteristics of high-context cultures to characteristics of low-context cultures, relying on "what is known," that is, research on characteristics of high- and low-context cultures (Figure 1). The measurable student outcome of this learning experience is ability to analyze information on high- and low-context cultures.

Figure 1
Definition and Characteristics of High- and Low-Context Cultures

- A *high-context culture* is a culture in which the individual has internalized meaning and information so that little is explicitly stated in written or spoken messages. In conversation, the listener knows what is meant. Because the speaker and listener share the same knowledge and assumptions, the listener can piece together the speaker's meaning. China is an example of a high-context culture.

- A low-context culture is one in which information and meaning are explicitly stated in the message or communication. Individuals in a low-context culture expect explanations when statements or situations are unclear, as they often are. Information and meaning are not internalized by the individual but are derived from context, e.g., from the situation or an event. The United States is an example of a low-context culture.

High-Context Culture

1. Implicitly embeds meanings at different levels of the sociocultural context.
2. Values group sense.
3. Tends to take time to cultivate and establish a permanent personal relationship.
4. Emphasizes spiral logic.
5. Values indirect verbal interaction and is more able to read nonverbal expressions.
6. Tends to use more "feeling" in expression.
7. Tends to give simple, ambiguous, noncontexting messages.

Low-Context Culture

1. Overtly displays meanings through direct communication forms.
2. Values individualism.
3. Tends to develop transitory personal relationships.
4. Emphasizes linear logic.
5. Values direct verbal interaction and is less able to read nonverbal expressions.
6. Tends to use "logic" to present ideas.
7. Tends to emphasize highly structured messages, give details, and place great stress on words and technical signs.

Sources: Retrieved January 16, 2006, from http://academic.brooklyn.cuny.edu/english/melani/cs6/tan.html

While technical action is based on objective information, *interpretive action* relies on interaction with others to share ideas and understand others' perspectives. It can be seen as a response to the question "So what?" For example, students take interpretive action when they role-play the part of an English-speaking student in a monolingual (Spanish) classroom. Students can ask themselves "how are my relationships with others affected by my inability to communicate with my peers and the teacher?" A measurable student outcome of this learning experience is ability to demonstrate language barriers to effective communication.

Reflective action goes beyond interpretive action to involve evaluation of alternatives. It is a response to the question "Now what?" Choices are made based on what is considered most appropriate for the situation. For example, students take reflective action when they observe the discrimination of some students on a school bus and devise a plan of action to end the discrimination. Measurable student outcomes of this learning experience include ability to formulate a plan and ability to advocate for others' rights. Indeed, students will encounter decisions and problems in all areas of their lives; process skills will be essential.

FACS teaching strategies

For decades, FACS teachers have been educated to employ teaching strategies that are consistent with multicultural education. Key strategies include small- and large-group discussions, cooperative learning, and simulated experiences (see Blankenship & Moerchen, 1979; Chamberlain, 1992; Chamberlain & Cummings, 2003;

Chamberlain & Kelly, 1975, 1981; Hatcher & Halchin, 1973). In addition, service learning is considered a specific component of FACS (see Chamberlain & Cummings, 2003).

Discussion. Discussions are planned experiences in which members of a group respond to lead questions and interact to express their experiences and opinions and listen to others (Chamberlain & Cummings, 2003). Group members "practice tackling an issue, rather than attacking the person discussing the issue" (p. 125). Discussion is key to understanding many FACS concepts, as there is often no single, answer (Fox, 1997). The answer to the questions "What?" and "How?" is often "It depends."

For example, students may discuss media portrayals of men, women, teens, and the elderly, then discuss the impact of the portrayals on identity formation and perceptions of others. Since students bring different views to the discussion based on their unique life experiences and family values, structures, and functions, they can learn how others are affected. A measurable student outcome of this learning experience is ability to compare and contrast personal perceptions of media portrayals with those of classmates. In addition, students can develop sensitivity to the impact of media portrayals on others.

Cooperative learning. Cooperative learning usually occurs in groups of three to five students formed according to criteria established for the project as well as goals for the functioning of the group (Chamberlain & Cummings, 2003). Cooperative learning encourages interdependence through the assignment of roles, group process, and accomplishment of a group goal or product, while students take responsibility for their own learning and tasks. Social skills, such as active listening, turn taking, and conflict management are required.

For example, Manning (1999/2000) proposed that implementation of cooperative groups can facilitate multicultural competence when teachers form heterogeneous groups. When assigned to examine textbooks for stereotypes and discrimination, group members can assist each other in perceiving blatant and subtle instances.

Through interaction, students help each other understand the concepts, (Banks, 2002) while facilitating students' socialization needs (NASSP's Council on Middle Level Education, 1989). Not only are students gaining understanding of others' perspectives, they are working to empower those who are marginalized by the dominant culture of the school or community. One measurable student outcome of this learning experience is ability to analyze literature for stereotypes while assuming responsibility for another student's learning.

Simulated experiences. Simulated experiences include a variety of strategies that bring subject matter to life by replicating situations in daily life. Skits, role-plays, sociodramas, case studies, visual situations, and computer simulations (Chamberlain & Cummings, 2003) are types of simulations in which students assume roles to grapple with practical problems in a safe environment (Blankenship & Moerchen, 1979). These situations may pertain to social issues that Beane (1993) considers relevant in the middle level curriculum, such as interdependence among peoples in near as well as global environments, cultural diversity in those environments, problems experienced by some in the physical, political, and economic environments, and the impact of technology on human relationships.

Simulated experiences have the potential to yield many benefits to students, including the abilities to gain intrapersonal and interpersonal insight, express feelings, improve communication skills, adopt a different perspective, and gain confidence. Moreover, students will be able to think critically, increase objectivity, make decisions, and solve problems (Chamberlain & Cummings, 2003).

For example, students may read a case study about residents of a run-down, poorly funded institution for the aging and disabled in their hometown. Students analyze and evaluate the case for the impact of the living conditions on the physical, cognitive, social, and emotional health of the residents. They investigate community resources and decide what can be done to improve the living conditions and present their plan at a mock city council meeting. A measurable student outcome of this learning experience is ability to propose changes to improve the health and well-being of individuals who cannot do it for themselves. In this example, students are not only gaining understanding of others' perspectives, they are practicing to advocate for those who are marginalized and lacking power to care for themselves.

Service Learning. Service learning is the application of knowledge and skills in the curriculum to community needs and goals (Chamberlain & Cummings, 2003). Learning occurs as students take part in the experience and later, as they reflect on the experience and its consequences (Wither & Anderson, 1994). The democratic process is essential to service learning where all students work together with the teacher to plan the project (Wither & Anderson, 1994).

Students benefit from participation in service learning in various ways. Academically, students are actively involved and con-

tribute to a solution, so learning tends to last longer. They gain skills in authentic situations; this has value in future educational and employment opportunities. Socially, students hone their interpersonal skills and learn how to work on a team. Personally, they feel a sense of accomplishment and self-worth. In addition, students experience emotions reflecting commitment to a cause and to particular people. As citizens, students may learn more about their community and increase their awareness of strategies for improving it (Chamberlain & Cummings, 2003).

For example, a popular service-learning activity in middle level schools is a recycling project (see "Reduce, reuse, recycle," 1996). Students may work with the municipal solid waste management agency to determine waste disposal problems in the community. Based on concepts and processes pertaining to waste management learned in class, students devise and carry out a project in which they collect waste to recycle. In addition, they plan and implement an educational program in elementary schools to prevent littering in the future. One measurable student outcome of this learning experience is ability to construct a recycling collection program. Another student outcome is ability to assume responsibility for the physical environment.

Students are actively involved and contribute to a solution, so learning tends to last longer.

This example illustrates service learning as well as cooperative learning. Moreover, it pertains to two of the values of multicultural education proposed by Bennett (2003)—"responsibility to a world community" and "reverence for the earth" (p. 16). FACS is concerned with individual, family, community, and global well-being in general and resource management in particular. Conserving and sharing resources such as energy, water, and soil punctuates the interdependence of humanity and its reliance on the physical environment for its survival.

Summary and Implications

The middle school years are optimal for multicultural education (Manning, 1999/2000). Students are in the throes of working through issues they face now (Beane, 1993) and anticipating issues they will encounter in the future (Chamberlain & Cummings, 2003). A successful middle school curriculum supports its students in these processes (Beane, 1993). In this, FACS can play a primary role.

FACS classes must no longer be viewed as useful for other subject areas' multicultural lessons in predictable and limited ways, such as cooking food or sewing costumes. These approaches limit students to recognizing superficial features or commercialized characteristics of other countries. Such token acknowledgment of cultures distorts and undermines their complex, dynamic nature and ignores the call for interpersonal knowledge and skills needed for effective daily functioning. Moreover, they ignore the unique, valuable contribution FACS can make to students' development of multicultural competence.

Multicultural education and family and consumer sciences are both concerned with interpersonal relationships. FACS teachers do not need to step outside their curriculum to make it multicultural. By the very nature of the discipline and its scholarship, they teach core concepts and skills in the context of a diverse society.

Furthermore, when FACS teachers are numbered among the colleagues of an advisory team, they are in a position to contribute to the themes and learning goals established for a group of students. Prepared for action with an appropriate philosophy, an essential body of core concepts, standards, and competencies, and a repertoire of appropriate teaching strategies, FACS teachers can do more than embellish others' multicultural education efforts; they can bring to front and center the very knowledge and skills students need for effective participation in a global society. From its philosophical foundation, through its national curriculum standards and curriculum processes, to its key teaching strategies, FACS makes a significant contribution to our children's competency to thrive in a multicultural world.

References

Association for Career and Technical Education. (1994). Family and consumer sciences vision and mission statement. Alexandria, VA: Author.

Banks, J. A. (2002). *An introduction to multicultural education* (3rd ed.). Boston: Allyn & Bacon.

Beane, J. A. (1993). *A middle school curriculum: From rhetoric to reality* (2nd ed.). Columbus, OH: National Middle School Association.

Bennett, C. I. (2003). *Comprehensive multicultural education theory and practice* (5th ed.). Boston: Allyn & Bacon.

Blankenship, M. L., & Moerchen, B. D. (1979). *Home economics education*. Boston: Houghton Mifflin.

Carnegie Council on Adolescent Development. (1989). *Turning points: Preparing American youth for the 21st century*. New York: Carnegie Corporation.

Chamberlain, V. M. (1992). *Creative home economics instruction* (3rd ed.). Peoria, IL: Glencoe MacMillan/McGraw-Hill.

Chamberlain, V. M., & Cummings, M. N. (2003). *Creative instructional methods for family and consumer sciences, nutrition & wellness*. Peoria, IL: Glencoe McGraw-Hill.

Chamberlain, V. M., & Kelly, J. (1975). *Creative home economics instruction*. New York: McGraw-Hill.

Chamberlain, V. M., & Kelly, J. (1981). *Creative home economics instruction* (2nd ed.). New York: McGraw-Hill.

Clausell, M. (1998). Challenges and opportunities for family and consumer sciences professionals in the new America. *Journal of Family and Consumer Sciences, 90*(1), 3–7.

Costa, A. L., & Liebmann, R. M. (1997). Difficulties with disciplines. In A. L. Costa & R. M. Liebmann (Eds.), *Envisioning process as content: Toward a Renaissance curriculum* (pp. 21–31). Thousand Oaks, CA: Corwin Press.

East, M. (1980). *Home economics: Past, present, and future*. Boston: Allyn & Bacon.

Fox, C. K. (1997). Incorporating the practical problem-solving approach in the classroom. *Journal of Family and Consumer Sciences, 89*(2), 37–40.

Greenwood, B. B., Darling, C. A., & Hansen-Gandy, S. (1997). A call to the profession: Serving culturally diverse individuals and families. *Journal of Family and Consumer Sciences, 89*(1), 36–41.

Hatcher, H. M., & Halchin, L. C. (1973). *The teaching of home economics* (3rd ed.). Boston: Houghton Mifflin.

Manning, L. (1999/2000). Developmentally responsive multicultural education for young adolescents. *Childhood Education, 76*(2), 82–87.

NASSP's Council on Middle Level Education. (1989). *Middle level education's responsibility for intellectual development*. Reston, VA: National Association of Secondary School Principals.

National Association of State Administrators of Family and Consumer Sciences Education. (1998). *National standards for family and consumer sciences education*. Decatur, GA: Vocational-Technical Education Consortium of States.

Pederson, P. (2004). *110 experiences for multicultural learning*. Washington, DC: American Psychological Association.

Reduce, reuse, recycle: A thematic module from the Indiana middle school curriculum framework for family and consumer sciences. (1996). Indianapolis: Indiana Department of Education.

Wither, J. T., & Anderson, C. S. (1994). *How to establish a high school service learning program*. Alexandria, VA: Association for Supervision and Curriculum Development.

BARBARA A. CLAUSS is an assistant professor of family and consumer sciences at Indiana State University, Terre Haute. E-mail: b-clauss@indstate.edu.

UNIT 6

Special Topics in Multicultural Education

Unit Selections

Key Points to Consider

- How can educators develop a better sense of cross-cultural conflicts and values?

- How does a child's home environment affect his or her ability to learn at school?

- How can educators help children from gay families find acceptance at school?

- How can educators better meet the needs of multiracial and multiethnic children?

Student Web Site
www.mhcls.com/online

Internet References
Further information regarding these Web sites may be found in this book's preface or online.

American Scientist
http://www.amsci.org/amsci/amsci.html
American Studies Web
http://lumen.georgetown.edu/projects/asw/
CYFERNet: National Network for Family Resiliency Program & Directory
http://www.agnr.umd.edu/nnfr/home.html
National Institute on the Education of At-Risk Students
http://www.ed.gov/offices/OERI/At-Risk/
U.S. Department of Education
http://www.ed.gov/pubs/TeachersGuide/

There are always special concerns relevant to particular academic areas of study that do not neatly fit into particular traditional categories of that area of study but that are very pertinent to it. Each year we try to focus in this section of this volume on selected special topics that have been of particular interest to those who live or work in multicultural settings. Topics are also chosen if they have a direct bearing on issues of equality of educational opportunity.

There is change in the journal literature as well as some thematic continuity from year to year in this area of study. The articles in this unit this year reflect a broad variety of topics that we believe readers will find informative and interesting. It is important and a poignant concern to witness how parents and others attempt to help children cope with adversity. There is great relevance in this for the field of multicultural education in America and other nations. The role of teachers, parents, and other community members is very important in terms of helping children to overcome disadvantageous living circumstances or backgrounds.

The special topics treated in this year's edition are, as usual, varied. There are six articles in the unit. The subjects treated are (1) how do citizens of a city gain influence over K–12 schooling in a privatized urban school environment, (2) how best to assess English Language Learners (ELLs) in mainstream classrooms, (3) the varieties of ways to do "standards-based" assessment in multicultural classrooms, (4) "building partnerships with the immigrant newcomer community," (5) the educational rights of native American and aboriginal peoples around the world, and (6) racial issues in American school disciplinary practices.

In "Public Education in Philadelphia: The Crucial Need for Civic Capacity in a Privatized Environment, the authors cite the changing demographics and economics of urban schooling. They seek to explore how citizens may achieve greater impact and influence on such urban school environments.

In "Assessing English Language Learners' Content Knowledge in Middle School Classrooms," the authors present a variety of alternative evaluation strategies available for teachers. They offer practical suggestions for teachers who have linguistic minority students in their classrooms.

In "Standards-Based Planning and Teaching in a Multicultural Classroom," the authors discuss the multiple meanings of the idea of "standards" in talking about "standards based" instruction. They offer several helpful suggestions for how teachers can do this.

In "Programming for Participation: Building Partnerships with the Immigrant Newcomer Community," the author examines a

Stockbyte/PunchStock

program that helps recent immigrants settle and integrate in Canada with the aid of the public library and school partnership.

In "Protecting Educational Rights of the Aboriginal and Indigenous Child: Global Challenges and Efforts," the author argues for the educational rights of the children of indigenous (native) peoples all over the world. The scope of this article is inclusive of the educational rights of Native American students. In his treatment of this subject, he makes a strong argument for the educational rights of *all* females.

Finally, in "Why Are 'Bad Boys' Always Black?" the author raises a critically important question regarding race relations in American schools, and how African-American males are singled out for excessive disciplinary punishment in the schools. She supports her report on this issue very well.

We believe these essays will be perceived as useful in strengthening our understanding of multicultural education and policy issues related to the topics covered in this year's special topics section. The essays in this unit are relevant to courses in educational policy studies, multicultural education, and cultural foundations of education. We hope that you will find all of the articles in this unit interesting and relevant.

Public Education in Philadelphia

The Crucial Need for Civic Capacity in a Privatized Environment

A broad coalition of educators and community groups is necessary to achieve equity and excellence in urban schools, Ms. Blanc and Ms. Simon argue. But the Philadelphia schools' system of privatization and strict contractual obligations presents obstacles to those goals.

SUZANNE BLANC AND ELAINE SIMON

Like many other U.S. cities, Philadelphia experienced a prolonged period of deindustrialization and job loss during the second half of the 20th century. As in other northern cities, the process of suburbanization went hand in hand with white flight, increased racial segregation of the city and its schools, and increasingly inadequate funding of the school system. During this period, education activists and school reformers were unable to rally the civic community in support of policies that would have helped to maintain equitable or high-quality education in Philadelphia's public schools.

Today, the city's long-term trends of job loss and depopulation appear to be reversing. The school district has also made rapid changes and has been at the forefront of a national trend toward private-sector involvement in urban education. However, there are reasons to question whether the form of public/private collaboration pursued in the School District of Philadelphia is an adequate basis for a policy agenda that can reverse the city's long-standing history of educational inequity based on race and social class.

Public Engagement with Urban Schools

In the 1990s, the work of Clarence Stone and his colleagues affirmed the importance of public participation in education, arguing that only broad-based public engagement with urban schools can overcome the problems stemming from underinvestment in the children of the poor. According to this line of research, individual decision making and market forces create a radically uneven distribution of educational resources in the United States. However, Stone and his colleagues argued that underinvestment in urban children is not inevitable: "The combined actions of the government and nongovernmental sectors can provide a compensatory response to underinvestment in children in urban school systems."[1] In an empirical investigation of 11 cities undertaking school reform efforts, these researchers found that school reform was more successful in cities with higher levels of civic capacity.

In the more successful sites, representatives of a range of sectors—including grassroots and community groups as well as the business community and traditional civic leadership—were willing to go beyond conventionally conceived self-interest. They worked together to develop a shared vision and plan for action, and they created a context in which ongoing collective problem solving could take place.

Other researchers have also argued that independent, locally based organizations familiar with local schools and school policies play critical roles in addressing issues related to educational equity. For example, in a national study of community organizing for urban school reform, Eva Gold and Elaine Simon demonstrated that organized community groups were able to mobilize their constituencies and develop networks of relationships in order to overcome persistent obstacles to school reform, such as continual turnover of leadership and competing priorities of local and state politicians.[2]

Several examples from Philadelphia's history suggest that in the second half of the 20th century, community and civic groups, as well as educators, identified viable solutions to key challenges facing the schools. However, none of these efforts was able to leverage the sustained civic capacity needed to address the critical issues of urban public education.

Challenges of racism, equity, and accountability. As African American migration to Philadelphia and other cities around the country increased after World War II, Philadelphia rapidly developed a highly segregated school district. It is often assumed that school segregation simply mirrors residential segregation in northern cities. However, school boundaries were commonly drawn to *create* segregated schools in neighborhoods that were racially mixed.

In Philadelphia, supporters of a liberal, integrationist vision of schools advocated for policies that could have strengthened Philadelphia's racially mixed neighborhoods, as well as its school system, by redrawing the existing school boundaries that created racially segregated neighborhood schools. The civic elite failed to support integration as a way to alleviate the conditions of overcrowding and lack of resources that were typical of black schools, and many white working-class communities across Philadelphia actively opposed school integration efforts.

Issues of community control. During the late 1960s and early 1970s, many African American activists in Philadelphia turned their efforts away from integration and embraced community control and an emphasis on black identity as ways to improve the schools serving African American children. The Philadelphia public schools soon became a central symbol in the ongoing battle pitting white communities and politicians against the proposals of African American activists and students. Former Police Commissioner Frank Rizzo won a key political victory in that battle when he ran a successful mayoral campaign that played on white fears about African American students and the educational aims of African American activists. During the same period, the Philadelphia Federation of Teachers gained recognition and strength among teachers, at least in part, by opposing calls for community control and African American studies in the Philadelphia schools.

Issues of accountability. In 1982, Constance Clayton became the first woman and the first African American to lead the School District of Philadelphia. As urban school districts across the country dealt with the consequences of increasing urban poverty and decreasing city revenues, *A Nation at Risk* stimulated national conversation about the need for academic excellence. During Clayton's tenure, the district adopted a standardized curriculum with the goal of increased instructional coherence.

Many of Clayton's reforms, which had the potential to support both excellence and equity, were welcomed by people both inside and outside the district. However, the school district remained an insular institution during Clayton's superintendency, with limited outreach to the public and limited public involvement with the schools. Eventually, a broad spectrum of civic groups, including representatives of the business community that had initially supported Clayton, grew frustrated with her leadership, aggravated in particular by Clayton's unwillingness to make information about student outcomes public.

Issues of equity. Local foundations and business leaders were initially enthusiastic about Children Achieving, a new systemic change initiative developed in 1995 by David Hornbeck, the incoming superintendent. Hornbeck placed increased state funding, educational equity for children of color, and increased accountability for student outcomes front and center in the reform effort. This initiative provided some openings for community-based groups to engage with the district in a meaningful way. However, the lack of consensus among local actors about specific strategies undermined the efficacy and sustainability of the reform. Hornbeck had limited success in rallying community groups and parents to increase state funding to Philadelphia's schools.

In 2000, Hornbeck left the district after having antagonized state officials through his battles over funding issues. In a report about Children Achieving, two of our colleagues at Research for Action noted that it is difficult to "build resilient civic coalitions necessary for improving urban schools, especially in the harsh circumstances of inadequate funding."[3]

Developing a Public Agenda in a Contracting Environment

In December 2001, after years of conflict between the city and state over education funding, the Commonwealth of Pennsylvania took over the School District of Philadelphia, declaring the city's schools to be in a state of academic and fiscal crisis. Since 2001, the Philadelphia district has created a new governance model—a partnership with the private organizations that were managing a significant proportion of the district's lowest-performing elementary and middle schools. Substantial improvement has been reported in a number of arenas since the state takeover. One notable and significant change has been a dramatic increase in the number of elementary and middle school students who perform successfully on Pennsylvania's standardized tests. Another significant change has been the introduction of a standardized curriculum and a sophisticated data management system that tracks student achievement.

However, other arenas were barely touched by the reforms enacted in the four years following the state takeover. This is particularly true in comprehensive high schools, where there have been few achievement gains and fewer than 50% of ninth-grade students graduate within four years. At all grade levels, the achievement gap between white students and African American and Latino students remains unacceptably high.[4]

Many observers in Philadelphia believe that the School District of Philadelphia has effectively responded to the pressure exerted by the state takeover and by the federal No Child Left Behind legislation. In their view, increased reliance on relationships with external partners and openness to the concept of outsourcing have made rapid change possible over the last four years. Paul Vallas, who was appointed CEO of the district following the state takeover, created a new Office of Development. This office was charged with handling contracts with outside organizations, fostering an "entrepreneurial spirit" in the district, and creating an environment conducive to productive relationships with for-profit and nonprofit groups.

During Vallas' tenure, district staff members have been able to develop relationships with businesses, universities, community groups, foundations, city programs, faith-based groups, and local cultural institutions, as well as with national for-profit corporations that offer services in such areas as school management, curriculum development, and technology. According to many district staff members and civic leaders, the number of new partnerships is an indication that the district is taking the initiative in addressing pressing issues.

While many in the civic community respond positively to the district's growing web of contract-based relationships, the evolving system of "partnerships" and contract-based relationships carries consequences for civic participation. The process of developing and approving contracts has been largely hidden from public view. The public plays no role in choosing which firms or organizations are selected and has little information about the rationale for particular choices.

In addition, the contracting process is changing the relationship between the school district and the grassroots organizations and community groups that have traditionally acted as independent voices for those who have historically been disadvantaged within the school system. Because higher-status nonprofits, such as universities and cultural institutions, have much to offer the district in terms of resources and legitimacy, they may be able to accept contracts without sacrificing their ability to exert pressure when and where they see fit. For grassroots and community groups that have little in the way of material resources to offer the district other than the services outlined in their contracts, it appears that the contractual relationship with the district may be narrowing their input.

For example, in June 2003 one local parent activist observed that the district had hired a number of parents to do the work that they were already doing as volunteers—changing their status from grassroots actors to district employees. This activist commented that at least one person hired by the district was told she could no longer perform her advocacy work because of a "conflict of interest" between her role as an advocate and her new role as a district employee. Later that same year, the director of a different organization noted that, when the district hires community leaders, community activists become much more careful about criticizing district policies.

> [Vallas has] been so effective at hiring people that we respect. So everyone has been very polite about how we in the Latino community attack the district. We don't want to hurt people that we respect and have a long history with, like [a local leader now working for the district]. . . . How would you attack the district when she's in such a high position there? Because when I attack the district, I'm also attacking someone I respect.[5]

Our evidence indicates that participation through contracts makes it difficult for some groups, especially small grassroots and advocacy organizations, to perform their traditional role as activists and critics, even while it offers employment to depressed communities and resources to financially strapped organizations. The result may be something of a tradeoff: wide-ranging dialogue and critique sacrificed for civic peace and resources for grassroots organizations.

Building Civic Capacity for the Future

Our overview of Philadelphia school history indicates that for more than 50 years, civil rights advocates, community activists, and leaders within the school district have been advocating for education policies that have the potential to challenge racial inequalities and support academic excellence in Philadelphia's public schools. However, past efforts have not been successful in building the momentum necessary for deep change within an urban school system. According to Clarence Stone and his colleagues, long-term improvement in an urban school district depends on sustaining a broad-based political coalition with a vision and commitment to urban children.

In recent years, the School District of Philadelphia has certainly been characterized by rapid change. We are concerned, though, that the pace of that change and the centrality of contractual relationships have actually inhibited the type of engagement needed to develop sustained momentum in support of public education. If Philadelphia schools are to successfully address longstanding issues of equity and quality for all children, we need to develop an agenda and a vision that can unite traditional civic elites and grassroots groups and at the same time extend well beyond the strict contractual obligations and responsibilities that characterize Philadelphia's public/private configuration.

Notes

1. Clarence Stone et al., *Building Civic Capacity: The Politics of Reforming Urban Schools* (Lawrence: University Press of Kansas, 2001), p. 12.

2. Eva Gold and Elaine Simon, "Public Accountability: School Improvement Efforts Need the Active Involvement of Communities to Succeed," *Education Week,* 14 January 2004, pp. 28, 30.

3. Jolley Bruce Christman and Amy Rhodes, *Civic Engagement and Urban School Improvement: Hard-to-Learn Lessons from Philadelphia* (Philadelphia: Research for Action, 2002), p. 57.

4. The following section is adapted from *Time to Engage? Civic Participation in Philadelphia's Reform,* by Eva Gold, Maia Cucchiara, Elaine Simon, and Morgan Riffer, published in 2005 by Research for Action.

5. Ibid., p. 11.

SUZANNE BLANC is a senior research associate at Research for Action in Philadelphia. **ELAINE SIMON** is co-director of the Urban Studies Program at the University of Pennsylvania. The authors wish to thank their Research for Action colleagues and the many local and national funders who are supporting this research. This article is part of Learning from Philadelphia's School Reform, a research and public awareness project examining Philadelphia's current wave of school reform. For more information, visit www.researchforaction.org.

Assessing English-Language Learners in Mainstream Classrooms

Mainstream classroom teachers need practical ways to assess English-language learners. Then they can evaluate students' progress and plan more effective literacy instruction.

Susan Davis Lenski, Fabiola Ehlers-Zavala, Mayra C. Daniel, and Xiaoqin Sun-Irminger

A great many classroom teachers in the United States find themselves teaching English-language learners (ELLs). The total number of ELLs in the public schools is more than 4.5 million students, or 9.6% of the total school population (National Center for Education Statistics, 2002). This number continues to rise because more than a million new U.S. immigrants arrive annually (Martin & Midgely, 1999). Not all communities have large populations of ELLs, but many do, and others will experience changes in the diversity of their populations, especially schools in the inner suburbs of metropolitan centers (Hodgkinson, 2000/2001).

Because assessment is a critical part of effective literacy instruction, it is important for classroom teachers to know how to evaluate ELLs' literacy development. Nevertheless, many teachers are unprepared for the special needs and complexities of fairly and appropriately assessing ELLs. To complicate the matter further, the U.S. federal No Child Left Behind Act (NCLB) of 2001 has established assessment mandates that all teachers must follow. Title I of NCLB requires that ELLs attending public schools at levels K–12 should be assessed in the various language domains (i.e., listening, speaking, reading, and writing). According to NCLB, ELLs must be included in statewide standardized testing. The results of the tests are reported in a segregated data format that highlights the achievement of each subgroup of students. As with all subgroups under NCLB, ELLs must make Adequate Yearly Progress (AYP) for the schools to meet state requirements (Abedi, 2004).

Over the years, ELLs have historically lagged behind their native–English-speaking counterparts, and this achievement gap is not likely to close in the near future (Strickland & Alvermann, 2004). ELLs come to public schools in large numbers, and they have unique learning and assessment needs. ELLs bring a wide range of educational experiences and academic backgrounds to school. They represent a variety of socioeconomic, cultural, linguistic, and ethnic backgrounds. In school, ELLs need to simultaneously develop English competence and acquire content knowledge. An overwhelming majority of assessment tools are in English only, presenting a potential threat to the usefulness of assessments when ELLs' lack of English prevents them from understanding test items.

Whether ELLs are newcomers to the United States or from generations of heritage language speakers, they are disadvantaged if assessment, evaluation, and the curriculum do not make allowances for their distinctive differences (Gay, 2001; Gitlin, Buendía, Crossland, & Doumbia, 2003; Greenfield, 1997). This article provides recommendations for literacy assessment practices for teachers of ELLs that will inform their instruction.

Toward Appropriate Assessment of ELLs

The assessment of ELLs is a "process of collecting and documenting evidence of student learning and progress to make informed instructional, placement, programmatic, and/or evaluative decisions to enhance student learning, as is the case of assessment of the monolingual or mainstream learner" (Ehlers-Zavala, 2002, pp. 8–9). Assessments of ELLs, however, are more critical. Many teachers have little experience with ELLs and may not understand the challenges faced by students in the process of acquiring English. Because assessment practices pave the way to making instructional and evaluative decisions, teachers need to consider all educational stakeholders (i.e., the students themselves, parents, administrators, and other teachers) as they plan to assess students from different cultural backgrounds.

Hurley and Blake (2000) provided guiding principles that teachers should consider when assessing ELLs:

- Assessment activities should help teachers make instructional decisions.
- Assessment strategies should help teachers find out what students know and can do . . . not what they cannot do.
- The holistic context for learning should be considered and assessed.
- Assessment activities should grow out of authentic learning activities.
- Best assessments of student learning are longitudinal . . . they take place over time.

- Each assessment activity should have a specific objective-linked purpose. (pp. 91–92)

Furthermore, because the NCLB legislation drives state standards, teachers should consider those standards as they assess ELLs. Standards can assist teachers in planning effectively linked instruction and assessment practices for ELLs at all levels of instruction and across the curriculum. In the absence of district or state standards, teachers can consult the standards that professional organizations, such as Teachers of English to Speakers of Other Languages (TESOL; 1997) have prepared (see www.tesol.org/s_tesol/seccss.asp?CUD=95&DID=1565). They may also consult the work other professionals have developed (Lenski & Ehlers- Zavala, 2004).

Assessing English-Language Learners

Teachers who assess ELLs must ask themselves a number of basic questions such as these: Who am I going to assess? How am I going to assess them? Why am I going to assess them? What specific aspects of literacy am I going to assess? When am I going to administer the assessment? Can I evaluate my students in my own classroom? In order to answer these questions, teachers should investigate their students' prior schooling before assessment.

Learn About ELLs' Literacy Backgrounds

English-language learners come to public schools with vastly different backgrounds. Teachers should never assume that students who share the same language will observe the same cultural practices or understand the same types of texts. Even speakers of the same language exhibit differences in their lexicon, in the grammar that they use, and in the formality and informality of expression that is acceptable in their everyday lives (Chern, 2002). ELL teachers should, therefore, become aware of their students' backgrounds before assessment takes place.

According to Freeman and Freeman (2004), ELLs fall into four categories that help teachers understand their background: newly arrived students with adequate formal schooling, newly arrived students with limited formal schooling, students exposed to two languages simultaneously, and long-term English-language learners. (See Table 1 for a complete description of these categories.) Knowing which category best describes an ELL can help teachers begin to learn about their students.

Understanding that ELLs come from different types of literacy backgrounds can help teachers as they develop appropriate assessments. Students' needs are mediated by who the students are, which includes their type of literacy background. Oftentimes, an understanding of students is fogged by the use of acronyms such as "ELLs," which, on the surface, seem to point at group homogeneity rather than heterogeneity. Differences are blurred in the use of such acronyms; consequently, there is always the potential to forget how diverse ELLs truly are. Understanding each ELL's background will help a teacher to choose the most appropriate assessment and instruction.

Predictability log. An ELL's knowledge base might include traditional and nontraditional literacies. Teachers can understand the types of literacies ELLs bring to the classroom by completing a predictability log (PL). A PL helps teachers understand their students' prior literacy experiences and the factors that helped shape them. (See Table 2 for an example.) According to Snyder (2003), assessing students' abilities to predict can assist teachers in creating a learning environment that is rich in predictable printed language. To use a PL, teachers should target the questions that are most relevant for the students' situations. Teachers can gather data for a PL from a variety of sources: by interviewing the students, talking with the students' parents, observing the

Table 1   Categories of English-Language Learners

Newly arrived students with adequate formal schooling

- Have been in the country for fewer than five years,
- Have had an adequate degree of schooling in their native country,
- Perform in reading and writing at grade level,
- Find it relatively easy to catch up with their native–English-speaking peers,
- Have difficulty with standardized tests,
- Have parents who are educated speakers of their L1 (native language),
- Developed a strong foundation in their L1,
- Demonstrate the potential to make fast progress in English, and
- Have found it easy to acquire a second or third language.

Newly arrived students with limited formal schooling

- Have recently arrived in an English-speaking school (fewer than five years),
- Have experienced interrupted schooling,
- Have limited native-language and literacy skills,
- Perform poorly on achievement tasks,
- May not have had previous schooling,
- May experience feelings of loss of emotional and social networks,
- Have parents who have low literacy levels, and
- Could have difficulty learning English.

Students exposed to two languages simultaneously

- Were born in the United States but have grown up in households where a language other than English is spoken,
- Live in communities of speakers who primarily communicate in their L1 or go back and forth between languages,
- Have grown up being exposed to two languages simultaneously,
- May have not developed academic literacy in either L1 or L2 (second language),
- Often engage in extensive code-switching, thus making use of both linguistic systems to communicate, and
- Have acquired oral proficiency in a language other than English first but may not have learned to read or write in that language.

Long-term English-language learners

- Have already spent more than five years in an English-speaking school,
- Have literacy skills that are below grade level,
- Have had some English as a second language classes or bilingual support, and
- Require substantial and ongoing language and literacy support.

Note. Adapted from Freeman and Freeman (2003).

students in a classroom context, and talking with others who know the students (e.g., family members, other teachers, community members). A bilingual specialist or someone who is fluent in the students' native language can also be of assistance in completion of the log. Whether the teacher or another adult gathers the data, the information can provide the teacher with a deeper grasp of the students' literacy backgrounds.

Using predictability logs. Information from PLs can help teachers understand that students who have been exposed to effective literacy practices in other contexts, such as their countries of origin, may be further along in their literacy development. Furthermore, in understanding that ELLs differ in the literacy practices of their native language (L1), teachers may be in a better position to determine whether those literacy practices are facilitating or interfering with the development of literacy in English—the learners' second language. This situation is contingent upon the degree of similarity or difference between English and the native language of the students. An example of this would be the knowledge students bring to the learning process regarding concepts of print. An ELL who is a native speaker of Spanish may benefit from having been exposed to concepts about print in Spanish because they are similar to those a native speaker of English would know (i.e., reading from left to right). Conversely, an ELL who is a native speaker of Arabic may display a different understanding of concepts about print learned in Arabic (i.e., reading from right to left).

Decide on the Purposes for Assessment

Once teachers know about a student's literacy background and knowledge base, they need to think about the reasons for further assessment. The purposes for assessment can be quite diverse; they can range from student placement to instructional decisions and from program development to program evaluation. It is critical that teachers identify the purposes for assessing their students before choosing the assessment instrument to be used.

As teachers consider the purposes for assessment, they should ask, "Does my assessment connect to the language and content standards and goals?" Teachers should also think about whether their assessment practices are consistent with their own instructional objectives and goals. When teachers think about the purposes for assessment beforehand, they can make better decisions about what information they should gather about their students.

Teachers can use language and content standards as the basis for what ELLs ought to know, and these standards then provide the purposes for assessment. For example, one of the TESOL standards is "Students will use learning strategies to extend their communicative competence" (TESOL, 1997, p. 39). Teachers can use this statement to develop an instrument to assess how well students are satisfying the standard. Figure 1 provides an example of an assessment that Ehlers-Zavala (second author) developed based on the standard.

Decide How to Assess Students

Teachers of ELLs should conduct multiple forms of evaluation, using a variety of authentic assessment tools (e.g., anecdotal records, checklists, rating scales, portfolios) to fairly assess the placement and progress of their students and to plan instruction. Authentic assessment tools will provide direct insights on the students' literacy development and showcase students' progress and accomplishments. Assessments also serve as mechanisms that reveal what instruction needs to be modified to help the students reach the necessary standards and goals.

Table 2   Predictability Log Questions

Language use

- What languages does the student know and use?
- What types of alphabets does the student know?
- What language and literacy experiences interest the student?

Knowledge

- What is the student's cultural background?
- What does the student enjoy doing out of school?
- In what areas or ways has the student helped classmates?
- What has the student said or what stories has the student told?

Events or experiences that matter to the student

- What has happened to the student recently that has been important?
- Have any major events occurred, especially recently, that have been of great interest to the student?

Narrative

- What kinds of stories does the student enjoy?
- What specific stories does the student know well?
- Can the student tell a story about a relative or a good friend?
- What activities is the student involved in?

Relationship

- What is the student's family situation?
- Who are the key family members in the student's life?
- Has the student left anyone behind in his or her home country?
- Who are the student's best friends?
- Is there anyone whom the student talks about frequently?
- Whom might you contact to follow up on one of the student's interests or needs?

Aesthetics and ethics

- What personal belongings does the student bring to class or wear?
- What objects or ideas appeal to the student?
- What values has the student expressed through actions or stories?

Note. Adapted from Snyder (2003).

Adopt a multidimensional approach including alternative assessments (AAs). Reading is a complex interactive process. According to O'Malley and Valdez Pierce (1996), the term *interaction* refers not only to the interactions between the reader, the text, and a given context but also to the interactions among the mental processes involved in comprehension. These range from the decoding of words on the printed page to making use of prior knowledge and "making inferences and evaluating what is read" (p. 94). Indeed,

> the assessment of reading ability does not end with the measurement of comprehension. Strategic pathways to full understanding are often important factors to include in assessing students, especially in the case of most classroom assessments that are formative in nature. (Brown, 2004, p. 185)

For this reason, it is important that teachers consider AAs to document ELLs' performance and growth in reading.

Student:

Date:

ESL Goal, ESL Standard: Goal 1, Standard 3

"To use English to communicate in social settings: Students will use learning strategies to extend their communicative competence" (TESOL, 1997, p. 39).

Progress indicator	Student performed task independently (√)	Student performed task with help (√)	Student was unable to perform the task (√)
Understands new vocabulary			
Recites poems			
Retells stories			
Uses new vocabulary in story retelling			
Formulates hypotheses about events in a story			

Figure 1 Sample checklist for reading (grades pre-K–3).

Alternative assessments provide teachers with a more complete picture of what students can or cannot do as they encounter reading materials. Through the use of AAs, teachers gain a direct view of the students' reading development in a variety of contexts and under different circumstances. AAs go beyond traditional testing, which provides a very narrow and discrete view of the students' capabilities when confronted with a reading task. They also evolve naturally from regular classroom activities and allow students the opportunity to show growth in literacy as they learn and practice.

Alternative assessment tasks are a more appropriate and fair way to measure ELLs' progress (Gottlieb, 1995; O'Malley & Valdez Pierce, 1996; Smolen, Newman, Wathen, & Lee, 1995). They provide teachers with the opportunity to identify what students need regarding reading instruction and literacy support. From information gathered as a result of AAs, teachers can devise a plan to instruct students in more meaningful ways because they have direct insights on the needs of each one. Finally, through AAs teachers can assess ELLs' literacy in more naturally occurring situations and thus document students' progress more thoroughly and progressively (Ehlers-Zavala, 2002).

As teachers attempt to put into practice multiple AAs, they may want to approach this task incrementally and consider the following practical suggestions:

- Learn what constitutes alternative or authentic assessment of ELLs. Examples of AAs generally include observations (i.e., anecdotal records, rating scales, checklists), journals (i.e., buddy journals, dialogue journals, reader response), conferring, questionnaires, portfolios, and self-assessments.
- Develop a philosophy of second-language acquisition that will assist you in the evaluation of ELLs.
- Know your district's curriculum of the program before planning assessments. The curriculum (specifically the reading curriculum) in any given school program must be sensitive to the students' needs, the institutional expectations, and the availability of resources. Because these will vary from setting to setting, it is nearly impossible to attempt to prescribe any guidelines or universal curriculum for all instructional settings (Grabe, 2004); thus, teachers must know the reality of their own localities.
- Implement the assessments once you have understood the features of the tools available and have determined the appropriateness of implementation at any given time.

- Plan assessments that yield data that can be used for evaluative and instructional purposes.
- Ensure that students understand how to use self-assessments (i.e., logs, journals).
- Use the results of your assessments to modify instruction.
- Communicate assessment results to the respective stakeholders (i.e., students, parents, administrators, community) in clear and meaningful ways.

The key to successful alternative assessment is thorough planning and organization (O'Malley & Valdez Pierce, 1996). As teachers plan, they should identify the purpose of the assessment, plan the assessment itself, involve students in self- and peer assessment, develop rubrics or scoring procedures, set standards, select assessment activities, and record teacher observations. For a helpful reminder of effective assessment practices, Figure 2 offers a teacher's bookmark on alternative assessment practices that Ehlers-Zavala developed.

Assess in nontraditional ways. Teachers should keep in mind that all assessments in English are also assessments *of* English. Because ELLs are in the process of acquiring language as they acquire content, teachers need to ensure that their assessment addresses the linguistic component of the learning continuum. Therefore, teachers should provide ELLs with opportunities to demonstrate knowledge in nontraditional ways (O'Malley & Valdez Pierce, 1996). Specifically, teachers might consider some of the following suggestions when assessing ELLs:

- Involve students in performance assessment tasks.
- Offer students opportunities to show and practice knowledge in nonlanguage-dependent ways through Venn diagrams, charts, drawings, mind maps, or PowerPoint slides.
- Promote participation in nonthreatening situations that encourage experimentation with the target language of study. Assess language learning in the participation activities.
- Before assessing students, teachers can help ELLs develop reading strategies that in themselves could constitute alternative forms of literacy assessment (Lenski, Daniel, Ehlers-Zavala, & Alvayero, 2004).
- Use the Language Experience Approach as assessment rather than just for instructional purposes (Lenski & Nierstheimer, 2004). As students read their language-experience stories, informally assess their oral reading fluency.

Modify traditional assessments. There will be times when teachers have to give ELLs traditional assessments. Some tests should not be modified because their results are based on standardized procedures. If in doubt, teachers should contact an administrator or bilingual teacher about which tests should or should not be modified. A rule of thumb, however, is that teacher-written tests can be modified for ELLs, but achievement tests should not be modified. When teachers modify traditional tests for ELLs, they learn what students know about the content without the barrier of language knowledge, and the assessment more accurately reflects what ELLs know and can do.

Teachers may consider the following assessment modifications appropriate for newcomers and ELLs who are in the process of acquiring English:

- Permit students to answer orally rather than in writing.
- Allow a qualified bilingual professional to assist with the assessment.
- Consider offering ELLs the possibility to demonstrate reading progress and growth through group assessments.
- Allow students to provide responses in multiple formats.
- Accept a response in the students' native language if translation support systems exist in the school or community.
- Allow ELLs to use a bilingual dictionary in the beginning stages of their language learning experience in English (United States Department of Education, Office for Civil Rights, 2000).

Teachers who are developing ELLs' literacy but still need modifications for accurate assessment information might consider the following suggestions:

- Have an aide record students' answers.
- Divide assessment time into small chunks.
- Use visuals.
- Add glossaries in English or the first language.
- Simplify vocabulary.
- Begin the assessment with several examples.
- Simplify assessment directions.
- Write questions in the affirmative rather than the negative and also teach sentence structures so that students are familiar with the language of testing.
- Give students breaks during assessments.
- Give directions in students' native languages.

Assessment Materials, Activities, and Language Issues

Assessment should be conducted through the use of authentic reading materials that connect to the students' real-life experiences in their personal and academic contexts. "Literacy is intimately bound up with their lives outside the classroom in numerous and complex cultural, social, and personal ways that affect their L1 and L2 identities" (Burns, 2003, p. 22). For ELLs, literacy in English can be an extension of their identity both in school and at home.

Assessment materials should also be adjusted to the student's English proficiency level because a text that is not comprehensible will only measure the vocabulary that a student does not know. A valid look at an ELL's literacy can only be accomplished through pragmatic integrative assessment. When teachers use purposeful communication and authentic material, the results of the assessment are more useful.

Clearly, materials used to informally assess ELLs may be different from those that a teacher would choose to assess the literacy level of mainstream students.

Know your curriculum and collaborate with other teachers when possible.

Determine what, who, why, how, and when to assess.

Ensure that your students understand your assessments.

Reflect on the results of your assessments.

Modify instruction in a meaningful way informed by your assessments.

Communicate the results of your assessments to stakeholders.

Use technology to facilitate your assessment practices.

Figure 2 A teacher's bookmark on alternative assessment practices

A book that fosters an emotional link between the student and the written word is an authentic text for that particular reader, even if it is not what would ordinarily be appropriate for a grade level. Such a book may not be an academic text. Instead, for a young reader, it could be a comic book about Spider-Man or another superhero. For an adolescent female of Cuban American descent, it might be the chronicle of a young teenager's immigration, *Flight to Freedom* (Veciana-Suarez, 2002). When students determine whether a text is authentic, they use many important thinking processes. As teachers talk with students about why books are authentic to them, they can learn a great deal of information about students' literacy interests (Carrell & Eisterhold, 1983; Davidman & Davidman, 2001).

Engage students in collaborative assessment activities. Collaborative work helps ELLs feel safe, work comfortably at a level where incoming stimuli are kept at a minimum, and demonstrate literacy to teachers in informal ways (Kagan & Kagan, 1998; Krashen,

1993, 2003). Because conversations between students can scaffold learning (Vygotsky, 1934/1978), collaborative assessment activities provide a powerful lens through which to view ELLs' literacy.

Collaboration permits students to showcase their talents and work in a manner that is a good fit with their individual learning styles and intelligence (Kagan & Kagan, 1998). As students collaborate, they should be free to code-switch without being penalized. Code-switching is moving between the native language and English during an activity and helps ELLs keep conversations moving. It is a natural occurrence among bilinguals, and there are many purposes behind its practice; for example, to stress a point in communication, to express a concept for which there is no equivalent in the other language, to indicate friendship, to relate a conversation, or to substitute a word in another language (Baker, 2001). Teachers should bear in mind that when code-switching compensates for lack of knowledge (e.g., of a word or a grammatical structure), ELLs should be helped to acquire the linguistic knowledge they lack. This type of instructional support should be given in a friendly manner to ensure that students do not feel they are being punished for using their native languages (Freeman & Freeman, 2003).

Teachers can also add an important collaborative component to the instruction and assessment of ELLs when they invite families and community members to participate in literacy projects (Moll & Gonzalez, 1994; Young & Helvie, 1996). For example, parents who are fluent in the native language and also know English can assist teachers in some informal assessment measures. Parents can talk with students in both languages and can alert teachers to difficulties that students face. Parents can also help students record lists of books that they have read. If parents do not know how to write in English, they can keep tape-recorded logs, or simply speak to teachers in the native language. Teachers who are unable to find bilingual parents can seek assistance from bilingual paraprofessionals or from local and state resource centers.

Use the students' native languages as an assessment resource. Students should be allowed to use their language abilities to complete literacy tasks (Brisk, 2002) and to express their knowledge in the language they know best when being assessed. Oftentimes, knowledge of the first language means that students possess linguistic skills that can assist them in mastering literacy tasks in the second language (Cummins, 1981). One of these tasks may relate to understanding the meaning of words. Sometimes students may think of what words mean in their first language and successfully guess the meaning of the equivalents in the second language. For example, a word like *compensation* may be understood by native speakers of Spanish if they know the Spanish term *compensación*. In this case, students may use a combination of letter–sound correspondence knowledge and pronunciation to figure out the meaning of the word. During assessment, ELLs may demonstrate their knowledge more accurately if teachers allow them to use their native languages to process their answers.

Encourage self-assessment

Self-assessments convey the message that students are in control of their own learning and the assessment of that learning. As students engage in self-assessment practices, they learn how their past learning is shaping their new learning. This type of assessment practice helps students understand that they can direct their learning, which paves the way to teaching students to become independent readers and learners.

As teachers use self-assessment with ELLs, they should keep in mind that ELLs vary in their linguistic ability and, by definition, are in the process of learning a language. Thus, teachers should be aware

Story title	Author
Connections to other books	
Connections to school learning	
Connections to self	

Figure 3   Connections chart

that ELLs might experience difficulties at first with self-assessments. In order to assist ELLs, teachers should provide them with support through substantial scaffolding activities. Teachers should model responses to self-assessment tasks and then provide students with group, peer, and finally independent practice. For example, a teacher might want to assess students' prior knowledge of a topic for a book students are going to read. Teachers might want to have students engage in self-assessment practices, but prior to asking students to do so, teachers need to model how to engage in a self-assessment activity. An example of a strategy that could be used for student self-assessment is a Connections chart (Lenski & Ehlers-Zavala, 2004). This strategy encourages students to read a story; stop at given points; and make connections to other books, past learning, and themselves. (See Figure 3 for an example of a Connections chart.) When students are engaged in this type of reflective activity, they learn how to use an important literacy strategy and provide teachers with information that could be used for making instructional decisions.

Effective Teaching Means Effective Assessments

English-language learners are not a homogeneous group; they can range from students who are emergent literacy learners in their first language to those who are proficient readers. Literacy in the first language mediates literacy in the second language (Odlin, 1989). Thus, literacy experiences that students may have had in their first language will influence their ability to acquire literacy in English. Because the range of literacy proficiencies may be quite vast in any classroom with ELLs, traditional testing formats are inadequate for the evaluation of the English literacy of the nonnative English speaker.

The most effective types of assessments teachers can use to make instructional decisions for ELLs are authentic performance-based assessments such as observations, journals, portfolios, and self-assessments. Performance assessment tasks allow teachers to simultaneously instruct and assess. When students undertake the process of completing an authentic performance assessment, the students plan, self-monitor, and evaluate progress continually, while creating a product. Throughout this process, the teacher is able to engage in ongoing informal assessment of the student's progress. No professionally prepared protocol will result in student learning if only a single test result is used to inform the development of the curricula. When authentic, performance-based assessments are administered throughout the year, they can provide not only a much more accurate picture of students' literacy development but also documented formative data that chart the students' literacy development.

Effective teaching, above all, is the key to the sustained achievement of all students, especially ELLs who struggle with reading. With effective teaching comes the teacher's ability to meet the needs of all students at all points in the educational continuum. Teachers must develop the ability to tailor instruction that helps all ELLs achieve English literacy. However, without a thorough understanding of students' background and current literacy levels, teachers will have difficulty providing effective instruction to meet the unique needs of ELL students.

Although instruction is the key to student learning, authentic assessment can help teachers understand the needs of their struggling readers who are English-language learners. Teachers can use assessment results to evaluate student progress and plan the direction classroom instruction and learning will take. Only when measurement, assessment, evaluation, and excellent teaching are present in classrooms will ELLs make real progress toward literacy.

References

Abedi, J. (2004). The No Child Left Behind Act and English language learners: Assessment and accountability issues. *Educational Researcher, 33,* 4–14.

Baker, C. (2001). *Foundations of bilingual education and bilingualism* (3rd ed.). Buffalo, NY: Multilingual Matters.

Brisk, M. (2002). *Literacy and bilingualism.* Mahwah, NJ: Erlbaum.

Brown, D.H. (2004). *Language assessment: Principles and classroom practices.* White Plains, NY: Pearson/Longman.

Burns, A. (2003). Reading practices: From outside to inside the classroom. *TESOL Journal, 12*(3), 18–23.

Carrell, P.L., & Eisterhold, J.C. (1983). Schema theory and ESL reading pedagogy. *TESOL Quarterly, 17,* 553–573.

Chern, C.-I. (2002, July). *Orthographic issues and multiple language literacies.* Paper presented at the IRA Multilingual Literacy Symposium, Edinburgh, Scotland. Retrieved February 16, 2006, from http://www. reading online.org/international/inter_index.asp?HREF=Edin burgh/ chern/index.html

Cummins, J. (1981). *Schooling and language minority students: A theoretical framework.* Los Angeles: California State University.

Davidman, L., & Davidman, P. (2001). *Teaching with a multicultural perspective: A practical guide* (3rd ed.). New York: Longman.

Ehlers-Zavala, F. (2002). *Assessment of the Englishlanguage learner: An ESL training module.* Chicago: Board of Education of the City of Chicago.

Freeman, D., & Freeman, Y. (2004). *Essential linguistics: What you need to know to teach reading, ESL, spelling, phonics, and grammar.* Portsmouth, NH: Heinemann.

Freeman, Y., & Freeman, D. (2003). Struggling English language learners: Keys for academic success. *TESOL Journal, 12*(3), 18–23.

Gay, G. (2001). Preparing for culturally responsive teaching. *Journal of Teacher Education, 53,* 106–115.

Gitlin, A., Buendía, E., Crossland, K., & Doumbia, F. (2003). The production of margin and center: Welcoming-unwelcoming of immigrant students. *American Educational Research Journal, 40,* 91–122.

Gottlieb, M. (1995). Nurturing students' learning through portfolios. *TESOL Journal, 5*(1), 12–14.

Grabe, W. (2004). Research on teaching reading. *Annual Review of Applied Linguistics, 24,* 44–69.

Greenfield, P.M. (1997). You can't take it with you: Why ability assessments don't cross cultures. *American Psychologist, 52,* 1115–1124.

Hodgkinson, H. (2000/2001). Education demographics: What teachers should know. *Educational Leadership, 57,* 6–11.

Hurley, S.R., & Blake, S. (2000). Assessment in the content areas for students acquiring English. In S.R. Hurley & J.V. Tinajero (Eds.), *Literacy assessment of second language learners* (pp. 84–103). Boston: Allyn & Bacon.

Kagan, S., & Kagan, M. (1998). *Multiple intelligences: The complete MI book.* San Clemente, CA: Kagan Cooperative Learning.

Krashen, S. (1993). *The power of reading.* Englewood, CO: Libraries Unlimited.

Krashen, S. (2003). *Explorations in language acquisition and use.* Portsmouth, NH: Heinemann.

Lenski, S.D., Daniel, M., Ehlers-Zavala, F., & Alvayero, M. (2004). Assessing struggling English-language learners. *Illinois Reading Council Journal, 32*(1), 21–30.

Lenski, S.D., & Ehlers-Zavala, F. (2004). *Reading strategies for Spanish speakers.* Dubuque, IA: Kendall/Hunt.

Lenski, S.D., & Nierstheimer, S.L. (2004). *Becoming a teacher of reading: A developmental approach.* Columbus, OH: Merrill Prentice Hall.

Martin, P., & Midgley, E. (1999). Immigration to the United States. *Population Bulletin, 54,* 1–44.

Moll, L.C., & Gonzalez, N. (1994). Critical issues: Lessons from research with language-minority children. *Journal of Reading Behavior, 26,* 439–456.

National Center for Education Statistics. (2002). *Public school student, staff, and graduate counts by state: School year 2000–01* (NCES Pub. 2003-348). Washington, DC: Author.

Odlin, T. (1989). *Language transfer: Cross-linguistic influence in language learning.* New York: Cambridge University Press.

O'Malley, J.M., & Valdez Pierce, L. (1996). *Authentic assessment for English language learners: Practical approaches for teachers.* Reading, MA: Addison-Wesley.

Smolen, L., Newman, C., Wathen, T., & Lee, D. (1995). Developing student self-assessment strategies. *TESOL Journal, 5*(1), 22–27.

Snyder, S.C. (2003). Foundations of predictability in L2 literacy learning. *TESOL Journal, 12*(3), 24–28.

Strickland, D.S., & Alvermann, D.E. (Eds.). (2004). *Bridging the literacy achievement gap grades 4–12.* New York: Teachers College Press.

Teachers of English to Speakers of Other Languages. (1997). *ESL standards for Pre-K–12 students.* Alexandria, VA: Author.

United States Department of Education, Office for Civil Rights. (2000). *The use of tests as part of high-stakes decision-making for students.* Washington, DC: Author.

Veciana-Suarez, A. (2002). *Flight to freedom.* New York: Orchard.

Vygotsky, L.S. (1978). *Mind in society: The development of higher psychological processes* (M. Cole, V. John-Steiner, S. Scribner, & E. Souberman, Eds. & Trans.). Cambridge, MA: Harvard University Press. (Original work published 1934)

Young, M.W., & Helvie, S.R. (1996). Parent power: A positive link to school success. *Journal of Educational Issues of Language Minority Students, 16,* 68–74.

Lenski teaches at Portland State University in Oregon. She may be contacted at 921 NW 115th Circle, Vancouver, WA 98685-4147, USA. E-mail sjlenski@pdx.edu. **Ehlers-Zavala** teaches at Colorado State University in Fort Collins, and **Daniel** teaches at Northern Illinois University in DeKalb. **Sun-Irminger** teaches at the State University of New York in Oswego.

From *The Reading Teacher,* by Susan Davis Lenski et al, Vol. 60, No. 1, September 2006, pp. 24–34. Copyright © 2006 by The International Reading Association. Reprinted by permission. www.reading.org

Standards-Based Planning and Teaching in a Multicultural Classroom

Chinaka S. DomNwachukwu

There seems to be a tension between the standards movement and the multicultural education movement in today's academic discourse. The fact, however, is that it is possible for teachers to develop standards-based lessons across various disciplines and effectively weave multicultural education into them. This approach is less time consuming than other multicultural education approaches and presents the possibility of standards-based instructional delivery at the highest level of cultural integration. In order to address this new approach, we must first understand traditional standards-based instruction and multicultural education.

Standards-Based Instruction

One of the fundamental points of confusion in understanding standards-based instruction is the assumption that it suggests a "one-size-fits-all" approach to teaching. Series of researches have looked at standards-based teaching. Some of these researches were cited by Wang and Odell (2002), who provided a variety of ways for looking at standards-based teaching. They cited Romberg (1992), Cobb (1994), and Cohen (1984) as presenting standards-based instruction as student-centered instruction that focuses on progressive ideas and constructivist ideas of learning and constructing knowledge; as active sense-making by students; and as collaborative inquiry.

According to this approach, knowledge is seen as "consisting of cultural artifacts constructed by individuals and groups" (Wang & Odell, p.484). If these ideas of standards-based instruction are to be taken at face value, one can logically argue that there could be a positive relationship that exists between standards-based instruction and multicultural education, contrary to the general perception.

According to Beverly Falk (2002), standards-based instruction and assessments can sometimes stimulate teachers and their students to "get clear about their purposes, to develop coherent goals for learning, and to make use of a range of instructional strategies to support students' varying approaches to learning" (p. 613). A more appropriate argument is that high standards, when required for all, may make it possible to invest resources into providing assistance to those who need extra help (Edsource, 2003).

The argument must be presented, however, that despite the possible symbiotic relationship that may be found between the standards-based instructional reform and the multicultural education movement, multicultural education seems to have suffered grave casualties in states where the standards-based reform movement has been the strongest. One of the fundamental issues that has often crippled the implementation of multicultural education in today's classrooms is time for another "subject." Many teachers and school administrators look at the idea of multicultural education as the inroad of a new subject into the school curriculum. This perception of multicultural education is based on the forms multicultural education has traditionally taken in schools.

Multicultural Education

James Banks (2003) has presented four levels of multicultural education, namely: contributions, additive, transformational, and social action approaches. According to him, the first level deals with heroes, holidays, and discrete cultural elements. Teachers conveniently infuse cultural themes like holidays and heroes into their curriculum. Banks refers to this approach as the easiest approach for teachers to integrate multicultural content into their curriculum, but one may argue against that assumption, because amidst the contemporary standards-based instructions, "scripted teaching," "pacing," and "bench-marking," it is more and more difficult to integrate cultural contributions and holidays into the main curriculum, unless it comes within the scripted teaching package.

At the second level, the additive approach, teachers add content, concepts, themes, and perspectives that are multicultural without changing the structure of their instructional materials. Teachers work hard to infuse multicultural themes, content, and perspectives into the main curriculum. When teachers do this, it often involves worksheets and reading materials on specific cultural activities related to the main topic being taught.

The problem with this approach is that whereas it may work perfectly well in history and social studies or language classes, it may be hard to do in mathematics, science, and other technical classes. In mathematics and science classrooms you may see multicultural games used to teach mathematics or science concepts, eg., Mankala (Okwe), an African game used in teaching addition, subtraction, and multiplication. When such games are used, their multicultural emphases are often lost, as generally nothing is done or said to connect the activity to the culture from which it originated.

The contemporary standards-based curriculum is crammed with lots of reading, writing, and arithmetic, as schools are struggling to meet the various state academic standards as well as score high on high-stakes tests. It is traditionally known that local schools hold the power on how they constitute and deliver instruction (Chatterji, 2002). With the standards movement and its accompanying evils of pacing and scripted teaching, that right and power has been significantly taken away from schools, and thus asking them to spend extra time teaching heroes and holidays or multicultural games is to require the impossible from them.

Added to the lack of time and space in the curriculum is the fact that the first two approaches have little or no value in transforming students' worldview or enhancing cultural appreciation, respect, and tolerance. These first two approaches are superficial, yet they place lots of demand on teaching time and curricular space.

In this age of standards-based instruction and assessments, any attempt to implement multicultural education which follows the first level will require a significant curriculum adjustment as teachers would be required to teach heroes, holidays, and cultural events outside of the main adopted state academic content standards. Some type of academic activities that take place as a part of the cultural emphasis programs are done as extra curricular activities rather than as part of the academic curriculum. At times when it is done as part of the academic curriculum, it might be the use of worksheets that have little or no connection to the academic standards. It is indeed an additional piece of work which many teachers don't have time and resources to undertake, given the pressures they face these days.

The second level is an improvement over the first, but remains significantly insufficient for today's classroom as many schools are demanding that all learning activities be tied to the academic content standards. When a teacher realizes that, even though the multicultural activity would be relevant and helpful to students but is not clearly tied to the standards, she would be reluctant to have a supervisor walk in on her doing an activity that she cannot readily link to the standards.

The last two approaches suggested by Banks—the transformation approach and the social action approach—do not necessarily require a separate curriculum. According to Banks (2003), in these two approaches "ethnic content is added to the mainstream core curriculum without changing its basic assumptions, nature, and structure" (p. 250). It is also at these two levels that we can see the possibility of integrating standards-based instruction and multicultural education. Let's look at these two levels.

The Transformation Approach

The transformative approach requires teachers to change the structure of their curriculum to enable students to engage concepts, issues, events, and themes from a multicultural perspective. Here teachers use the mainstream subject areas like mathematics, the arts, and language and literature to acquaint students with the ways the common United States culture and society has "emerged from a complex synthesis and interaction of the diverse cultural elements that originated within the various cultural, racial, ethnic, and religious groups that make up U.S. society" (Banks, 2003, p. 235). Here students engage and critique issues and concepts which deal with diversity and social justice. They learn to take a stand.

The Social Action Approach

Bank's fourth level, the social action approach, allows a student "to make decisions on important social issues and take actions to help solve them" (p. 229). The last two are best implemented by weaving culture appreciation and cultural awareness issues into the existing curriculum: mathematics, language arts, history/social studies, and science. Using this approach, the teachers are able to teach the standards and follow whatever pacing guides are stipulated by their districts, while at the same time teaching equity and social justice without having to look for extra time in their day to teach such multicultural awareness.

It is in the planning of their instruction of the basic subjects that teachers are able to weave in multicultural education. A legitimate question that follows would be "how is this done?" In the section that follows, we will explore how teachers can develop standards-based lessons across various disciplines and effectively weave in multicultural education.

Lesson Planning for the Multicultural Classroom

Lesson planning in a multicultural classroom needs to depart from the exclusively traditional subject matter focus to a broader view of the need of the classroom community. The basic steps for preparing a lesson often vary from one teacher to the other, one teacher education institution to another, yet the basic required elements remain the same.

There are seven steps that would be found in any standard lesson plan, the order may vary, but the content remains the same: (1) goals and objectives, (2) materials and resources, (3) anticipatory set or entry, (4) instructional input, (5) guided practice, (6) independent practice, and (7) assessment/evaluation. Using these steps, we will explore ways to integrate multicultural education into standards-based instructional planning and teaching.

Step 1: Goals and Objectives

For a standards-based lesson plan in the state of California, for example, two basic tools are mandatory for teachers to familiarize themselves with: The goals should usually be derived from the State Academic Content Standards which address the concepts being taught and the State Framework for that subject matter. These are two separate but closely related documents. Oftentimes the two are combined in one volume, but they are nevertheless two separate entities.

The framework provides guidelines and "research-based approaches" for implementing the standards. It is an organized approach to implementing the standards from Kindergarten to twelfth grade. The standards, however, provide the required learning and curriculum content needed for each grade level. The two combine to make for a standards-based curriculum.

For standards-based instruction, the standards remain the first point of call. The California Academic Content Standards provide us with the broad and specific goals to be pursued in every lesson. Assume that a California art teacher wants to teach art critique and analysis to her 7th grade class. Let's plan the lesson. The lesson is anchored on the 7th grade California academic content standard for visual and performing arts, standard 4.0 (Aesthetic valuing), which reads *"Students analyze, assess, and derive meaning from works of art, including their own, according to the elements of art, the principles of design, and aesthetic qualities."*

Let's narrow our focus down to substandard 4.2, which reads, *"Analyze the form* (how a work of art looks) *and content* (what a work of art communicates) *of works of art."* The standards provide us with the goal of the lesson, which specifies where this lesson is going, yet the teacher is required to isolate certain measurable objectives that would convince her at the end of this lesson that the destination was reached. This refers to the learning objectives. In a multicultural classroom there is need to ensure that our objectives consider cognitive as well as affective domains of learning (Tiedt & Tiedt, 2002, p. 41).

The objective is where the teacher articulates her expectations from students in relation to the stated goals, and it is also here that she articulates any multicultural and behavioral objective she wants to achieve through this lesson. In keeping with Banks' third and fourth levels of multicultural education, the objectives here must not only be measurable, they must have transformational and social action focus.

The task of the teacher is to teach a standards-based lesson, cleverly infusing multicultural education in such a way that students' worldviews are not only transformed, but they are led to do something to positively impact the world around them. What is social action? Banks (2003) explains that

> When you identify concepts and generalizations, you should select those that will help students make decisions and take personal, social, or civic actions that reduce prejudice and discrimination in their personal lives, in the school, and, when possible, in the other social settings in which they function. (p. 109)

Social action, therefore, is an action that is taken with the objective of enhancing the social status of another person or group of persons. Whatever thing we do to enhance the social status of another person or group is a social action. A social action objective, therefore, is an objective that aims at enhancing an individual's or group's social status.

In the case of this art lesson, this teacher may want to state the following academic objective, *"Students will be able to create a collage of pictures representing the theme of homelessness, and subsequently identify the thoughts and feelings associated with each art work."* Homelessness is in itself a social as well as multicultural issue, as it addresses a people's group within the larger society. The homeless represent marginal life and destitution. However, the objective does not contain any social action.

Should the lesson end here, the academic goal would be fully met, but the multicultural impact will be very minimal.

To take it to the higher level, a second objective may need to be added as follows: *"After identifying the thoughts and feelings that those homeless scenes represent, students will list positive actions society can take to engage and mediate those feelings and thoughts, and the problem of homelessness in general."*

This second objective brings in transformation, as students are led to critically engage the topic in question and propose solutions. However, there is no explicit social action yet. To bring in the social action part of the objective, let's add that, *"Students will hold an exhibition of their art work on homelessness and the suggested strategies that can be used in addressing it. This may assist people to begin to adjust their attitudes towards the homeless."* Thus a simple art lesson can produce change of attitude and a changed society. This is social action.

The goals and objectives parts of a lesson may be considered the most crucial part, as time needs to be spent articulating academic and social objectives and merging them into one lesson plan. One of the areas in which teachers may face challenges is articulating a valid social action for primary grade students.

In responding to this challenge, Banks argues, "Primary grade students cannot take actions that will reduce discrimination in the larger society. However, they can make a commitment to not tell or laugh at racist jokes, to play with and make friends with students from other racial, ethnic, religious groups . . . " (2003, p. 108).

Banks seems to be expressing a narrow view of social action in submitting that primary grades "cannot take social actions." Social action can be undertaken at any grade level. Choosing not to tell or laugh at racist jokes is an action. Primary grade students can and do engage in age appropriate social actions.

According to Taylor and Whittaker (2003), "once the major goal for implementing a change process have been chosen and prioritized, the steps for achieving these goals must be delineated" (p. 76). According to them, a plan of action may involve reference to the time and place of the action, like next classroom, assembly ground, community, or neighborhood. This specific detail is not expected to be part of the objectives statement. It is usually best presented as part of the independent practice. Moving on from goals and objectives, therefore, let's go to the next level.

Step 2: Materials

The materials that will be needed for this lesson would include poster boards, magazines and newspapers (which will have pictures of the homeless from across all gender and ethnicities), glue sticks, markers, pens and pencils, and paper to write with.

Step 3: Anticipatory Set/Entry

This step is often called "entry" as it excites, arouses interest in, and prepares the students for the learning experience. A relevant story that can accomplish these for this lesson and provoke student curiosity about the homeless or art appreciation can be selected. Kathleen Krull's *Lives of the Artists: Masterpieces, Messes (and What the Neighbors Thought)* could make a good anticipatory set. The story is read and briefly discussed, and the teacher quickly transitions into the lesson. Another form of anticipatory set may be to preview the lesson by checking to know what the students already know on the topic so as to avoid repeating what they already know.

One good way to do this is to use the KWL chart. This chart asks students for what they already know on the subject (K), what they want to know about the subject (W), and what they have learned (L). The good thing about the KWL chart is that it serves as an anticipatory set while also serving as a way to summarize and assess learning. In this case students can tell what they already know about collages, the homeless, etc. They can state what they want to learn about each of the concepts to be addressed. At the end they will summarize what they learned in terms of art analysis and critique, as well as the homeless.

Step 4: Instructional Input

This is the place where the teacher presents and explains basic concepts, definitions, and clarifications which students need in order to comprehend the lesson. Here is where new concepts are introduced. According to Barba (1998), decisions about your instructional strategies need to depend on the characteristics of your students, information to be learned, and your goals and objectives. This is the right place, as you plan, to specify what scaffolds you intend to use in delivering instruction to special needs students or English learners.

For this lesson, the teacher will need to define and explain such words as collage, homelessness, and aesthetic valuing. Word study (along with pictures) may be additional scaffolds for students who are English learners. The teacher will need to present a variety of collages for illustration. She needs to explain to students how the collages were created by pulling together different shapes and forms that were otherwise unrelated. She could separate the various parts of a collage to demonstrate to students what a collage means and how they are formed.

She now needs to demonstrate the process involved in making collages by starting a collage from the scratch and finishing it as students watch. This is called modeling. After the demonstration, the first part of her direct instruction has ended.

Step 5: Guided Practice

Here, the teacher hands the students a set of arts activity materials containing blank paper and cut out parts from various magazines. Each student would have the same set of items. The teacher will then lead them to make a collage giving them step by step direction. The instructions on the activity can also be typed up and given to individual students.

The teacher walks around, making sure everyone is following her instruction. She ensures that each step is clear and comprehensible to everyone. When everyone has completed that task, she is ready to discuss. She leads them through a discussion of the art principles (form and content) as well as social/multicultural issues represented by the collages they had made. She models for them how to analyze a piece of art and how to decipher their hidden messages. This modeling by the teacher assures that the whole process is clear to the students.

Given the fact that the homeless presents the object of analysis and critique, a discussion of the hidden messages in the art piece would reveal the plight of the homeless and the social questions it should provoke. This way, the discussion of the multicultural objectives of this lesson is not pursued outside of the scope of the lesson's academic goals and objectives—form and content of art.

Step 6: Independent Practice

At this point, the students have fully experienced the process of making collages as well as deciphering the hidden messages through analysis and critique. They have also discussed the social implications of the feelings aroused by homelessness and how the art pieces portray them. Now they are going to create their own unique collages and use them to communicate unique messages about homelessness.

It will be the task of classmates to decipher the message contained in other classmates' art work as they work in pairs or small groups to analyze their works. Part of the independent practice may be to work individually or in small groups to produce collages that would present positive ways to respond to the feelings and faces of hopelessness in the homeless.

It could also be a written piece that analyzes the feelings and thoughts. The two pieces of work can then be published to the public (which could be school community, school bulletin board, open house day, community center, etc) for viewing. Now social action is completed. The message has been communicated outside the classroom.

Step 7: Assessment and Evaluation

At this point, the teacher may choose to require a written piece of analysis of at least one piece of art from each student. Each assessment may be placed side by side with the artist's own piece of communicative intent, and the success may depend on how closely the critic comes to the artist's communicative intent. The evaluation may also be anchored on the exhibition. Written comments can be solicited from viewers and such comments would indicate whether the artists were successful in presenting the two views of homelessness through their works of art or not.

Extending the Lesson

Extending the lesson beyond visual and performing arts, a language art lesson can be developed for the same 7th grade classroom with good multicultural twist using the following goals and objectives:

Goals and Objectives

Standard: Students will write a summary of a reading material (California 7th grade academic content standard 2.5).

Objective: Students will identify and write the main idea of the story "Bums in the Attic" from the book *The House on Mango Street,* with supporting details.

Social action: Students will go to neighborhood grocery stores and solicit enough supplies to make 101 lunches for the homeless. The supplies will be donated to a homeless shelter.

Additional Samples of Standards-Based Multicultural Lessons

Lesson 1: Racial Percentage Grade: 5

I. Goals and Objectives:

a. *Goal:* Standard 1.3. (Data Analysis)—Use fractions and percentages to compare data sets of different sizes.

b. *Objective:*
- Students will search information online regarding American racial distribution.
- Students will research the internet for the racial make-up of their city.
- Students will discuss the racial make-up of their city and identify ethnicities that are absent or inadequately represented in their city, and explore ways to attract them to the neighborhood to make for more diversity.
- The class will write a letter to the mayor of their city presenting their suggestions on how to attract other ethnicities to their community. The list will also be taken to the city library and posted for public reading.

II. Materials:
- Basic instructional tools (ex. overhead projector, compass, protractor).
- Computers with online access.
- Textbook.

III. Anticipatory:
Teacher will read the story "Nino's Pizzeria."

IV. Instructional Input:
Teacher will first teach students how to convert between fraction, decimal, and percentage. Then teacher will do a poll and find out about classroom students' racial distribution and use percentage to present the data collected in a list and in a pie chart.

V. Guided Practice:
Teacher will guide students to take a poll of the entire school's student population and break them down to percentages to show the ethnic distribution.

Then they will search online about the racial distribution of a U.S. city of their choice, find out the percentage of each race in that city and draw a pie chart. (They might start to notice that America is a melting pot, and that sometimes it is not easy to clearly indicate which race one person belongs to).

VI. Independent/Group Activities:
Groups of students will research the internet for the demographics of their city and report to the class on the ethnic make-up of their city in fractions and percentages. The following day, using their research results, students will work in groups to compare the percentage of each racial group in their cities to that of different U.S. cities. They will discuss why certain population of people are missing in their city, and scantly represented in another. Issues like equal housing opportunities law,

housing segregation, and economic opportunities will be discussed. Each group will devise ways to attract the under-represented group to their city. This list will be sent to the Mayor of their city, taken to the city library, and posted for public reading.

VII. Evaluation/Assessment:
- The homework will be graded in the next class session to see if students get the math concepts.
- Students will share their findings on the racial distribution of a U.S. city in a list and in pie chart, in groups of 4. Each student will be graded by teacher and also by their peer on their online project final product.
- The list of polarizing issues in our city and things that can be done to combat them will merge into one whole class project before it is published. The success of this work will inform the teacher on the success of collaborative activities as well as students' ability to engage sensitive social issues and find solutions to them.

Lesson 2: Language Arts Grade: 9

Goals:
Writing Strategies: 1.0. Students write coherent and focused essays that convey a welldefined perspective and tightly reasoned argument. The writing demonstrates students' awareness of the audience and purpose. Students progress through the stages of the writing process as needed.

Listening and Speaking: 1.1. Formulate judgments about the ideas under discussion and support those judgments with convincing evidence.

Writing: 1.1. Establish a controlling impression or coherent thesis that conveys a clear and distinctive perspective on the subject and maintain a consistent tone and focus throughout the piece of writing.

Objectives:
Students will research, discuss, consider, and take a position on current issues faced by Native Americans, in light of historical and contemporary facts. They will lead and participate in small group and class-wide discussions that exhibit cogent thought, that will serve as a theme for a position paper, in the form of a persuasive letter. Further, they will select a public medium or representative to whom they will write and mail a persuasive letter that seeks to effectively stimulate the recipient to consider their position and take the suggested action.

Materials:
1 DVD and 2 Videotapes of *Dances With Wolves* and one Videotape of *Incident at Oglalla* (Students will have two scheduled opportunities after school to view *Dances,* as well as option to check out two copies; *Incident* will be viewed in-class.

3 x 5 index cards.

Multi-media equipment, including Internet access w/overhead projection, is installed and operating.

Class Activity

Day 1 (*Warm-Up*)

Entry: Students: In writing journal brainstorm images, words, and phrases you associate with Native Americans.

Guided Discussion/Instructional Input: Teacher & Students: View *Incident at Oglalla.* (ref. *American Indian Stereotypes in the World of Children,* Hirschfielder)

Day 2 (*Instructional Input*)

Debriefing/Discussion: Teacher & Students: *On Incident at Oglalla.*

Guided Practice: Students: In groups of 3–4, discuss film and compose consensus opinion in one paragraph on any issues considered.

Instructional Input Assessment/Debriefing: Teacher & Students: *On Dances with Wolves.*

Day 3 (*Guest Speaker*)

Warm Up/Instructional Input/Guided Practice: Teacher & Students: Prepare questions for guest speaker.

Guest Speaker: Dr. Cornell Shayan, Assistant Professor in the Department of Teaching and Leadership, School of Education at the University of Kansas.

Discussion: Students: Questions for Dr. Shayan.

Assignment

Teacher Assesment:

Someone in your family asks: I saw a bumper sticker that said 'Free Leonard Pelletier,' who is he?

Write a one page summary of who he is and why he is in prison.

Independent Practice:

Research via the Internet/library a current topic or event directly associated with Native Americans; may include historical perspectives, casinos, reservations, taxes, employment, education, alcoholism, standard of living, etc.

Select a topic, keep track (via 3 × 5 cards) of your references and write one paragraph that summarizes your topic and position.

Journal Entry Prompt:

In what way/s will you think differently about Native Americans after today's speaker?

Social Action:

Complete a position paper on the plight of the Native Americans and propose ways the Federal Government can improve their lives. Send your finished position paper, in the form of a letter, to your representative in Congress.

This lesson plan presumes block schedule, i.e., 90 min. class; may be modified for conventional 50 min. period by increasing number of days

Also presumed, students had prior introduction to the structure of a persuasive essay (as described in the lessons in the table above).

References

Banks, J. A. (2003). Approaches to multicultural curriculum reform. In J. A. Banks & C.A.M. Banks (Eds.) *Multicultural education: Issues and perspectives* (pp.242–261). Hoboken, NJ: John Wiley & Sons.

Banks, J. A. (2003). *Teaching strategies for ethnic studies.* Boston: Pearson Education Group.

Barba, R. H. (1998). *Science in the multicultural classroom.* Boston: Allyn & Bacon.

Chatterji, M. (2002). Models and methods for examining standards-based reforms and accountability initiatives: Have the tools of inquiry answered pressing questions on improving schools? *Review of Educational Research, 72*(3), 45–386.

Cobb, P. (1994). Where is the mind? Constructivist and sociocultural perspectives on mathematical development. *Educational Researcher, 23*(7), 13–20.

Cohen, E. G. (1984). Talking and working together: status, interactions, and learning. In P. L. Peterson, L. C. Wilkerson, & M. Hallinan (Eds.), *The social context of instruction: Group organization and group processes* (pp. 171–187). New York: Academic Press.

Edsource. (2003, September/October). Standards in focus. *Leadership. 33*(1), 28–31.

Falk, B. (2002). Standards-based reforms: Problems and possibilities. *Phi Delta Kappan, 83*(8), 612–620.

Kohn, A. (2001). Fighting the tests. *Phi Delta Kappn, 28*(5), 348–360.

Romberg, T. A. (1992). Problematic features of the school mathematics curriculum. In P. N. Sackson (Ed), *Handbook of research on curriculum* (pp. 749–788). New York: Macmillan.

Taylor, L. S. & Whittaker, C. R. (2003). *Bridging multiple worlds: Case studies of diverse educational communities.* Boston: Pearson Education Group.

Thompson, S. (2001). The authentic standards movement and its evil twin. *Phi Delta Kappan, 82*(5), 358–362.

Tiedt P. L., & Tiedt I. M. (2002). *Multicultural teaching: A handbook of activities, information, and resources.* Boston: Allyn & Bacon.

Wang, J., & Odell, S. J. (2002). Mentored learning to teach according to standards-based reform: A critical review. *Review of Educational Research, 72*(3), 481–546.

CHINAKA S. DOMNWACHUKWU is an associate professor in the School of Education and Behavioral Studies at Azusa Pacific University, Azusa, California.

Programming for Participation
Building Partnerships with the Immigrant Newcomer Community

CHRYSS MYLOPOULOS

Public libraries are gradually getting more involved in partnerships with community-based organizations with which they share the same vision, mission, and philosophy regarding services to their culturally diverse communities. The benefits from such an involvement can be significant in areas such as:

- Knowledge sharing and exchange
- Expanding the scope of service
- Promotion of the service
- Accessing community resources

There has also been a growing recognition of partnerships as a value that provides opportunities for city-supported services such as public libraries to form alliances or to link up with other sectors, including the private sector, and strengthen their image as an important community resource accessible to the immigrant public.

Under the umbrella of multicultural library services, the Toronto Public Library got involved in partnerships focusing on immigrant settlement services and on facilitating access to information related to newcomer and immigrant needs. As a result of this relationship the public library has become very close to the immigrant services sector, which has grown in sophistication and importance over the past years, and engaged them in the planning of programs and services.

The Immigrant Settlement Services

The immigrant services sector resembles a "community of practice"—to borrow and apply a term coined by Etienne Wenger, a pioneer in communities of practice related to corporations and their organizational structure. It is a community that includes a group of people who know each other, connect in a helping way, and work toward developing a sense of common good practices when dealing with newcomer individuals and groups. Through sharing of insights and experiences these communities have also managed to create a valuable knowledge network around common problems faced by newcomers, offering possible solutions as well as approaches.

The settlement sector is valuable in serving as a sounding board for organizations that need expertise and information on the "unique realities of immigrants and refugees" (OCASI fact sheet, 1996). According to a report written by Francis Frisken and Marcia Wallace of York University in Toronto, immigrant settlement "is recognized as a localized phenomenon and as a highly localized activity that intersects with the activities of a large number of local political institutions and a network of community agencies." An organization such as the public library needs to recognize the role of this community and acknowledge its expertise and the invaluable contributions it makes toward the settlement and integration of the new immigrants. In particular, the library also needs to recognize the fact that the settlement sector's firsthand knowledge of newcomer communities can help, first by informing the library's decisions about the type of services needed and second, in bringing the newcomers closer to the library.

Most important of all, the public library as a local political institution should join the settlement sector in this network and contribute its expertise, knowledge, and other skills as well as its facilities to maximize the benefits to the immigrant community. As the document "A Social Development Strategy for the City of Toronto" (2001) points out, "Local community cultural centers, . . . libraries . . . are important community resources which must be accessible for public use."

The Toronto Environment: Facts and Figures

Before I describe the settlement program in which the Toronto Public Library is involved, I would like to give a snapshot of the immigrant and refugee communities in the city. The 2001 Census revealed that 49 percent of Toronto's total population of 2,456,000 was born outside Canada, 46 percent of residents reported a mother tongue other than English, and close to 30 percent of city residents primarily speak a language besides English at home.

The director feared that having consulting and referral services for immigrants in the library would lead to other social agencies demanding library space. Clearly this view demonstrated a lack of understanding of the nature of immigrant settlement services, and the significance and contributions of the settlement workers working at the library and bringing hundreds of people closer to this institution.

According to Statistics Canada, the major recent source countries for immigration were China, India, Pakistan, Philippines, Korea, Sri Lanka, United Arab Emirates, Iran, Saudi Arabia, and Romania. In regards to the refugee population between 1991 and 2001, Toronto received approximately 100,000 refugees belonging to all categories, such as refugee claimants and Geneva Convention refugees. Averaged on an annual basis, Toronto receives between 5,000 and 10,000 refugees, accounting for 30–35 percent of the total refugees coming to the country.

How the Partnership with the Immigrant Sector Started

The Settlement and Education Partnerships in Toronto (SEPT) program, as it relates to public libraries, grew out of the close connection that existed between the Multicultural Services in the East Region of the Toronto Public Library (formerly Scarborough Public Library before the amalgamation of all regional libraries into the Toronto Public Library in 1998) and the immigrant settlement sector. When the SEPT program was first introduced, it operated only in schools. Yet many immigrants arrived close to the end of the school year, and it became evident that the settlement workers needed a space to meet the newcomers and their families during summer. The library, a public and neutral place with many branches located all over the city, was thought to be a good place for this program during the summer months.

However, when the multicultural coordinator of the East Region first approached the new East Region director in the spring of 1999 and requested that consideration be given to the idea of the library becoming the place for the summer SEPT program, the idea was met with a negative response. The director feared that having consulting and referral services for immigrants in the library would lead to other social agencies demanding library space. Clearly this view demonstrated a lack of understanding of the nature of immigrant settlement services,

and the significance and contributions of the settlement workers working at the library and bringing hundreds of people closer to this institution. It also underscored a shortsightedness regarding the value of such a partnership in a culturally diverse and immigrant-based city.

The director's refusal delayed the involvement of the library for a year, and it was not until the next year, in June 2000, when SEPT, adopting another strategy, officially approached the administration of the amalgamated Toronto Public Library to request a sharing of facilities. The administration collectively accepted the recommendation, approved the hosting of the program that year, and suggested an evaluation of the program in 12 months to determine its future. In 2001 the program began in a coherent organized fashion.

The Partnership: SEPT Program

SEPT is a primary example of a partnership and the first of its kind between federal levels of government (Citizenship and Immigration Canada) and public institutions (schools, public libraries, parks and recreation facilities) funded by federal, provincial, and city taxes and widely supported by all three as a result of the continuous advocacy by the immigrant settlement sector of the city. SEPT is most closely a partnership between the Toronto School Boards and agencies in the immigrant settlement sector funded by Citizenship Immigration Canada. Settlement workers employed by community agencies work as the school settlement workers (SSWs) of the SEPT Program. The schools and the agencies have formed seven clusters to coordinate the work of SSWs. The program started in 1998–9 with settlement workers assigned to selected schools. After five years in operation it has been expanded to include both public and Catholic schools and employ more workers. The public library and Parks and Recreation joined the SEPT summer program in 2000.

The purpose of the program is to assist newcomers during their initial adjustment period by using schools as a base to meet newcomers; by providing settlement information, translation and interpretation; and by linking and referring new immigrants to programs in schools and community.

Organizational Structure

SEPT currently has a coordinator from the immigrant sector community, a Steering Committee, a cluster coordinator, a Library SEPT coordinator, and SEPT liaisons from each local library. The schools and the agencies in each of the seven clusters have agreed that one agency will act as the lead. The agency hires the cluster coordinator, who works closely with the school principals and coordinates the work of SSWs. The lead agency also hires the school settlement workers.

The school settlement workers (SSWs) are based in elementary and secondary schools during the school year and link newcomer families and students to services that promote settlement. Using the school as a base, they meet with parents and children, provide information and answer questions, and link parents with various programs within the school and the community. SSWs help newcomers learn about services and community programs and overcome difficulties they may experience when integrating into the society.

SEPT Program at the Library

The library summer program was approved in 2000, and it was a pilot program in 2000–2001. It was approved on a long-term basis in 2002 and has expanded from 15 to 29 libraries. During the two summer months of July and August, the library offers its facilities in 29 library locations to settlement agencies and their staff to provide consultation and information and referral in the immigrant's home language for a few days a week.

The purpose of the partnership is to allow the SSWs to use the public library as a base to meet families during the summer, when school is not in session. During these meetings, the SSWs provide settlement information, translation, and interpretation; assist newcomers with information and referrals to a wide range of services in the city; and identify and try to resolve their more specific needs. Secondarily, because of their extended outreach activities, the SSWs bring people to the library, promote awareness and understanding of the library as a community resource, and extend support for the services and programs at the library.

Benefits of SEPT Program at the Local Library

The settlement workers are an excellent resource for the staff. They benefit and assist the local library in:

- communicating with members of the community in languages other than English
- reaching out to the newcomers and attracting them to the library
- creating awareness of library resources and services in the newcomer/immigrant community
- providing staff with background information about the cultural diversity of the community
- informing staff about reading interests and information needs of newcomers and other immigrants
- assisting the library in organizing information/orientation programs
- assisting in the preparation of joint library/SEPT promotional materials in newcomers' languages

Benefits of Developing a Partnership with SEPT

As we see above, there are definite benefits for individual libraries hosting a SEPT program. But the partnership with SEPT benefits the library as an organization by:

- building up contacts and developing an ongoing liaison with immigrant serving community-based agencies and the School Boards

- tapping the most recent information that is gathered either by settlement agencies or School Boards on newcomer groups and languages
- using this information to inform allocation of resources, programs, and services

What Kind of Information Is Requested?

Through this program hundreds of newcomers visited the library and were introduced to its programs and services. In all, 3,000 newcomers came to the library for SEPT meetings in 2000, 2001, and 2002. There was a 60 percent increase in 2002 over the previous year. Eighty-five percent of the newcomers had been in Canada less than six months.

Newcomers, both immigrants and refugees, requested information and referrals in the following areas, identifying and reaffirming their information priorities:

- Employment, language training
- Education and the school system
- Libraries and recreation
- Health, childcare, housing, immigration rules, and finances

Success Factors within the Library

Over the first three years of operation we concluded that the success of the program at the libraries had to do with a number of factors. The first was the awareness of the program on the part of library staff. Presentations by SEPT program staff at library staff meetings were crucial in this respect. Following the initial presentation, regular meetings between library staff and the SSWs helped to establish an ongoing communication and a feeling of partnership.

Logistical factors included availability of space and other facilities such as desks and tables, computers, and phone access. Staff time had to be allotted to provide a local library orientation to the SSWs stationed at each library. Successful libraries also organized library orientation tours and group education programs for newcomers, which introduced the library catalog, the collection, and facilities for using the Internet. Finally, the successful libraries engaged in promotional activities and arranged an informational display on settlement resources, such as a poster with SEPT service hours at the library.

External Success Factors

In addition to factors originating within the library, there were others related to the community and SEPT organization. These included the location of the library in a neighborhood with many new immigrants, the accessibility of the library, especially to public transportation, the lack of competing settlement agencies in the area, consistent and organized outreach to targeted communities on the part of the SEPT program, and frequent and regular SEPT service hours at the library. Other factors had to do with the SSWs themselves: that there were enough to staff the library-based program, that they educated themselves to take full advantage of the library's resources, and that they had sufficient facility in the languages spoken in the surrounding area.

Success Measures/Indicators

Each year the program is evaluated by Citizenship and Immigration Canada-appointed evaluators, but in addition to the federal-level evaluation, the library uses criteria that relate to the purpose of having the program at its facilities. The following indicators have been used to determine whether the program was successful from the library perspective:

- Number of people who were introduced to the library by SSWs
- Participation of the immigrants in library orientation activities and events and in other "user education programs" with the assistance of SSWs
- Referrals to and participation in library programs such as children's summer programs
- Information offered by SSWs to library staff on demographic changes in the community
- Building ongoing liaison with SSWs and their respective agencies and participation of the library in orientation programs during the school year
- Library publicity provided in other languages with the assistance of SSWs for translation and distribution

The success of the partnership of SEPT with the Toronto Public Library during the two summer months has led to discussions on similar partnerships with the public libraries in other cities and regions. The program has now expanded to the cities of Hamilton, Kitchener/Waterloo, and Ottawa, and the Peel and York regions in the Province of Ontario.

It is very encouraging to see that the value of a collaborative partnership between public libraries and the immigrant services sector is finally recognized and pursued. This is the true meaning of practicing multiculturalism at the public library.

Sources

Ethnocultural Portrait—2001 Census. (2001). Toronto: Urban Planning and Development Services.

Frisken, F. and Wallace, M. (2001). *Immigrants and Municipal Services: Client Perspectives.* Toronto: York University.

Immigration Overview: Facts and figures. (2002). Ottawa: Citizenship and Immigration Canada.

Scarborough Network of Immigrant Service Organizations. (2000). *Building Effective Partnerships: A Resource Manual for Community Agencies.* Toronto: Scarborough Network of Immigrant Service Organizations.

Toronto Community and Neighborhood Services. (2001). *A Social Development Strategy for the City of Toronto.* Toronto: City of Toronto.

CHRYSS MYLOPOULOS was the multicultural services specialist at the Toronto Public Library from 1981 to 2003. She presented an earlier version of this article at a symposium on immigrant and refugee communities at the joint meeting of the Canadian Library Association and the American Library Association in Toronto in June 2003. E-mail address: chryss@cs.toronto.edu.

Protecting Educational Rights of the Aboriginal and Indigenous Child

Global challenges and efforts: an introduction

JYOTSNA PATTNAIK

The terms "indigenous" and "aboriginal" are used interchangeably in this issue to refer to original or long-term inhabitants of a geographical area. In this international theme issue, we will adhere to the definition formulated by J. Martinez Cobo (1987), Special Rapporteur for the subcommission of the United Nations Working Group on Indigenous Populations:

> Indigenous communities, peoples, and nations are those which, having a historical continuity with pre-invasion and pre-colonial societies that developed on their territories, consider themselves distinct from other sectors of the societies now prevailing in those territories, or parts of them.

This issue focuses on the need to design educational programs that address the unique linguistic, geographical, economic, and cultural affiliations, as well as the needs, potentials, and interests, of each individual indigenous child and his/her family and community.

According to the UN, some 300 million indigenous people inhabit more than 70 countries in the world. However, the impact of what some would call social Darwinism has led to the disappearance of many aboriginal communities, prompting concern that if the rights of indigenous people are not protected, many more communities will quickly disappear. Education has been acknowledged as an important human right that is key to the survival and prosperity of indigenous groups, the preservation of cultural values, the elimination of discrimination, and the realization of social justices (Tomasevski, 2003).

My Personal Connections with the Theme Issue

The idea for the theme issue stems from my personal experiences with aboriginal cultures in my native country. I grew up in a state in India that is home to a number of aboriginal groups. I have had the opportunity to listen to aboriginal people who worked in my parents' home and learn about their customs and beliefs. I also had the opportunity to teach aboriginal children and interact with parents from these communities. As a teacher, I followed the "assimilation" model of fitting aboriginal children into the dominant group's educational system. I witnessed the plight, struggle, and hardship of the children and their families as they strove to adapt to an unfamiliar and very different culture. I also noticed aboriginal children dropping out of school because of severe corporal punishment (in response to non-attendance and academic failures), academic pressure, and the competitive nature of Indian schooling; practices that were unfamiliar to aboriginal children in their communities. I have supported and mentored aboriginal children in spite of societal perceptions and uncertainty that existed (and still continues) regarding their mental ability and educational future. Because of my own academic interest in and alignment with postmodern thoughts and critical theories, I have engaged myself in reading and reflecting over issues that relate to education of children from marginalized groups across the globe. I strongly believe that the groups that have received the least attention from scholars, policymakers, educators, and educational researchers are the aboriginal communities worldwide. This international focus issue is an effort to reverse this trend.

Rationale for Choosing the Issue's Theme

The articles for this international focus issue were selected because they: 1) draw attention to the impact of colonization on aboriginal children, 2) share some successful efforts by international organizations and indigenous communities to counter these effects, 3) highlight the uniqueness of various aboriginal cultures, and 4) share diverse educational approaches.

Colonization and Its Impact

In recent years, pressure from national and transnational organizations has forced many governments around the world to adopt economic, educational, and legislative provisions to protect the rights of minority groups within their territories. However, aboriginal peoples continue to suffer the aftereffects of colonization, including blatant human rights violations (Sodoti, 2000). Colonization has had linguistic, cultural, economic, educational, social, political, and physical effects on these small indigenous cultures. From their study based on indigenous people in Latin America, Hall and Patrinos (2005), the authors of a recent World Bank study, report that indigenous people still have less education, being indigenous increases an individual's probability of being poor, the educational outcomes are substantially worse for indigenous learners, and indigenous women and children continue to have less access to basic health services.

Researchers report low academic achievement and high dropout rates, depression, and high rates of substance abuse among indigenous youth (Clarke, 2002). Daes (2001) describes these symptoms as a "spiritual erosion" among indigenous youth and traces their roots to indigenous groups' historical experiences with colonization. Educational experts attribute the educational failure of indigenous children to a host of school-related factors, such as cultural discontinuity and omission of aboriginal languages in the curriculum; irrelevant content and pedagogy; and an unavailability of schools for aboriginal children in remote areas in developing countries (Barman, 1996; Mattson & Caffrey, 2001; Ogbu & Simons, 1994; Singh, 1997; Smith, 1999; Sodoti, 2000).

Rays of Hope

Against this bleak scenario stand efforts at various levels to address challenges faced by indigenous communities and children.

UN intervention. Transnational bodies such as the UN have made numerous efforts to highlight indigenous issues and put pressure on national governments to address them. The UN declared 1993 to be the Year of the World's Indigenous Peoples. That same year, it published the Draft Declaration on the Human Rights of Indigenous Peoples. In 1994, the UN General Assembly proclaimed 1995–2004 as the International Decade of the World's Indigenous People in order to solicit and strengthen international cooperation on problems faced by indigenous people in such areas as human rights, the environment, development, education, and health. While the Convention on the Rights of the Child, adopted in 1989, focuses on the rights of all children, Article 30 explicitly recognizes the right of indigenous children to enjoy their traditional culture, practice their own religion, and use their traditional language. In the year 2000, the UN Permanent Forum on Indigenous Issues was established by UN Economic and Social Council (ECOSOC). Furthermore, UNICEF has implemented many projects worldwide that focus on health, nutrition, education, rural development, poverty reduction, and improvement of the status of women and children. Although these efforts have raised awareness about indigenous issues, there is still much work to be done.

Successful educational initiatives. In recent years, some indigenous scholars and organizations have demanded that state and national governments include the contents of indigenous knowledge, indigenous history, philosophy, and values as integral aspects of their cultural and educational policies and programs for indigenous children. These efforts have led to the creation of some successful culturally appropriate indigenous educational programs across the globe, such as the preschools that originated from the Kohango Reo movement in New Zealand, the Yipirinya School in Australia, and the Bodo language medium schools in India.

Understanding the Uniqueness of Aboriginal Cultures

It is important to make a distinction between aboriginal groups and other minority cultures. Aboriginal people have a special status outlined in the constitutions of many countries. In addition, the historical as well as the contemporary issues, experiences, needs, and aspirations of aboriginal people are very different from other minority groups. In fact, as Mattson and Caffrey (2001) argue, "Policy and practice that is based on multiculturalism may further marginalize aboriginal people, as it obscures the special status of aboriginal people as the original inhabitants of the land" (p. 11). However, non-aboriginal people frequently are unaware of and/or unwilling to accept constitutional provisions made for them.

In addition, non-aboriginal people tend to perceive aboriginal communities as a homogeneous singular entity. Yet tremendous linguistic, historical, cultural, socio-economic, and political diversity exist among and within aboriginal communities.

In recent years, there has been a greater acknowledgment and acceptance of aboriginal knowledge, beliefs, and worldviews. Instead of perceiving aboriginal language, consciousness, and knowledge as irrelevant to modern educational thought and practices, educators now argue that indigenous beliefs on ecological and environmental sustainability will serve the needs of the greater society (Cajete, 1994), and they chart the many unique contributions of indigenous knowledge and practices to modern medicine, agriculture, sociology, and politics.

Diverse Educational Perspectives and Programs

Currently, a wide range of educational perspectives and programs focus on indigenous children. Some aboriginal communities have resisted the mainstream educational models, and have reconceptualized schooling and implemented educational programs that assert their own cultural parameters. Others argue for achieving a synthesis between the traditional informal patterns of education of the aboriginal cultures with more formal and structured approaches.

Mainstream education programs around the world have been criticized for their focus on the dominant group's knowledge, beliefs, and practices. In response, many educational institutions in the United States, Canada, and Australia adopted a form of curriculum reform that Banks (1997) dubbed as "additive," and that others refer to as the "cultural tourism" approach. Scholars now argue for replacing this superficial approach to multicultural education with a critical approach (e.g., the "place-based learning" initiative, Smith, 2002) that encourages teachers to perceive curriculum, pedagogy, and literacy as vehicles to understand and challenge the unequal distributions of privilege, power, and domination (Brady & Kanpol, 2000), and that encourages them to integrate minority cultures into all aspects of the curriculum (Jones & Moomaw, 2002).

Overview of the Articles

The issue begins with a keynote speech by Ole-Henrik Magga, the Chairperson of the United Nations Permanent Forum on Indigenous Issues (submitted to *Childhood Education* by John Gordon Scott, secretariat of the Permanent Forum on Indigenous Issues Division for Social Policy and Development). The speech acknowledges the challenges faced by indigenous children around the world with regard to educational access and success and discusses strategies to tackle these issues. The speech is a call to the international community to make greater efforts to achieve indigenous education goals. The issue also includes an interview with Dr. Ajit Mohanty, noted Indian psycholinguist, conducted by the guest editor. The interview captures the status of aboriginal languages and cultures in India, successful efforts to revive aboriginal languages through instruction in the mother tongue, and criticisms of state and national governments' language policies in education.

The other articles selected for this issue are organized around some major themes. These articles reflect very well the current discourse on aboriginal and indigenous education around the world. While written within a global discourse and with an international audience in mind, these articles also point to the relationship between the discursive, the structural, and the pedagogical within particular local contexts. More articles were accepted for this issue than we had room to print, so we will be revisiting the topic in upcoming issues of *Childhood Education*. The themes that are discussed are drawn from all the articles selected for the theme issue.

Continuing Misconceptions and Colonization of Indigenous Children and Communities

Some authors in this issue have addressed the continuing colonization of indigenous children and communities, describing how the dominant cultures use the public education system to colonize indigenous cultures. For example, the article by Behera and Nath vividly captures the failure of the residential schooling initiative undertaken by the state government in Orissa, India, to educate aboriginal girls. The intolerable living conditions, rampant corruption, and violation of human rights inside the dormitories, as well as the regimented curriculum and culturally inappropriate school routines, contribute to a cruel process whereby individual lives lose their relevance. For aboriginal girls, training in the dominant educational system becomes a liability rather than a door for upward mobility and economic advancement.

Too often, teachers and preservice teachers trivialize indigenous cultures instead of deconstructing stereotypes and biases against indigenous communities and giving voice to authentic

indigenous cultural beliefs and practices within the school's dominant curriculum. The article by Simpson and Clancy identifies factors that contribute to the marginalization of Aboriginal children in Australia. Simpson and Clancy describe how the dominant literacy practices in educational settings, such as the use of Standard English and incompatible cultural and linguistic practices, seriously challenge the literacy learning of Aboriginal children in preschool settings.

The economic impact of colonization is evident in the extreme poverty among indigenous population worldwide. The 2005 World Bank Study reports that few gains were made in income poverty reduction among indigenous peoples during the preceding decade (Hall & Patrinos, 2005). In his article, Singh draws readers' attention to the impact of extreme poverty on the educational processes and outcomes of isiZulu indigenous learners in Durban, South Africa. Singh's article echoes researchers Fiske and Ladd (2004) in his concern that South Africa is still far from creating a racially equitable educational system for its minority children.

Factors That Prevent Aboriginal Children's Academic Success

Some authors focused their discussion on the question, "What prevents aboriginal children's success, either academic or psychosocial, in school?" Children's lack of a smooth transition to school—whether from preschool or from home—has been identified as one of the challenges for academic success, especially for children from diverse cultural backgrounds.

Based on the findings of her research with urban Native American children ages 9 to 18 in the midwestern United States, Powers identifies factors that contribute to underachievement among indigenous children in the upper grades and provides practical suggestions to address these issues. Powers reminds school personnel to perceive urban indigenous children, who have been removed from their tribal homelands for three or four generations, differently than their rural counterparts, who are closer to their cultural roots.

Stories of Survival and Spiritual Regeneration

In contrast to the stories of imposed powerlessness, some authors share stories of collective efforts in indigenous populations to regain possession of indigenous knowledge, scholarship, identity, and destiny by discarding what Blaut (1993) calls the "colonizer's model of the world." As linguists rightly point out, the passion and commitment for language maintenance, revival, and revitalization needs to come from language minority communities themselves (Fishman, 2001). Education is an important means to the survival of small indigenous cultures, and indigenous communities must bear the ownership of designing and implementing appropriate educational processes for their children.

In this issue, the article by Pearce and colleagues very eloquently illustrates Varadharajan's (2000) observation that amidst the experiences of blatant dispossession and deracination, aboriginal history simultaneously entails the story of survival and spiritual regeneration. With a story telling approach true to aboriginal collective consciousness, the article shares the story of a new aboriginal Charter School, Mother Earth's Children's Charter School, in Western Canada, an example of an indigenous community reclaiming its educational system, implementing culturally appropriate practices, and involving all members of the community in this process. The authors hope that the article may serve as a source of inspiration and wisdom for aboriginal communities around the world.

Co-authors Aquino and Kirylo contribute a story about the revival of the Guarani language in Paraguay. These efforts are based on a strong conviction that the survival of a minority culture depends on the use of its native language, both written and oral, especially by children in school and community settings.

Chang based her article on an ethnographic account of a kindergarten program for the Atayal people in Taiwan. The article discusses five projects that resulted from the Taiwanese government's policy on education of aboriginal children and demonstrates how governmental policies can be very well translated into culturally responsive educational practices in the hands of committed teachers and community members.

Recommended Practices and Successful Approaches

Throughout this issue, the authors make some recommendations for addressing the needs of aboriginal learners.

Culturally appropriate educational practices. Henderson (2000) urges teachers to understand the restrictive nature of the Eurocentric curriculum and its impact on indigenous children and use this knowledge to incorporate aboriginal teachings and traditions into dominant educational contexts. Authors in this issue have suggested that successfully educating indigenous children depends on offering culturally appropriate curriculum and pedagogy. Indigenous scholars unanimously agree that "student achievement and performance in school and pride in aboriginal communities and heritages are directly tied to respect for and support of the students' aboriginal languages" (Battiste, 2000, p. 199).

Literature-based intervention. Teachers can adopt a literature-based intervention approach to integrate authentic cultural information on indigenous cultures in their curriculum. Quality children's books that provide authentic representations of aboriginal peoples, and appropriate activities based on these books, are invaluable teaching tools.

Community involvement. The education of aboriginal learners in formal settings has been described as a process that involves recovery, spiritual healing, and rediscovery. Therefore, the role of elders as healers, transmitters, innovators, and purveyors is crucial in the education of aboriginal children (Corbiere, 2000). Elders can expertly incorporate aboriginal healing and teaching strategies to reach aboriginal learners. They have shared their collective wisdom and experiences through storytelling in many educational programs (Meyer & Bogdan, 2001). Elders also can play an important role in promoting resiliency among indigenous children (HeavyRunner & Marshall, 2003).

Teacher preparation and indigenous teachers. Researchers report that culturally responsive teachers play an important role in the sociocultural and academic success of their indigenous learners (Jeffries & Singer, 2003). It is important to note that most teachers of aboriginal children come from non-aboriginal backgrounds. The incongruence between non-aboriginal teachers and their aboriginal students makes it imperative that teacher education programs prepare culturally responsive teachers. To be effective with aboriginal students, teachers must show their commitment to the children through high expectations, cultural sensitivity, reflectivity, commitment to building home-school partnerships, and acquisition of bilingual and pedagogical proficiency. Indigenous teachers offer the following advantages: enhanced learning opportunities for indigenous children when teachers and children share the same language and culture, enhanced teacher-student relationship, increased school retention for indigenous youth, and greater connectivity to indigenous communities (McCarty & Watahomigie, 1999; Swisher & Tippeconnic, 1999).

Conclusion

The authors of the 2005 international focus issue of *Childhood Education* have shared their passion, experiences, and insights on the issue of education of the aboriginal child. As the guest editor, I hope that the issue, with its international focus and human rights mission, will contribute to the continuing global efforts toward realizing the freedom, self-determination, and equal treatment of indigenous people. It also may open up public and political space for transcultural and transnational dialogue/debates and promote advocacy for the education and well-being of aboriginal children around the world.

References

Banks, J. (1997). *Teaching strategies for ethnic studies* (6th ed.). Boston: Allyn & Bacon.

Barman, J. (1996). Aboriginal education at the cross-road. The legacy of the residential schools and the way ahead. In D. A. Long & O. P. Dickason (Eds.), *Vision of the heart: Canadian aboriginal issues*. Toronto: Harcourt Brace.

Battiste, M. (2000). Maintaining aboriginal identity, language, and culture in modern society. In M. Battiste (Ed.), *Reclaiming indigenous voice and vision* (pp. 192–208). Toronto: University of British Columbia Press.

Blaut, J. M. (1993). *The colonizer's model of the world: Geographical diffusionism and Eurocentric history.* New York: Guilford Press.

Brady, J. F., & Kanpol, B. (2000). The role of critical multicultural education and feminist critical thought in teacher education: Putting theory into practice. *Educational Foundations, 14*(3), 39–50.

Cajete, G. (1994). *Look to the mountain: An ecology of indigenous education.* Durango, CO: Kivak.

Clarke, A. S. (2002). Social and emotional distress among American Indian and Alaska Native Students: Research findings. *ERIC Digest.* (ERIC Document Reproduction Service No. ED 459 988)

Cobo, J. M. (1987). *Study of the problem of discrimination against indigenous populations.* E/CN.4/Sub.2/1986/7/ Add.4, Volume V. United Nations.

Corbiere, A. O. (2000). *Reconciling epistemological orientations: Toward a holistic Nishnaabe (Ojibwe/Odawa/Potawatomi) education.* (ERIC Document Reproduction Service No. ED 467 707)

Daes, E-I. (2001). Prologue: The experience of colonization around the world. In M. Battiste (Ed.), *Reclaiming indigenous voice and vision* (pp. 192–208). Toronto: University of British Columbia Press.

Fishman, J. (2001). Why is it so hard to save a threatened language? In J. Fishman (Ed.), *Can threatened languages be saved?* (pp. 1–22). Clevedon, UK: Multilingual Matters.

Fiske, E. B., & Ladd, H. F. (2004). *Elusive equity: Education reform in post apartheid South Africa.* Washington, DC: Brookings Institution Press.

Hall, G., & Patrinos, H. A. (2005). *Indigenous peoples, poverty and human development in Latin America: 1994–2004.* Retrieved May 25, 2005, from http://wbln0018.worldbank.org/LAC/lacinfoclient.nsf/8d6661f6799ea8a48525673900537f95/3bb82428dd9dbea785257004007c113d/$FILE/IndigPeoplesPoverty_Exec_Summ_en.pdf

HeavyRunner, I., & Marshall, K. (2003). Miracle survivors: Promoting resilience in Indian students. *Tribal College Journal, 14*(4), 14–18.

Henderson, J. Y. (2000). Challenges of respecting indigenous worldviews in Eurocentric education. In R. Neil (Ed.), *Voice of the drum: Indigenous education and culture* (pp. 59–80). Manitoba, Canada: Kingfisher.

Jeffries, R. B., & Singer, L. C. (2003). Successfully educating urban American Indian students: An alternative school format. *Journal of American Indian Education, 42*(3), 40–57.

Jones, G. W., & Moomaw, S. (2002). *Lessons from Turtle Island: Native curriculum in early childhood classrooms.* St. Paul, MN: Redleaf Press.

Mattson, L., & Caffrey, L. (2001). *Barriers to equal education for aboriginal learners. A review of the literature: ABC Human Rights Commission report.* Vancouver: British Columbia Human Rights Commission.

McCarty, T. L., & Watahomigie, L. J. (1999). Indigenous community-based language education in the USA. In S. May (Ed.), *Indigenous community-based education* (pp. 79–94). Philadelphia: Multilingual Matters.

McSwan, D., Clinch, E., & Store, R. (2001). Otitis media, learning and community. *Education in Rural Australia, 11*(2), 27–32.

Meyer, J. F., & Bogdan, G. (2001). *Our "first education."* (ERIC Document Reproduction Service No. ED 476 011)

Ogbu, J. U., & Simons, H. D. (1994). *Cultural models of school achievement: A quantitative test of Ogbu's theory. Cultural models of literacy: A comparative study. Project 12.* (ERIC Document Reproduction Service No. ED376 515)

Singh, U. K. (1997). *Tribal education.* New Delhi, India: Common Wealth.

Smith, D. (1999). Educating inner-city aboriginal students: The significance of culturally appropriate instruction and parental support. *McGill Journal of Education, 34*(2), 155–171.

Smith, G. A. (2002). Place-based education: Learning to be where we are. *Phi Delta Kappan, 83*(8), 584–594.

Sodoti, C. (2000). *Rights for all. The human rights of rural citizens. Keynote address.* (ERIC Document Reproduction Service No. ED 455 058)

Swisher, K. G., & Tippeconnic, J. W. (1999). *Research to support improved practice in Indian education.* (ERIC Document Reproduction Service No. ED 427 915)

Tomasevski, K. (2003). *Education denied.* London: Zed Books.

Unger, R. M. (1986). *Passion: An essay on personality.* New York: The Free Press.

Varadharajan, A. (2000). The repressive tolerance of cultural peripheries. In M. Battiste (Ed.), *Reclaiming indigenous voice and vision* (pp. 142–149). Toronto: University of British Columbia Press.

JYOTSNA PATTNAIK is Professor and Director, Early Childhood Education Master's Program, California State University Long Beach.

Why Are "Bad Boys" Always Black?
Causes of Disproportionality in School Discipline and Recommendations for Change

CARLA R. MONROE

C uriosity about the crowd forming on the next block attracted me to the scene in time to witness Kevin's[1] arrest. I watched him struggle futilely against the police officer's determined hold of his upper body. Kevin's winced expression was briefly visible as the handcuffs were placed around his restrained wrists. His body seemed limp and defeated as he was moved from the grassy plot into the back of the police car, sobbing. As the climax of the arrest slowly subsided, clipped thoughts and questions flooded my mind. Kevin was an eighth grade kid from my school. I had never seen a 13-year-old in the back of a police car; definitely never anyone that young in police custody. Why? What happened? What now? Unfortunately, I had arrived too late to know how the arrest had been set in motion. Some of the other onlookers said that Kevin had tried to rob someone; others commented that the incident was drug related. As strands of truth and speculation shaped Kevin's story, I turned and walked back to the school campus. He was in my second period class. I knew that I would learn the details of the story at work.

The form of notification soon arrived from the district office. Beside Kevin's name were the expected words. *Status: Suspended. Location: Juvenile detention.* The document provided a crisp and matter-of-fact conclusion to the story. Yet, my own experiences with Kevin, coupled with observations by students and colleagues, raised complicated questions about the situation. Already struggling academically, what effect would Kevin's incarceration have on his intellectual development? How would he readjust to mainstream society and school following his release? What life implications did juvenile detainment hold for a young adolescent, particularly a black male? Unfortunately, such questions surround the lives of many African American youths as crime continues to be a familiar component of the nation's urban landscape.

I was a middle-school teacher employed in a large urban school district when the events related to Kevin's arrest unfolded. I taught in a predominately African American institution in which some of my students were middle- and working-class and others were from decidedly low-income backgrounds. Improving student outcomes, both inside and outside school walls, was a shared institutional concern. Yet, young people such as Kevin symbolized the ways in which articulated goals frequently failed to become reality.

At first glance, Kevin's predicament may appear to reside beyond the boundaries of the public education enterprise. However, numerous social scientists have identified compelling connections between students' schooling experiences and negative outcomes such as delinquency (Noguera 2003; Voelkl, Welte, and Wieczorek 1999). Examinations of low-income communities further suggest that antisocial behaviors surfacing during adolescence often become a trenchant component of youths' experiences across the lifespan, thereby heightening their likelihood of entering the juvenile and criminal justice systems (Simon and Burns 1997). Notably, studies conducted with middle-school learners have linked school disciplinary patterns with trends in delinquency and recidivism (Gottfredson, Gottfredson, and Hybl 1993; Skiba, Peterson, and Williams 1997). The present overrepresentation of African American males in the U.S. justice system (Wacquant 2000), combined with racial disproportionality on measures of school discipline (Applied Research Center 2002), provide compelling reasons for continued scrutiny of connections between the two areas.

Although previous studies have revealed powerful insights about the salience of culture, particularly race, in schools and society, few scholars have explored how culturally-based constructs relate to school discipline. In this article I expand on current research by examining factors that contribute to the discipline gap, or the overrepresentation of black, male, and low-income students on indices of school discipline. Whereas researchers commonly agree that cultural mismatches create conditions for systematic school failure, less is known about how societal forces may inform teachers' perceptions of African American student behaviors. There is a particular need to understand how and why teachers' views of these students, particularly males, mediate their disciplinary actions in the classroom. Specifically, how do images of African American men and boys in society at large relate to teachers' notions about effective disciplinary strategies based on student race and gender? Moreover, how do prevailing norms and practices in society at large influence the shape of disciplinary problems in schools? This article is grounded in a consideration of the criminalization of black males, race and class privilege, and zero tolerance policies as key forces in the genesis and evolution of the discipline gap. The article concludes with recommendations for how educators and policymakers should approach disciplinary concerns for middle-school learners.

Why the Discipline Gap? A Synopsis of Research Findings

Nationally, African American students are targeted for disciplinary action in the greatest numbers (Johnston 2000). According to quantitative reports, black pupils are statistically two to five times more likely to be suspended than their white counterparts (Irvine 1990). Qualitative findings simultaneously indicate that teachers confine reprimands and punitive consequences to black children even when youths of other races engage in the same unsanctioned behaviors (McCadden 1998). Skiba et al.'s (2000) research further reveals that African Americans receive harsher punishments than their peers, often for subjectively defined offenses. Inequities in school discipline are most pronounced among boys (Ferguson 2000).

Because school trends reflect currents of the national contexts in which they exist, core causes of the discipline gap are both internal and external to schools. In this section, I discuss three conditions that contribute to current disparities. They are (a) the criminalization of black males, (b) race and class privilege, and (c) zero tolerance polices. Each is discussed at length.

Criminalizing African American Males

Popular views of African American life are connected to threatening images with predictable regularity. Both media and scholarly portrayals of contemporary black life often highlight cultures of violence, drugs, anti-authoritarianism, and other social deficiencies. When confining attention to urban black males, threatening and criminal archetypes frequently ground their perceived existence, particularly in low-income environments (Canada 1996). Notably, unflattering prototypes tend to emerge from youths' efforts to assert their identities and protect themselves in disenfranchised communities (Anderson 1999). For example, in analyzing the relationship between self-presentation and power, West writes that

> for most young black men, power is acquired by stylizing their bodies over space and time in such a way that their bodies reflect their uniqueness and provoke fear in others. To be "bad" is good not simply because it subverts the language of the dominant white culture but also because it imposes a unique kind of order for young black men on their own distinctive chaos and solicits an attention that makes others pull back with some trepidation. This young black male style is a form of self-identification and resistance in a hostile culture; it also is an instance of machismo identity ready for violent encounters. (1994, 128)

West's analysis captures a fundamental dilemma facing many young black males. Although attempting to assert self-affirming identities in adverse environments, behaviors among African American youths often fuel pejorative stereotypes that distinguish black males as troublesome and threatening. Grant (1988), Noguera (2002a, 2002b), and others have argued that negative views of black males largely emanate from environmental dynamics that circumscribe how young African American boys' identities are perceived both inside and outside their communities.

When examining research literature on school discipline, the criminalization of black males appears to provide a powerful context for the discipline gap. On one level, researchers widely recognize that teachers frequently approach classes populated by low-income and African American youths with a strong emphasis on controlling student behaviors. Custodial tendencies tend to be most pronounced with low-ability level and male students (Gouldner 1978). On a second level, practitioner responses to incidents of perceived misbehavior tend to reside at either extreme of the disciplinary continuum. That is, when disciplining African American students, teachers are likely to demonstrate reactions that appear to be more severe than required. Additionally, there is evidence that practitioners may devote little effort to addressing behavioral concerns in their infancy when nonpunitive techniques are likely to be effective (Emihovich 1983). Such tendencies are less likely to be true with white students.

Although many factors influence teachers' work, previous research has marked practitioner perceptions and accompanying expectations of youths as key mediating influences in their decisions concerning discipline (Bennett and Harris 1982). Many teachers may not explicitly connect their disciplinary reactions to negative perceptions of black males, yet systematic trends in disproportionality suggest that teachers may be implicitly guided by stereotypical perceptions that African American boys require greater control than their peers and are unlikely to respond to nonpunitive measures. Although movements to address diversity in teacher education programs are useful means of heightening teachers' awareness of racial issues, the trenchancy of the discipline gap suggests that education professionals insufficiently interrogate connections between generic perceptions of black males and their treatment in the classroom.

Race and Class Privilege

Educational expectations, practices, and policies reflect the values of the individuals who create them. As a consequence, judgments about student disruption are imbued with cultural norms. Because white and middle-class individuals occupy most positions of power in educational settings, decisions concerning behavioral expectations and infractions are set forth by a culturally-specific bloc. Juxtaposing the leading reasons for disciplinary referrals with qualitative research findings make the culturally-influenced nature of school discipline clear. For instance, Skiba et al.'s (1997) analysis of nineteen Midwestern middle schools revealed that disobedience, conduct, disrespect, and fighting were the most common reasons for teachers to write disciplinary referrals. Yet, empirical comparisons of cultural interaction styles indicate that teachers regularly interpret African American behaviors as inappropriate when the actions are not intended to be so (Hanna 1988; Weinstein, Curran, and Tomlinson-Clarke 2004; Weinstein, Tomlinson-Clarke, and Curran 2003). Examples include viewing overlapping speech as disrespect, play fighting as authentic aggression, and ritualized humor as valid insults.

Limited racial and socioeconomic diversity in educational circles of power has inhibited professionals' recognition of school disciplinary practices as socially defined constructs. Because prevailing beliefs and practices often proceed unchallenged, the culturally based nature of school discipline has remained an unquestioned component of school life. Moreover, structural oversights have facilitated explanations for disciplinary action that assign culpability to the children involved. Altering present disciplinary trends demands improved cross-cultural competency among classroom practitioners regarding behavioral norms in African American communities. Unfortunately, teacher preparation programs often fail to encourage candidates to expand their vision of culturally responsive pedagogy beyond academic material to include classroom management and student discipline. Teacher preparation and professional development programs that remain innocent community-based practices for African American students risk perpetuating approaches that have little relevance for pupils who are most at risk for disciplinary action.

Zero Tolerance Initiatives

Convictions that a stern approach to school discipline would curb inappropriate—particularly criminal—behavior have speeded the national growth and implementation of zero tolerance policies. In fact, a reported 94 percent of U.S. public schools have adopted such initiatives (Johnson, Boydon, and Pittz 2001). Yet, analyses of zero tolerance efforts indicate that the policies may be yielding unintended consequences to a greater extent than they eradicate inappropriate behaviors. The exacerbation of racial discrepancies currently ranks among the most serious concerns. Educators' unwillingness to draw distinctions between severe and minor offenses and the breadth with which zero tolerance approaches are applied appear to be primary sources of the problem (Skiba and Peterson 1999).

What appears to be a more significant challenge, however, is educators' general inattention to the value of working cooperatively with parents and communities to construct schools where disruption is minimized overall. Rather, by most accounts, institutional decisions concerning student behavior are reached in isolation of input from other relevant stakeholders. Even parental efforts to legally challenge punishments have failed to make an incision in rigid interpretations of the policies (Dohrn 2001). Although teachers lack the institutional authority to alter principals' and policymakers' decisions, practitioners should appreciate the power that falls within their purview: whether to write a disciplinary referral at all. Encouraging teachers to address behavioral concerns in their classes would be a significant stride toward lowering suspension and expulsion rates.

Recommendations for Middle School Professionals

Closing the discipline gap requires reshaping individual and institutional orientations and practices. This section contains four broad recommendations designed to guide middle-school educators' efforts to address disproportionality.

1. *Provide opportunities for teachers to interrogate their beliefs about African American students.* Racial and gender stereotypes often undergird teachers' interactions with students. As a result, many teachers, consciously or unconsciously, believe that boys present more disciplinary problems than girls, and that black students are more likely to misbehave than youths of other races. Because school structures seldom provide opportunities for practitioners to interact and observe alternative classroom environments, teachers' perceptions frequently proceed unquestioned and may be crystallized by incidents that affirm preexisting stereotypes.

In-service professional development efforts focused on discipline should be designed to identify and critique teachers' perceptions of students of color, particularly African American boys. Such workshops should be designed to attract a wide-ranging cadre of teachers from alternative school environments, and conducted by racially diverse facilitators. Enabling teachers to share their views and experiences in a multiracial environment provides opportunities for teachers to be exposed to experiences and approaches that may challenge marginalizing beliefs about African American youths. Moreover, these efforts are powerful means of encouraging teachers to recognize culturally-based behaviors that are not intended to be disruptive.

2. *Incorporate and value culturally responsive disciplinary strategies.* The field of education is replete with programs and approaches designed to elicit desirable student behavior, yet the disproportionate percentage of disciplinary action targeting African American students raises twin questions. With whom are these models successful? And why have they failed to reverse negative trends among culturally diverse students from high poverty backgrounds?

Many classroom and institutional disciplinary approaches suffer from a basic inattention to cultural context. Because common techniques and expectations are moored in middle class, white norms, numerous approaches fail to prove useful with students of color. In fact, many prevailing techniques are at odds with the very disciplinary practices to which many African American students are exposed, particularly low-income youths. Eradicating the discipline gap requires theorists, researchers, and practitioners to familiarize themselves with culturally specific behavioral norms, and incorporate culturally familiar behavior management strategies into their practice. For example, successful teachers of African American students tend to incorporate demonstrations of affect and emotion, as well as culturally based humor, into their interactions with students (Irvine 2003). Empirical findings further suggest that culturally responsive teachers are more comfortable in their roles as disciplinarians, less likely to write disciplinary referrals, and have stronger relationships with students and parents than their counterparts (Cooper 2002; Monroe and Obidah 2004).

3. *Broaden the discourse around school disciplinary decisions.* Despite provisions that permit school officials to address disciplinary concerns on a case-by-case basis, there is significant evidence that most organizational leaders elect not to do so. Rather, many administrators uphold narrow applications of disciplinary consequences. Consider a few of the following examples:

- In Ohio a fourteen-year-old student was suspended for giving Midol tablets to a classmate. The recipient of the pills was suspended as well and required to complete a drug awareness class.
- A Georgia middle-school student was suspended for bringing a Tweety Bird key chain to school on the basis that the trinket violated policies concerning weapons.

Concentrating decisions about expulsions and suspensions in the hands of a few has restricted opportunities to raise concerns about troubling disciplinary procedures. Stated more plainly, the closed nature of school discipline precludes important stakeholders from questioning dubious reasons for suspensions and expulsions in addition to disturbing racial and gender patterns that accompany sanctions.

Flattening the organizational hierarchy by creating advisory boards for school discipline would be a useful means of closing the discipline gap on several levels. First, the board may serve as a means for monitoring demographic trends in referrals and highlighting discriminatory patterns that emerge. Identifying problems early in the school year would be a strong step toward preventing recurrent problems across the year. Secondarily, schools would structurally enable well-qualified individuals to provide important feedback on how to serve students' and teachers' needs most effectively. Urban institutions would be well served to select advisory members from well-regarded teachers as well as parent and community volunteers who are familiar with the school and its constituents.

4. *Maintain learners' interest through engaging instruction.* A clear and logical correlation exists between student discipline and academic achievement. Throughout the nation, there is evidence that students who are disproportionately targeted for disciplinary action are the same pupils who perform poorly on most measures of achievement. For example, Skiba and Rausch (2004) analyzed the relationship between standardized tests scores and suspension and expulsion rates for students in the state of Indiana and found that schools with high out-of-school suspension rates had a lower percent of students passing the math and English/Language Arts section of the Indiana State Test of Educational Progress (ISTEP). The correlation held true even after the researchers controlled for poverty and the percentage of African American students enrolled. Correlations between discipline and achievement were strongest at the secondary level.

Student behavior is intimately connected to the quality of instruction in the classroom. When students are intellectually immersed in learning tasks they are less likely to engage in behaviors that detract from the instruction at hand. Ladson-Billings' (1994) seminal study of effective teachers of African American students cited several pedagogical tools that teachers may use to guide their efforts. Among other findings, she noted that academic materials drawn from students' home environments anchored teachers' instruction and set the stage for inviting lessons that students found relevant, meaningful, and affirming. Although not focused on classroom discipline specifically, Ladson-Billings' research holds particular relevance for the discipline gap.

When students perceive that their lives and experiences are valued, they are less likely to engage in behaviors that express resistance against alienating school forces. Moreover, youths are provided opportunities to appreciate benefits gleaned from sharpening their scholastic skills and broadening their knowledge base. Additionally, relying on students' intellectual capacity as a means of addressing discipline draws on intrinsic behavioral motivations—an approach that tends to be effective with low-income students of color (Noguera 2001).

Conclusion

Educators across the nation share a common dilemma. Research inquiries completed since the 1970s provide evidence that black males are disciplined with greater frequency and severity than their peers. The glaring persistence of such patterns challenges educators to approach their work with African American youth in new ways. Although many problems are connected to cultural mismatches between teachers and students, there remains a broader conversation to explore with regard to societal factors that provide fertile ground for the discipline gap. Based on prior scholarship, I assert that disproportionality in school discipline is in large part a function of macro-level problems such as the criminalization of black males and race and class privilege. At the school level, zero tolerance policies provide a conduit by which a significant percent of students are systematically removed from school for subjectively defined offenses. Unfortunately, few policymakers and school officials appear to weigh decisions to expel or suspend students against research evidence regarding the culturally influenced nature of school discipline or harmful outcomes associated with removing students from school, such as delinquency. Rather, most accounts suggest that school officials uphold rigid interpretations of zero tolerance initiatives.

Ending racial disparities in school discipline is a formidable responsibility. Yet, encouragingly, some school systems are taking strides to eliminate the discipline gap (Denn 2002). Growing evidence supports the view that school inequities involving African Americans are best addressed through race-conscious approaches at the teacher preparation and professional development levels. Providing opportunities for teachers to interrogate their own beliefs about student groups as well as culturally based expectations concerning discipline are powerful means of shifting present trends in disproportionality. To date, there is mounting evidence that culturally responsive teachers, particularly African American practitioners, play pivotal roles in promoting transformative outcomes among students. School systems would be well served to employ such individuals in leadership roles that enable them to mentor practicing colleagues as well as to have a voice in decisions concerning discipline.

Note

1. "Kevin" is a pseudonym.

References

Anderson, E. 1999. *Code of the street: Decency, violence, and the moral life of the inner-city.* New York: W. W. Norton.

Applied Research Center. 2002. *Profiled and punished: How San Diego schools undermine Latino and African American student achievement.* Oakland, CA: Applied Research Center.

Bennett, C., and J. J. Harris III. 1982. Suspensions and expulsions of male and black students: A study of the causes of disproportionality. *Urban Education* 16 (4): 399–423.

Canada, G. 1996. *Fist stick knife gun: A personal history of violence in America.* Boston: Beacon.

Cooper, P. 2002. Does race matter? A comparison of effective black and white teachers of African American students. In *In search of wholeness: African American teachers and their culturally specific classroom practices,* ed. J. J. Irvine, 47–63. New York: Palgrave.

Denn, R. 2002. How one school almost succeeded. *Seattle Post-Intelligencer,* March 15.

Dohrn, B. 2001. "Look out kid/It's something you did": Zero tolerance for children. In *Zero tolerance: Resisting the drive for punishment in our schools,* ed. W. Ayers, B. Dohrn, and R. Ayers, 89–113. New York: New Press.

Emihovich, C. A. 1983. The color of misbehaving: Two case studies of deviant boys. *Journal of Black Studies,* no. 13:259–74.

Ferguson, A. A. 2000. *Bad boys: Public schools in the making of black masculinity.* Ann Arbor: University of Michigan Press.

Gottfredson, D. C., G. D. Gottfredson, and L. G. Hybl. 1993. Managing adolescent behavior: A multiyear, multischool study. *American Educational Research Journal* 30 (1): 179–215.

Gouldner, H. 1978. *Teachers' pets, troublemakers, and nobodies: Black children in elementary school.* Westport, CT: Greenwood.

Grant, C. A. 1988. The persistent significance of race in schooling. *Elementary School Journal* 88 (5): 561–69.

Hanna, J. L. 1988. *Disruptive school behavior.* New York: Holmes and Meier.

Irvine, J. J. 1990. *Black students and school failure: Policies, practices, and prescriptions.* New York: Praeger.

———. 2003. *Educating teachers for diversity: Seeing with a cultural eye.* New York: Teachers College Press.

Johnson, T., J. E. Boyden, and W. J. Pittz. 2001. *Racial profiling and punishment in U.S. public schools,* http://www.arc.org/erase/downloads/profiling.pdf (accessed June 14, 2003).

Johnston, R. C. 2000. Federal data highlight disparities in discipline. *Education Week,* June 21.

Ladson-Billings, G. 1994. *The dreamkeepers: Successful teachers of African American children.* San Francisco: Jossey-Bass.

McCadden, B. M. 1998. Why is Michael always getting timed out? Race, class, and the disciplining of other people's children. In *Classroom discipline in American schools: Problems and possibilities for democratic education,* ed. R. E. Butchart and B. McEwan. Albany: State University of New York Press.

Monroe, C. R., and J. E. Obidah. 2004. The influence of cultural synchronization on a teacher's perceptions of disruption: A case study of an African American middle-school classroom. *Journal of Teacher Education* 55 (3): 256–68.

Noguera, P. A. 2001. Finding safety where we least expect it; The role of social capital in preventing school violence. In *Zero tolerance: Resisting the drive for punishment in our schools,* ed. W. Ayers, B. Dohrn, and R. Ayers, 202–18. New York: New Press.

———. 2002a. The trouble with black boys: The role and influence of environmental and cultural factors on the academic performance of African American males. *In Motion,* May 13, http://www.inmotionmagazine.com/er/pntroub1.html (accessed March 9, 2005).

———. 2002b. Joaquin's dilemma: Understanding the link between racial identity and school-related behaviors. *In Motion,* December 1, http://www.inmotionmagazine.com/er/pnjoaq1.html (accessed March 9, 2005).

———. 2003. Schools, prisons, and social implications of punishment: Rethinking disciplinary practices. *Theory Into Practice* 42 (4): 341–50.

Simon, D., and E. Burns. 1997. *The corner: A year in the life of an inner-city neighborhood.* New York: Broadway Books.

Skiba, R., and R. Peterson. 1999. *The dark side of zero tolerance: Can punishment lead to safe schools?* http://www.pdkintl.org/kappan/ski9901.htm (accessed November 4, 2001).

Skiba, R., and M. K. Rausch. 2004. The relationship between achievement, discipline, and race: An analysis of factors predicting ISTEP scores. Center for Evaluation and Education policy, July 9. Bloomington, IN.

Skiba, R. J., R. S. Michael, A. C. Nardo, and R. Peterson. 2000. The color of discipline: Sources of racial and gender disproportionality in school punishment. Indiana Education Policy Center Policy Research Report #SRS1. Bloomington, Indiana: Indiana Education Policy Center.

Skiba, R. J., R. L. Peterson, and T. Williams. 1997. Office referrals and suspension: Disciplinary intervention in middle schools. *Education and Treatment of Children,* no. 20:295–315.

Voelkl, K. E., J. W. Welte, and W. F. Wieczorek. 1999. Schooling and delinquency among white and African American adolescents. *Urban Education* 34 (1): 69–88.

Wacquant, L. 2000. Deadly symbiosis: When ghetto and prison meet and mesh. *Punishment and Society* 3 (1): 95–134.

Weinstein, C., M. Curran, and S. Tomlinson-Clarke. 2004. Toward a conception of culturally responsive classroom management. *Journal of Teacher Education* 55 (1): 25–38.

Weinstein, C., S. Tomlinson-Clarke, and M. Curran. 2003. Culturally responsive classroom management: Awareness into action. *Theory Into Practice* 42 (4): 269–76.

West, C. 1994. *Race matters,* New York: Vintage.

CARLA R. MONROE is an assistant professor at Wheelock College in Boston, Massachusetts.

UNIT 7

For Vision and Voice: A Call to Conscience

Unit Selections

Key Points to Consider

- What would be possible if schools permitted teachers more autonomy in how they assess their students?

- What can teachers do to help students develop a sense of social consciousness and social responsibility?

- How can teachers help students to develop their talents and to develop a vision of hope for themselves? How can teachers help students to develop a sense of public service?

- What are the most important challenges confronting multicultural educators in the new century?

Student Web Site
www.mhcls.com/online

Internet References
Further information regarding these Web sites may be found in this book's preface or online.

Classroom Connect
http://www.classroom.net
EdWeb/Andy Carvin
http://edwebproject.org
Online Internet Institute
http://www.oii.org

We are situated as people in the context of a social matrix of many dimensions, including social class, gender identity, culture, race, age, ideological position, life experiences, and beliefs. We have a special obligation to encourage our students to create the best visions for their lives that they can imagine and to help them lift up their voices and their spirits in the pursuit of their dreams. We must do this for all students, not just the marginalized. No child or teenager should have to feel unwanted or hopeless. As matters of social conscience and moral principle, we must recognize and affirm our duty as teachers to make the best effort possible to teach our students well.

We look forward to a future of multicultural education with a degree of optimism, although aware that there are serious challenges before us. The winds of xenophobia are blowing across the land again; concern regarding immigration is at a fairly high level. Yet this concern was present in all earlier decades in American history when rates of immigration were running at as high levels as they are now. We all agree that there is much work to be done to accomplish the goals of multicultural education. There is, however, great hope that these goals will be achieved as our population moves steadily toward becoming ever more unique as a multicultural civilization. We are going to become less and less like Western Europe and more and more a very unique national wonder such as the world has not seen before. The next 30 to 40 years will bring that vision into reality.

We need a vision for the future of our schools that includes a belief in the worth and dignity of all people. We need to clarify our vision in such a way that it has a holistic character, which takes into account the ever more culturally pluralistic social reality that we are becoming. As part of this effort we need to consider the French revolutionary concept of fraternity. Fraternity and its female counterpart, sorority, refer to brotherhood and sisterhood. We need a new birth of fraternity and sorority in our national life that will enable us to truly care about what happens to one another. We need very much to communicate that sense of caring to the young people who attend our schools, for they truly are our social future. The teaching profession needs a good dose of fraternity and sorority as well. Teachers need to work together in solving problems and supporting their respective professional efforts on behalf of students.

The future of teaching and learning from a multicultural perspective should include more emphasis on cooperative learning strategies that encourage students to develop a sense of community and fraternity that will transcend competition with one another and create a sense of trust and caring among them. We need to stop making students compete with one another and encourage them to work together. We need to learn to team together and teach together more than we have in the past, and we need to have the professional autonomy (independence of professional judgment) to be able to do so at our own discretion and not because someone told us to do so.

There needs to be more democratization of the day-to-day governance structures of schools so that competent teachers can enjoy

the same levels of personal, professional autonomy that their colleagues in teacher education enjoy. A multicultural vision of the future of education will embrace the concept that the strengths and talents of all students need optimum development. The problems and weaknesses of all students need resolution and assistance. We need to see young people as a treasured human resource whose needs for safety, health, and cognitive and affective development are to be met by our best efforts as educators. Educators need to expand their responsibility to their students to include a commitment to each student's best possible development as a person; we will both see and help make our student clients whole. We will be concerned about more than their intellectual development, although this is our primary role; we will also see schooling as having a therapeutic mission. Diverse cultural backgrounds and learning styles will be accepted and nurtured as we treat students as brothers and sisters in a shared national community of educational interests.

Finally, a multicultural vision of the future of education will include a strong commitment to develop a powerful, critical sense of social consciousness and social responsibility between teachers and students. Students will be encouraged and assisted to define and to reconstruct their personal worlds so that they are empowered to see the world as it is and to make it better if they can. Educational settings of society are important terrain in the struggle to reconstruct public life along more egalitarian social policy lines. A multicultural vision of our educational future will encourage teachers to adopt a pedagogy of liberation that champions the development of critical social awareness among students, and which empowers them to evaluate critically all that they may experience. Education will have a liberating intent; the goal will not be just to teach children to reason critically, but to reason critically in the light of a clear vision of social justice worthy of all of their rights as citizens. The struggle to see a multicultural vision for our schools adopted by the teaching profession has always been closely aligned with the broader struggle for civil liberties and human dignity.

The Culturally Responsive Teacher

To engage students from diverse cultural and linguistic backgrounds, we must see them as capable learners.

ANA MARÍA VILLEGAS AND TAMARA LUCAS

Belki Alvarez, a young girl one of us knows, arrived in New York from the Dominican Republic several years ago with her parents and two siblings. After a difficult start in the United States, both parents found jobs; their minimum-wage earnings were barely enough for a family of five to scrape by month to month. As the oldest child in the family, Belki soon had to assume caretaking responsibilities for her younger brother and sister. At only 8 years old, she was responsible for getting her siblings ready for school, taking them there each morning, bringing them back home at the end of the school day, and caring for them until her parents came home from work.

On weekends, she worked with her mother at the community street fair to make extra money for the family by selling products prepared at home. She astutely negotiated prices with customers and expertly handled financial transactions. Belki often spoke enthusiastically about having her own business in the future. She spoke Spanish fluently at home and in the community, and she often served as the English language translator for her parents.

Belki's teachers, however, did not know this competent, responsible, enthusiastic girl. They perceived her as lacking in language and math skills, having little initiative, and being generally disinterested in learning.

Such profound dissonance between her in-school and out-of-school experiences is not unique to Belki. Sadly, this is typical for an increasing number of students in U.S. schools today.

Over the past three decades, the racial, ethnic, and linguistic demographics of the K–12 student population in the United States have changed dramatically. In 1972, 22 percent of all students enrolled in elementary and secondary public schools were of racial/ethnic minority backgrounds (National Center for Education Statistics [NCES], 2002). By 2003, racial/ethnic minority students accounted for 41 percent of total enrollments in U.S. public schools. In six states and the District of Columbia, students of color are already in the majority (NCES, 2005). The immigrant student population has also grown significantly in the past 30 years. Currently, one in five students speaks a language other than English at home, and the majority of these students are learning English as a second language in school (Center on Education Policy, 2006).

A Framework and a Vision

Successfully teaching students from culturally and linguistically diverse backgrounds—especially students from historically marginalized groups—involves more than just applying specialized teaching techniques. It demands a new way of looking at teaching that is grounded in an understanding of the role of culture and language in learning. Six salient qualities (see Villegas & Lucas, 2002) can serve as a coherent framework for professional development initiatives in schools seeking to respond effectively to an increasingly diverse student population.

Understanding How Learners Construct Knowledge

Our conception of culturally and linguistically responsive teaching is grounded in constructivist views of learning (National Research Council, 2000). From this perspective, learners use their prior knowledge and beliefs to make sense of the new ideas and experiences they encounter in school. A central role of the culturally and linguistically responsive teacher is to support students' learning by helping them build bridges between what they already know about a topic and what they need to learn about it.

For example, Belki will learn more from a social studies unit on immigration if her teacher draws on her very real experience as a newcomer to the United States. The teacher might ask her and other immigrant students in the class to describe their experiences learning a new language and compare living in the United States to living in their native countries. The teacher could build on those narratives to introduce relevant concepts, such as factors that lead people to immigrate and phases in the immigration process. The teacher could invite immigrant parents to the class to share their experiences. By involving the students and their parents in these ways, the teacher would not only help students build bridges to learning but also strengthen the connections between home and school. If the teacher does not tap into the experiences of students in the class and instead teaches the unit by focusing solely on the experiences of earlier immigrant groups coming to the United States—such as the Germans and Irish—the material will be much less relevant and engaging.

Learning also involves questioning, interpreting, and analyzing ideas in the context of meaningful issues. With this in mind, an English teacher in a community in the U.S. Southwest that had a large Latino population designed a unit on immigration to the United States. The students were asked to write a letter to the editor of a local newspaper expressing their views on the topic. To write the letter, the students realized that they needed to understand the issues more deeply. So they summarized relevant newspaper articles and developed and administered a questionnaire in their neighborhoods to learn about the community's views on immigration. They debated in class the proposal to build a fence along the United States/Mexico border. Working in groups, they wrote letters to the editor and then assessed their drafts using a rubric that focused on grammar, clarity of position taken, and development of supporting arguments. After receiving the teacher's feedback, the students revised and sent their letters. The students were deeply engaged in a process that helped improve their writing skills.

In embracing constructivist views of learning, we do not mean to suggest that there is no place in schools for direct instruction, memorization, and basic skills instruction. When such transmission-oriented strategies predominate, however, their pedagogical value diminishes, much to the students' disadvantage. Such an approach to teaching does not give students opportunities to actively engage in learning and integrate new ideas and frameworks into their own ways of thinking. Therefore, students are less likely to learn to think critically, become creative problem solvers, and develop skills for working collaboratively—all qualities that are essential for success in life and work.

Learning About Students' Lives

To teach subject matter in meaningful ways and engage students in learning, teachers need to know about their students' lives. We are not suggesting that teachers learn generic information about specific cultural or social groups. Such thinking leads to stereotypes that do not apply to individual students.

Instead, teachers need to know something about their students' family makeup, immigration history, favorite activities, concerns, and strengths. Teachers should also be aware of their students' perceptions of the value of school knowledge, their experiences with the different subject matters in their everyday settings, and their prior knowledge of and experience with specific topics in the curriculum. For example, Belki's teachers would benefit from knowing that she and her family are immigrants, that she often serves as the English language translator for her parents, that she aspires to own a business some day, and that she expertly manages financial transactions at the weekend street fair.

Effective strategies for learning about students' lives outside school include conducting home visits, creating opportunities

in the classroom for students to discuss their aspirations for the future, posing problems for students to solve and noting how each student goes about solving them, and talking with parents and other community members. For instance, Belki's teacher might have asked her to give examples of how she uses math outside school. The teacher could have learned even more by visiting the street fair. By observing her animated interactions with customers, the teacher would have seen that Belki is a fluent Spanish speaker with sophisticated negotiation skills and some important math skills.

The vast majority of teachers in the United States are white, middle class, and monolingual English speaking. In most cases, their lives differ profoundly from the lives of their students. Although information-gathering strategies are simple enough to develop, it is more challenging for teachers to learn how to interpret what they discover about students through their data gathering. To make productive instructional use of this information, teachers must possess two fundamental qualities: They must have sociocultural consciousness and hold affirming views toward diversity (Nieto, 1996).

Being Socioculturally Conscious

We define sociocultural consciousness as the awareness that a person's worldview is not universal but is profoundly influenced by life experiences, as mediated by a variety of factors, including race, ethnicity, gender, and social class. Teachers who lack sociocultural consciousness will unconsciously and inevitably rely on their own personal experiences to make sense of students' lives—an unreflective habit that often results in misinterpretations of those students' experiences and leads to miscommunication. For example, students from cultures with a less individualistic and more collectivist worldview than that of mainstream U.S. culture may be overlooked in class and assumed to be less capable than their mainstream peers because, in general, they do not seek individual attention and praise.

Teachers need to know something about their students' family makeup, immigration history, favorite activities, concerns, and strengths.

To develop sociocultural consciousness, teachers need to look beyond individual students and families to understand inequities in society. In all social systems, some positions are accorded greater status than others, and such status differentiation gives rise to differential access to power. Teachers need to be aware of the role that schools play in both perpetuating and challenging those inequities. Professional development carried out in groups and guided by an experienced facilitator who is knowledgeable about multicultural issues can be instructive. Activities might involve reading about the differential distribution of wealth and income in the United States or reflecting on the well-documented fact that a person's social class is the best predictor of academic success and future social standing

(Natriello, McDill, & Pallas, 1990). To see the powerful connections between social and education inequities, participants could read *The Shame of the Nation: The Restoration of Apartheid Schooling in America,* by Jonathan Kozol (2006). By reading and discussing accounts of successful teaching and learning in diverse settings (see Garcia, 1999; Ladson-Billings, 1994; Nieto & Rolón, 1997), teachers can develop a vision of how schools can challenge such inequities.

Holding Affirming Views About Diversity

Unfortunately, evidence suggests that many teachers see students from socially subordinated groups from a deficit perspective (Nieto, 1996). Lacking faith in the students' ability to achieve, these teachers are more likely to have low academic expectations for the students and ultimately treat them in ways that stifle their learning. They are more apt to use drill, practice, and rote-learning activities at the expense of more challenging work that demands the use of higher-order thinking skills. They are also less likely to call on the students in class, give them sufficient wait time to respond thoughtfully to questions, or probe incomplete answers for clarity.

Teaching is an ethical activity, and teachers have an ethical obligation to help all students learn.

By contrast, teachers who see students from an affirming perspective and truly respect cultural differences are more apt to believe that students from nondominant groups are capable learners, even when these students enter school with ways of thinking, talking, and behaving that differ from the dominant cultural norms. Teachers who hold these affirming views about diversity will convey this confidence by providing students with an intellectually rigorous curriculum, teaching students strategies for monitoring their own learning, setting high performance standards and consistently holding students accountable to those standards, and building on the individual and cultural resources that students bring to school. For example, instead of setting out to "correct" students' language through the use of decontextualized drill and worksheet activities, the English teacher who asked her students to write to the newspaper editor helped her students develop their writing skills by involving them in purposeful and intellectually stimulating tasks.

Using Appropriate Instructional Strategies

Teachers can activate students' prior knowledge by asking them to discuss what they know about a given topic, as Belki's teacher could have done by having the immigrant students in the class share their personal experiences with immigration. Teachers can embed new ideas and skills in projects that are meaningful to the students, as the English teacher who helped students improve their writing skills through researching immigration did.

Teachers can also give English language learners access to the curriculum by drawing on the student's native language resources. They can provide students who are literate in their native language with material to read in that language to help them build background knowledge for specific content. They can encourage students to use bilingual dictionaries. They can prepare study guides for instructional units that define relevant vocabulary and outline key concepts in English, using simplified language. They can also use more visual cues and graphic organizers and incorporate more hands-on activities into their lessons.

Using pertinent examples and analogies from students' lives is another instructional strategy that helps students build bridges to learning. For example, one of us recently observed a teacher introducing the concept of rhythm in poetry by having students analyze the rhythm in a well-known hip-hop recording and then engaging the students in a similar analysis of a poem by Robert Frost. In U.S. history classes, teachers can help engage students from historically marginalized groups by having them examine the curriculum to determine whose perspectives are and are not presented. This would work well, for example, with a textbook treatment of slavery. If the students determine through an analysis of the text that they are learning little about the real experiences of slaves, they can read one of the many published slave narratives to deepen their understanding. As these examples suggest, the job of the culturally and linguistically responsive teacher involves engaging all students in learning for understanding.

Advocating for All Students

Numerous practices embedded in the fabric of everyday schooling put students from nonmainstream groups at a disadvantage. These include a school culture of low expectations for students from low-status groups, inadequate general and multicultural learning materials, large class sizes, assignment of the least-experienced teachers to classes in which students need the most help, insensitivity toward cultural differences, questionable testing practices, and a curriculum that does not reflect diverse student perspectives.

To continue to move toward greater cultural and linguistic responsiveness in schools, teachers must see themselves as part of a community of educators working to make schools more equitable for all students. Teaching is an ethical activity, and teachers have an ethical obligation to help all students learn. To meet this obligation, teachers need to serve as advocates for their students, especially those who have been traditionally marginalized in schools.

For example, teachers involved in school- or district-level textbook review committees could ensure that selected textbooks and supplemental materials appropriately reflect the diversity of experiences and perspectives in the student population. Those who have input into the design of professional development activities could identify specific areas in which the faculty might need professional growth. Topics might include how to implement strategies for learning about students' lives, become socioculturally conscious, build on students' interests outside school to advance curriculum goals, and tap community resources in teaching. Responsive classroom teachers could also request common planning time with the English as a second language teacher to coordinate instruction in ways that maximize content learning for their English language learners.

Just Imagine

Certainly, individual teachers can enhance their success with students from diverse backgrounds by working on their own to cultivate these qualities of responsive teaching. However, the framework that we have presented here will have the greatest effect on a school if teachers and school leaders develop a shared vision of the culturally and linguistically responsive teacher.

Teachers need to serve as advocates for their students.

Imagine Belki Alvarez's school life if her teachers had explored these six qualities and shared ideas for applying them in their teaching. They could have capitalized on her entrepreneurial skills to help her learn mathematical concepts. They would have seen her as a capable learner and understood the relevance of her life experiences for her school learning. They might have tapped her experience as the English translator for her family by having her translate for other Spanish-speaking students in the class who spoke minimal English. Approaching a student's education in these culturally and linguistically responsive ways—rather than emphasizing deficits—has the potential to truly engage all students in learning, both in school and beyond.

References

Center on Education Policy. (2006). *A public education primer: Basic (and sometimes surprising) facts about the U.S. education system.* Washington, DC: Author.

Garcia, E. E. (1999). *Student cultural diversity: Understanding and meeting the challenge.* Boston: Houghton Mifflin.

Kozol, J. (2006). *The shame of the nation: The restoration of apartheid schooling in America.* New York: Three Rivers Press.

Ladson-Billings, G. (1994). *The dreamkeepers: Successful teachers of African American children.* San Francisco: Jossey-Bass.

National Center for Education Statistics. (2002). *Digest for education statistics tables and figures.* Washington, DC: U.S. Government Printing Office. Available: http://nces.ed.gov/programs/digest/d02/dt066.asp

National Center for Education Statistics. (2005). *Digest for education statistics tables and figures.* Washington, DC: U.S. Government Printing Office. Available: http://nces.edu.gov/programs/d05/tables/dt05_038.asp

National Research Council. (2000). *How people learn.* Washington, DC: National Academies Press.

Natriello, G., McDill, E. L., & Pallas, A. M. (1990). *Schooling disadvantaged children: Racing against catastrophe.* New York: Teachers College Press.

Nieto, S. (1996). *Affirming diversity: The sociopolitical context of education.* White Plains, NY: Longman.

Nieto, S., & Rolón, C. (1997). Preparation and professional development of teachers: A perspective from two Latinas. In J. J. Irvine (Ed.), *Critical knowledge for diverse teachers and learners* (pp. 89–123). Washington, DC: American Association of Colleges for Teacher Education.

Villegas, A. M., & Lucas, T. (2002). *Educating culturally responsive teachers: A coherent approach.* Albany, NY: SUNY Press.

ANA MARÍA VILLEGAS (villegasa@mail.montclair.edu) is Professor of Curriculum and Instruction. TAMARA LUCAS (lucast@mail.montclair.edu) is Associate Dean of the College of Education and Human Services and Professor of Educational Foundations at Montclair State University, Montclair, New Jersey.

Toward a Pedagogy of Transformative Teacher Education

World educational links

Judith Reed and Deborah J. Black

As a classroom teacher, I used to believe that valuing diversity in the classroom meant learning about our differences and similarities and finding ways to work together. Creating a peaceable classroom for learning became central in my teaching. I taught strategies for conflict resolution, developed culturally responsive curriculum that promoted cross cultural understandings, and worked to help my students build self-esteem. Now as I reflect on my own past practice, I have come to believe that teaching the skills for a peaceable classroom without a focus on social justice and activism is a way of managing behaviors, silencing the marginalized, and maintaining the status quo. My limited worldview as a privileged person shielded me from seeing how my "peaceable classroom" failed to expose the inequities inherent in our political-economic system. Worse, by ignoring gross inequities or treating them as mere "differences," I was actually abetting the forces of injustice. From this painful realization and critical reflection on my own practices, I dared to imagine how teaching could be different.

—WEL faculty member

Imagine for a moment teachers whose core guiding principle is Paulo Friere's (1970) notion of praxis: "reflecting and acting on the world to transform it."

Imagine for a moment teachers who foster critical inquiry and critical reflection using readings and experiences that challenge students' assumptions, beliefs, and knowledge about the world.

Imagine teachers who respond to oppression differently—not reinforcing it or turning a blind eye—but teachers who challenge all forms of exploitive oppression.

Imagine for a moment the personal engagement in transformative learning that would prepare teacher-activists to help build schools that create "a social movement against oppression" (Kumashiro, 2004, xxv).

In describing below an innovative model for teacher education, the authors hope to contribute to an interrogation of teacher education, class, and culture within the current political and economic system.

Introduction to the WEL Program

Inaugurated at Keene State College in New Hampshire in May 2002, World Educational Links (WEL) prepares future educators for anti-oppressive teaching, critical pedagogy, and social activism. It provides post-baccalaureate initial teacher certification (either elementary or secondary) and a master's degree through a 12-month integrative immersion model.

The typical teacher education program provides an academic curriculum consisting of pedagogical methods, child development, philosophical foundations, exceptionality, literacy—each delivered in a credit-based module in the college classroom, and generally prior to any actual teaching experience. In the WEL program, this knowledge base is gained within the context of a full-year immersion experience in a school, four days a week for the entire public school year. One day a week interns attend seminars on campus. Working with experienced mentor teachers, they are fully immersed in the life of the school.

WEL is innovative in its delivery model, but more so in its transformative mission and its focus on teacher-as-activist. The goal is transformative learning through a reconstruction of social-political-historical knowledge, demonstrated through language and action on the part of the learner. The immersion model is seen as vital not only to the delivery of traditional teacher education curriculum, but to the potential for transformation that WEL offers its interns.

Three areas of inquiry are woven throughout the content of the WEL Program:

(1) Deconstructing the current educational system within its historical and political context.
(2) Deep inquiry into issues of equity and social justice in a multicultural world.
(3) Constructing a new perspective on our essential task as educators.

Implicit in these three tasks is a difficult process of self-scrutiny. This self-examination is impelled by an accumulation of evidence concerning the intern's privileged position[1] in an unjust social order that is founded on the existence of just such privilege.

Deconstructing the Current Educational System Within Its Historical and Political Context

Underlying almost any discussion of school policy and practice are unvoiced assumptions about the function and purpose of public education in the United States. As interns de-construct the educational establishment, they engage in an interrogation of these assumptions and of the competing goals of different players and policymakers. Rather than ideals of social equity, or even individual advancement, schooling in this political-economic system, with its emphasis on teaching differentiated job skills and on producing a stratified workforce through vocational and professional tracking, is seen as primarily serving to maintain societal stability, the status quo (Labaree, 1989).

As they navigate the settings in which they must function as educators, interns are encouraged to interrogate the organizational framework that shapes how teachers do their work, the organizational features that typically define a school as a school. For example,

- students grouped in classrooms by age,
- school day divided into periods, usually with bells at the start and end of each,
- content divided into certain discrete disciplines,
- students grouped by ability and assumed potential.

These rules for what constitutes "school" are, to most within the system, so broadly accepted and unexamined as to be insidiously invisible (Tyack & Cuban, 1995). The structure of schooling is so "routine and common place" that it goes unquestioned. After all, this is what schools are "supposed" to look like. This is common sense (Kumashiro, 2004, xxi–xxii). Upon closer examination, interns may agree that certain of these features are actually not important for learning and some even impede most learners. Interns typically rail against them while expressing a sense of impotence regarding their intransigence.

Who Benefits?

This becomes a crucial question that we come back to again and again as we help interns process the deficiencies they see in the real world of the school, the limits they collide with, and the intractability of these factors. Central to the WEL program is the task of providing to interns a wide lens for viewing the historical-political context of the educational system in which they find themselves.

The practice of academic tracking provides one good example. Flying in the face of the evidence that tracking benefits those in the high track but not the low track students (Oakes, 1985), tracking persists. High track students disproportionately represent the dominant culture, those who enjoy privileged social and economic status. Students of color and students from low-income families are much more likely to be placed in lower tracks. Tracking creates what Sleeter (2001) calls "zones of privilege" that have distinct racial and economic compositions.

In this example, as in countless others in the course of the year, interns experience, recall, and discuss how public education exclusively benefits the members of the dominant group, overriding commonly expressed ideals of democratic equality or social mobility.

Deep Inquiry into Issues of Equity and Social Justice in a Multicultural World

Confrontation with injustice is a crucial factor in a child's developing sense of social responsibility (Berman, 1997), and more specifically in developing an anti-racist white identity (Tatum, 1997). WEL interns are confronted with injustice repeatedly and relentlessly throughout the year. This objective is reflected in the summer readings given when interns first enter the program and continued intensely all year long through videos, workshops and guest speakers.

Interns are thus faced with information that most of them did not learn in high school history classes, or even college (e.g., Golden et al., 1992; Rodney, 1981; Zinn, 2003). They are asked to reflect upon why it might be that, though European immigrant groups have experienced initial discrimination, most have been accepted within two or three generations, while our society has failed to accept people of color over countless generations (Takaki, 1993).

They explore the development of racial identity among Blacks, among Whites (Tatum, 1997). They view and reflect on videos such as *Broken Rainbow* (Florio & Mudd, 1986), showing how the Navajo people have been "relocated" en masse in very recent times; *Children in American Schools* (Hayden & Cauthen, 1996), illustrating Kozol's (1991) exposure of the consequences resulting from gross inequities in school funding; and *The Color of Fear* (Wah, 1994), a deep conversation about the historical construction of racism in the U.S. and its hold on everyone.

Midway into the second semester, WEL interns take a field trip to the Global Kids exposition in New York City. This event features performances and workshops led by inner city youth, including immigrants from around the world, organizing and speaking out. It gives interns a more intimate brush with the world of difference from which many of them have been insulated. Importantly, it also provides a model for enabling young people to take the reins in effecting social change. (See www.globalkids.org/index.shtml).

Confronted thus with myriad examples of inequity and oppression, interns begin to question why these social inequities are so pervasive and persistent. They are challenged to explore the power structures that produce and maintain inequity. They are asked to consider, once again, the key question: *who benefits from the status quo?* Recognition of the power and privilege available to most WEL interns by virtue of the accident of birth becomes painfully inescapable.

Most interns anticipate a year of intense hard work, but few if any are prepared for the distress they might face in coming to realize what place they occupy as members of the oppressor class in a grossly unjust world. A precept of the WEL program is that teachers must be deeply educated about issues of equity and social justice, and ultimately about the oppressive role of the dominant White system and structure to which most of them belong, if public educators are to become a force for social change.

Most teachers enter the profession with dreams of "making a difference," but typically this amounts to a "food and festivals" approach. There is little interrogation of the dominant discourse, into which they are continually co-opted. For example, while democratic community may be espoused within the classroom group, standardization, tracking, and testing continue unimpeded in the overall school system. These contradictory messages emanate from and are managed by the teacher. In an effort to immunize them to the effects of the school culture in which they find themselves participating, WEL interns are challenged to wrestle with contradictions existing and moving in society, but also reflected deep within themselves.

Re-Constructing Our Essential Task as Educators

A contextual understanding of the educational system, and a deep inquiry into issues of equity and social justice, lead to a reexamination of the essential task of an educator. To underpin that process, interns are asked to examine and acknowledge their own position within the cultural-political-educational status quo (Howard, 1999) and to critique their "positionality as a beneficiary of the United States educational system" (McIntyre, 1997, p. 13).

Even if they have never uttered a bigoted comment, the quality of life that they enjoy, from the clothes they wear, to the food they eat, to the cars they drive, comes to them at the expense of others. This realization has strong implications for their personal sense of social responsibility, but it inevitably also raises a professional issue: What is the responsibility of an educator within this political-economic system?

The following essential questions are implicit in the content of the program all year long:

- Are you here because you want to make the world politically and economically more equitable?
- Will you make your teaching a tool for such social change, or a force for the status quo?
- Is it your job to help your *students* feel empowered to identify and address issues of social inequity?
- Is teaching a fundamentally political act?

Pedagogical principles promoted and practiced in the WEL program are consistent with an affirmative answer to the above questions and with principles of social equity (see Berman, 1997; Charney, 2002; Lieber, 2002). These elements allow a critical investigation of the present system of political and economic exploitation and offer possibilities for different relationships among human beings:

- Community building replaces "management" of student behavior. Developing among students a commitment to the common good and to fostering caring relationships: this is seen as a core task and a constant mission in every classroom.
- Participatory classroom processes provide students with choice and authority in the classroom, on both individual and collective levels. Interns learn methods for helping students assume responsibility in the classroom.
- Democratization of knowledge means valuing student knowledge and the co-construction of knowledge. Interns learn ways to create a student-centered classroom based in a constructivist pedagogy.
- Critical inquiry and critical reflection become possible and perhaps even inevitable as students participate in a democratic community of learners. Interns are encouraged to challenge their students to question the assumptions and knowledge presented in their very textbooks.

As they attempt to practice such principles, interns begin to understand the larger picture in their schools, and they are able to see that one powerful way a school may inhibit innovation in the classroom is embedded in the very structures of the school. For example, an intern in a self-contained 5th grade wanted to design an integrated, project-based unit during his solo week, but was stumped by a schedule which broke the day into segments, never longer than one hour, some as short as a half hour, and often with some students out of the room for band or tutoring or the like. When he brought his complaints to seminar, WEL faculty responded, "Do you see how the system operates to prevent you from exercising creative autonomy?"

Interns are daunted by the task of implementing "idealistic" practices that support an anti-oppressive ideology and "best practice" pedagogical theory in inhospitable settings. They are inclined to point the finger at the "unreasonable" expectations of WEL faculty and/or at school administrators whom they hold responsible for creating the strictures.

The faculty interpret this blame-laying as a form of resistance to the necessity for activism (Gay & Kirkland, 2003). Interns are encouraged to take a larger view of such difficulties, to see the task ahead as greater than a single classroom, more than just writing and implementing good lesson plans. Rather, lesson plans, based on a theoretical understanding of systemic contradictions in society, become the mechanism for larger changes.

The goal is for interns to begin to see themselves as activists, seeking ways around the countless petty impediments and finding allies to help remove them, developing a strategic understanding of the nature of the powerful forces keeping teachers from controlling the conditions under which they carry out responsibilities that are vital to the building of an inclusive, humanistic global society.

Transformative Learning: The Inner Process

A few brief vignettes will show a progression of transformative moments involving participants in the first two years of the program.[2] An active acknowledgment of one's own position of privilege in an unjust world is primal. Second, knowledge of injustice is found to be necessary but not sufficient; it needs to lead to action. Third, taking action is frightening, and the fears must be faced and acknowledged. Finally, one can't expect to feel prepared to tackle this material with students *before* one sets out to do so; becoming does not precede doing.

What, Me—A Racist?

The seminar topic was Beverly Daniel Tatum's (1997) book, *"Why Are All the Black Kids Sitting Together in the Cafeteria?"* The interns were asked what they learned from the book, which treats the development of racial identity among both people of color and White people. After a moment of silence Kevin volunteered, "I learned that I'm a racist. I'm a White male, so I'm a racist. It's a really unsettling idea. I don't much like it."

"Yeah," put in Diane. "I found myself feeling thankful that at least I'm not male, just White."

In her book, Tatum draws heavily on Janet Helms's (1990, 1995) analysis of the development of racial identity among Whites. The above comments reflected a new awareness of racism and White privilege, typically accompanied by "the uncomfortable emotions of guilt, shame, and anger" (Tatum, 1997, p. 97).

Knowledge Needs to Lead to Action

A guest presenter at a campus seminar asked the interns to tell how the program was enabling them to teach about issues of social justice. Ellen said that the program had given her new knowledge about important social issues, but that she'd also come to understand that knowledge is not enough—you have to take action.

Gary Howard (1999) proposes that taking action can be seen as a final stage in a journey that, in the WEL program, began when students were asked to be *honest* about who they were and to reflect critically on their privileged social position in the world. Interns were exposed to stories and information that allowed them to *empathize* with others placed in a subordinate social position. This then positioned them to move toward *advocacy* and, finally, into *action* in the form of activism.

Taking Action Is Scary

Chuck had somehow never managed to incorporate any social equity material into his high school Social Studies classes. Finally, during Black History Month, he did initiate a class discussion about racial and ethnic slurs overheard in the hallways. The students were eager to speak and uninhibited in their response, detailing the common use of such language in their homes and at school, some defending its use as unobjectionable because it was not aimed at anyone in particular. Chuck reported in seminar that he came away from this 30-minute discussion totally wrung out. He said it was the hardest, scariest thing he had done so far all year. He felt he'd opened Pandora's Box and didn't know what to do with what came out.

Taking this first step was enormously important, and talking about it with the rest of his cohort was equally important. For a White middle class male creating a second career, well defended all his life from the harsher realities of unexamined bigotry and ignorant racism, this felt like sticking his toe into shark-infested waters. He wasn't sure he'd survive total immersion.

While the fear and courage of the White intern were acknowledged by the WEL faculty, the interns were reminded that others who are not members of the dominant group are not afforded the "luxury of nonengagement," regardless of any fears they may harbor (Howard, 1999, p. 58).

You Can't Wait Until You Feel Completely Prepared

In the first year of the program Karen decided to do a unit on Kwanza, which developed into a program for the entire elementary school, with guests whom she brought in to help. She was highly praised in the school for this work, and it was a peak experience for her. Moreover, when she wrote about it, her reflections revealed an important piece of wisdom. She said that this is hard material to learn about. It takes a lot of deep self-scrutiny and it's very uncomfortable. She said in effect, "I'm just beginning to do that hard work, but I can't wait until it's done before I start teaching about it. I'm just going to have to teach it while I'm learning it."

This same theme played out in the second year, when Terri spoke in seminar about feeling unprepared to teach about prejudice and racism, fearing she might do damage by responding poorly. Others chimed in with similar sentiments. After listening to these

hesitations for a time, Damon suggested they simply needed to "get over it." "You'll never really feel ready. You just have to do it." The WEL faculty member cautioned, "Don't let these fears become an excuse to do nothing."

Consistent with the findings of Gay and Kirkland (2003), WEL interns tended to resist both the work of critical self-reflection and the task of addressing inequities in schools. Early and often, WEL faculty challenged the unconscious attitudes and "maneuvers" that interns exhibited in seminar discussions and written reflections. They reminded interns that it is a political choice of no small consequence to take no action, to remain silent, particularly in light of their new consciousness.

Praxis: Learning to Teach for Equity and Social Justice

As the year unfolded, the first two cohorts of WEL interns gradually transformed the way they framed knowledge and learning, translating their own personal critical inquiry and reflection into their work as budding teacher-activists. For example, the march of traditional holidays through the school calendar provided interns with opportunities for critical inquiry into the meanings and symbolisms of holidays and the nature of holidays as exclusive or inclusive within the school community.

Columbus Day fell at a time when most were still figuring out which way was up at their school sites. Articles like "Discovering Columbus: Re-reading the Past" (Bigelow, 1998) and "We Have No Reason to Celebrate an Invasion" (Harjo, 1998), sparked a heated discussion, but most interns expressed little hope of finding an entry point for sharing their new understanding with students in the school.

By Halloween, many were finding a way to critique what they were witnessing in the schools. Seminar discussions at this time included descriptions of the stereotypes that abounded in the costumes selected by elementary school children: for example, Native Americans (Indians with feathers, tomahawks and "war paint"), or elderly women (witches with warts and broomsticks). However, most interns just watched this occasion pass them by, with belated regrets that they had failed to call attention to it.

Then came Thanksgiving, a holiday whose oppressive features are reinforced by myriads of teachers across the nation annually. Inspired by the work of anti-oppressive educators such as those at Rethinking Schools, a few interns created lessons ranging from giving thanks Native-American style, to confronting directly the conventional Christopher Columbus mythos.

Christmas overwhelmed all but the most assertive, though most gave the usual nod to Hanukkah and Kwanza. Meanwhile, however, the readings and discussions in seminar had sensitized the interns to oppressive practices and policies in school and to the numerous examples of how the curriculum marginalized groups of people. The interns were now positioned to create learning experiences for their students that engaged them in critical inquiry.

January brought Black History Month, but by then some interns were able to dissect this reliance on occasional holidays and special months, and during the second semester most developed ways to incorporate multicultural and social justice material into the mainstream mandated curriculum, regardless of the time of year. Having begun with a new lens for viewing the holiday practices at schools, they had moved to the transformative level of curriculum reform

(Banks, 2001), as reflected in both their language and their classroom practice (Jennings & Smith, 2002). The following are just a few among many examples:

- In a lengthy unit on immigration, Ellen created opportunities for second graders to celebrate global cultures and to explore issues of cultural identity.
- In an eighth grade unit on the Industrial Revolution that focused on life in a New England mill town, Alan led a discussion of the differences between Irish- and African-American assimilation.
- Damon's lesson on the Boston Massacre required fifth grade students to engage in a critical interrogation of attitudes and perspectives implicit in different artistic renditions of the event.
- Robin's full-blown original role play on "Westward Expansion" challenged another fifth grade class to compare and contrast the viewpoints of multiple members of society: European settlers from different socio-economic classes, native Americans, African slaves.
- Seth showed *Mickey Mouse Monopoly* (Sun, 2001) to his sophomore English class and facilitated a heated and intensely engaging discussion of the images of race, class and gender that are presented in children's cartoons.
- When his turn at solo teaching came up, Kevin was given to understand that he might, for that week, cover the material however he chose, though the content was prescribed. In particular, he was assigned the topic of "light and sound" as his science unit. Kevin planned a thematic study of India, beginning with an impersonation of Ghandi and a recital on the sitar. (The topic of "sound" was already well under way.) All week his students were immersed in a study of Indian culture. Simultaneously, he addressed the content of the core curriculum and made sure the students learned principles governing light and sound.

Taking Stock
An Ethic of Activism

"Before, I thought that teachers should stay away from politics and any political agendas, since school is the place to simply acquire academic knowledge," wrote Gail near the end of the year, "but now I see myself making so many political decisions in a single teaching day that it hardly excludes politics from teaching."

Writing about Freire's *Pedagogy of the Oppressed* (1970), Diane reflected that "encouraging dialogue, leadership, and questioning in students is helping them find their own way to truths, and to being active, engaged citizens *who can create change*" [emphasis added].

This is exactly the pedagogy that the WEL program seeks to impart, and also to employ in working with the WEL interns. To this end, interns encountered in the WEL program an ethic of activism which supported, encouraged and sometimes drove them in their fledgling efforts at social change through public education.

Looking Forward

As they disperse and enter professional life within a vast social institution whose function is to maintain the status quo, will these new teachers resist the pressure to conform? Will they comport themselves as teacher-activists in their new professional world?

Taking the pulse of the cohort near the end of the second academic year, WEL faculty felt guardedly optimistic regarding the transformative effects of the program. Many interns had been attracted to the program because of the one-year time frame and the master's degree that would accompany teacher certification. The focus on equity and cultural issues was understood but not necessarily important to them at the outset. Barriers to self-reflection and critical thinking regarding racial, ethnic, and cultural diversity (Gay & Kirkland, 2003) did persist among some WEL interns.

However, some eschewed the "luxury of ignorance" (Howard, 1999, p. 58), opening themselves to the barrage of new images and perspectives, and allowing themselves to adopt a new way of framing social-political knowledge. These interns experienced an internal revolution that not only influenced their teaching practice, but often affected their lives in far-reaching and sometimes difficult areas, including family relationships.

Initial results seem to validate the efficacy of a teacher education model that integrates theory with practice in an immersion experience, rather than providing theory in the college classroom apart from meaningful fieldwork. Mentors and WEL faculty alike considered the interns from each cohort to be very well prepared as teachers, and graduates have been successful in finding employment.

In sum, WEL has yielded promising results among its first two cohorts. Initial lessons have been learned about fostering the development of a new consciousness and about helping interns transform knowledge into action. Further study is called for regarding:

(1) how to deepen the transformational process for a largely Euro-American student population faced with a non-Eurocentric curriculum;

(2) the performance of WEL graduates in their first teaching jobs and beyond;

(3) the importance of faculty composition;

(4) partnerships with cooperating schools and the transformative effects of the program on mentor teachers and partner schools; and

(5) the potential for systemic transformation within the institution, simultaneous with the effects of institutional resistance on the program.

Notes

1. The first two WEL cohorts consisted of 13 to 16 exclusively Euro-American students.

2. Participants' names are fictional, though the activities described are authentic.

References

Banks, J. (2001). *Introduction to multicultural education.* Boston: Prentice Hall.

Berman, S. (1997). *Children's social consciousness and the development of social responsibility.* Albany, NY: State University of New York Press.

Bigelow, B. (1998). Discovering Columbus: Rereading the past. In B. Bigelow & B. Peterson (Eds.), *Rethinking Columbus: The next 500 years.* Milwaukee, WI: Rethinking Schools.

Charney, R.S. (2002). *Teaching children to care: Classroom management for ethical and classroom growth.* Greenfield, MA: Northeast Foundation for Children.

Florio, M., & Mudd, V. (1986). *Broken rainbow.* Los Angeles: Direct Cinema.

Freire, P. (1970). *Pedagogy of the oppressed.* New York: Seabury Press.

Gay, G., & Kirkland, K. (2003, Summer). Developing cultural critical consciousness and self-reflection in presevice teacher education. *Theory Into Practice,* (42)3.

Golden, R., McConnell, M., & Mueller, P. (Eds.). (1992). *Dangerous memories: Invasion and resistance since 1492.* Chicago: Chicago Religious Task Force.

Harjo, S. S. (1998). We have no reason to celebrate an invasion: An interview with Susan Shown Harjo. In B. Bigelow & B. Peterson (Eds.), *Rethinking Columbus: The next 500 years.* Milwaukee, WI: Rethinking Schools.

Hayden, J., & Cauthen, K. (Producers). (1996). *Children in America's schools.* Colombia, SC: South Carolina ETV.

Helms, J. E. (Ed.) (1990). *Black and White racial identity: Theory, research, and practice.* Westport, CT: Greenwood.

Helms, J.E. (1995). An update of Helms's White and people of color racial identity models. In J. G. Pointerotto, J. M. Casas, L. A. Suzuki, & C. M. Alexander, *Handbook of multicultural counseling* (pp. 181–198). Thousand Oaks, CA: Sage.

Howard G. (1999). *We can't teach what we don't know: White teachers, multiracial schools.* New York: Teachers College Press.

Jennings, L.B., & Smith, C.P. (2002). Examining the role of critical inquiry for transformative practices: Two joint case studies of multicultural teacher education. *Teachers College Record, 104*(3), 446–481.

Kozol, J. (1991). *Savage inequalities: Children in America's schools.* New York: Crown.

Kumashiro, K. (2004). *Against common sense: Teaching and learning toward social justice.* New York: Routledge Falmer.

Labaree, D. (1989, Fall). The American high school has failed its missions. *Michigan State University Alumni Bulletin, 7*(1), 3, 14–17.

Lieber, C.M. (2002). *Partners in learning: From conflict to collaboration in secondary classrooms.* Cambridge, MA: Educators for Social Responsibility.

McIntyre, A. (1997). *Making meaning of Whiteness: Exploring racial identity with White teachers.* Albany, NY: State University of New York Press.

Oakes, J. (1985). *Keeping track: How schools structure inequality.* New Haven, CT: Yale University Press.

Rodney, W. (1981). *How Europe underdeveloped Africa.* Washington, DC: Howard University Press.

Sleeter, C.E. (2001). *Culture, difference & power.* In J. A. Banks (Ed.), *Multicultural Education Series.* New York: Teachers College Press. (CD-ROM)

Sun, C.F. (2001). *Mickey Mouse monopoly.* Northampton, MA: Media Education Foundation.

Takaki, R. (1993). *A different mirror: A history of multicultural America.* Boston: Little, Brown & Co.

Tatum, B.D. (1997). *"Why are all the Black kids sitting together in the cafeteria?"* New York: Basic Books.

Tyack, D., & Cuban, L. (1995). *Tinkering toward utopia: A century of public school reform.* Cambridge, MA: Harvard University Press.

Wah, L.M. (1994). *The color of fear.* Oakland, CA: Stir-Fry Productions.

Zinn, H. (2003). *A people's history of the United States: 1492–present.* New York: Perennial.

JUDITH REED is an assistant professor and **DEBORAH J. BLACK** is an associate professor, both in the Education Department at Keene State College, Keene, New Hampshire.

From *Multicultural Education,* Winter 2006, pp. 34–39. Copyright © 2006 by Caddo Gap Press. Reprinted by permission.

Researching Historically Black Colleges

A History with Archival Resources

MATTHEW J. PARIS AND MARYBETH GASMAN

In 1978 Atlanta University president Benjamin Mays noted, "If America allows black colleges to die it will be the worst kind of discrimination and denigration known in history. To decree that black colleges, born to serve [blacks] are not worthy of surviving now that white colleges accept [blacks] would be a damnable act."[1] In spite of setbacks and challenges, Black colleges and universities have continued to thrive. Government support and philanthropic efforts have produced positive results. Even more important has been a renewed appreciation of historically Black colleges and universities as both a traditional and a transformative educational experience for African Americans. Recent scholarship has examined various aspects of the history of black higher education, including administration, curriculum development, philanthropy, faculty relations, and architecture. One problem immediately encountered in researching Black higher education, however, is the diffuse locations of archival sources. While it is reasonable to assume that the archival documents for Howard University and Spelman College reside at their respective institutions, other records prove more difficult to find. The archival sources for the philanthropic and church organizations that established these colleges, for example, can be scattered among institutional archives, research universities, and personal papers. In this article, we have located much of the relevant archival resources and linked them to a general history of historically Black colleges and universities. As the reader, it is essential that you consult the endnotes as well as the text of this article, as the archival sources are included in the references.

The Beginnings of Black Education and Black Colleges

From their arrival on the shores of the United States, Black people have thirsted for knowledge and viewed education as the key to their freedom. These enslaved people pursued various forms of education despite rules, in all Southern states, barring them from learning to read and write. A few Black colleges appeared immediately prior to the Civil War, such as Lincoln and Cheyney universities in Pennsylvania and Wilberforce in Ohio.[2] With the end of the Civil War, the daunting task of providing education to over four million formerly enslaved people was shouldered by both the federal government, through the Freedmen's Bureau, and many Northern church missionaries.[3] As early as 1865, the Freedmen's Bureau began establishing Black colleges, resulting in staff and teachers with primarily military backgrounds. During the postbellum period, most Black colleges were colleges in name only; these institutions generally provided primary and secondary education, a feature that was also true of most historically White colleges—starting with Harvard—during the first decades of their existence.

As noted, religious missionary organizations—some affiliated with Northern White denominations, such as the Baptists and Congregationalists, and some with Black churches, such as the African Methodist Episcopal and the African Methodist Episcopal Zion—were actively working with the Freedmen's Bureau.[4] Two of the most prominent White organizations were the American Baptist Home Mission Society and the American Missionary Association, but there were many others as well.[5] White Northern missionary societies founded Black colleges such as Fisk University in Nashville, Tennessee; Atlanta University (now Clark Atlanta) in Atlanta, Georgia; and Spelman College, also in Atlanta.[6] The benevolence of the missionaries was tinged with self-interest and sometimes racism. Their goals in establishing these colleges were to Christianize the freedmen (convert formerly enslaved people to their brand of Christianity) and to rid the country of the "menace" of uneducated African Americans.[7] Among the colleges founded by Black denominations were Morris Brown in Georgia, Paul Quinn in Texas, and Allen University in South Carolina.[8] Unique among American colleges, these institutions were founded by African Americans for African Americans.[9] Because these institutions relied on less support from Whites, they were able to design their own curricula; however, they were also more vulnerable to economic instability.

With the passage of the second Morrill Act in 1890, the federal government again took an interest in Black education, establishing public Black colleges.[10] This act stipulated that those states practicing segregation in their public colleges and universities would forfeit federal funding unless they established agricultural and mechanical institutions for the Black population. Despite the wording of the Morrill Act, which called for the equitable division of federal funds, these newly founded institutions received less funding than their White counterparts and thus had inferior facilities. Among the 17 new "land grant" colleges were institutions such as Florida Agricultural and Mechanical University and Alabama Agricultural and Mechanical University.[11]

Support from the Titans of Industry

At the end of the nineteenth century, private Black colleges had exhausted funding from missionary sources. Simultaneously, a new form of support emerged, that of White Northern industrial philanthropy. Among the leaders of industry who initiated this type of support were John D. Rockefeller, Andrew Carnegie, Julius Rosenwald, George Peabody, and John Slater.[12] These industry captains were motivated by both Christian benevolence and a desire to control all forms of industry.[13] The organization making the largest contribution to Black education was the General Education Board (GEB), a conglomeration of Northern White philanthropists, established by John D. Rockefeller Sr. but spearheaded by John D. Rockefeller Jr.[14] Between 1903 and 1964, the GEB gave over $63,000,000 to Black colleges, an impressive figure, but nonetheless only a fraction of what they gave to White institutions. Regardless of their personal motivations, the funding system that these industrial moguls created showed a strong tendency to control Black education for their benefit, to produce graduates who were skilled in the trades that served their own enterprises (commonly known as industrial education).[15] Above all, the educational institutions they supported were extremely careful not to upset the segregationist power structure that ruled the South by the 1890s. Black colleges such as Tuskegee and Hampton were showcases of industrial education.[16] It was here that students learned how to shoe horses, make dresses, cook, and clean under the leadership of individuals like Samuel Chapman Armstrong (Hampton) and Booker T. Washington (Tuskegee).[17] The philanthropists' support of industrial education was in direct conflict with many Black intellectuals, who favored a liberal arts curriculum. Institutions such as Fisk, Dillard, Howard, Spelman, and Morehouse were more focused on the liberal arts curriculum favored by W. E. B. Du Bois than on Booker T. Washington's emphasis on advancement through labor and self-sufficiency.[18] Whatever the philosophical disagreements may have been between Washington and Du Bois, the two educational giants did share a goal of educating African Americans and uplifting their race. Their differing approaches might be summarized as follows: Washington favored educating Blacks in the industrial arts so they might become self-sufficient as individuals, whereas Du Bois wanted to create an intellectual elite in the top ten percent of the Black population (the "talented tenth") to lead the race as a whole toward self-determination.[19]

Beginning around 1915, there was a shift in the attitude of the industrial philanthropists, who started to focus on those Black colleges that emphasized the liberal arts. Realizing that industrial education could exist side by side with a more academic curriculum, the philanthropists opted to spread their money (and therefore their influence) throughout the educational system.[20] The pervasive influence of industrial philanthropy in the early twentieth century created a conservative environment on many Black college campuses—one that would seemingly tolerate only those administrators (typically White men) who accommodated segregation. But attention from the industrial philanthropists was not necessarily welcomed by institutions like Fisk University, where rebellions ensued against autocratic presidents who were assumed by students to be puppets of the philanthropists.[21] In spite of these conflicts, industrial philanthropists provided major support for private Black colleges up until the late 1930s.

The pervasive influence of industrial philanthropy in the early twentieth century created a conservative environment on many Black college campuses—one that would seemingly tolerate only those administrators (typically White men) who accommodated segregation.

At this time, the industrial philanthropists turned their attention elsewhere. In response, Frederick D. Patterson, then president of the Tuskegee Institute, suggested that the nation's private Black colleges join together in their fund-raising efforts. As a result, in 1944 the presidents of 29 Black colleges created the United Negro College Fund (UNCF).[22] The UNCF began solely as a fund-raising organization but eventually took on an advocacy role as well.

The Impact of *Brown v. Board of Education*

Until the *Brown v. Board of Education* decision in 1954, both public and private Black colleges in the South remained segregated by law and were the only educational option for African Americans. Although most colleges and universities—the University of Mississippi being a notable exception—did not experience the same violent fallout from the *Brown* decision as Southern public schools, they were greatly affected by the decision. The Supreme Court's landmark ruling meant that Black colleges would be placed in competition with White institutions in their efforts to recruit Black students.[23] With the triumph of the idea of integration, many began to call the need for Black colleges into question and label them vestiges of segregation. However, desegregation proved slow, with public Black colleges maintaining their racial makeup well into the current day. In the state of Mississippi, for example, the *Fordice* case was mired in the court system for almost 25 years, with a final decision rendered in 2004. The case, which reached the United States Supreme Court, asked whether Mississippi had met its affirmative duty under the Fourteenth Amendment's Equal Protection Clause to dismantle its prior dual university system. Despite ample evidence to the contrary, the high court decided that the answer was yes. Although the *Fordice* case applied only to those public institutions within the Fifth District, it had a ripple effect within most Southern states, resulting in stagnant funding levels for public Black colleges and limited inroads by African Americans into predominantly White institutions.[24]

After the *Brown* decision, private Black colleges, which have always been willing to accept students from all backgrounds if the law would allow, struggled to defend their image of quality in an atmosphere that labeled anything all-Black as inferior. Many Black colleges also suffered from "brain drain," as predominantly White institutions in the North and some in the South made efforts to attract the top ten percent of their students to their institutions once racial diversity became valued within higher education.[25]

The Black college of the 1960s was a much different place from that of the 1920s. The leadership switched from White to Black, and because Blacks had more control over funding, there was greater tolerance for political dissent and movements for Black self-determination. On many public and private Black college campuses throughout the South, students were staging sit-ins and protesting against segregation and its manifestations throughout the region. Most prominent were the four Black college students from North Carolina A & T, who refused to leave a segregated Woolworth lunch counter in 1960.[26]

The Federal Government's Increased Attention

During the 1960s the federal government took a greater interest in Black colleges. In an attempt to provide clarity, the 1965 Higher Education Act defined a Black college as "any . . . college or university that was established prior to 1964, whose principal mission was, and is, the education of black Americans."[27] The recognition of the uniqueness of Black colleges implied in this definition has led to increased federal funding for these institutions.

Another federal intervention on behalf of Black colleges took place in 1980, when President Jimmy Carter signed Executive Order 12232, which established a national program to alleviate the effects of discriminatory treatment and to strengthen and expand Black colleges to provide quality education.[28] Since then, every United States administration has provided funding to Black colleges through this program. President George H. W. Bush followed up on Carter's initiative in 1989, signing Executive Order 12677, which created the Presidential Advisory Board on Historically Black Colleges and Universities to advise the president and the secretary of education on the future of these institutions.

Black Colleges Today

Currently, over 300,000 students attend the nation's 105 historically Black colleges (40 public four-year, 11 public two-year, 49 private four-year, and 5 private 2-year institutions). This amounts to 28 percent of all African-American college students. Overall, the parents of Black students at Black colleges have much lower incomes than those of parents of Black students at predominantly White institutions.[29] However, many researchers who study Black colleges have found that African Americans who attend Black colleges have higher levels of self-esteem and find their educational experience more nurturing.[30] Moreover, graduates of Black colleges are more likely to continue their education and pursue graduate degrees than their counterparts at predominantly White institutions.[31] Despite the fact that only 28 percent of African-American college students attend Black colleges, these institutions produce the majority of our nation's African-American judges, lawyers, doctors, and teachers.[32]

Black colleges in the twenty-first century are remarkably diverse and serve varied populations. Although most of these institutions maintain their historically Black traditions, on average 13 percent of their students are White. Because of their common mission (that of racial uplift), they are often lumped together and treated as a monolithic entity, causing them to be unfairly judged by researchers, the media, and policy makers. Just as predominantly White institutions are varied in their mission and quality, so are the nation's Black colleges. Today, the leading Black colleges cater to those students who could excel at any top-tier institution regardless of racial makeup. Other institutions operate with the needs of Black students in the surrounding region in mind. And some maintain an open enrollment policy, reaching out to those students who would have few options elsewhere in the higher education system.

Notes

1. Benjamin Mays, "The Black College in Higher Education," in *Black Colleges in America: Challenge, Development, Survival,* edited by Charles V. Willie and Ronald R. Edmonds (New York: Teachers College Press, 1978).

2. Lincoln University of the Commonwealth of Pennsylvania was first founded as the Ashmun Institute in 1854. As Lincoln president Horace Mann Bond stated, it was "the first institution anywhere in the world to provide a higher education for male youth of African descent." Lincoln's graduates include Thurgood Marshall, Langston Hughes, and Kwame Nkrumah. Lincoln University Archives and Special Collections includes alumni directories and magazines as well as materials related to the African Diaspora. Policies and procedures for the Lincoln Archives and Special Collections can be found at their web site at www.lincoln.edu/library/specialcollections/.

   Cheyney University was founded in 1837 with funds bequeathed by Quaker philanthropist Richard Humphreys. The school began in Philadelphia as the Institute for Colored Youth and provided classical education for qualified young people. The university joined the State System of Higher Education in 1983. The University Archives is open by appointment only. More information is available at the school's web site at www.cheyney.edu.

   One of the oldest historically Black colleges, Wilberforce was founded prior to the end of slavery in 1856. The Ohio university was named in honor of British abolitionist William Wilberforce. The school was founded and for years maintained through a cooperative agreement between the African Methodist Episcopal Church and the Methodist Episcopal Church. Archival records for Wilberforce University can be found in the Stokes Memorial Library at Wilberforce, www.wilberforce.edu. Source: Ronald Butchart. *Northern Schools, Southern Blacks and Reconstruction: Freedmen's Education, 1862–1975.* Westport, Conn.: Greenwood Press, 1980.

3. The Bureau of Refugees, Freedman and Abandoned Lands, often referred to as the Freedmen's Bureau, was created in the War Department in 1865. The bureau supervised all relief and educational activities relating to refugees and freedmen. The bureau records were created or maintained by bureau headquarters, the assistant commissioners, and the state superintendents of education. Archival records for the Freedmen's Bureau are located in state archives and the National Archive and Records Administration. The Freedmen's Bureau Records Preservation Act of 2000 provides funds and a mandate to preserve these records and make them accessible to the public. An online index with many full-text records can be found at Freedmen's Bureau online, www.freedmensbureau.com.

4. The African Methodist Episcopal Church was created in 1816 by a group of African-American delegates from the Methodist Episcopal Church meeting in Baltimore, Maryland. By 1866 the organization had expanded to ten conferences and 75,000 members. In the years immediately preceding and following the Civil War, the AME began a concentrated effort to provide educational opportunities for young people. These efforts focused on the development of scholarships and the creation of church-sponsored schools. In 1863 the organization took control of Wilberforce University in Ohio. From 1870 to 1886 the AME established six colleges and universities throughout the South.

Archival materials related to the African Methodist Episcopal church are located within the Department of Research and Scholarship of the African Methodist Episcopal Church. The Zale Library at Paul Quinn College in Dallas, Texas, includes an extensive collection of materials covering the Tenth Episcopal District. The collection dates cover 1868 to 1984.

The African Methodist Episcopal Zion Church (AMEZ) emerged from the Methodist Episcopal Church (later known as the United Methodist Church) as a response by African-American congregants to racism in the Church. In 1796, James Varick and 30 other Black members of the John Street Methodist Church in New York began to hold separate meetings from the White parishioners, eventually building their own church in 1801. In 1820 they voted to officially leave the Methodist Episcopal Church. The church was widely known among African Americans as the "freedom church" because of its strong stance in favor of abolition. Its archives and national headquarters are located in Charlotte, North Carolina.

5. The American Baptist Home Mission Society (ABHMS), organized in 1832, united all branches of the Baptist denominations in an effort to proselytize in the western territories and states. After the Civil War, the group directed its efforts to establishing theological seminaries and universities in the Southern states. From 1870 to 1880 the group established a number of Black higher education institutions, including Shaw University (Raleigh, North Carolina), Wayland Seminary (Washington, D.C.), Benedict Institute (Columbia, South Carolina), and Leland University (New Orleans, Louisiana). The ABHMS also created the Atlanta Baptist College, which grew into Morehouse College. Archival records for the American Baptist Home Mission Society are located at the Society's National Ministries office in Valley Forge, Pennsylvania.

The American Missionary Association (AMA) was formed in 1846 by an interdenominational group of abolitionist missionaries. Many of the organization's founders were involved in the defense of the Amistad Africans from 1839 to 1841. During and after the Civil War, the AMA established hundreds of schools for freedmen, including institutions of higher education such as Fisk University, LeMoyne-Owen College, Atlanta University, and Tougaloo College. Archival records for the AMA are located at the Amistad Research Center at Tulane University in New Orleans. The original archives consist of approximately 350,000 manuscript pieces, including financial reports, field reports, correspondence, and organizational publications. The original archives have been micro-filmed and extensively indexed. The Amistad Research Center survived Hurricane Katrina with little damage and is now open to visitors.

6. Fisk University, Franklin Library, Special Collections, 100 Seventeenth Ave. North, Nashville, TN 37208-3051; Phone: (615) 329-8500. Atlanta University (now Clark Atlanta University) was founded in 1865 by the American Missionary Association, with later assistance from the Freedman's Bureau. The university is the oldest graduate institution serving a predominantly African-American student body. Its archival records are housed at the Robert W. Woodruff Library, part of the Atlanta University Center. In addition to housing several colleges' archives, the Atlanta University Center holds collections pertaining to many significant African Americans, including C. Eric Lincoln, Countee Cullen, and John Henrik Clarke. In addition, the archives has a substantial collection of civil rights organization papers.

Spelman College was founded in 1881 with assistance from the Women's American Baptist Home Mission Society. It is the oldest Black women's college in the United States. In the 1960s Spelman students were heavily involved in the civil rights movement and the Student Non-Violent Coordinating Committee. Spelman is part of the Atlanta University Center consortium that includes Clark-Atlanta University, Morehouse College, Spelman College, Morehouse School of Medicine, Morris Brown College, and the Interdenominational Theological Center. Records for Spelman College are kept in the Spelman College archives.

7. James D. Anderson, *The Education of Blacks in the South, 1860–1935* (Chapel Hill: Univ. of North Carolina Press, 1988).

8. Founded in 1885, Morris Brown College was the first educational institution in Georgia under sole African-American patronage. The school was named in honor of the second consecrated Bishop of the African Methodist Episcopal Church. The strong relationship between the AME and the school remains today. Records for Morris Brown College are kept in the college's archives.

Paul Quinn College in Dallas, Texas, was established in a one-room building in 1872, by African-American circuit riders, for the education of newly freed slaves. The school remains affiliated with the African Methodist Episcopal Church. The Zale Library at Paul Quinn College contains university archives and archival material related to the African Methodist Episcopal Church. The library also contains the Ethnic Cultural Center for African and Hispanic Americans, which includes books on the African Diaspora and other issues relevant to both ethnic groups. Policies and procedures of the library can be found at their web site at www.pqc.edu/zale_library.htm.

Allen University is the first institution of higher education in South Carolina founded by African Americans for the express purpose of educating African Americans. It was established in 1870 by the African Methodist Episcopal Church and retains a close relationship with the church today.

9. Anderson, *Education of Blacks.*

10. The Morrill Act of 1862 established land-grant institutions of higher education for Whites. The 1890 Act required states with segregated higher education systems to establish land-grant institutions for Blacks. Seventeen of the 19 land-grant HBCUs were established as a result of the 1890 Act. A copy of the Morrill Act of 1890 can be found at www.higher-ed.org/ resources/ morrill_acts.htm.

11. Florida A & M was originally established as the State Normal College for Colored Students in 1887. The school received funds under the Second Morrill Act and changed its name to Florida Agricultural and Mechanical College for Negroes. In 1971 FAMU was recognized as a full partner in the public higher education system in Florida. The Coleman Library at FAMU includes an African American Collection of over 20,000 titles, with a microform reproduction of the Collection of Negro Literature and History from the New York Public Library's Schomburg Collection. Policies and procedures for accessing these collections can be found at their web site at http://famu. edu/acad/coleman/collections.html.

The archives for Alabama A & M University are located on campus in the James H. Wilson Building, which also houses the State Black Archives Research Center and Museum. The Archives/Museum Center is open to visitors Monday through Friday, 9:00 A.M. to 4:30 P.M. For information about exhibits, resources, programs, museum, and tours call (256) 372-5846 or fax (256) 372-5338, or write to the State Black Archives Research Center and Museum, P.O. Box 595, Normal, AL 35762.

12. For extensive information on John D. Rockefeller and his heirs, visit the Rockefeller Archives Center, 15 Dayton Avenue,

Sleepy Hollow, New York 10591; Fax: (914) 631-6017; e-mail: archive@rockefeller.edu. The center's reading room is open Monday through Friday, 9:00 A.M. to 4:45 P.M. An explanation of their procedures and protocols can be found at their web site, www.archive.rockefeller.edu.

Born in Scotland in 1835, Andrew Carnegie moved to the United States at age 12. He made his fortune in the steel industry in Pennsylvania. Throughout his lifetime, he gave to many causes including Black colleges—in particular those espousing an industrial philosophy. Carnegie's personal papers are archived at the Library of Congress in Washington, D.C., the New York Public Library, and the Heinz History Center in Pittsburgh.

The Julius Rosenwald Fund was established in 1928 by the head of the Sears & Roebuck Company. Rosenwald was impressed with the work of Booker T. Washington and the Tuskegee Institute. While the fund originally emphasized the construction of small rural schools, its activities soon extended to include a wide array of educational opportunities. Archival records for the Julius Rosenwald Fund are located in the Special Collections of the Franklin Library at Fisk University in Nashville, Tennessee. The archive traces the history of the Rosenwald Fund from its incorporation in 1917, to its demise. The personal papers of Julius Rosenwald are located in the Department of Special Collections at the University of Chicago.

The Peabody Education fund was created in 1867 to support the development of public education in the South. George Peabody donated $2 million. The majority of the funds supported teacher training for African-American and White schools in the segregated South. Over the next 10 years the Peabody Education fund would contribute $636,000 to develop elementary, secondary, and higher education in the South. The Peabody Education Fund merged with the Slater Fund in 1914, and both became part of the Southern Education Foundation in 1937. Archival records for the Peabody Education Fund are located in the Archives and Special Collections at Vanderbilt University in Nashville. The collection covers the years 1870–1918 and includes correspondence, subject files, pamphlets, and proceedings of the trustees. The personal papers of George Foster Peabody are located in the Manuscript Division of the Library of Congress These cover the years 1894–1937.

The John F. Slater Fund was the first philanthropic fund devoted to education for African Americans. John F. Slater, a wealthy Connecticut textile merchant, created the fund in 1882 with a gift of $1 million. Grants from the Slater Fund helped to develop private Black colleges and stimulated vocational and industrial training. The John F. Slater Fund became part of the Southern Education Foundation in 1937. Archival records for the John F. Slater Fund are part of the Southern Education Foundation records. Those records are located in the Robert Woodruff Library at the Atlanta University Center.

13. Anderson, *Education of Blacks;* William Watkins, *White Architects of Black Education: Power and Ideology in America, 1865–1954* (New York: Teachers College Press, 2001).

14. The General Education Board was a Northern philanthropic organization incorporated in 1903. Supported financially by John D. Rockefeller, the board coordinated efforts to establish a public education system in the Southern states. The majority of these funds were expended on programs that exclusively benefited Whites. Archival records for the General Education Board are located at the Rockefeller Archive Center in New York. Along with the General Education Board, there were two other prominent funds for the education of African Americans. These were the Negro Rural School Fund and the Southern Education Fund.

Established by Anna T. Jeanes in 1907, the Negro Rural School Fund (also called the Anna T. Jeanes Fund) worked to maintain and assist rural schools for African Americans in the South. In the early years the fund established the Jeanes Teachers program. Jeanes Teachers traveled to rural areas in the South with high populations of minorities and taught classes on industrial subjects. Over the years the focus evolved to help improve the educational programs through curriculum development. Teacher archival records for the Negro Rural School Fund can be found with the Southern Education Foundation records in the Robert Woodruff Library at Atlanta University Center.

The other fund was the Southern Education Foundation (SEF). It was created in 1937 through the consolidation of four philanthropic educational foundations: the George Peabody Fund (1867), the John F. Slater Fund (1882), the Negro Rural School Fund (1907), and the Virginia Randolph Fund (1937). The Southern Education Foundation continued the mission of its predecessors—to increase educational opportunities for African Americans and other disadvantaged citizens in the South. The SEF continues that work today. Archival records for the Southern Education Foundation are also located in the Robert Woodruff Library at Atlanta University Center. The records include documentation of its four predecessor organizations as well as SEF activities up to 1979. The records include correspondence, financial papers, administrative records, and photographs.

15. Anderson, *Education of Blacks;* Watkins, *White Architects.*

16. Tuskegee Institute was founded in a one-room shack in 1881, near Butler Chapel AME Zion Church. Thirty adults represented its first class. The famed Booker T. Washington was the institution's founder and first teacher. Tuskegee rose to national prominence under the leadership of Washington, who headed the institution from 1881 until his death at age 59 in 1915. The university archives are located in the Washington Collection, on the third floor of the Hollis Burke Frissell Library. To contact the archives, send an e-mail to tuarchives@tuskegee.edu.

Hampton University was founded in 1868 by General, Samuel Chapman Armstrong with the goal of providing "education for life" and "learning by doing." The archives for the institution are located in the William and Norma Harvey Library and can be contacted via e-mail at Library@hamptonu.edu. Source: David Levering Lewis, *W. E. B. Du Bois: Biography of a Race, 1868–1919* (New York: Henry Holt, 1994).

17. Samuel Chapman Armstrong, a Civil War general, founded Hampton Normal and Agricultural Institute in 1866. Hampton was established to provide education and training for former slaves with a strong emphasis on Christian principles. Armstrong was involved in educational and philanthropic activities throughout his career. Williams College in Massachusetts has an extensive collection of Armstrong's papers and manuscripts. Finding aids and an overview of the collection can be found at the web site at www.williams.edu/library/archives/manuscriptguides/armstrong.html.

In the last years of the nineteenth century, Booker T. Washington built the Tuskegee Institute into one of the leading African-American educational institutions. Its programs emphasized industrial training and economic independence. Washington's autobiography, *Up from Slavery* (1901) remains a classic American memoir.

18. Dillard University can trace its heritage to two separate schools. The American Missionary Association founded Straight College in 1869. The Freedman's Aid Society and the Methodist Episcopal Church established the Union Normal School the

same year. The schools merged into Dillard University in 1930. The Will W. Alexander Archives includes first editions of African-American writers such as Langston Hughes, Countee Cullen, and Frederick Douglass. The collection includes papers and minutes of the AME church and numerous historical documents pertaining to the history of Straight College, New Orleans University, and Dillard University. The university and its library suffered extensive damage in Hurricane Katrina, and as of spring 2006, on-campus facilities have not reopened.

Howard University was founded in 1866 by the First Congregational Society of Washington, D.C., to prepare African-American ministers. In 1867, during the last session of the 39th Congress, a charter officially incorporating Howard University was passed. Today Howard, one of the most prestigious Black universities, boasts a diverse student body and strong endowment. The university's archives are located in the Moorland Spingarn Research Center on campus. The manuscript division is open Monday through Friday by appointment and can be accessed at www.howard.edu/library/moorland-spingarn as well.

Morehouse College was founded in 1867 as the Augusta Institute in Augusta, Georgia. The seminary moved to Atlanta in 1879 and over the next 100 years became one of the leading liberal arts colleges for African Americans. Morehouse is part of the Atlanta University Center consortium that includes Clark Atlanta University, Spelman College, Morehouse School of Medicine, Morris Brown College, and the Interdenominational Theological Center. Archival records for Morehouse College can be found in the Robert Woodruff Library at Atlanta University Center.

An author, editor, activist, and academic, W. E. B. Du Bois is an iconic figure in American intellectual thought and African-American history. Du Bois received his Ph.D. in sociology from Harvard in 1895. Over the next 60 years he was a powerful advocate for social and political equality for African Americans. His teaching career included academic appointments at Fisk and Atlanta University. Du Bois's books *The Souls of Black Folk* (1913) and *Color and Democracy* (1945) are landmark works in American intellectual history. An extensive collection of his papers can be found in the W. E. B. Du Bois Library, Special Collections and Archives, at the University of Massachusetts. The collection covers the years 1803–1979 and includes writings, speeches, correspondence, audiotapes, and motion pictures. Source: David Levering Lewis, *W. E. B. Du Bois: Biography of a Race, 1868–1919* (New York: Henry Holt, 1994).

19. David Levering Lewis., *W. E. B. Du Bois: Biography of a Race, 1868–1919* (New York: Henry Holt, 1994).

20. Anderson, *Education of Blacks.*

21. Anderson, *Education of Blacks.*

22. The United Negro College Fund was incorporated in 1944 in an effort to unite private Black college and universities for fund-raising on a national level. Pioneered by Tuskegee president Frederick D. Patterson, the UNCF quickly established itself as an effective fund-raising organization. The UNCF continues today as a consortium of private, accredited, four-year historically Black colleges and universities, offering scholarships, mentors, internships, and other education-related programs. Archival records for the UNCF are located in the Robert Woodruff Library at Atlanta University Center. The records cover the years 1935–1983, with the bulk of the material covering 1944–1965. These records include reports and publications of member institutions, speeches and publications of administrative officers, pamphlets, news releases, and administrative records. Duplicate copies of the UNCF records can be found at the Library of Congress, Manuscript Division, 101 Independence, Ave. SE, Room LM 101, James Madison Memorial Bldg, Washington, DC 20540-4680. The Manuscript Reading Room is open weekdays and Saturday from 8:30 A.M. to 5:00 P.M. It is closed on federal holidays. A further explanation of policies and procedures can be found at the Library of Congress Manuscript Reading Room web site, www.loc.gov/rr/mss.

23. Marybeth Gasman, "Rhetoric vs. Reality: The Fundraising Messages of the United Negro College Fund in the Immediate Aftermath of the *Brown* Decision," *History of Education Quarterly* 44, 1 (2004).

24. M. Christopher Brown, *The Quest to Define Collegiate Desegregation: Black Colleges, Title VI Compliance, and Post-Adams Litigation* (Westport, Conn.: Greenwood, 1999).

25. Gasman, "Rhetoric vs. Reality."

26. North Carolina A & T was originally established in 1891 as the Agricultural and Mechanical College for Negroes in Greensboro. It was designated a regional university in 1967 and merged into the University of North Carolina in 1972. The Archives and Special Collections for North Carolina A & T can be found in the Ferdinand D. Bluford Library on the Greensboro campus. The University Archives tries to collect materials related to the African-American experience in the local area. Policies and procedures for the archives can be found at their web site, www.library.ncat.edu/info/archives/archives.html.

27. A copy of the Higher Education Act of 1965 can be found at www.higher-ed.org/resources/HEA1.htm.

28. A copy of the initiative and more information can be found at the Department of Education web site, www.ed.gov.

29. Harold Wenglinsky, *Historically Black Colleges and Universities: Their Aspirations and Accomplishments* (Princeton, N.J.: Educational Testing Service, 1999).

30. M. Christopher Brown and Kassie Freeman, *Black Colleges: New Perspectives on Policy and Practice* (Westport, Conn.: Praeger, 2004).

31. Wenglinsky, *Historically Black Colleges and Universities.*

32. American Association of University Professors, "Historically Black Colleges and Universities: A Future in the Balance," *Academe* (January–February 1995).

MATTHEW J. PARIS is the educational reference librarian at the University of Southern Illinois, Edwardsville. **MARYBETH GASMAN** is assistant professor of higher education at the University of Pennsylvania.

Test Your Knowledge Form

We encourage you to photocopy and use this page as a tool to assess how the articles in *Annual Editions* expand on the information in your textbook. By reflecting on the articles you will gain enhanced text information. You can also access this useful form on a product's book support Web site at *http://www.mhcls.com/online/*.

NAME: _____   DATE: _____

TITLE AND NUMBER OF ARTICLE: _____

BRIEFLY STATE THE MAIN IDEA OF THIS ARTICLE:

_____

LIST THREE IMPORTANT FACTS THAT THE AUTHOR USES TO SUPPORT THE MAIN IDEA:

_____

WHAT INFORMATION OR IDEAS DISCUSSED IN THIS ARTICLE ARE ALSO DISCUSSED IN YOUR TEXTBOOK OR OTHER READINGS THAT YOU HAVE DONE? LIST THE TEXTBOOK CHAPTERS AND PAGE NUMBERS:

_____

LIST ANY EXAMPLES OF BIAS OR FAULTY REASONING THAT YOU FOUND IN THE ARTICLE:

_____

LIST ANY NEW TERMS/CONCEPTS THAT WERE DISCUSSED IN THE ARTICLE, AND WRITE A SHORT DEFINITION:

We Want Your Advice

ANNUAL EDITIONS revisions depend on two major opinion sources: one is our Advisory Board, listed in the front of this volume, which works with us in scanning the thousands of articles published in the public press each year; the other is you—the person actually using the book. Please help us and the users of the next edition by completing the prepaid article rating form on this page and returning it to us. Thank you for your help!

ANNUAL EDITIONS: Multicultural Education 08/09

ARTICLE RATING FORM

Here is an opportunity for you to have direct input into the next revision of this volume.
We would like you to rate each of the articles listed below, using the following scale:

1. **Excellent: should definitely be retained**
2. **Above average: should probably be retained**
3. **Below average: should probably be deleted**
4. **Poor: should definitely be deleted**

Your ratings will play a vital part in the next revision.
Please mail this prepaid form to us as soon as possible.
Thanks for your help!

RATING	ARTICLE
	1. Five Trends for Schools
	2. In Urban America, Many Students Fail to Finish High School
	3. In Rural America, Few People Harvest 4-Year Degrees
	4. Colorblind to the Reality of Race in America
	5. Metaphors of Hope
	6. Hitting the Ground Running
	7. The Biology of Risk Taking
	8. Dare to Be Different
	9. The Cultural Plunge
	10. Ain't Nothin' Like the Real Thing
	11. Collaborative Recruitment of Diverse Teachers for the Long Haul—TEAMS
	12. Asian American Teachers
	13. The Human Right to Education
	14. Knowing, Valuing, and Shaping One's Culture
	15. Beyond Promise: Autobiography and Multicultural Education
	16. Expanding Appreciation for "Others" Among European-American Pre-Teacher
	17. Whose World Is This
	18. A Developing Identity
	19. Making Connections with the Past
	20. Affirming Identity in Multilingual Classrooms
	21. Myths and Stereotypes about Native Americans
	22. Transcending Spaces: Exploring Identity in a Rural American Middle School

RATING	ARTICLE
	23. As Diversity Grows, So Must We
	24. Arts in the Classroom: 'La Llave' (The Key) to Awareness, Community Relations, and Parental Involvement
	25. Rewriting "Goldilocks" in the Urban, Multicultural Elementary School
	26. Assessing English Language Learners' Content Knowledge in Middle School Classrooms
	27. Promoting School Achievement among American Indian Students throughout the School Years
	28. Family and Consumer Sciences Delivers Middle School Multicultural Education
	29. Public Education in Philadelphia
	30. Assessing English-Language Learners in Mainstream Classrooms
	31. Standards-Based Planning and Teaching in a Multicultural Classroom
	32. Programming for Participation
	33. Protecting Educational Rights of the Aboriginal and Indigenous Child
	34. Why Are "Bad Boys" Always Black
	35. The Culturally Responsive Teacher
	36. Toward a Pedagogy of Transformative Teacher Education
	37. Researching Historical Black Colleges

BUSINESS REPLY MAIL
FIRST CLASS MAIL PERMIT NO. 551 DUBUQUE IA

POSTAGE WILL BE PAID BY ADDRESSEE

McGraw-Hill Contemporary Learning Series
2460 KERPER BLVD
DUBUQUE, IA 52001-9902

ABOUT YOU

Name   Date
_____

Are you a teacher? ☐ A student? ☐
Your school's name
_____

Department
_____

Address   City   State   Zip
_____

School telephone #
_____

YOUR COMMENTS ARE IMPORTANT TO US!

Please fill in the following information:
For which course did you use this book?
_____

Did you use a text with this ANNUAL EDITION? ☐ yes ☐ no
What was the title of the text?
_____

What are your general reactions to the Annual Editions concept?
_____

Have you read any pertinent articles recently that you think should be included in the next edition? Explain.
_____

Are there any articles that you feel should be replaced in the next edition? Why?
_____

Are there any World Wide Web sites that you feel should be included in the next edition? Please annotate.
_____

May we contact you for editorial input? ☐ yes ☐ no
May we quote your comments? ☐ yes ☐ no